My Future Is in America

My Future Is in America

Autobiographies of Eastern European Jewish Immigrants

EDITED AND TRANSLATED BY

Jocelyn Cohen and Daniel Soyer

*Published in conjunction with
the YIVO Institute for Jewish Research*

New York University Press

NEW YORK AND LONDON

Translation copyedited by Sarah Swartz.

NEW YORK UNIVERSITY PRESS
New York and London
www.nyupress.org

Library of Congress Cataloging-in-Publication Data
My future is in America : autobiographies of Eastern European Jewish
immigrants / edited and translated by Jocelyn Cohen and Daniel Soyer.
p.   cm.
"Published in conjunction with the YIVO Institute for Jewish Research."
Includes bibliographical references and index.
ISBN-13: 978-0-8147-4019-4 (cloth : alk. paper)
ISBN-10: 0-8147-4019-7 (cloth : alk. paper)
1. Jews—Europe, Eastern—Biography. 2. Jews, East European—United
States—Biography. 3. Immigrants—United States—Biography. 4. United
States—Ethnic relations. 5. Europe, Eastern—Ethnic relations.
I. Cohen, Jocelyn. II. Soyer, Daniel.
DS135.E89M9 2005
920'.0092924073—dc22   2005018192

New York University Press books are printed on acid-free paper,
and their binding materials are chosen for strength and durability.

Manufactured in the United States of America

10 9 8 7 6 5 4 3 2 1

Contents

Acknowledgments

In the course of work on this project, we have amassed many debts. First of all, as it is written, "Without bread there is no Torah." A major grant from the National Foundation for Jewish Culture (NFJC) enabled us to eat as we took a full year to sift through the extensive collection of autobiographies generated by YIVO's 1942 contest, make our selections, and draft the translations. A grant from the Lucius N. Littauer Foundation helped us finish a second part of the NFJC project: an inventory of the collection. We are also grateful to Fordham University for financial assistance. None of this material aid would have been forthcoming, however, if YIVO had not recognized the value of the autobiographies and the worthiness of their publication. Thanks to Lisa Epstein, then research director at YIVO, for first approving the project; to Elise Fischer for producing the grant proposal; and, especially, to Carl Rheins, YIVO's executive director, for the faith he has shown in the project and for his unstinting and generous support.

"And without Torah there is no bread." No individual, and certainly not the editors, has mastered all of the knowledge—linguistic, cultural, historical—necessary to understand everything in the autobiographies, much less to translate and annotate them. We therefore leaned heavily on many colleagues with widely divergent areas of expertise. Professors Anita Norich, David Fishman, and Arthur Goren constituted our official advisory panel and afforded us the benefit of their insights into European and American Jewish history and Yiddish literature. Sarah S. Swartz was our discerning editor, whose familiarity with the subject matter made her comments all the more acute.

YIVO's chief archivist, Fruma Mohrer, shares credit for the translation of the autobiography of Bertha Fox.

Thanks especially to the members of the YIVO staff whom we pestered constantly: Nikolai Borodulin for help, not only with the Russian language, but also with Russian and Yiddish bibliographic queries; Shaindl

Fogelman for cultural references; Hershl Glasser for answering endless queries concerning Yiddish words and expressions, folkways, and customs; Yeshaye Metal for putting up with constant requests for reference assistance as well as dense ignorance concerning the foundational texts of traditional Judaism; Chana Mlotek for help identifying Yiddish songs; Leo Greenbaum for his reference help and acquaintance with modern Jewish social movements; David Rogow, Solomon Krystal, Samuil Goldenberg, and Hinde Jacobs for answering questions about Yiddish; Lyudmila Sholokhova for reference and linguistic assistance; Aaron Taub for his bibliographic assistance as well as his knowledge of religious texts; Marek Web for his help with Polish language and geography; and Vital Zajka for his apparent familiarity with every single Slavic dialect. Other members of the YIVO staff were also helpful. Andrew Demers, Ella Levine, and Linh Nguyen provided administrative support. Aviva Astrinsky, Gunnar Berg, Krysia Fisher, Brad Sabin Hill, Herbert Lazarus, and Fruma Mohrer provided reference support. Special thanks to Jesse Aaron Cohen for tracking down many of the photographs. Roberta Newman and Yankl Salant offered constant encouragement and enlightenment on various issues. Thanks, too, to the able staff of the autobiography inventory project: Donna Gallers, Judith Liberman, Gloria Donen Sosin, and Judith Wolfsohn.

Colleagues not on the YIVO staff also proved indispensable. Tony Michels and Cecile Kuznitz commented on the introduction. Jeffrey Shandler offered advice based on his experience with a similar YIVO publication. Zalman Alpert offered his extensive knowledge concerning Hasidic and rabbinic dynasties. Eve Jochnowitz answered questions about Jewish food, and Ellie Kellman about Yiddish literature. Steven Zipperstein responded to queries about Odessa, Sheva Zucker about Winnipeg, and Gilbert Sandler about Baltimore. Itzik Gottesman helped with Jewish folkways. Thanks to the folks at *American Woodworker* and at the *Galveston County Daily News*. We are also grateful to Jennifer Altermatt of the Children's Hospital, Boston, and Jeanne Abrams of the Rocky Mountain Jewish Historical Society.

Thanks also to New York University Press for seeing merit in this book, and especially to Jennifer Hammer and the two anonymous readers for press, who turned out to be Mark Raider and Beth Wenger.

It has been an honor to work with the writers' children and grandchildren, a living link to the stories in this collection, who generously made possible the publication of this volume: Caila Abedon, Miriam Arnowitz,

Suzie Bobele, Menucha Boomer, Howard Carasik, Hannah Cukell, Ellen Elias, Noel Fox, Alfred Goldstein, Lawrence Goldstein, Charlotte Gordon, Ruth Margolin, Fay Minkin, Sylvia Neff, Reuven Opher, Michael Silverman, Lillian Spitzer, Abe Weiner, Sam Weiner, William Weiner, Celia Weiss, and Betty Weissbecker.

Finally, a *yasher-koyekh* to Max Weinreich and to the autobiographers for all their efforts.

A Note on Annotations and Transliteration

In the autobiographies that follow, explanations of terms are given, when needed, in the notes, except when the term in question is mentioned in more than one autobiography. In such cases, an asterisk (*) is appended to the term in the text and its definition is found in the Glossary.

Yiddish words are transliterated according to the YIVO system of romanization. English words of Yiddish or Hebrew origin found in Merriam-Webster's Collegiate Dictionary, 10th edition, are spelled as they are in the dictionary. Hebrew words follow the style of the Jewish Publication Society. (When a writer cites from a traditional Hebrew or Aramaic text, however, the transliteration follows a generalized Ashkenazi pronunciation.)

Introduction

Yiddish Social Science and Jewish Immigrant Autobiography

Jocelyn Cohen and Daniel Soyer

The life histories in this book are the product of a remarkable collaboration between a scholarly institution and an immigrant community. In
1942, the Yiddish Scientific Institute (known by the acronym YIVO)—
which itself had relocated to New York from Vilna, then part of Poland,
only two years earlier—called on Jewish immigrants to write their autobiographies.[1] The call took the form of a contest: the writers were to send
their manuscripts to YIVO, which would then judge them and award
prizes. In response, more than two hundred Jewish immigrants took part
in the contest by writing their life stories. These garment workers, shopkeepers, housewives, communal activists, professionals—and even a couple of writers—had come from all parts of Eastern Europe and settled in
the cities and towns of the United States and Canada in the late nineteenth
and early twentieth centuries. Now, as they seized the opportunity to write
their stories, they thanked the sponsoring institution for providing them
with a forum in which to express themselves. As Minnie Goldstein wrote
to Max Weinreich, YIVO's guiding intellectual light at the time of the contest, "I have lived my whole life with these events in my heart, and many
times I thought that if I had someone to tell my life story to my heart
would have been less burdened."[2] Sixty years later, it is clear that YIVO was
serving posterity as well as its contemporary public. We too are lucky that
these writers had a chance to unburden their hearts and tell us their life
stories.

The autobiographies included in this book capture the collective,
many-textured experience of a generation that witnessed great upheaval in

Eastern European Jewish life and ushered in a new era in American Jewish history. Presented here as complete stories, these personal narratives offer special insight into the transition between the Old and New Worlds, revealing new perspectives on some well-studied aspects of Jewish immigration history and also opening new areas of inquiry. The autobiographers offer their own views on religion and political revolt; on the struggle for literacy and worldly knowledge beyond traditional Jewish learning; on masculinity and femininity; on family relationships and the domestic sphere; on upward social mobility and the price of success; and on the definition of success itself. Reflecting on these and other themes, the writers struggled to establish a sense of continuity in their lives in the midst of wrenching and fundamental social change. Taken collectively, these autobiographies present a dynamic portrait of an immigrant generation in its encounter with an epic historical moment, and they testify to the power of storytelling as a historical practice.

Weinreich believed that American Jews had much to learn from the immigrant generation, whose members had successfully negotiated the transition from tradition to modernity and from Europe to America. The immigrants, Weinreich believed, formed a living bridge to the Jewish past and its rich cultural resources, without which a creative and vibrant Jewish identity could not survive. This anthology aims to bring that profound legacy to a new audience by presenting just a small selection of the immigrants' stories to the English-reading public. It hopes to convey some of the immigrants' strength and the intensity of their struggle not only to forge new lives for themselves in America, but also to construct a modern Jewish identity.

The Yiddish Scientific Institute (YIVO)

The story of how these autobiographies came to be written begins with YIVO and with the ideas of Max Weinreich (fig. 1). Founded in 1925 and based in Vilna, YIVO was one of the bright lights of Polish Jewish cultural life in the period between the world wars. The institute's founders, including Weinreich, were dedicated scholars who worked not only *on* Yiddish, but also *in* Yiddish, the much-maligned vernacular of Eastern European Jewry.[3] YIVO's leaders believed that the Jews of Eastern Europe constituted a distinct people, and that this people had a right to develop its national culture in the countries where it lived. Language was central to YIVO's

Fig. 1. Max Weinreich, director of research at the YIVO Institute for Jewish Research and the guiding light of the 1942 autobiography contest. Courtesy of the YIVO Institute for Jewish Research

conception of Jewish peoplehood. Most Eastern European Jews spoke Yiddish, a language that embodied the history of the Jewish people in Central and Eastern Europe and distinguished its speakers from the surrounding populations. But as the Jews' everyday language, Yiddish had always had low social status in comparison with Hebrew, the language of Jewish learning and prayer, and with such highly regarded European languages as German and Russian. One of YIVO's chief aims was to raise the prestige of the Yiddish language, and therefore of its speakers. The institute also sought to serve the Jewish people by giving them knowledge about themselves. Above all, YIVO's leaders recognized the urgent need to document all aspects of Jewish life, both in the past and the present.

Weinreich soon emerged as the institute's leading intellectual. Trained as a linguist, he hoped to construct a new academic field to study the interaction between "personality and culture"—that is, between the individual and his or her social environment. His interest in the developing personality, especially of members of ethnic minority groups, led him to champion the use of life stories in social scientific research. Such documents seemed well suited to the study of the individual's total development over time, and also more likely to capture the individual's subjective understanding of his or her life, which was of prime importance to Weinreich. Ultimately, Weinreich intended his research to have practical meaning for the Jewish people. With the decline of traditional Jewish culture in the modern world, Weinreich believed, social science would have to provide the positive group identity, cultural pride, and sense of historical continuity that Jews needed as a minority group.

Weinreich's research interests coalesced in three autobiography contests that YIVO sponsored in the 1930s for Jewish youths in Poland. Weinreich intended to use the assembled autobiographies to investigate the problems that young Jews faced and to find positive aspects of their experience that could be built upon.[4] Tragically, Jewish youth quite literally had no future in Poland, and neither did YIVO in Vilna. But the institute survived by transferring its center to New York, where Weinreich and several other YIVO scholars had managed to flee. As an immigrant institution, YIVO struggled to find a place for itself in its first couple of years in the United States. Thus, while YIVO continued to research and publish work on Eastern European Jewry, it also took special pains to sponsor projects that focused on American Jewish life.

The Immigrant Autobiography Contest of 1942

One of YIVO's first major American-centered projects was an autobiography contest patterned after its earlier efforts in Poland. The institute thus turned to a tried-and-true method, but this time applied it to a new constituency with which it had a natural affinity—Eastern European Jewish immigrants who not only spoke Yiddish, but also sympathized with YIVO's mission of social research. Weinreich realized that the Jewish Socialist and labor movements built by the immigrants served to reinforce their faith in education, knowledge, and culture. As Weinreich put it, "Among those elements with a connection to Yiddish, we do not find, perhaps, a clear understanding of the meaning of research. But neither is there fear of it. On the contrary, the respect for learning lives on, a respect that combines the old Jewish reverence for Torah study with the Socialist labor movement's faith in science as a bearer of progress."[5]

Large-scale immigration to the United States had been cut off, first by World War I and then by a series of restrictive laws enacted in the 1920s, so that by 1942 the immigrant population was an aging one. Although the autobiography contest thus represented a shift in emphasis from youth to middle and old age, it would provide the kinds of material that YIVO wanted. First, immigrant autobiographies would certainly link American Jewry's present with its past, both in America and in Eastern Europe. Second, they would provide clues about the success and failure of various strategies for adjusting to American conditions and for retaining healthy Jewish identities. They could also be used to preserve cultural memory for current and future generations of American Jews cut off from their Eastern European roots.

In late May 1942, YIVO issued the call for a new autobiography contest on the theme "Why I left Europe and what I have accomplished in America." The announcement, which appeared in YIVO's own journal as well as in a number of Yiddish-, English-, and German-language Jewish publications, expressed the organizers' view that the mass migration of the previous six decades constituted a nearly unprecedented historical revolution in Jewish life. It also stressed their belief in the historical importance of the everyday lives of ordinary people. While historians had described the general contours of the migration, and while some famous immigrant leaders and intellectuals had written their memoirs, the "great masses of immigrants, those who struggled and with their own hands built their personal lives and communal institutions in the New World, have not yet had their say."[6]

The announcement explained the rules of the contest and advised contestants on how and what to write. The competition was open to any adult Jew who had not been born in the United States or Canada. The top six winners would receive monetary prizes ranging from twenty to one

hundred dollars. Another nineteen writers would win book prizes. Participants were asked to write a minimum of twenty-five notebook-sized pages
and to sign their works only with pseudonyms, enclosing their real name
in a separate envelope. The announcement suggested a long list of topics
that writers could cover, following more or less the life cycle of an individual and stressing issues that had to do with work, social mobility, and aspirations for children. Above all, the call asked that the autobiographies be
"detailed," "precise," and "sincere."

The results were gratifying to the organizers. By the end of the contest,
more than two hundred autobiographies had been assembled, together
with many letters, photographs, diaries, and other personal documents
submitted by participants. Analyzing the returns, the YIVO staff found
that 176 of the works had been written by men and 47 by women; that just
over half had come from New York, while the others had arrived from 62
other places in the United States, Canada, Mexico, Argentina, and Cuba;
and that the majority of the writers were between 51 and 70 years of age.
The writers came from all over Eastern Europe, as well as from Germany
and Palestine, and they had arrived in America in every decade from the
1880s to the 1940s, though most had come in the years of mass migration
between 1882 and 1924. Ninety percent of the works were written in Yiddish, with the rest in English, German, or Hebrew.[7]

The participants were both eager to write and uneasy about undertaking so daunting a task. Some reported that they had felt "inspired" after
reading about the contest, but they still sometimes hesitated to write, fearing that they were not up to the task. Weinreich responded patiently to
many inquiries about technical matters, and he encouraged the writers to
persevere. In some cases, he corresponded with participants even after
they had submitted manuscripts, urging them to flesh out their narrative
and posing specific questions for them to answer. Above all, he reassured
the contestants that their lives really did matter and that they had much to
contribute to scholarship. "There is no human life," he told one nervous
autobiographer, "that is not interesting to science."[8]

What ultimately motivated the participants to write? Many of the autobiographers were entering late middle and old age, when it is common for
people to take stock of their lives. They felt a need to assess for themselves
the very question that the contest theme posed: What, indeed, had they
accomplished in America? Writing their autobiographies also gave them
the opportunity to link their childhoods in Europe with their adulthoods

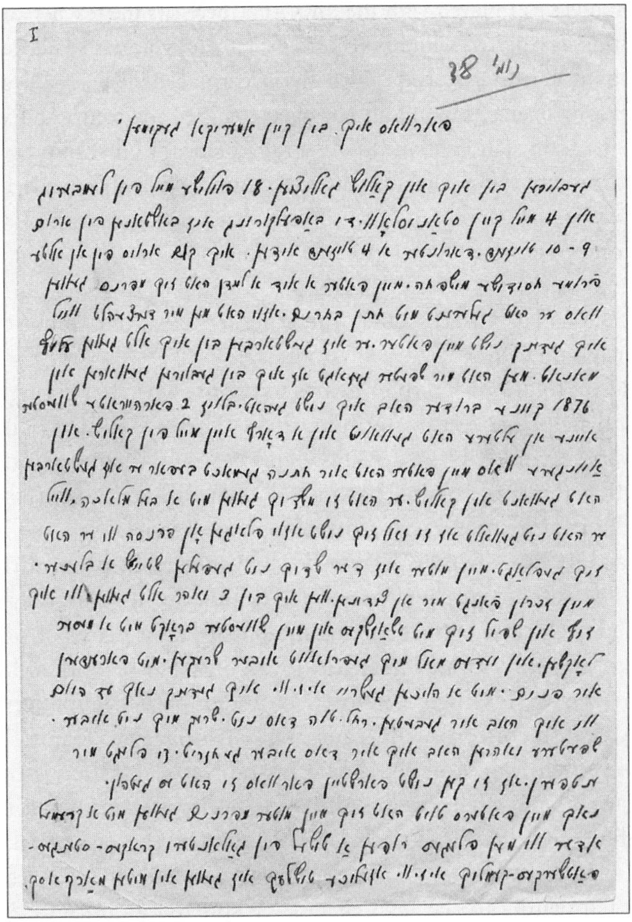

Fig. 2. The first page of Benjamin Reisman's manuscript. Courtesy of the YIVO Institute for Jewish Research

in America. The act of writing itself proved a deeply emotional experience, as autobiographers explored memories long buried. As first-prize-winner Ben Reisman (fig. 2) put it,

When I sat myself down at my desk, my God! No exaggeration. Not as in a dream, but as if in reality, I once again became that baby watching his sister make noodles as I played with the toys. And there sits the teacher, Simkha, instructing us children with his beautiful sorrowful voice. . . . And I cry as I write about it, as I cried then when I was learning Bible. . . . As I wrote I involuntarily opened my mouth and then clenched my teeth. And when I was at the train station about to leave for America, I burst into tears as I parted from my young wife and my sister. And, remarkably, while I wrote that I was saying goodbye, I cried so hard that I had to wait quite a while until I calmed down enough to resume writing.

Writing thus had a cathartic effect for some writers. They were finally able to "unburden their hearts."[9]

This desire to unburden their hearts to people who they thought would understand helped to motivate the writers. They would have liked their children and grandchildren to know more about their lives, but some doubted that this was possible because of their different historical experiences and, in some cases, because of a language barrier.

It is hard to know what role World War II played in prompting people to write. The autobiographers responded to the war in various ways. Some maintained such close emotional attachments to their places of origin that they worried openly about the fate of loved ones left behind and pictured vividly to themselves their hometowns under Nazi occupation. Others combined Jewish concern with American patriotism by closing their narratives with their hopes for the defeat of the Nazis and the victory of the Allies. Many do not mention the war at all, perhaps feeling that it was not part of their own lives and therefore not part of the assignment. A few mention explicitly that the knowledge, however vague, that something terrible was happening to the Jews of Europe spurred a desire to describe a vanishing way of life that they had known. At the same time, the war confirmed the writers' good fortune in having become American and validated their decision to emigrate decades earlier.

The contest also offered the writers a chance to gain recognition and honor, and some had high hopes that their manuscripts would win prizes and even be published. But, winner or not, most contestants found it very gratifying to hear that their lives had significance for history. On September 15, 1943, YIVO distributed the awards at a gala ceremony with several hundred people in attendance. All of the writers received certificates (fig. 3), which delighted them. A number indicated their intention to frame these "diplomas" and hang them on the wall. As several contestants put it,

Fig. 3. All participants in the 1942 contest received a certificate like this one. It recognizes that the participant has "taken part in the contest of the Yiddish Scientific Institute, 'Why I Left the Old Country and What I Have Accomplished in America,' and has submitted an account on this theme. The contest jury has decided to acknowledge the account as a document that conveys important material on the history of Jews in recent times. The account has been permanently entered into the store of scientific materials at Yivo and will be used by historians and social psychologists in research and publications. Yivo expresses gratitude to the writer of the account and appreciation for his contribution to Yiddish science." Courtesy of the YIVO Institute for Jewish Research

writing their autobiographies was itself one of their most important accomplishments in America.

In the end, only a few works saw publication, in whole or in part.[10] In the six decades since the contest, the autobiographies have resided in the YIVO archives, consulted occasionally by scholars. But this "eternal treasury of Jewish studies and Jewish culture," as Weinreich called it, remained largely unknown and inaccessible to the wider public.

Jewish Immigrant Writers and Genres of Autobiography

Weinreich and the writers all agreed that the autobiographies made compelling reading. As Minnie Goldstein told Weinreich, she had never expected to win a prize, "but I knew one thing, that if I had read such a history written by someone else . . . it would have really sparked my interest." They still fascinate today. True, not all of the autobiographies are equally engaging, but each and every one of them has something essential to say about one or another aspect of the Jewish experience. Most importantly, how the authors wrote and structured their narratives reflects how they understood their lives.

As they wrote, the participants consciously or unconsciously followed several distinct European and American autobiographical traditions. One of these traditions emerged out of the Haskalah, or Jewish Enlightenment, which began in Germany in the late eighteenth century and spread to Eastern Europe in the nineteenth century. Just as the general European Enlightenment gave rise to the autobiographical form for which Rousseau's *Confessions,* written in the late eighteenth century, served as the paradigm, the Haskalah gave rise to a new tradition of Jewish autobiography. In the maskilic[11] autobiography as it developed in Eastern Europe, the story details the writer's education and coming into worldly knowledge beyond or in opposition to traditional Judaism. The figure of the yeshiva student secretly reading "forbidden literature" under threat of punishment is perhaps most emblematic of the excitement, danger, and appeal of the Haskalah to the youth of the elite eager to quench their thirst for knowledge of the world beyond the yeshiva walls.

Although the writers of the YIVO autobiographies all came of age after the Haskalah had lost momentum in the 1880s, the maskilic theme of the pious youth's loss of faith and cultural reorientation through the secret study of heretical literature remained common at the turn of the twentieth century and beyond. The difference was that youths were now likely to be attracted to one of the political movements that succeeded the Haskalah as vehicles for the modernization of Eastern European Jewry.

Indeed, the maskilic story of individual enlightenment blends well with what might be called a genre of Socialist autobiography. Many of the writers of the YIVO autobiographies were, in fact, profoundly influenced by the Socialist movement both in Eastern Europe and in the United States. The Socialist autobiography, as it developed in Europe, is the story of the young worker who remains oblivious to the ruthless, impersonal forces of capitalist exploitation at work in his or her life, until an encounter with the Socialist message inspires "conversion" to Socialism and a lifelong commitment to Socialist principles.[12]

The Socialist autobiographical genre is strongly represented in the YIVO collection in large part because the Workmen's Circle, a Socialist-oriented Jewish labor fraternal order, enthusiastically endorsed the contest. Bertha Fox could not have been alone in first reading about the contest in the Workmen's Circle organ, *Der fraynd*, "after a day of house-work."[13] The stories of Workmen's Circle members fit well into the Socialist genre of autobiography. Many of them write about their encounter with Socialism as a form of conversion, during which the Socialist message penetrates their soul and precipitates an immediate shift in their worldview and priorities. Most importantly, the Workmen's Circle endorsement offered writers an alternative interpretation of the contest's problematic theme of "accomplishment," which may otherwise have discouraged those whose lives did not reflect conventional notions of success. The order's members could judge their success in life not only by their upward mobility, but also by their roles in helping to lift up the masses of Jewish workers by building the movement's impressive network of working-class institutions.

The struggle to achieve basic literacy, especially in the case of some of the women, or to acquire worldly knowledge and understanding, as in the case of some of the men who had been deeply embedded in the traditional world of the yeshiva, was another important aspect of the writers' lives. Rose Silverman describes how she painstakingly taught herself to read and write Yiddish, using a prayer book and a published letter-writing manual. Minnie Goldstein taught herself to read Yiddish as an adult, using the Yiddish daily newspaper *Forward*'s famous advice column, the *Bintl brief* (Bundle of Letters). Her pride—mixed with surprise—in having won a prize in an essay contest is moving testimony to the strength of her desire for both literacy and recognition. By contrast, Aaron Domnitz, who had a solid education in the traditional Jewish texts, describes his growing interest in modern literature and natural science—an interest that gradually helped lead him out of the traditional milieu.

The Socialist autobiographies also highlight the importance of organizations in the lives of the authors. In both Europe and America, the Socialist movement infused the lives of many of the writers not only with structure, but also with meaning. As these participants describe their youths in Europe, they chronicle daily life in an underground movement that met their dual needs for political activism and social interaction in equal measure. Socialist organizing in the United States was not nearly so romantic. Not only was it legal, but it also tended to focus on such mundane tasks as winning local elections and gathering subscriptions for the party press. Indeed, disappointment in the American movement's lack of passion is a characteristic theme in the autobiographies of radicals. Nevertheless, after an initial period of adjustment, immigrant radicals transferred their allegiances. Some joined the Socialist Party, but the organization that really won the loyalty of many writers was the Workmen's Circle.

Coexisting uneasily with the Socialist autobiographical approach was yet another model: the uniquely American story of the poor immigrant of any nationality who "pulled himself up by his bootstraps" and "worked his way up" from humble origins to achieve unprecedented economic success. This narrative is often associated with the popular nineteenth-century novelist Horatio Alger, whose protagonists overcome great obstacles through their strength of character to cross class barriers. Real-life figures such as the Scottish immigrant turned steel magnate Andrew Carnegie gave this legend of democratic opportunity a new focus for the significant immigrant population only then shedding its "greenhorn" status.

This immigrant "bootstraps" narrative resonated strongly with a number of the YIVO autobiography writers (perhaps abetted by the official theme of the contest, which focused on "accomplishment"). Many of those who started out in the workshop eventually came to the conclusion that working "for someone else" was no good. Business was the surest way up, though it could mean almost anything from peddling to owning a factory. By the 1920s, many of the writers were "successful" by their own estimation. Not only did they own their own businesses and homes, but many had also begun to invest heavily in real estate. Reflecting the emergent consumer culture in which they lived, these autobiographers report the purchase of increasingly expensive consumer goods, houses, and home furnishings as they work their way up the income ladder. Strikingly, authors often combined the story of their upward mobility with that of their continued commitment to the Socialist cause.

As the writers in this anthology navigated their way across the borders of class and culture, they engaged the various narrative forms discussed above in creative tension. They learned these ways of approaching autobiography from a range of sources: from their extensive reading of modern Jewish literature; from the political movements in which they participated;

from the American Yiddish press; and from the sophisticated new media of consumer culture, including advertising, film, and radio.

Jewish Immigrant Autobiography

The stories told by the YIVO writers contrast sharply with the better-known immigrant memoir literature in a number of ways. For the most part, for example, the YIVO writers were adults when they arrived in the United States and their perspectives and experiences therefore differ from those of better-known writers who came as children. Perhaps most significantly, the YIVO collection includes the life stories of a number of "immigrant mothers"—women who had already married and given birth to children in the Old Country. Many of these women lacked the ability to write in English (or even Yiddish) and were not as conspicuous in the public sphere as were young, unmarried women. When immigrant women's voices have found their way into the historical record—either through published autobiographies or, later, through oral history projects—they have tended to be those of the "immigrant daughters" who arrived in the United States as young girls and subsequently mastered the English language.

Among the most famous Jewish immigrant autobiographies are those by Mary Antin and Rose Cohen. Antin's *The Promised Land*, published in 1912, focuses on the early recognition and cultivation of the author's literary talents in public school and serves as a song of praise for her adopted country. Antin's story is one of near-complete assimilation, as she marries a Gentile and immerses herself in "American" life. Rose Cohen's *Out of the Shadow*, published in 1918, begins as a matter-of-fact account of sweatshop life that more closely resembles the stories in this collection in its lack of self-conscious reflection—at least until the point when she enters the sphere of the settlement house and comes under the powerful influence of Protestant philanthropic endeavors. Cohen's radical assimilation is less complete and more conflicted than Antin's, but the assimilationist thrust of her autobiography is nonetheless clear.

Both Antin and Cohen wrote for an English-speaking, gentile audience as cultural brokers, with the goal of giving outsiders an "authentic" perspective on Jewish immigrant life. The result is a flattening out of the historical narrative and a loss of cultural specificity as unfamiliar terms, events, and concepts are either translated loosely into rough Anglo-American equivalents or omitted altogether. By contrast, the YIVO autobiographers, writing in Yiddish for a Yiddish-speaking audience of fellow immigrants, relate stories about the past rich in detail concerning the culture and history from which they emerged.

Perhaps most importantly, unlike writers such as Antin and Cohen, with their explicitly assimilationist message, the YIVO autobiographers assert continuity between past and present within their own lives. They would never have proclaimed, as Antin did in her foreword, that their past selves had died to enable to them to be born anew in the United States. To a large degree this search for continuity is a function of the YIVO writers having been adults when they emigrated. Moreover, for those politicized in Eastern Europe, radicalization in the social movements of the Old Country rivaled emigration itself as the most significant transformative experience of a lifetime. This is not to argue that the writers did not in fact change fundamentally. Rather, they take it as their task to weave their lives into a coherent whole in the face of a profound disjuncture between past and present.

The well-known published memoir literature also has little to say about relations among husbands, wives, and children (at least from the immigrant parents' point of view). The YIVO autobiographies, to the contrary, give an intimate view of gender relations in marriage, from the joys of shared domesticity to deep conflict over money, religion, emigration, and politics in both Europe and America. In discussing their lives in Europe, the authors provide detailed, complex, and often unsentimental accounts of childhood, courtship, and relations with parents. Likewise, the autobiographies document the struggles of immigrant parents to maintain a living link to their children and to pass on to them at least some of what they called their "*gayst,*" their spirit. The loss of easy communication between the generations was an ironic by-product of the parents' frequent success in seeing to it that their children got a good education and entered prestigious careers. Indeed, the women especially saw their children's upward mobility as their proudest accomplishment.

Ironically, Orthodox Jews shared with radicals the problem of educating their American children in their own spirit. In Eastern Europe, the United States had gained a reputation as a *treyfene medine,* a non-kosher country. But some newcomers struggled mightily to keep the Sabbath, an observance made difficult by Sunday blue laws and by the six-day work-week common at the beginning of the century. Indeed, as the stories of

Shmuel Krone and Chaim Kusnetz show, some members of the immigrant generation strove to maintain their religious principles under the pressures of American materialist culture.

This hardly exhausts the list of important aspects of immigrant life on which the autobiographies shed new light. As YIVO's research director, Weinreich argued so strongly for the centrality of life stories to social science partly because he believed that they represented the complexity of real life more fully than other kinds of documents. Readers and researchers will no doubt continue to come to the autobiographies with their own questions—and, in many cases, the autobiographies will reward them with important clues to the answers.

Translating and Reading the Autobiographies

This volume can present only a small handful of the more than two hundred manuscripts in the YIVO collection. The editors used several criteria for selection. First, those manuscripts chosen for inclusion had to be good stories. Second, they had to be interesting for their historical significance —not only because they touched on great events, but also because they said something about changes in everyday life. Third, the editors tried to make the sample included here at least somewhat more representative of the general immigrant population than is the collection as a whole— not only in terms of gender, but also in political and religious orientation, class status, age, time of migration, region of origin, and place of settlement.

The translation of these texts also presented a number of challenges. Writing in Yiddish for an insider audience, the writers often took it for granted that readers would share their historical and cultural reference points. And having lived through a time of tremendous change and crossed cultural and geographic boundaries, the authors had historical experiences of exceptional variety. To fully understand all of their stories, one must have some familiarity with traditional Judaism; with Eastern European Jewish folkways; with modern political movements; with various trades and occupations; and with the histories of Eastern Europe, North America, and the Middle East. One must also know something of the geography not only of these broad regions, but also of the cities and towns from which the writers came and in which they settled. Few readers today, including the editors, have all of that knowledge. We were able to rely on the assistance of experts in all the necessary fields. We hope that the notes and Glossary will help the reader navigate the material.

The very fact that the authors were writing in Yiddish presented its own unique challenges. Like most Yiddish speakers, the writers also knew the languages of their native and adopted homelands with varying degrees of fluency. Thus their Yiddish is laced with expressions from Russian, Polish, German, and English. Sometimes, writers manipulated their use of these languages quite consciously. Those who had received a good traditional education, for example, knew at least a smattering of Hebrew and Aramaic as well. Following custom, they quote in the original from the Talmud and the Bible, thus demonstrating their status as educated Jews. These layers of language help give the writing some of its special flavor.

Ultimately, Max Weinreich was right. These texts deserve to be published precisely because the writers and the worlds in which they lived deserve to be remembered. This volume seeks to preserve a bit of that memory and present it to a new audience.

NOTES

1. In the mid-1950s the institute changed its English name to YIVO Institute for Jewish Research. YIVO is an acronym for the institute's Yiddish name, *Yidisher visnshaftlekher institut*, which has remained unchanged. For the sake of consistency, the institute will be referred to as YIVO throughout.

2. Minnie Goldstein to YIVO, October 4, 1943, unsorted material, American-Jewish Autobiographies Collection, Record Group 102, YIVO Archives.

3. On YIVO and Max Weinreich, see Lucy S. Dawidowicz, *From That Place and Time: A Memoir, 1938–1947* (New York: W. W. Norton, 1989); Barbara Kirshenblat-Gimblett, "Coming of Age in the Thirties: Max Weinreich, Eduard Sapir, and Jewish Social Science," *YIVO Annual* 23 (1996): 1–103; Cecile Esther Kuznitz, "The Origins of Yiddish Scholarship and the Yivo Institute for Jewish Research (Lithuania)" (Ph.D. dissertation, Stanford University, 2000).

4. Marcus Moseley, "Life, Literature: Autobiographies of Jewish Youth in Inter-war Poland," *Jewish Social Studies* 7:3 (spring/summer 2001): 1–51; Jeffrey Shandler, *Awakening Lives: Autobiographies of Jewish Youth in Poland before the Holocaust* (New Haven: Yale University Press, 2002); Max Weinreich, *Der veg tsu undzer yugnt: yesoydes, metodn, problemen fun yidisher yugnt-forshung* (Vilna: YIVO, 1935).

5. Max Weinreich, *Di yidishe visnshaft in der hayntiker tsayt* (New York: YIVO, 1941), 11. On the immigrant autobiography contest, see Jocelyn Cohen, "Discourses of Acculturation: Gender and Class in East European Jewish Immigrant Autobiography, 1942" (Ph.D. dissertation, University of Minnesota, 2000); Daniel Soyer,

"Documenting Immigrant Lives at an Immigrant Institution: The YIVO Autobiography Contest of 1942," *Jewish Social Studies* 5:3 (Spring/Summer 1999): 218–43; Moses Kligsberg, "Socio-Psychological Problems Reflected in the YIVO Autobiography Contest," *YIVO Annual* 1 (1946): 241–49; Kligsberg, "Jewish Immigrants in Business: A Sociological Study," *American Jewish Historical Quarterly* 56:3 (March 1967): 283–318.

6. "A konkurs af oytobiografies fun imigrantn," *Yivo bleter* 19:2 (March–April 1942): 281–82. See also the draft English-language version, American-Jewish Autobiographies Collection, unsorted materials, RG 102, YIVO Archives.

7. "Der kontest af oytobiografies fun yidishe imigrantn in Amerike" / "The Yivo Contest for the Best Autobiographies of Jewish Immigrants to America," *Yedies fun Yivo / Newsletter of the Yivo* 1 (September 1943): 3, 4*.

8. Max Weinreich to Harry Sprecher, July 4, 1942, letter accompanying autobiography #20, American-Jewish Autobiographies Collection, RG 102, YIVO Archives.

9. Ben Reisman (Yosem Halevi Me'ir Kalush) to Weinreich, undated, American-Jewish Autobiographies Collection, unsorted materials, RG 102, YIVO Archives.

10. Israel Pressman, *Der durkhgegangener veg* (New York, 1950), published in English as "Roads That Passed: Russia, My Old Home," *YIVO Annual* 22 (1995): 1–80; Isaac Donen and Gloria Donen Sosin, *A New Life Is Coming Soon: The Story of My Father's Life* (White Plains, N.Y.: Kalita Press, 1992); Falek Zolf, *Oyf fremder erd* (Winnipeg: Israelite Press, 1945), published in English as *On Foreign Soil*, trans. Martin Green (Winnipeg: Benchmark Press, 2000); Yankev Finklshteyn, "Zikhroynes fun a 'fusgeyer' fun Rumenie keyn Amerike," *Yivo bleter* 26:1 (September–October 1945): 105–28.

11. From the Hebrew *maskil*, "enlightened one." See Glossary.

12. The Socialist autobiographical form incorporates elements of the Protestant Evangelical conversion narrative, and likely reflects the influence of the German Social Democratic movement over the political culture of labor movements in Europe and the United States. See Mary Jo Maynes, *Taking the Hard Road: Life Course in French and German Workers' Autobiographies in the Era of Industrialization* (Chapel Hill: University of North Carolina Press, 1995).

13. Autobiography #193, part 1, page 1, American-Jewish Autobiographies Collection, RG 102, YIVO Archives.

Chapter 1

Success or Failure?

Minnie Goldstein (Mashe)

b. 1882, Warsaw, Poland
To U.S.: 1894; settled in Providence, R.I.

Minnie Goldstein's struggle to achieve basic literacy was a difficult one. In her native Warsaw, Goldstein (fig. 4) spent most of her time on the street, and in New York she went to work as soon as she arrived at the age of twelve. She never received any formal education. Only as an adult did she learn to read and write, first Yiddish and then English. Although she asks the scholars at YIVO to judge whether she has been a success or a failure, Goldstein clearly believes she has been a success. Starting with virtually nothing, she has acquired several houses, learned how to read and write two languages, become active in communal affairs, and "fooled the doctors" by virtually curing her son of the debilitating effects of polio.

My parents and I were born in Poland. I am a sixty-year-old woman. I have always liked to dress neatly and cleanly. I love to take long walks in the fresh air. In the summer I love to bathe and swim in the ocean. People tell me that I do not look older than forty-eight. My mother brought me to America when I was twelve years old. I was married in America.

As far as I recall, my parents and their parents were all natives of Warsaw. I was born to respectable parents. My grandmother and grandfather had a large business in Warsaw. They had a wholesale shoe and rubber business on Nalewki Street, which was the biggest business district in Warsaw at that time. I found out that my grandmother came from a family of poor workers, and that her parents had died very young leaving her as a young orphan with a little sister. At the age of twelve, she went to work in a shoe business as an errand girl, and there she stayed until she worked her

Fig. 4. Minnie Goldstein. Courtesy of the YIVO Institute for Jewish Research

way up to become a saleslady. Then she opened her own shoe store. She got married, but always remained a businesswoman. Though she did not have any education, she knew how to pray well and was very pious.

My grandfather came from a very respectable family, but his parents had become very poor. My grandmother's business went very well. Together they had twelve children, but their children did not live long. Of all those children, only my mother survived. The rebbe* advised my grandmother to have my mother raised in a poor household with many children, until she got older. And when my mother became older, her mother brought her home and told her that she (my grandmother) was her real mother. Their house was always empty. Only the servant was at home, while the mother and father were at the store until late. My mother felt terribly lost.

Well, the time came, and my mother married a yeshiva* student. She had a dowry, and it was agreed that the groom's parents would provide the couple with board. But before long she gave birth to two children in two years and her husband became sick and died. My mother was still very young, all of nineteen years, when her first husband died. When my mother married my father he was a young man of twenty, also a yeshiva student. Since my mother wanted to take care of her children, she lent out the money that she had from her first marriage as a first mortgage on a house. Her father-in-law said that he wanted to keep his son's children, since she was marrying again. Her father-in-law also had a second mortgage on the same house, and was the children's guardian. When property fell steeply in value, some sort of deal was made, and the house was sold at auction. In short, the children's grandfather received the money that belonged to the children and then sent the children to my mother.

My parents were always physically weak people. My father saw that it could not go on like that for too long—taking board from my grandmother and warming the bench studying. So he started to rent out houses and my grandmother took in one of my mother's children. My mother also bore my father two children—my brother and me.

Time passed. My father's business did not go well. My grandmother continued to help but it helped like a hole in the head. My parents were not making a living. Then my grandfather died, leaving my grandmother alone with her first grandchild, a young boy. For as long as I can remember, there was always worry in my parents' house when I was a child—that there was no rent money . . . that times were bad—until my grandmother convinced my father to open a kind of a little shoe business. Nor did this bring in any fortune. Then my grandmother said to my father, "Bring the goods from your business and we'll work together." But her business was not going so well either.

Well, they became partners, and things went a little better, but this did not last long. My half-brother felt that he would have been much better off if my father had not been a partner, and he convinced my grandmother that the business was going under. Arguments started. My grandmother yelled, my mother cried, and my father kept quiet. I once heard my mother say that she was certain that merchandise was missing from a couple of crates in the store. But my father said, "Oh, don't talk nonsense." More time passed and the arguments and crying continued. Once, around two o'clock at night, I heard my mother say to my father, "Hershl, please, let's get dressed and go to the store. I'm telling you, my heart tells me that my son and my mother are removing merchandise." Well, they went over and actually found them carrying merchandise from the store. Well, my father immediately left the partnership with my grandmother and tried it on his own. But again it did not work out. My grandmother still had to help us with a couple of dollars a week.

Suddenly, my mother noticed that my father was walking around with a small book in his hand. He was walking back and forth, reciting from the book in English and translating into Yiddish: "Good morning, gentlemen. *Gut morgn, here.*" He walked back and forth, learning the words. So my mother asked him, "Tell me, what do you need to know that for?" My father kept quiet, but he never failed to learn a couple of words each day, until my mother insisted that he tell her what he intended to do and why he needed to know English words. Then he told her that he was getting ready to go to America.

"What are you talking about? You're going to America? You're a weakling and you don't have a trade. And you don't have any money. Who goes to America anyway? Those who run away from home because of some sort of crime, or those who are banished there by the government. What does someone like you have to do with America? They need only heavy laborers there and you can't do anything."

"Well, that's exactly what I want. I want to go to a country where heavy labor is no disgrace. I want to go to a country where everyone is equal, where the rich also work, and work is no disgrace. I want to go to America, where a Jew does not have to take off his hat and wait outside to see a Pole. In other words, I want to go to a country where I can work hard and make a living for my wife and children and be equal to everyone."

Well, no matter how much my mother tried to convince him that, since there was no one from their family in America, he would have no one to turn to for money, it did no good. He went on with his English dictionary. And one morning at about four o'clock, there was a loud knock on the door. I heard my father say to my mother, "Brayndl, dear, the coachman is here. I have to go." Well, I do not remember whether my mother accompanied him to the train, but I think that he left by himself. In the morning, my mother told me that if anyone asked me where my father was, I should say that I did not know. My mother said that she would tell strangers that my father had gone abroad on business, because she was very ashamed that her husband had gone to America.

My mother's name was Brayndl. My Father's name was Hershl. My mother was something of a nervous and excitable woman. She would often yell, and sometimes also curse. But my father often said that she was a stunning woman. My father had a very refined outlook. He was someone who was happy with whatever came his way. He used to tell me, "My child, if you look upward, you'll never be happy. But if you look downward, you'll see it can be worse and you'll always be happy with your life." He did not like people who were proud of their money or of how smart they were. He was a quiet, honest, sincere person.

Well, my grandmother had by now kept my mother's first two children —a son and a daughter—for a long time. And now that my father had left, she also took in the third grandchild—my real brother—and gave my mother five rubles a week on which to live. My mother rented a room from others for herself and for me. My grandmother and mother often fought. My grandmother screamed, "What do you want from me? I'm keeping three of your children, and I'm giving you five rubles a week! I am an old woman! With your two weddings and with me giving you money every week, you've already cost me ten thousand rubles!" My mother cried and yelled, "Who asked you to give me a yeshiva student for a husband?" My mother and I lived far away from my grandmother.

Now the bitter years of my childhood began. I remained alone in the room with my mother. No one even spoke of sending me to learn to read or write. My mother was always nervous and angry. She was very tired of staying home. She kept talking about how my father had gone away, about how she had trouble with my grandmother, about how her eldest son had betrayed her. This was why my father had no choice but to go to America. I was then around ten years old, but I understood my mother's and my situation as though I were a girl of twenty. Well, my mother could not stay in the room; she kept wandering around, leaving me two or three *groshns** each day to buy a roll with some stewed plums, which was called *povidle* in Warsaw. I ate rolls for breakfast and dinner, and again for supper also, because my mother came home when I was already sleeping. And if I felt like a snack, I would buy a piece of candy for one *groshn,* but then I would have to eat a plain roll. I was always hungry. Now who was it who said that hunger is stronger than iron? I fell upon a plan. I started to walk through the streets and whenever I saw a piece of pear or apple that someone had thrown away without finishing, I would pick it up and eat it.

When I was a child I looked a lot older than I was. I loved to play with children who were much older, and this got me in a lot of trouble. I recall my childhood boyfriends and girlfriends saying to me, "Come, let's go to a far away street. You'll go up to a coachman and tell him that you were sent to call a coach, and we'll all get in and take a long ride. And when we tell him that we're going to call the man who needed the coach, we'll run away." Well, they really did run away, but I got caught and the coachman brought me to my mother and I got a good beating.

Another time, several children said to me, "Mane, come with us to the marketplace (the marketplace near the Żelazna Brama—the Iron Gate). We'll pluck the cherries off the sticks there, so we'll have cherries to eat and a couple of *groshns* as well." Well, this looked to me like a good business, because we got a job there. I heard the market woman tell my girlfriends, "I'll give each of you two *groshns,* but don't nibble on any cherries!" Well, I sat down and got to work, and I noticed that my friends were putting cherries in their mouths whenever the woman went away for a moment. Well, I was so hungry that I thought to myself, "I'll just take one cherry so my mouth stops watering so much." Well, the woman caught me putting the cherry in my mouth, and she grabbed me by the shoulders and looked me straight in the eye, and said to me, "Come here, you little thief. I saw it in your eyes right away—that you are a thief. You're not getting a *groshn.* Now go!" That woman still appears before my eyes. Right then and there I made up my mind never again to take anything that did not belong to me.

Well, I wandered around like a lost soul. My father wrote letters with very bad news. And when a couple of weeks went by without my mother having received any letters from him, she could not sleep at night. Since she was very pious and had read somewhere that children had the power of prophecy, she kept waking me up and asking me to tell her if a letter from my father was coming for her. As young as I was, I still understood her position and I sympathized with her more than I did with myself. I was always very good to her. It happened once that I told her that a letter from my father was coming and that she would get it in a couple of days. And that is really what happened: She got a letter from my father! From then on I had no nights either, and I became so sleepy that I could not keep my eyes open. So she took spit and rubbed it on my eyes so that I would wake up and tell her when she was going to get a letter from my father.

My mother came home very sad one night, sat down next to me in the room, and started to weep and wail so hard that I too started to cry and wail. But she did not tell me why she was wailing like that, and I was so scared that I will never forget it. In the morning, my mother could not get out of bed. She spit up half a glass of blood. To this day, I do not know what she was crying about. Had she had a run in with my grandmother? Or had my father written her about his bitter situation? (This was when my father had already been in America for two years.) I heard my mother say that my father was not even making enough to feed himself, so what was he staying there for? He should come home!

My father had sold everything he could to get a couple of dollars to go to America. And when he arrived in Castle Garden,* he had two dollars in his pocket. A representative of the Hakhnoses Orkhim* brought him there. (I think that this organization is now called ORT.*)[1] They gave him something to eat and a free place to stay at night, with the right to go out and see people and come back. But it was only for a couple of days. He had with him a long cloth coat with a fur collar and lining which he had received from my grandfather as a wedding present. First he sold that coat for a couple of dollars. Then he found lodgings with a family with children on Hester Street. The apartment consisted of a bedroom and a kitchen. The children slept in the bedroom with the husband and wife, and my father slept in the kitchen with three other boarders.

At first, my father was eager to learn a trade and started to learn to be a shoemaker. But after he had worked for a couple of days, the boss came to him and said, "Mister Hirsh, don't knock yourself out for nothing. You're not suited to the work. You're too slow. Your hands are too clumsy to be a shoemaker." So he left that trade and tried another trade. But the same thing happened. The boss sent him away again. It went on like this for two years. My mother kept on writing him that he should come home, but he replied, "I promised myself that I would never set eyes on Warsaw again, and I'll keep my word." But it went so bitter for him here that he was living on one dry roll a day. And no one knew, because he was not the sort of person to complain and did not know the meaning of the word "borrow." If there was no money, one simply did not eat—until an idea occurred to him. He took a wooden box, bought some baby shoes, took up position on Hester Street, and sold the shoes at a profit of five or ten cents a pair. Gradually, he started to make a profit, and wrote my mother much better letters.

Before very long the women of Hester Street found out that my father would sell them a pair of shoes for thirty cents, while they had to pay fifty cents in a store for the same pair of shoes. Well, he started to earn some money, so he rented a small store. This was on Hester Street, between Essex and Ludlow. It was in an alley between the houses, which was closed off in the evening. My father put up a tent outside the store, with various children's shoes. As soon as he had arrived in America, he had taken out his first citizenship papers. Now he started to do business and felt fortunate with his success. He started to write to my mother that she should come with me to join him in America.

Then trouble started up again at home. My mother went around anxiously and kept complaining to me, "What does your father want from me? Do I have the strength to withstand the strain of traveling to America? What good will a person like me be there, when I can't even wash out a glass? And how can I leave behind my aged mother, who is over seventy years old, and my three children?" (My half-brother and half-sister were already married.) By then, my father had already started to send some money home to my mother. My grandmother also gave my mother money weekly for as long as my mother was in Warsaw, and I had to go pick it up every week. When my grandmother saw me coming, her blood ran cold. She saw me as a nuisance, which I could not understand. "Why is grandmother so angry when she sees me coming?" I felt that if my mother was sending me for the money, she must certainly have it coming.

Well, my father had been in America for four years before my mother decided to leave my brother behind with his grandmother and go with me to America. And then another pack of troubles started for me. My mother knew a woman who traded in silks in Germany. The woman bought merchandise in Warsaw, and she and my mother agreed that since the woman knew how to do these things, she would smuggle us over the border. The woman had already made an agreement with the conductor on the train, and she told my mother what to say when the conductor came up to her. But my mother got so scared when the conductor came up to her that she said everything all wrong. The woman started to tremble as if she had the highest of fevers. When we got off the train, she asked my mother, "How can a woman like you undertake such a long journey?" But we traveled on.

We said goodbye to the woman and arrived in Berlin very early in the morning. When we got off the train, a tall German stood there, dressed in a railroad employee's uniform and angry as a mad dog. He led us into a small house. My mother said to me, "I am afraid this man wants to rob us. Come, let's leave." As soon as we started to leave, the German ran over with a whip in his hand and told us to go back. "If you don't, I'll beat you."

And when we did go back in, the angry German locked the door. My mother was very scared, and said to me, "You see, he's locked us in. He wants to rob us and then perhaps to kill us." And she started to cry. Well, watching her, I also cried. An hour later the German came, opened the door, let in twelve young Poles, and locked the door once again. My mother recognized that the young men were also going to America, so she asked them in Polish, "Why is the German locking us in?" One of them answered, "I can't understand why he is locking us in either. Maybe he is some sort of robber. Well, we'll see. If he doesn't open the door in a little while, I'll break the window and we'll get out. We'll take both of you out with us." After an hour of fear, a train arrived with a lot of people, and they all came into the same house. Soon our train arrived, and we went on our way.

We rode on until we came to Rotterdam. It was Friday night, and my mother and I had to board a small boat along with many other people, and go to the place where everyone waited until their ships departed. But my mother did not want to board the ship because it was Friday night, so a man showed her a hotel and we stayed there.[2] And what about food? Since it was a gentile hotel and the dishes were not kosher* it was forbidden even to drink coffee or tea. Luckily, the Jewish man who had shown my mother the hotel came on the Sabbath to see how we were doing, and my mother asked him to try to buy us some food. So he brought us some dry bread and a smoked herring. We sat there and waited for four days for our ship to leave for America.

Our hotel windows looked out onto the ocean. The stormy waves scared my mother very much and she almost decided to send me off on the ship alone, while she returned to Warsaw. When I heard this, I cried so hard that she changed her mind once again. We would both go.

My father had written that we should not eat anything for a couple of hours before we boarded the ship, but I was really starving. I spotted a man with a pushcart selling peanuts. I asked my mother if she knew what they were, because I had never seen peanuts in Warsaw. My mother told me that she did not know either, but she thought they must be some sort of nut. So I begged my mother for some money to buy some nuts. If I am not mistaken, they used *pfennigs* there. She gave me two *pfennigs* and the man gave me a whole bag of peanuts. Well, as soon as I tasted the delicious, dried peanuts, I could no longer control myself, and I ate them all up as I sat on the ship. And when the ship started to toss, I became terribly sick, so I climbed into the upper bunk and lay there. My mother lay in the bottom bunk.

Before long my mother started to feel very sick and she spoke to me: "Manele, I feel very bad. I'm done for. Come up on deck with me, because I'm suffocating here." Well, as bad as I felt, I forgot about myself and I crawled out of bed to help my mother out of her bed, and dragged myself up on deck with her. Water sprayed from the waves. The ship's ropes were stretched across the deck. The sailors were not to be seen on deck. And I was dragging myself around the ship with my mother! We barely managed to drag ourselves back down to our beds.

My mother became very weak, and the same man who had brought us to the hotel in Rotterdam came to my mother's aid once again. My mother asked him to meet with the captain and ask him how much he would want for both of us to move to second class. Since the man had been in America once already, he knew whom to turn to. The captain told the man that if my mother had changed her ship ticket to second class before, she would only have had to pay for half a ticket for me. But now she would have to pay for two whole tickets. Well, my mother paid for a ticket for herself, and I stayed in third class. My mother said to me, "Manele, don't be afraid. The food they give you to eat in third class won't do you any harm, and you'll come to me in second class and be with me every day." But when I wanted to go see my mother, they did not let me in. I did not see my mother for a couple of days.

One morning they told me that a steward had come down from second class and was looking for me. He took me to my mother in second class. I had not been with her for ten minutes before the steward came right up to my mother and told her that time was up and that I already had to leave. I do not remember how long our trip on the ship took, but I remember that I saw my mother only a couple more times the whole rest of the way.

I do remember one thing that happened. I once told my mother that the people in third class were asking me why I came to eat there when I ate with my mother in second class. My mother said to me, "I don't eat here either, because, as you know, everything here is as *treyf** as a pig. I only drink a bowl of soup every day with a piece of bread. I consider it medicine to keep body and soul together.[3] You are hungry," she said to me. "I'll order them to bring me something to eat, and I'll give it to you." So she told the steward to bring her a plate of potatoes and onions. Well, don't ask! He brought a plate of potatoes and fried onions, along with a nice steak! He put it down and went away. My mother sat there looking at me and said, "You see what he brought me? Why are you looking at it that way? You would eat it, wouldn't you, you *treyf* soul! It's because of you and your father that I was driven out of my home. And it's because of you that I have to go to America." So, she called over the steward and told him that this was not what she had ordered. She wanted him to bring her plain boiled potatoes and raw onions. And since the steward was a young German, he went off very angrily, saying to himself, "Damn Jews! All they eat are onions!" And he brought the plain potatoes and the onions.

Well, thank God, we arrived at Castle Garden in America. Since my mother was traveling second class, she was allowed to leave right away. But I had to stay until someone came to pick me up. I do not remember how long it took, but I do remember that everyone else had left, and that only I remained behind, along with the people who were being sent back home. When I saw them wringing their hands and crying, I was overcome with fear. I could only figure that my mother had gotten lost somewhere and that I would be sent back home to Warsaw. But, with God's help, my father arrived and picked me up from Castle Garden. He told me that he had been very frightened when he saw my mother coming in a coach without me. And why had it taken so long to come and pick me up? Because he did not have anyone to mind the store.

My father rented a couple of rooms across from the store on Hester Street. I felt very happy now that we were all together. But—what can you do?—I was not lacking for work. I had to help my father in the store. Business was going very well. He was now also selling grown-up men's and women's shoes. I worked from very early to late at night with my mother at home and with my father in the store. And there was no talk at all of sending me to school.

When I got a little older, I was very ashamed that I could not even write my English name. Once, I said to my poor father, "You taught my half-sister in Warsaw to read and write Yiddish and Polish, and German as well. Why don't you at least teach me a little English?" He told me that he had a lot more time in Warsaw than he did here. "But come sit down and I'll teach you." But no sooner had I sat down with my father than my mother interfered and said, "What do you have to teach her to write for? She'll be a lot better off if she doesn't know how. Look at me with all of my knowledge of Yiddish, Polish, and German! I was driven from my home and now I'm in America where even the stones are not kosher! But just look at Mrs. Fertig downstairs. She can't sign her name, yet she sits in a big trimming store, respected and esteemed by everyone. Come here, Manele, better go bring me a pound of sugar." And my mother sent me away and I had to go.

Afterwards, my father said that he would let me go to night school. Well, since I looked much older than my age, I met girls in night school who were much older than I. They invited me to their home. They were honest children of working-class parents. Theirs was a happy home. The girls and a couple of neighbor boys dropped in there. When my parents found out that I was going there sometimes, they stopped me from going to night school and said they would hire a private teacher for me. But this never happened.

And another thing: My father was always a very quiet and happy person, while my mother was one of those people who had complaints against the world. It seems that I take after my father, one hundred percent. I have believed in working hard all my life, and I make the best of what comes my way. I was my parents' youngest and also most beloved child. Yet I cannot remember a single day during my childhood when I was taken care of as a child should be, or when I had enough to eat—even here in America. I just worked hard and heard my mother say that she was weak and unhappy. But since I possessed my father's nature, I grew into a pretty, healthy girl with dark brown eyes and red hair, despite the fact that I had lived through such a childhood.

Many boys fell head over heels in love with me, as they say. And of all of them, I picked a poor worker boy, my own age. He was very much in love with me and very good to me. He did not smoke or drink. But he had one big fault: Whenever he had even a couple dollars, the money immediately slipped through his fingers. He did not even know himself what he had done with the money. We married on the couple of dollars that I made sure we had saved up before the wedding.

Since in those days one did not work more than four months of the year, I knew that I had to start to do something right away.[4] We bought a candy store on Fifty-third Street. My husband either worked or went to look for a job, and I tended the store. Our rooms were together with the store, so I cleaned the rooms and cooked supper when there were no customers. And I learned to read the "Bintl brif" in the *Forward*.*[5] Meanwhile, a child arrived. I went on like that for five years. Then I saw that whatever I saved, my husband would spend, so we sold the store and took rooms on Fifth Street in New York. Before long I became the mother of another son. But, in all of my years of marriage, I never let a single day go by without sitting down and learning something. My husband was then earning very little, but we lived happily.

A better job became available for my husband in Providence [Rhode Island], so we moved here. My husband earned a little more, and had less slack* time. And the children studied very well in school and in *heder*.* I blessed my husband with a third son. The child was born nice and healthy like the other two children. I thought to myself, now that I could write Yiddish and read a Yiddish newspaper, I would start to learn a little English.

But a very great misfortune befell us. Our youngest child became very sick, and within twenty-four hours he could not sit up or raise a hand or a foot.[6] He was then nine months old. This hit me so hard that I often thought to myself, "None of the doctors give any hope that our son will ever be able to stand on his own little feet, or that he will be able to put a piece of bread in his mouth with his own hands. He will have to spend his whole life in bed. Yet he remains fully conscious. And he will be able to understand his situation so well. How will I be able to live, seeing that I have brought such an unfortunate soul into the world? Would it not be much better to take the child into bed with me, turn on the gas, and go to sleep forever together with the child?" But I did not have the courage, and I could not bear to cause my parents, my husband, and my children so much pain. And I thought to myself that the child would get better. "I know that I have not committed any wrong in my life, and the child certainly hasn't, so God will surely help him regain his health." Well, I gave a lot of money to the doctors and I could not afford to hire anyone to help me with the housework. The child alone could have used two nurses—one during the day and one at night. And what with the other children, and my husband, and cleaning the house. . . .

Well, we had a couple of hundred dollars in the bank, so I said to my husband, "Morris, I see that none of these doctors are helping the child at all. And the way they talk to me is making me sick, because they have nothing to give him. And the work is too hard even for three women, let alone for me by myself. It will kill me to go on like this. We should buy a little farm in the country, I tell you. You'll work in the city, and I'll stay with the children on the farm." My husband is not a bad person, and he was happy to toil away to make things easier for me and the children. We bought a farm in Connecticut, and things went slowly. But in three years time, I saw a great improvement in our child. He could now help himself a little with one hand and sit for a couple of minutes after you sat him up. It took me four years together with the children on the farm. The child improved greatly, and I saw that I had fooled the doctors.

Then I sold the farm and made a profit of 1,600 dollars. We moved back to Providence, where my husband was working. My situation was still quite difficult, but another year passed and my child continued to improve, and life became a little easier. Every minute that I could tear myself away I would take to the *Forward*, as a fish takes to water. We bought a house and I became a landlady. My mother died and my father was with me for eight more years. We bought another house in Providence. My husband did not deal with the houses at all. He did not even know what the mortgages were on the houses, and he certainly did not know the tenants. All of the workers who do jobs for me—the plumbers, painters, carpenters —like to work for me, because I do not take up too much of their time, and I pay them right when they finish the job. I can honestly say that I do not owe anyone a dime, and this makes me feel very good.

My first son entered college and studied well. He graduated from Boston University as a lawyer. Then my second son entered college at Brown University. This was at the time of the Depression. Times were not too good. Well, my son got a four-hundred-dollar scholarship each year for four years, and joined the biggest honor societies and graduated with the highest honors. And then our youngest son entered college. Times were not much better then either. My youngest son also got scholarships for four years, and also joined the biggest societies and graduated with the highest honors. And now we have one son who is a lawyer and two sons who are chemists.

Four times, every couple of years, my husband started his own business in his line. But he did not succeed. Not only did he lose the money with which he went into business each time, but for many years thereafter he also had to pay off the people to whom he owed money. So he went out of business and remained a worker to this day. But this did not bother me, because I was always happy to help, and we always had enough to live on. I felt very fortunate to know that with my help I was able to succeed in giving our children such a good education. I knew that it would not have been possible without my assistance.

My eldest son passed the bar as a lawyer in New York and stayed there to live. Once, when I went to New York, he said to me, "Mother, I want to take you to a show tonight. Would you object if I brought along a friend— a girl?" I told him that I would be very happy if he took her along. After the show, he asked me how I liked the girl, and I told him that she seemed like a very nice girl, and also very pretty. But, after all, she was not Jewish. "So why do you have to go with her? Aren't there enough Jewish girls who are looking for a boy like you—tall, handsome, and a lawyer?" So he assured me that she knew that he would not marry her. He just passed the time with her sometimes.

Once, he called me on the phone to ask if I would mind if he came home and brought along a girlfriend. I told him to come. I recognized that she was the same girl whom he had brought to the show. So I said to him, "Sol, why are you playing with fire? Why don't you give her up? You'll fall so in love with her that you'll suffer a lot when you tear yourself away from her. And why are you taking up her time?" So he replied that if he went with a Jewish girl he would soon have to marry her, because Jewish girls did not want to wait too long. And since he was still a law clerk and was not making much money, he could go out with her as long as he wanted. And she knew it. They had an agreement. When he wanted to leave her, it would be alright. Well, a couple of years went by and they got married. Once, when I went to New York, he told me the news that he had married the gentile girl. This hit me very hard.

I started teaching myself to read and write English. I did not have too much time for this, because my youngest son still demanded a lot of my time and I had to tend to the house, and shop for the house. And I had just become a landlady of two houses. But I continued to study every single minute that I could find. Then God provided and our President Roosevelt instituted morning classes, English schools, through the W.P.A.— two hours a day, twice a week, for older people.[7] I immediately used the opportunity and started to go to school. I found studying very difficult after going through such a hard life. But I tried as hard as I could, and used every single minute.

Our teacher once told the class that there was an S.A. contest in the schools, and if any of us wanted to take this on, we could be in the contest too.[8] I was the only one who told the teacher that I wanted to try. The teacher sent off my work. Some time passed, and I had already completely forgotten about it when a woman knocked on my door. I opened the door, and the woman said to me, "You've won an honorable mention, and I've come to teach you how to proceed, because you will have to get up and recite your piece. I am a teacher," she said. Well, I did not believe my ears, because I was sure that I could not write English well enough to have earned an honorable mention. But it was really true. I read my writing to the ladies, and they presented me with two books. My happiness was indescribable.

I read the Yiddish *Forward* every day. I have read a couple of English books. One book was called *You Can't Do Business with Hitler.* I read the *Reader's Digest.* I get the *Ladies Home Journal* every month. I like very much to read the questions there that people ask our First Lady, Mrs. Roosevelt, and also Dorothy Thompson's articles. I also sometimes read a monthly Zionist paper. I am now reading Hitler's book, *Mein Kampf.*[9] When I look at the book I am overcome with fear, but I think that every Jew should read the book to see what that mad dog is barking at the Jews. And I still go to school when I have a chance. I belong to the Workmen's Circle* women, and to the women's society. And I am a member of the Consumptives' Home.[10] One son has now enlisted in the navy, and my eldest son is about to enlist. My husband makes a living. I would be happy, if it were not for the war.

Before I got married, I worked as a baster on men's vests from six in the morning until seven at night with a heavy iron in my hand. I often ask myself, do today's children know how hard and bitter their parents' lives were? We love our children very much, and they also love us very deeply and show us respect. But I often ask myself whether it is right that poor parents work so hard to make chemists and lawyers of their children. Who knows? It may be that if I could live my life over again I would do the same for my children as before. But I now feel that when parents have to toil so hard to achieve this, they have no right to do so. And instead of putting every penny into their children, they should also make things a little easier for themselves.

Dear friends, after you read my life story, I would give you a thousand thanks if you wrote me whether my life up to now has been a success or a failure, because only such people as you can judge the best. Many thanks.[11]

NOTES

1. Goldstein is mistaken. The Hakhnoses Orkhim (Hebrew Sheltering House Association) was a predecessor of the Hebrew Sheltering and Immigrant Aid Society (HIAS).

2. Travel is forbidden on the Sabbath, which begins at sundown Friday.

3. Food taken for medicinal purposes by someone who is in danger of dying need not be kosher.

4. Work in many industries, including the garment industry, was seasonal.

5. Beginning in 1906, the "Bintl brif" (Bundle of Letters) was an extremely popular advice column in the *Forward*.

6. The child was stricken with infantile paralysis, also known as polio. Polio was common in the United States until effective vaccines were introduced in the 1950s.

7. Part of President Franklin D. Roosevelt's New Deal, the Works Progress Administration (WPA) was primarily a jobs program, so the classes that Goldstein attended were most likely intended mainly to provide work for unemployed teachers.

8. Goldstein means "essay."

9. *You Can't Do Business with Hitler* (Boston: Little, Brown, 1941), by Douglass Phillips Miller (b. 1892). Eleanor Roosevelt (1884–1962) contributed a monthly question-and-answer column, "If You Ask Me," to *Ladies Home Journal* from 1941 to 1949. Journalist Dorothy Thompson (1894–1961) espoused anti-fascist views through her widely read syndicated column. In his autobiography, *Mein Kampf* (My Struggle, 1925), Adolf Hitler set forth his anti-Semitic ideas.

10. In late 1928, in an effort to draw more women into the work of the order, the Workmen's Circle decided to encourage the formation of women's clubs. Goldstein also belonged to an independent local women's society and to an association that supported one of several Jewish-sponsored homes for tuberculosis patients ("consumptives").

11. The last paragraph is taken from a supplement to her autobiography that Goldstein wrote at YIVO research director Max Weinreich's urging.

Chapter 2

Why I Came to America

Ben Reisman (The Levite Orphan from the City of Kalush)

b. 1876, Kalush, Galicia
To U.S.: 1896; settled in Pittsburgh, Pa.

In YIVO's 1942 contest, Ben Reisman (fig. 5) won first prize for this detailed, lively, and nuanced autobiography. An orphan, Reisman had a close, but troubled, relationship with his extended family, a theme that runs throughout his account and is closely bound up with his resentment at having been forced to cut short his traditional Jewish education to apprentice as a tinsmith. In the United States, he became active in the Socialist movement and continued to work at his trade. He led a happy family life and expresses pride in his wife and children. Reisman eventually went into business for himself and prospered. Nevertheless, he exhibits the ambivalence of a Socialist businessman and remains critical of the materialism of some members of his extended family. We have significantly abridged Reisman's narrative due to space considerations.

I was born in Kalush, Galicia, eighteen Polish miles from Lemberg and four miles from Stanislav.[1] The population consisted of nine or ten thousand people, including around four thousand Jews.

I come from an old, pious Hasidic* family. My father, a learned Jew, made a living as a teacher of young men of marriageable age. At least that is what I was told, because I don't actually remember my father. He died when I was eleven months old. I was told that I was born in 1876. I had no brothers, just two married sisters. The older one lived in a village one mile from Kalush. And the younger one, whom my father had married off before he died, lived in Kalush. He matched her with an artisan because he

Fig. 5. Benjamin Reisman with his wife, Kay, c. 1920. Courtesy
of the YIVO Institute for Jewish Research

did not want her to suffer as he had suffered from not being able to make
a living. My mother did not like the match: "What? A tinsmith?"

After my father's death my mother made a living from a small store or,
as it used to be called, a "table" with fancy goods—belts, ribbons, beads,
combs, etc. There were many such tables in the middle of the marketplace
and many Jewish families made a living from that sort of trade. My
mother rented the table from a certain Yitskhok Rayner, an ardent Hasid

learned in Gemara.* We lived with my sister. She paid the rent, but when she did not have the money, my mother would give it to her. My mother was quite learned in Yiddish. She was very knowledgeable when it came to the Torah* portion with Rashi's* commentary. When I was four years old she taught me the Hebrew alphabet, showing me each letter in the prayer-book, starting with *alef, beys,* and so on.

When I was four and a half, she handed me over to Moyshe Cow (that's what they called him) for instruction. When I was six years old, he started to teach me Khumesh,* the first five books of the Bible. Yes, I remember to this day a Sabbath day when my mother brought me to school for the first time to be tested in the Torah portion that begins with *va'yikro,* "The Lord called to Moses."[2]

And I started out, "*Va'yikro,* and he called out." And my teacher immediately asked me: "Who called out? Was it Hoshaye the Sexton calling people to prayers?" I answered that God had called out to Moses and spoke to him from the Tent of Meeting, and so on. When I finished, my mother took me in her arms and kissed me, saying to the teacher that she hoped to God that her dear Binyomen would grow up to be a scholar.

And it was not long before she sent me to a more advanced teacher to study Khumesh with Rashi's commentary, and, if possible, a bit of the rest of the Hebrew Bible, the Tanakh.* This is what she said to my new teacher. His name was Simkhe, a fine Jew, tall and with a splendid beard. On his head, he wore a *spodek,* the kind of high fur cap that learned men used to wear, higher than a *shtrayml.*[3] The teacher's wife, Brayntse, a pious and kosher* woman, also knew a bit of Khumesh, and when the teacher was instructing us, she sometimes also took part.

It seems to me that Simkhe's teaching with children had no equal. He used to teach us each passage of the Khumesh with an appropriate melody, so he really drew us children in. I remember the sweet melody of the Song of Songs at Passover* time. He had a different tune for each Torah portion. I still have sweet memories of the time on a winter night when we were learning the passage "*kol be'ramah nishmo, Rokhl mevako al boneha*—Rachel cries for us, her children who are dispersed in exile."[4] I was then seven years old and the words, "*kol beramah nishmo,*" as the teacher called them out and translated them, made such a sad impression on me that I, the little Israelite, burst into tears. I sobbed so hard that the teacher's grandson, Hirshl, burst out laughing. The teacher bawled him out and turned to me. "Say it again, Binyomen, *kol beramah nishmo.*" And he immediately added the words of consolation, "*Rokhl, mini kolekh* *mibekhi,* stop your voice from crying. Your children will return to their old Zion." These words of consolation comforted me.

Every Sabbath, my mother would to test me in the weekly Torah portion. In the summer, Simkhe would teach me the *Ethics of the Fathers.* I used to begin, "*Rabi omer, ezohi derekh yeshoro sheyovor lo ho-odom. Kol shehi tiferes le-oso ve'tiferes lo min ho-odom.*"[5] My mother, may she rest in peace, would hear me out as I interpreted what my teacher had said. Then she said to me, "Listen, my child. I will explain to you what Rabbi meant." And she began: "In our town, there are many Jews who study Gemara day and night—Red Yankev, for example, and Yosl Kurts, and Shapse Mendl —and contribute a lot to the synagogue and the study house. But they demand high interest from any poor person who comes to them to borrow a few guldens.* They tear out his soul, yet they are known as scholars. This is what Rabbi is referring to when he asks, 'Which is the right way that a man should choose unto himself?' and immediately answers, 'One which is an honor to the person adopting it, and an honor to him from men.' He means, only those who feel in their hearts that they do themselves as much credit as people think they do. Now, my child, it is time to say the afternoon prayer."

At that time, my mother made a good living. She even lent money to non-Jews, and they paid her back by bringing her eggs, potatoes, onions, and the like. Naturally, she gave all of it to my sister (her daughter) with whom we lived. My mother did not want me to go to a secular school. She thought that later she would turn me over to a good writer to learn how to write.

My sister was not very good to me. She was not a bad person by nature. I remember that my mother spoke with her several times about me. My sister married young, at seventeen, about the same time that I was born. At the time about which I am writing she was about twenty-four years old and was thinking to herself that if I had not been born she would have inherited our mother's estate. In any case, she did not like me.

My brother-in-law was then a fine, robust, honest twenty-eight-year-old man. He loved my mother, his mother-in-law, very much. She once helped him out by lending him five hundred guldens at a very low rate. Rent did not cost him much, so he could save and make something of himself.

Soon I turned eight and my mother handed me over to a teacher of Gemara. Zekharye the Teacher was a fine man, tall as a pine tree, with snow-white hair. His wife, Zekharye's Etshe, helped them make a living.[6]

She had a small mill, where a gentile woman used to grind buckwheat into pellets and granules. And so, from the teacher's work with children and from the mill, they eked out a hard living. The teacher often sighed, "Oh, maybe God, blessed be He, will help me some day." I began to study Gemara with Rashi's commentary at eight. My *heder* was near the large study house. In those days, young men would study heartily in the study house. The melodies of Gemara study could be heard outside. I would often drop into the study house and listen.

And then, suddenly, my mother became ill. After several weeks of lying in bed she died. I still remember, it was a Friday. My mother's body lay on the floor with candles at her head. I sat on a small bench and cried bitterly, "Mamma, in whose hands are you leaving me?" My brother-in-law was working in a village at the time. Only my sister and my uncle Yankev, my mother's brother from Novitsa, were there. When the Sabbath was over, my mother was buried.[7] Coming back from the cemetery my uncle said to me, "I can't do anything for you, Benetshe. Just see to it that you don't make Rokhl angry, because she is the only one in the family who is so ill-tempered." He said that he did not know whom she took after.

So now I was an orphan and it was she who was to watch over me. My mother left a little bit of money, as well as some merchandise. My sister sold the goods to a neighbor who dealt in the same merchandise. My sister kept all of the money, though it was supposed to be for me to pay tuition and other expenses.

In the meantime, I went to *heder*. I started the Talmud* tractates Bava Metsia, Bava Kama, Ketubot, Gitin, and Kidushin, cutting down on Bible study to several hours on Thursdays.[8] Among my friends in *heder* was Getsl Foygl, the son of Shimshen Foygl, a great prayer leader and Torah reader in the synagogue, as well as a good scholar of the Gemara. When we were studying a *mishna,* Getsl's father would go through it with Getsl in the evening. When it came time to recite the *mishna* with our teacher, naturally, Getsl more or less knew it. Our teacher would bawl me out every time.

That is how it was with my little friend Moyshe Rentslshteyn as well. Moyshe's father was also a scholar who would go over the *mishna* with him, so he also sometimes knew how to interpret more of the words. During the first few months when the time came for me to recite for the teacher, I would sweat, but later it became easier for me. I overtook my friends in learning to such an extent that when the teacher wanted to take on a new pupil, and he wanted to show how well his pupils learned, he would take me along with him on the Sabbath to read from the Khumesh and the Gemara for the boy's father.

We would study from eight in the morning until eight in the evening. In the winter, we walked home by the light of a lantern. Early Friday mornings, we would study until it was time for morning prayers.

I studied for two more years with Zekharye the Teacher. Then I went to study with Meshel the Teacher, a Jew with a sharp mind and a great talmudist. He took on only selected children who already knew how to study Gemara well. But for my parents' sake, he took me on as a pupil.

In the almost two years since my mother's death, I had not experienced any mistreatment from my sister. But I did notice, here and there, children my age being caressed and kissed tenderly by their mothers and I would envy those children. Later, I became indifferent.

I was ten and a half years old when I began to study with Meshel the Teacher. I entered a completely different atmosphere from the one I was in with Zekharye. The big boys who sat over the Gemara knew me well, because Zekharye's house and Meshel's house were very close together. So they were good to me. The teacher started to teach me the chapter of the tractate Bava Batra* that begins "A presumptive title to houses . . . ," together with the commentaries of Rashi and the *Tosefos,** the additional commentaries.[9] This was a difficult Gemara for older people, but my teacher was happy with the way I learned. After about five or six weeks of study, he sent me almost every Sabbath to my parents' relatives to be tested. About two months later, he told me to study on my own, allowing me to ask just three questions for each *mishna.* Well, I had to obey my teacher. I began to drill it into my young mind. On the third day, I recited the *mishna* for my teacher. He was happy. After all, it was the first time I had studied alone, and it was such a difficult Gemara. So, there were certain chapters that the teacher taught to all of us boys together. But several select students, including me, studied Gemara on our own.

Once I was sitting and reading the *mishna* that begins, "If a man sells a house . . . ,"[10] and the teacher was studying the chapter "A presumptive title to houses" with another youth—the Innkeeper's Zekharye he was called. Zekharye says, "*Omar Robo shato,* he drank . . ." The teacher was dozing off. Suddenly he sat up and said to him, "Wait. Don't rush, Zekharye. Say it again." So he began, "*Omar Robo,* Rabba said, *shato,* he drank." Here the teacher said, "*Komayso,* he got drunk." Zakharye repeated. "*Mokhil,* he lay in the mud. *Inish,* he made a *tsimes.**"

I could no longer hold it in and I burst out laughing. The teacher addressed me, "Binyomen, what are you laughing at? Let's hear how you would interpret the passage." I read, "*Shato komayso mokhil inish*.[11] The issue has to do with title over land and fruit when one has held it for two or three years." After I had interpreted the passage, the teacher addressed Zekharye, "Tell your father that I want to see him tomorrow in the small study house."

After studying with Meshel the Teacher for half a year, I was really happy with his teaching. In the beginning, it was very hard for me. But later I learned a lot from him. And I also got more out of it spiritually. As winter approached, I thought I would learn really a lot in the second half of the year. In the meantime, the holidays arrived and I hoped that after the holidays I would return to *heder*. I was about to turn eleven years of age. On the day of Simhat Torah,* my brother-in-law said to me, "Binyomen, now you will stop going to *heder*. You're not going to make a living from studying. You will learn the trade." My sister was sitting there, and she said, "Quite so. How much longer can you go to *heder*?" Neither my tears nor my pleas had any effect. I was over and done with *heder*.

On the first day, they told me to clean out the store and the house, and to do other little chores. My teacher Reb* Meshel sent one of his pupils to find out why I had not come to *heder*. Of course, they told him that I had begun to learn the tinsmith's trade. When the teacher heard that, as I was told later, he took it to heart. And when the pious Jewish circles found out that I had been torn away from the *heder* it created an uproar. They told me that I should trade off days eating my meals with the local household-ers. But I did not want to "eat days.*" Secondly, what I wanted had nothing to do with it. And so, at the age of eleven, I started to train as a tinsmith.

Several months earlier, my brother-in-law had brought a journeyman from Lemberg by the name of Mates. He was a native of Rohatyn, in Galicia, a good tradesman and, as it turned out, a very honest man. My brother-in-law worked mainly in the villages making new roofs for churches. Every Friday he would come home for the Sabbath and ask my sister if I had obeyed her and if I had been a good boy. And it was seldom that she said that I had been obedient.

As I wrote before, there were three boys in the house: my sister's two boys, Mordkhe and Menashe, and I. I was two years older than Mordkhe. Next door to us lived a respectable man named Red Dovid with his two sons. They made boxes for the merchants who sent eggs to Germany. The neighbors' children would go into the yard and play with the wooden boards, making and taking apart little houses. I wanted to play with the boards sometimes too. In my heart I was dying to put together a little house. But I was afraid of my sister. Once I snuck out the back door and spent half an hour putting a very fine little house together. When Toybe the Poppy-Seed-Candy-Lady came by she shouted out, "Binyomen's house is the nicest! I have to go tell Rokhl to come and look." I ran right into the house, with Toybe behind me saying, "Rokhl, go take a look at the nice little house that Binyomen set up. He will grow up to be a good builder." Rokhl threw a sarcastic glance at me. When Toybe had gone, she said to me, "You have nothing else to do but to play around? Go do such and such."

My brother-in-law arrived on Friday as always. We came home from services and made the blessing over the wine. It was quiet. I thought to myself, can it be that she won't complain about me to him today? We finished eating the fish quietly. My young heart pounded for joy, or was it for fear? We ate the soup. My brother-in-law asked, "Well, how was Binyomen this week? Good?"

"I couldn't stand him. He was lying around in the yard playing with the boards."

My brother-in-law responded—wham!—with a good smack. I burst out in tears and sobbed loudly, crying "Mama, mama." I didn't eat my meat, but lay down on my little bed crying and fell asleep.

I helped out in the house and every Thursday I polished the eight-armed chandelier, the Hanukkah* menorah, and so on. Occasionally, I used to watch Mates work. When Mates went off somewhere, I took to the workbench and made a little lantern. Mates arrived back just when I had finished. "What did you make?" he asked. I answered, a bit fearfully, "A little lantern." He wanted to grab it away from me. But I held on to it firmly until my fingers dug into the teeth that held the glass in place and the teeth cut into my fingers and drew blood. I let out a terrible scream of pain. My sister came in from the kitchen and only then did he let me go. And as I remember she did not speak to him for a week.

My brother-in-law bought a house, and thus began my hard work. He borrowed five hundred guldens where we lived and added another five hundred guldens, and bought a house for six thousand guldens. He made a down payment of a thousand guldens and was left with a debt of five thousand. For the sake of convenience I will say "dollars."

At the same time, they enrolled the children in school. Mordkhe was also enrolled. I cried, "Why don't you enroll me in school like Mordkhe?" She did not give me a straight answer. I cried bitterly. "Why are you crying? Go sweep out the house," she said. I answered her, "Enroll me in school, and I will do everything." Just then Arn the Potter came in, and she complained to him that I would not obey her. "He wants us to send him to school."

"He really should go to school," he responded, glancing at me with pity. I never went to school or to a writing teacher. It may have been that in other cities, the municipality saw to it that children had to go to school. But the city of Kalush was then immersed in darkness. And everyone was out for himself. No one cared that many orphans like myself remained ignorant. With a heavy heart, I looked on in pain as Mordkhe went to school every day while I remained ignorant. The first few days, I had a good cry. Then, I told myself that I had to find a way to teach myself how to read and write.

In the meantime, we were supposed to move into the new house in about two or three months. We bought a wheelbarrow, and every day I packed various things and pushed the wheelbarrow day in, day out. Yes, sometimes even at night. And it was quite a long way. This lasted until we had moved into our new house. And that is when my hard work began. My brother-in-law wanted to enlarge the cellar, so the earth had to be excavated. My brother-in-law helped me dig and I carted the dirt far away with the wheelbarrow. In the evenings I used to help Mates in the work-shop. I could already make many small things from sheet metal.

It was a Thursday evening. Mates had finished a job and I was to deliver it quite a distance away. On the way back, a cold, hard rain was falling. I came in cold and soaked, so I got undressed and climbed into bed. Wood was burning in the oven, and Mates went up to the oven, took a shovel full of ashes mixed with live embers, and threw them at me on the bed. I got out of bed and started to yell. So my sister and brother-in-law came in and gave him a good talking to. He answered that there was a lot of work to be done and I was lying in bed. Well, I could not be mad at him for long, since he was my teacher and a good tradesman as well.

Once, my sister asked me, "Would you like to stay with your uncle Yankev for a week?" I said yes. The next day, I went on foot to my uncle in Novitsa. It was a two-hour walk. My uncle, my aunt, everyone was glad to see me. My aunt pampered me and my uncle instructed me. I told him that I would like to learn how to write.[12] So he took a shingle and a piece of chalk and wrote "*alef, beys*," and so on, and I started to learn how to write Yiddish. The girls wrote the a-b-c on a piece of paper for me, and I would erase it and write. Within about four or five days, I was able to write the following words: "Dear uncle, I received your dear letter in good order." I could also write several Polish words.

Friday evening after dinner, my uncle read a religious book, while I read the weekly Torah portion, *Ve-yeshev*, "Now Jacob was settled," together with the commentary of Rashi.[13] Rashi says, "*Bikesh Yankev leyashev be-shalva.* Jacob wished to live at ease, but this trouble in connection with Joseph suddenly came upon him. When the righteous wish to live at ease, the Holy One, blessed be He, says to them: 'Are not the righteous satisfied with what is stored up for them in the world to come that they wish to live at ease in this world too?'"[14]

I did not like Rashi's interpretation. My uncle noticed that I was very absorbed in Rashi. I asked him if the righteous really had to have a bad time in this world in order to attain a place in the next world. He answered that when a righteous person goes through many troubles in this world, he sits on high in Heaven under the wings of the Divine Presence in the other world. My uncle's answer did not satisfy me.

Instead of one week, I spent two weeks with my uncle. These were weeks of love and gentleness as I had not experienced since my mother, may she rest in peace, had died. I did not want to go home at all. On Monday, a gentile neighbor was going to town with a horse and wagon, so he took me along. My uncle's family gave me a chicken, butter, potatoes, and more, to bring along. As we came into town, I looked at the signs on the stores. I simply beamed: I could read the signs, the names of the stores and what they had to sell! Some signs were hard for me, but I could read them.

Well, back to work. The household was suffering without a cent, though outsiders thought that my brother-in-law was a wealthy man. Just as soon as a dollar was earned, it went to pay the interest, and bit of the principal, on the house. In short, we were scraping by. I would take things made out of sheet metal to sell. I had to sell something. First of all, there was not enough to eat. Secondly, I was simply afraid to come home with empty hands. That is how it was for months and years.

My sister's boy, Menashe, became sick and died on the nineteenth of Kislev. At the *shiva*,* the traditional weeklong mourning period, my brother-in-law's mother was truly a woman of valor. While I worked in the store, I overheard her saying to Rokhl and Moyshe Avrom, "Be good to the children and also to Binyomen. Don't curse and don't shout." But I thought to myself, it's no use; that is their nature.

In the meantime, Mates treated me better after I returned from my uncle's house. He could not read or write, so I would write to his parents in Rohatyn for him. Now he no longer needed one of the neighbors to write for him. Of course, my writing at the time was good for nothing, but at least it could be read. Secondly, I could already do quite a bit of work and helped him out a lot.

Mordkhe went to school and his school friends would visit, bringing their books, and do their homework together. As they prepared their lessons, I would follow along in such a way that no one would notice. And the boys really did help me out a lot. In this way, I learned how to read German.

Whenever I had free time, I spent it studying, sometimes by myself, sometimes with someone else's help. A friend of mine, Yisroel Kinstler, was reading a German book. He also taught me a lot. He would visit, and, sometimes, he would leave the book with me. The book was about Columbus and his discovery of America. When Mates was not in the workshop, I started to read the book, not very fluently, of course, but I was reading. My sister was in back, in the house. While I read, I gave a couple of raps with the hammer. But she heard that the raps of the hammer did not sound natural, like they would if I were making something to sell, so she snuck into the store. She found me reading the book, which she immediately tore out of my hands. "So is this book going to make a living for me, eh?" she asked. In the meantime, Mates arrived and she complained to him about me.

A short time later, Gitl, the daughter of Lilien's Brayntse, who lived opposite us, came in. Her husband, Avrom, would buy old sacks, fix them up, and resell them. She wanted me to make her a small metal sign with her name, but it wasn't to cost more than fifty kreuzers.* "Good," I said. "I'll make it for you." Well, I won't say that the sign was first class, but she was happy and she paid me the fifty kreuzers. My sister was standing nearby. I handed her the money, looking her straight in the eye. "You didn't want to send me to school and you don't let me learn on my own. But you take my money." Turning her head a little and putting the fifty kreuzers in her pocket, she understood my look.

Near us lived a great talmudist, Berish Kinstler, the grandfather of Yisroel Kinstler who had lent me the German book. On the Sabbath, he would study the five books of Moses with a group. I would go almost every week. (He had known my parents well.) After one study session, he said to me that when I had time, I should come to him and he would instruct me in Gemara, Khumesh, and other sacred books. I responded that I never had time. Even Saturday evenings, I had to work until Passover. Only in the summer would I have time in the evening. And so I studied with him in the summer evenings and I learned a lot from him.

When people asked me how my sister and brother-in-law treated me, I would reply, "Just fine." I never confided in anyone. Once I was fixing an umbrella that had a broken spring in its handle. I made a small tube with a cut where the spring had to push in and out. I was almost finished when my brother-in-law called out, "Binyomen, let's take a look. Show it to me." I handed him the umbrella. He took a look at it and said, "You made a little too much of a cut for a spring," and gave me such a ringing slap on the left cheek that I saw stars. But I think that he had pangs of conscience about it, because that was the first and last time he slapped me.

In general, he was not a bad person. After all, whenever I put on a new suit for a holiday, he derived pleasure from it. He was very honest. Apparently he was influenced by my sister into lashing out at me for any little thing.

Summer came and I was free in the evenings. I would go to Reb Berish Kinstler every evening and study. There was a fire in town and many houses burned down. Afterwards, we made sheet-metal roofs and I learned a lot about roofing. By then, I had begun to put on *tfilin.** Quietly, no one knew, except at home. I was now taken along on long trips to the villages and cities to put tin, zinc, or copper roofs on churches. We would go on foot, sometimes for a day and a night, sometimes for two days and two nights. Everything we earned went toward paying for the house and nothing was left for travel expenses.

Mordkhe, my sister's boy, also started to learn the trade. I was already working on churches with a helper. If there was a Jewish innkeeper or lessee of an estate, we ate with him. And if there was not, we would bring our own bread. We received potatoes, eggs, and milk free from the priest or the gentile peasants. We worked in this way for almost the entire summer. When autumn arrived, we still did not have a cent because the several hundred dollars that my brother-in-law made went toward the house. Even so, we kept on hoping that we would be finished with the payments any minute, and that our lives would become easier.

I knew well that if people knew how hard I myself worked for the whole family, they would ask me, "Why do you stay with your sister and brother-in-law? Go to another city, work for yourself, and be free." [But there were several reasons that I did not leave.] First of all, journeymen came almost every week from various cities, big and small: good, hard-working workers, looking for work. They would spend several days with us, eating and sleeping in exchange for work. Then they were given small change and rode, or walked, on, looking for work. Secondly, I understood that [if I looked for work elsewhere] it would be impossible for me to lead a thoroughly Jewish life or to look into a religious book once in a while. And above all I did not have the heart to leave them at a time when we were all plugging away. And besides, being here meant that I belonged to a household and was not far from home. Of course, I hoped that the house would soon be paid for.

So, we used to come home and I would only then start worrying about preparing for the holiday. It was not proper for my brother-in-law to chase after work in town, since everyone considered him a wealthy man. . . .

Finally, with God's help, my brother-in-law made the last payment on the house. On the intermediate days of Sukkot,* we invited to our *sukkah** Leybtsikhe's Reb Dovid (that's what they called him), a Hasid who lived in the house attached to ours, and Sholem Yeshaye, the clockmaker's son-in-law, from across the street. We ate and drank wine, and everyone was merry. No small matter—to pay off the house after so many years of drudgery. Both Hasidim got good and merry. Leybtsikhe's Reb Dovid was a Chortkover Hasid and Reb Sholem was a Belzer Hasid. Suddenly they got into a heated discussion about their rebbes* and began to fight.[15] Reb Sholem did not like Reb Dovid's remark about the Belzer Rebbe so he reached out and gave him a slap, and Reb Dovid gave him one back. Sitting on the other side of the table and wanting to separate them, I moved the Sabbath candles that were in my way. Both Hasidim noticed this and shouted at me with alarm, "Binyomen, it is Friday evening!" And they took up their cups of wine and began to sing pretty Hasidic Sabbath songs. And so we sat late into the night. On Monday, I fasted because I had forgotten that it was the Sabbath and had moved the lamps with the burning candles.

Leybtsikhe's Reb Dovid's house was under the same roof as ours. Between his house and ours was a common hall with doors to both our houses. Reb Dovid lived in front where he had a small tavern. His brother lived in the back and dealt in lumber. His name was Lipe and he made a lot of trouble for us. In the spring, we would cultivate our part of the yard and plant various vegetables. That way we had enough for our own use for eight to ten months. But Lipe would throw anything that was of no use to him, and plain old garbage, into the garden. He was a nasty person. No one liked him. His own brother hated him.

In the month of April, Reb Dovid entered the middle room where my sister and brother-in-law were sitting. I was in the workshop doing my work. "Listen," Reb Dovid began to my brother-in-law, "you have trouble from my brother. I get no pleasure from him. We can both get rid of him. My advice is that you buy my house. You will have gotten rid of a bad neighbor and will be the landlord over the whole house. You will rent it out and, with time, it will pay for itself." I heard these words from Dovid and my head started to swim. Mordkhe was also in the store and over-heard what Reb Dovid said. He did not like it either. What? Start again with all the drudgery?

"Reb Dovid," my brother-in-law said, "I don't have any money. As you know, I just paid off my house."

"You can take out a loan on both houses from the mortgage bank in Lemberg," replied Reb Dovid. "It will all be one structure and belong to you. You can buy it easily."

Both my sister and brother-in-law responded that they would think it over and let him know. When Reb Dovid left, I remained silent. But Mordkhe said, "Father, do you want to start again with houses?"

"But maybe it is a good idea," he responded. "It will pay for itself."

"But father, the house must be repaired first, even redone, before the mortgage bank will lend you money. Where will we get it from?"

"We will see," he answered.

It was in the evening during the intermediate days of Passover, at about twelve o'clock. There was a knock on the door. I got out of bed to open the door. My brother-in-law entered, apparently a bit soused, and ran over to my sister.

"Congratulations to us! I have already bought the house. I even already paid it off."

"How did you pay it off?" my sister asked.

"With notes," he answered. "And I have already applied to the mortgage bank for a loan."

When I heard everything he told my sister, I nearly leaped out of the bed. Rivers of tears began to stream from my eyes. Good heavens! What will become of us? Must I really work my young life away for them in order to earn my piece of bread? Mordkhe was not happy either, but at least he was their own child and in the long run this would be part of his inheritance.

The day after Passover, my brother-in-law went looking for work. The next day, I was supposed to travel quite a ways to a village by the name of

Sinitshol, not far from Maramaros, near the Hungarian border. I had to go by train to Dolina and from there proceed on foot for one day and night. It did not scare me at all to walk for a whole night; I was already used to it. Before I left, I asked my sister, "How long am I going to have to work for houses and more houses? What will become of me?" She gave me an angry look and said nothing. And with a goodbye, I left for the train station.

From Dolina, I arrived in Veldzizh, a town set between forests and high mountains, at about six in the evening. I did not feel like going further. I went to the priest to spend the night because we had worked for him, and we still had to do a lot more work for him.

It is worth mentioning that I had the opportunity to work for many priests. If the priest was a friend of the Jews, then the whole village full of peasants would be good to the Jews. But if the priest was an anti-Semite, then, generally, the village Gentiles were not friendly toward the Jews. Certainly, there were exceptions.

The next evening, I arrived at my job. I always loved my work, especially in the country in the fresh air of the fields and orchards. So I became deeply absorbed in my work. I would do such a beautiful job on the cupolas that the engineer gave my brother-in-law work for that very reason. Of course it was unpleasant for me to work on churches, but I consoled myself that the Gemara allowed such work for the sake of making a living.

We, or I, used to sleep on haystacks. Sleeping on a haystack for a whole summer made me very strong and robust. The heavy work did not bother me. For food, we would get milk, eggs, yellow meal, and more from the priest. We made a tin pot for ourselves in which we boiled the milk and poured in the yellow meal and mixed it up. It was quite tasty!

I worked for about four or five weeks until I ran out of materials. So I told Mr. Marr, the sexton of the church, that I was going home and asked him for expense money. He gave me two guldens. I was finished with my work on Wednesday at four o'clock. At six o'clock, I set out on foot, a walking stick in hand.

I arrived at Veldzizh on Thursday at eleven in the morning and went to see the priest. He told me that his coachman was going to Dolina at two o'clock and could take me. I got a nice rest. At two o'clock, we set out with a noble pair of horses, arriving at the train station at six in the evening. The train was supposed to arrive at seven-thirty. It was very unpleasant for me to be going home. The train arrived five minutes later. I went up to the official to buy a ticket, when it suddenly occurred to me, who knew whether I would find everything ready for the Sabbath?[16] Perhaps something was missing? But I could be home in less than two hours with the train, while to go on foot would take eight or nine hours. And I had already walked such a long way. These thoughts came to me in a flash. One more minute to go. I run to buy a ticket. I have my hand in my pocket ready to pay for the ticket. I hear the train whistle. But what if something is still missing for the Sabbath? I hold back. The train is already here and people are getting on. Now it is too late to buy a ticket. The train begins to move. I give a lightening-fast leap. But I am thinking, what if there is no wine for *kiddush*?* I jump back and start out on foot.

On the way, I meet a Gentile. Though he must go on a different road, he takes me onto his wagon. Even a mile less to walk is worth something.

I arrived very early, at four o'clock in the morning. I knocked on the door. I heard from within an angry voice yelling and coming to the door. My brother-in-law opened the door and yelled at me: "Here he is. Such an inheritance my sister-in-law left me! What right did you have to question Rokhl why I bought the second house, eh?" The entranceway was dark and to the side of the door was the cellar. So I quietly opened the cellar door and climbed down the stairs into the cellar. I made myself comfortable and relaxed. When it quieted down, I left the cellar and quietly lay down in bed.

At ten o'clock in the morning, I went to work. Later, the shoemaker brought over a pair of shoes for one of the children. He had to be paid, but there was not enough to pay him. He wanted to take the shoes back until he was paid for the new soles he had put on. I spoke up, saying, "I have money. I will pay you."

I had guessed right. There was nothing to make *kiddush* over—neither wine nor whiskey. I called over Moyshe Avrom. "Mr. Marr gave me two guldens, but I went on foot the whole way. Here, take the money."

My brother-in-law's brother, also a tinsmith, happened to be there. He was already married, having married young. (It is worth noting that at that time a young man of twenty-two or twenty-three was already almost an old bachelor.) He was seven years older than I, a quiet person and a good tradesman. He had his store and workshop not far from us. He had an apprentice. Like other tinsmiths, he made little money from his store. Sometimes, when we had a lot of work with the churches, my brother-in-law would hire him and pay him like a regular worker. He was the youngest son of good and decent parents who had their own large house, where he lived without paying rent. His name was Efroim. We often worked together, but sometimes he would be in one village and I would be in another. And we got along amicably. He had not touched the four hundred guldens he got as a dowry. He used to lend it out at interest. And so he also made loans to my brother-in-law, that is, his brother, Moyshe Avrom.

One Saturday night I was marking the end of the Sabbath. I was in the middle of reciting *Ish khosid hoyo bli,* "a righteous man was without . . . ,"[17] when the door flew open and a ringing shout came in my direction: "Why did you tell Bunem's Yisroel that Moyshe Avrom is buying up houses when he doesn't have a kreuzer to his name?" I leaped up as if I had been scalded. "What are you talking about, Efroim?" My brother-in-law and sister listened to us quarrel. "You did so tell," shouts Efroim, "and the proof is . . ." My brother-in-law gritted his teeth with anger. "Is that so? Are you going around telling people bad things about me?" My sister looked at me and at Efroim, and at us both, with an inquisitive gaze. "Efroim, you are a liar," I blurted out. And I threw myself at him, fearing that I would tear him to pieces. Suddenly, I lunged toward the chandelier and grabbed the fixture as if I wanted to take it and throw it at him. At the same time, I took my time in order to give him time to escape. And that is what really happened. By the time I had the fixture in my hand, he was out the door.

I could not calm down for a long time. Why would Efroim think up such a lie about me? Why? My brother-in-law called my sister into another room and they spoke together for some time. They returned to me and said, "Go, get back to work already." So they understood that Efroim had invented that lie by himself. But what did he gain from such a lie?

That night I could not work. I asked my sister and brother-in-law to let me go out that evening simply to take a walk outside in the fresh air. They gave me permission. I went out in the fresh air and recovered a bit. And I thought again, why? What brought Efroim to invent such a lie about me? He must have had a reason. I could not sleep that night.

Two days before I had returned home from my work in Sinitshol on Friday morning, a commission had come from the mortgage bank in Lemberg to evaluate the houses for a loan. In the meantime, Moyshe Avrom needed several hundred guldens. Well, he asked Efroim for a loan. (And he absolutely needed the money.) Efroim responded, "I'll give you a loan on condition that you take me in as a partner to the work on the churches. You will get sixty percent and I will get forty percent."

"What do I need a partner for," Moyshe Avrom responded. "You work and I'll pay you in addition to your interest. I walk around for months, and sometimes several years, before I get a church to work on, and you want to be a partner just like that? Where is the fairness in that, Efroim? And in addition I have Binyomen. In two or three more years, I will have to marry him off."

But Efroim stuck to his position: "I will not give you a loan otherwise." Moyshe Avrom had no choice and promised him forty percent of the business. (Whether he actually got forty percent is another question.)

All of this took place while I was away in the village. And Efroim, knowing that I was not happy that they were buying a second house, found out what kind of reception I had gotten when I came from the village. So he thought that this was his opportunity to get them to send me away altogether. Then he would always work together with Moyshe Avrom, fifty-fifty. So he came out against me with such a big and silly lie. Oh God! Circumstances, circumstances. What they can bring quiet and honest people to do! A couple of weeks went by. We spoke again, but never a word was spoken about his deed.

One weekday, I went to pray in the study house. Leyb Prints, Hirsh Prints's son, came up to me. (They said that I was born at Hirsh Prints's house.) "Binyomen," he said, "I've been waiting for you. I didn't want to come to your house, because I want to speak with you alone. You have that bit of a place that your mother left you. I want to buy it from you. I know that it belongs to you and not to Rokhl."

"For three hundred guldens I'll sell it to you," I said.

"It's not worth more than 125 guldens. Rokhl doesn't even have to know."

"No, I won't sell it so cheaply." And we parted.

The mortgage bank approved a loan for several thousand guldens on the houses. I heard the news when I returned home from a job. My brother-in-law had to go to Lemberg to draw up the papers with a lawyer. Mordkhe and I worked for two days and came home with twenty-four guldens. "Listen," my sister and brother-in-law asked, "did they pay you?"

"Yes," I said, "twenty-four guldens."

"Give it here. Moyshe Avrom is going to Lemberg tonight." I handed her the money and she gave it to Moyshe Avrom. God only knows how I felt in my heart at that moment. I thought to myself, this is just the beginning of my hard toil. Oh God, what will become of me? Will I ever get out of this vale of tears?

I returned to work in Sinitshol, but this time with Mordkhe. He needed to learn the trade better so that he could be left alone on a job. We worked diligently for four weeks. My brother-in-law was with us for two or three days, and then went home with Mordkhe to work there. I remained behind to finish the job completely. Three days before Shavuot,[18] I finished the work. The master builder was there at the time and was very happy with my work. "Even though you're still young," he said to me, "you could work on your own, not for Moshko. I myself would give you work." I did not make anything of it. I went home as usual, partly by train and partly on foot.

A matchmaker started to come to propose matches for me. He said that this one wanted to give me a five-hundred-dollar dowry, and that that one also wanted to pay so much. But nobody paid much attention to him.

My brother-in-law Moyshe Avrom had an older sister, Royze. Her husband, Berl (they were related), was a butcher. He worked for others while Royze, his wife, raised geese. She also used to make sure that the needy had hallah* for the Sabbath, and so on. Her husband, Reb Berl, was an able student of the Gemara. He was also a prayer leader and Torah reader, simply a refined person. They had three children, two sons and a very pretty girl. She was somewhat taller than I, with a pretty head of dark brown hair and big black eyes. Above all, she was well educated in both Yiddish and Polish. Her name was Etshe Keyle. From our childhood on, they had convinced themselves that their Etshe Keyle would be my bride. There is no telling how a person will delude himself.

Reb Berl's meat store was opposite us, a little up the street, and he would visit us in his spare time. After all, he was also member of the family. It was very early one Friday. My sister had just put the bread and the hallah in the oven and I was still lying on my hard bench-bed. "Rokhl," he said, "you know that I would like to find a match for my dear Etshe Keyle."

"Well," Rokhl responded, "May God send you her true mate."

Reb Berl had not expected such an answer. He thought that she would respond that Binyomen and Etshe Keyle would make a good couple. He told his wife, Royze, and Royze told her mother and also my sister's mother-in-law.

Rokhl's answer did not please them. So the mother-in-law spoke with her son, that is, with my brother-in-law. "My son," she said, "see that the match is made between Binyomen and Etshe Keyle. After all, this is Etshe Keyle! And there is no other girl like her in the world." That is what she said to my brother-in-law, her son.

"Mama," answered Moyshe Avrom, "you don't have to tell me what a precious girl Etshe Keyle is, may I have such good fortune. First of all, they are still young children. Second, I am not against the match, but we still have time to talk about it. Third, it will be as Rokhl wants it to be."

Well, she knew Rokhl and how stubborn she was, so the old mother left. Rokhl simply told all of them that they should leave her alone. Binyomen would never marry Etshe Keyle. Etshe Keyle and her mother felt very bad about this.

Several months passed. I was sitting and working. In came Maltshe, Berl Zekharye's wife, the son of my teacher Zekharye and also a teacher. She went straight to Rokhl in the other room. Well, who knows what one woman says to another? They spoke together for some time. When the woman left, Rokhl came into the room where I was and said to me, "They will accomplish nothing by such fantastic methods! Royze sent Maltshe to say that she, Maltshe, saw her mother in a dream and that her mother told her to go see Rokhl and tell her not to impede the match between Binyomen and Etshe Keyle. They won't scare me!"

I think to myself, "Me, they don't ask! What do I have to say about it?"

At the same time, I hurried to find some sort of work. We needed to bring some money into the house, just so we could eat. The small children had grown up. Noyekh and Leyb were already going to *heder* and about to finish third grade. They could already repair small things. Leyb, the older one, especially, took things around to sell—a baking pan, a frying pan, and the like. There were also three girls: Hendl, a pretty, lovely girl who could read and write Yiddish nicely; Peshi, a plump girl, who went to school; and the youngest, Khave, who was very cute. Rokhl was still getting pregnant. Yes, I can hardly remember a time when my sister, may she rest in peace, was not pregnant. So you can understand how hard up my brother-in-law was. Yet he still wanted to buy a second house and make the whole household suffer for it—and not just for a year or two with the hope of paying off the debt. The bill was already in; it was only a matter of the interest. And there was nothing to live on. When we ate up part of the rent money, we would run to borrow more to pay off the interest. That is how we were all afflicted.

It was winter. I was working until ten or eleven at night. What could I do? But why did I have to stand there working away with my hammer on Saturday night, right after the conclusion of the Sabbath, when people went to visit one another and chat? Not for an order, oh no. I would have been happy to prepare an order for someone. But to sit and hammer for the sake of hammering, that was the last straw. I told them that if there was no order to fill I did not feel like working on Saturday night. Mordkhe and Noyekh went places. I should also be at liberty to go out a little sometimes. And I took my coat and went out. My sister and brother-in-law shouted, "Don't you dare come back to sleep in the house!"

I go to the synagogue of the Stretyner Hasidim, where every Saturday night they organized a celebration to "usher out the Sabbath Queen."[19] I enter. Oh God, how lively and cheerful it is. They sing such sweet tunes. What a pleasure! And there are also good things to eat and drink. Yitskhok Rayner's son Mekhl sees me, leads me to the table, and says to me, "Binyomen, eat something and have a drink and help us sing along." I sing along and really have a good time. And they discuss a little Torah, until eleven-thirty.

The Hasidim started to split up. Where should I go to sleep? I had been forbidden to return home to sleep. What should I do? The sexton was putting out the lights. So where should I go? I thought of the "sufferers" who had to report to be examined for military service and who were staying up the whole night in the study house.[20] I ran to the study house. I walked for about five minutes and met some sufferers carrying wood that they had stolen from householders' sheds. I followed them to the study house and went in. A wonderful warmth, an iron oven red with fire. Some people were jumping, others were dancing. I took a sacred book and sat down at the table. Motl, the son of Kopl the Scribe, saw me. "Binyomen, what are you doing in the study house so late? Aha! You've gotten into a fight with Rokhl and Moyshe Avrom, eh?"

I spent the night in the study house on a bench. Motl was up the whole night with all of the sufferers. In the morning after the second service, he said his prayers and went home. He stopped by our house and told them that I had slept in the study house. Not knowing what to do next, I said my payers, picked up a Gemara, and studied. I was deep into the Gemara, when a hand nudged me. I raised my head. It was Moyshe Avrom, my brother-in-law. "Come home. Come." At first, I did not know how to answer him. "Let me finish the *mishna*," I answered, not looking him in the face. Fifteen minutes later, I was back home.

It was after twelve o'clock. The children and I were eating breakfast. In comes a tall, attractive, and very intelligent woman, Hinde, Reb Kopl the Scribe's wife. She went right up to Rokhl and said to her, "My Motl told me that Binyomen slept in the study house. What happened?"

"Nothing happened," Rokhl answered. "Eh! A foolish boy. He gets mad and runs to sleep in the study house."

"Is that so?" said Hinde. "He got angry."

Meanwhile, Hinde noticed that the children were eating bread with butter, while I was eating dry bread. "Rokhl," Hinde asked, "How is it that Binyomen eats dry bread and the children eat bread with butter?"

"Binyomen hates butter," Rokhl answered.

"Is that so Binyomen?"

I lowered my head and shook my head "yes." The truth was that we could not afford to buy butter. But for the little children at least a half cup of butter had to be bought each week.

It was already the beloved springtime. Nature was reviving. I also revived after the long, hard winter. I was going to Lalin, a village past Veldzizh, to cover a new church. Dovid Lehrer, who worked for Efroim, Moyshe Avrom's brother, was sent with me. He was about the same age as I. He was not yet well acquainted with covering cupolas on churches. That was why they were sending him with me. And I was very happy to show him everything. He was a very refined and quiet boy. With his looks, it would have been more appropriate for him to be sitting in a yeshiva* studying a folio of the Gemara rather than to be working on a church.

It may be that I was not the first orphan to be sold as a slave, never to have the freedom to go out for a while whenever and wherever I wanted. In short, my soul was completely out of my hands—until the long-awaited summer arrived and I went away from home. Whether the work was in another city or in a village, it did not matter. Then I had the freedom to decide when to start work and when to finish. And the main thing was that I had freedom after work to go wherever I wanted. Even Moyshe Avrom was not the Moyshe Avrom of home. At work in the villages, he treated me very gently, and this was his natural gentleness. He was by nature a good person (there was never any question of his honesty). But as soon as we arrived home, Moyshe Avrom became another person.

It was very pleasant to work with Dovid. He was something of a scholar, so we had things to talk about. We made our own meals, as always in the country, namely, eggs, milk, yellow meal, potatoes, and spring water. And we had free fruit. We slept almost in the open air on stacks of hay. Lalin is situated on a mountain surrounded by large and dense forests. Who can describe the delicious air there? We worked together until Shavuot, although we had not yet finished, and arrived home on the eve of the holiday. Dovid wished that he could always work outside with me. When I got home nobody recognized me, I looked so good.

Berl Zekharye's wife showed up again with her dream. One morning, I was saying my prayers when the door flew suddenly open. She was barely able to pant out, "Heh, heh, Rokhl, R-r-rokhl."

"Well? Out with it. What happened, Maltshe?"

"Oy, oy, your mother came to me in a dream today at dawn, and told me very firmly, 'Go immediately to Rokhl and tell her that I cannot rest until a match is made between Binyomen and Etshe Keyle.'"

My sister answered her very plainly. "Dreams do not scare me, Maltshe. And never come to me again with any dreams. Have a good day." And she left her standing there and entered the house.

Maltshe went through the store, where I was, and shuffled out without even looking at me. Poor Royze! What would she not do to see her dear Etshe Keyle happy, as she saw it. Poor mother! Yes, both were to be pitied, the mother and the girl. As far as I was concerned, I thought that I would never marry and make a girl have to scrape out a living, seeing how the tinsmiths in my city and other cities slaved away. Precisely because I loved Etshe Keyle, so I thought, I pleaded with God to send her a good match, not a tinsmith.

I returned to Lalin to finish the work. I traveled by train for a while and then went by foot—alone. Dovid had work to finish in his workshop. He would come a week later.

I arrived at the inn, ate breakfast, and was no longer in a hurry. I relaxed, and actually considered staying until the next day. The innkeeper knew me. A good fellow—he also told me to stay the day, because there was a possibility that someone else would be going to Lalin and I would be able to go along. I stayed to take a rest there. Mirl, the innkeeper's wife, prepared lunch for me and a pretty daughter of hers—with two long black braids, plump red cheeks, and black eyes—set the table with the spoon, fork and knife, and salt shaker. She must have been about two years younger than I. And we ate a good, delicious dairy lunch.

Later, I went into the innkeeper's room, where there was a case of religious books. I took one out—the *Yalkut*—and sat down at the table to read.[21] At about two o'clock, the door opened and the girl, Rivkele, was holding a tray in her hands. She placed a small dish with a piece of honeycomb and a glass of red water next to me. She said that her mother told her to bring me the piece of honeycomb and the glass of raspberry syrup water. "Drink. It's very good." I put a piece of honeycomb in my mouth. Rivkele stood right next to me and just as I was enjoying the honeycomb, she bent over, gave me a firm kiss, and ran out of the room. That was the first kiss that I ever had from a girl.

Astonished, I was left holding pieces of honeycomb in my hand and in my mouth. Yes, and I turned red from embarrassment—in front of myself and the four walls.

After a while, when I had recovered, I ate the honeycomb and drank the glass of raspberry syrup water. But I immediately closed the *Yalkut* and put it back in the bookcase. I sat down again at the table, and pondered what had happened to me in those few minutes, but I could not explain it at all. Afterwards I recovered a bit, and I asked myself which was sweeter: the honeycomb with the pretty holes left by the bees, the glass of raspberry syrup water, or Rivkele's kiss?

Soon I started to think that it was not right for me to have such thoughts. I immediately recalled a passage in the Gemara tractate Yevamot which states, "*Haaleym eynekha me-eshes kheyn pen tilokheyd be-metsu-daseho.*"[22] In plain language that can be expressed as, "Divert your eyes from a beautiful married woman, because you may get into trouble." And the same can be said of a maiden. I immediately said to myself, I won't stay here today. I went into the public room and went up to the innkeeper and told him that I was going on my way.

A week later, Dovid came. I told him what had happened to me on my way there. Other than him, I told no one. We finished the work in four weeks, and went home.

In the meantime, the great scholar and scribe, Reb Kopl, had died, leaving behind a widow and two girls. Keyle was the older, and Alte, a sickly girl, was the younger. His son Motl was already married and living in Solotvina. It tugged at my heart when I heard it. First, I had been like a member of the family. And second, I used to make the little tubes for the knife handles for the son, Motl, because since Motl had married he had learned to make the handles on the lathe. Reb Kopl had loved me and called me Binyomentshe.[23] After his death, his wife Hinde sold eggs at the market.

The older girl, Keyle, actually worked for her uncle, Moyshe Loker, at thread and ribbons. Moyshe Loker also did lathe work for the spools for the thread. The factory belonged to Leybtshe Shpindels and to Aba Milsh-teyn's son. But Moyshe Loker ran it because he had spent more than a year in such a factory in Vienna and had learned more or less how to run it. Taking with him the engineer from the Vienna factory, he had come to Kalush and proposed his plan to the Shpindelses and the Milshteyns. They liked the plan and built the factory. So that meant that Keyle worked for her uncle, a highly educated Jew. The factory paid girls from four to six guldens a month. But Keyle received six guldens a month. Motl returned to Kalush and went to work as a turner. We also had a lot of work from that factory: pipes, various lamps, and so on.

And alas, a short time later Hinde, Keyle's mother, also died. She had caught cold in the market. And everyone in town took pity on the two poor orphan girls. They had another uncle, Hirsh Loker, a rich man. It is worth noting that it was said of the Lokers that they had the nobility of those of aristocratic birth. There was no question that they were learned. When Hirsh Loker led services during the High Holidays,* he would break the hearts of all the members of the congregation and they would cry their eyes out. His business was selling haberdashery goods to stores—belts, ribbons, thread, combs, and so on.

Before his sister Hinde died, he became very ill. Hinde and their brother Moyshe Loker sat by his sickbed. From his sickbed, Hirsh said, "Hinde, stand over here by me. Moyshe, stand next to her. Hinde, take my hand. If I recover, with God's help, I will marry off Keyle." These words brought tears to the eyes of his brother Moyshe and his sister, and the whole household just cried. Aunt Ester also approached him and said, "Yes, Hirsh, may you have a full recovery. I will help marry off Keyle."

With God's help, Hirsh Loker did recover, and they tried to match Keyle up with me. One day, Red Dovid the Teacher's wife came in. She called my sister into the other room and told her that she had a rare match for Binyomen, one with the highest pedigree: Keyle. "True," my sister said to her, "she is very smart and pretty. But, after all, she is a poor orphan."

"Rokhl," answered the matchmaker, "what are you saying? I wouldn't come empty-handed. Listen, the house belongs to both girls. One half belongs to Alte, and the other half to Keyle. Hirsh Loker will contribute 150 guldens, and a brother of Reb Kopl, a rich man, has promised a hundred guldens. Is that so bad? And how about her fine background?"

Rokhl came into the store and related to me what the teacher's wife had told her. I answered, "Rokhl, go tell her to find a better match for pretty Keyle."

Rokhl went to tell the teacher's wife that she would talk it over with Moyshe Avrom. Keyle's brother Motl also met with Moyshe Avrom at services and spoke to him about it. Later Motl asked me directly, "Tell me frankly, Binyomen, do you want to marry my sister?" At first, I did not know how to answer. I said that I also wanted to think about it, because it wasn't a question of Keyle; after all, one has to be careful about getting married.

In the beginning, as I said, Leyb Prints wanted to give me 125 guldens for the place I had inherited. We met again. Now he wanted to give me 150 guldens, but on condition that we both go immediately to Dovidl Robin, the local document writer and draw up the papers right away. He offered me a fifty-gulden down payment. I considered a bit, then said to him, "Leyb, it's sold."

We went to Dovidl Robin, who drew up the papers. I signed and he gave me a fifty-gulden note; when the deal was approved by the court I would get the other hundred guldens.

I took the fifty and ran to Reb Rafoyl Hirsh, who sold kerosene and salt, and gave it to him to hold for me until I needed it. (When I went to *heder* he used to examine me.) When I got home, I did not say a word. Two weeks later, my sister came from the market, where she found out that I had sold the place for 150 guldens. "Binyomen," she asked me, "is it really true?"

"Yes, Rokhl," I said.

"Where are the fifty guldens?" she asked.

"I gave them to Rafoyl Hirsh to hold," I answered. She did not say another word.

Four weeks later, they needed 150 guldens. My sister went over to Leyzer, a dry-goods dealer, and asked to borrow 150 guldens from him. Well, he only had one hundred. She came back with the hundred guldens and said to me, "Binyomen, I must have your fifty guldens. You know that I need it right away." I felt sick.

"Yes," I said, "of course I know. But what will become of me? My work will always go to the devil."

"Binyomen," she said very softly and quietly, "I'll give it back to you. You know what? You take it out of your work yourself."

Well, I softened and went to Rafoyl Hirsh and brought back the fifty. But I knew that I would never see those fifty guldens again, simply because it wasn't there.

Once, when I was in the factory installing some pipes, Moyshe Loker called me into his office and told me that if I married Keyle I would get all the work at the factory. An idea came into my head.

"Reb Moyshe," I said completely frankly, "tinsmiths struggle bitterly to make a living. If Keyle agrees that I go to America right after the wedding, then we can make an engagement. And I want to talk it over with Keyle myself." He thought it over. Then he replied, "Maybe this makes sense."

Now about Keyle. She was two and a half years younger than I, and almost as tall. She had a very refined face with a small mouth, red cheeks, a small well-shaped nose, and small blue-gray eyes. When she laughed, it seemed as if she closed her eyes. She had a big head of light blond hair, and it was a pleasure to watch her as she combed it. Girls from good homes and young women used to stop her and ask how she combed such a fine head of hair. And sometimes she used to make two big braids. So she was wonderfully beautiful. But her uncle, Hirsh Loker, forbade her to wear long braids, because it was too frivolous, not fitting for Kopl the Scribe's daughter or for the Loker family. Well, Hirsh Loker had to be obeyed. She knew how to pray well and could write Yiddish, Polish, and a little German. In short, she had all the virtues.

Well, my sister agreed. I discussed with Keyle my plan to go to America right after the wedding. I was surprised by her answer, namely, that she would be very happy to go to America, that this had been her dream all along. So what was the problem? She could not open her mouth in front of Uncle Hirsh, because he said that only impious people went to America.

With good fortune, we became engaged. While the engagement ceremony was taking place, I thought to myself, will I have enough for a ship's ticket and several guldens to leave for Keyle until I am able to send her a ticket? Who knows? These were the thoughts that lay in my head as I became engaged. The irony was that one day earlier I had worked for Khanele's Brayntshe and earned just as much as the engagement and the banquet cost. And there were good things to eat; my sister can cook and bake well. Once again, it appeared as if Moyshe Avrom was a wealthy man.

Right after she became engaged, Moyshe Loker said to Keyle that he was certain that Binyomen must have money stashed away. "Why do you think that?" Keyle asked him. "Just because," he answered. Keyle told me about this. I told her the truth, that, so far, I did not have a kreuzer. This conversation took place in the factory in Uncle Moyshe's office.

Keyle's Uncle Hirsh pestered her continually. Why? Sometimes because she combed her hair too frivolously, sometimes because she dressed up too much. Finally, she went away to an uncle who was a ritual slaughterer in Bogdan, Hungary.

Moyshe Loker returned from Vienna and moved in with us in the newly bought house. He spoke with his brother Hirsh, telling him to marry off Keyle as he had promised to do when he was sick. Uncle Hirsh answered, "I have put aside fifty guldens, and when Hirshl of Antinye, a rich man and a brother of Kopl the Scribe, sends me a hundred guldens I will add the other fifty." Moyshe Loker wrote to Hirshl in Antinye. A week later, when Hirsh Loker received only fifty guldens from Hirshl of Antinye, he became so angry that he wanted to return it. "He was supposed to send me a hundred!"

Moyshe spoke up. "Hirsh, better not to send it back. You know that Hirshl is a great miser. He won't send you back the fifty guldens." Hirsh followed Moyshe's advice and did not send it back. Uncle Moyshe Loker wrote a letter to Keyle telling her to come home because being in Bogdan did her no good. I did not know about the letter.

Keyle came home, looking like a beautiful springtime rose. She had been treated very tenderly. And what's more, her Uncle Khaym the ritual slaughterer wanted Keyle to marry his son, a scholar. But she said that she would not break our engagement. Once, Uncle Khaym was playing with one of his younger sons and he took two metal pans, clapped them together and said, "You see, Mordkhenyu, Keyle will marry a tinsmith." But it was no use clapping pans together. Keyle did not want to marry her cousin. She told me about this later.

I settled with Leyb Prints on the house and brought the hundred guldens that I received to Reb Rafoyl Hirsh. One night, Moyshe Loker called me in to see him. Keyle was also there. "Binyomen," he said to me, "let's try to find a way to force Hirsh to hold a wedding. Do this. Pretend you want to break off the engagement and send the engagement contract back to Hirsh. Well, we'll see. I don't think that he will allow it."

"What do you say, Keyle?" I asked.

"I agree," she answered. "Let's try it."

Hirsh Loker received the engagement contract. Keyle arrived and pretended not to know what was happening. He accosted her and said, "Keylutshikl, Binyomen has sent you back the engagement contract." Keyle did not move. He said to her, "Don't worry, you can find a tinsmith any time." Perhaps he was happy; it would not cost him any money.

Keyle and I once again met with Uncle Moyshe. We searched for a new plan to force Hirsh's hand. Uncle Moyshe said, "I have another idea, so let's try again. Binyomen, go to the rabbi and send for Hirsh. Tell the rabbi, with Hirsh present, how when he was sick he gave his sister his word that he would marry off Keyle. And now the orphan is hanging around with nowhere to go."

"Uncle," I said, "call Hirsh Loker to the rabbi? First, he prays with the rabbi and is the prayer leader. So how can the rabbi force him?"

"Yes, but he won't be able to deny what you say."

The next day, I went to the rabbi. He entered. "Good afternoon, rabbi." I told the rabbi of my complaint. The rabbi heard me out and said, "Reb Hirsh will certainly keep his promise. Oh, you demand that he marry the girl off now? Well, Reb Hirsh knows whether he can do it now or later. You can't be forced to marry her either." Hirsh Loker left the rabbi with a smile on his face.

Well, there I was, again at Uncle Moyshe's house. They were waiting, curious to hear how Hirsh had explained himself to the rabbi. I told them that the rabbi did not even want to hear my complaint and we parted with nothing.

For over a year, they were unable to marry off Leyb; it was not working out. One fine winter's day, Aunt Reyzl and some other relatives burst into Hirsh and Aunt Ester's house. Yes! With a shout! "Hirsh and Ester," they yelled, "you will never lead Leyb to the wedding canopy as long as you fail to marry off Keyle. And you, Ester, don't you see that God is not allowing you to marry Leyb off first?" Hirsh Loker heard the angry women out and said, "Reyzl and Khaytshe, don't preach to me. Ester, make tea. We'll drink." But their talk actually did scare Aunt Ester. Well, what *was* preventing her from leading her beloved son to the wedding canopy? What? Money was no obstacle. The 1,200-gulden dowry had been put aside for a long time. Half his wedding clothes had also been prepared. It must really be the hand of God.

At the time, I was working in Zhuravno, about four miles from Kalush. It was Adar, the week of the Torah portion that begins, "When you take a census of the people of Israel."[24] My brother-in-law had received three hundred guldens so far from the priest for a job that came to 1,400 guldens. When we came home for the Sabbath, my sister gave us the news that I would be getting married on the first day of the month of Nisan.[25] They were already preparing, with good fortune, the bride's wedding clothes. And the men's tailor would soon come to measure me for a long frock coat and some clothes. The hat maker would also come to measure me for a *shtrayml*.

Only God in Heaven knows how I felt at the time. I burst out crying and oceans of tears poured out of me. I could barely stop myself. Many bridegrooms prepare themselves for months before they go very happily to the wedding canopy. Most of them already have some sort of purpose in life, or they have prospects for some sort of business. But they let me

know that I was going to get married only nine or ten days before the wedding! They did not give me any opportunity to work out my own plan.
They just took two orphans and married them off without asking them a
thing.

Opposite us lived Brayntshe's Gitl. She had one room, in which she
both mended old sacks and cooked. The bed was there too, and she and
her husband Avrom slept there. Five days before my wedding, they had to
move out. So I rented the room from Gitl's mother for several weeks, until
I would leave for America.

It was the eve of the first of Nisan, 1896. I was supposed to get married
in the evening. I sent Keyle several guldens by messenger so she could buy
whatever she needed. I rehearsed a bit of a sermon, because such a thing
might still occur to Hirsh Loker. To tell the truth, I went to the wedding
canopy with a heavy heart, because very soon I would have to go my way
on a distant journey across the sea.

Well, with good fortune, the ceremony was over. They announced the
gifts. Uncle Hirsh gives the bride two baking spoons. . . . This one gives
two guldens, that one gives one gulden. Altogether, thirty-five guldens
in wedding gifts, with uncle's two spoons. I handed it over to my bride.
I did not give a sermon, because I was not asked to do so. Uncle danced
the *mitsve-tants*.[26] People dispersed. I went home to sleep, and my bride,
already now my wife, went to her home to sleep. After Brayntshe's Gitl
moved out, it took two days until the room was cleaned out. And, in a
propitious moment, we moved in. There was one thing I was happy about:
that Keyle was my first love, unlike the case with some of my friends. For
that reason, I was happy.

We wondered why Motl was not at the wedding. One morning, we
received a letter from America that he had arrived in New York and his
address was 179 Eldridge Street. Well, my Keyle was in seventh heaven. I
would have someone to pick me up from the ship. We sat down to calculate our fortune, how much I could leave for Keyle until I was able to send
her money from America. And here is the calculation:

150 guldens from my brother-in-law
100 guldens with Rafoyl Hirsh
46 guldens from Moyshe the Baker's son, who was getting married and
    bought my jacket and *shtrayml*
296 guldens in total

I would leave Keyle a hundred [guldens], and have 196 guldens left for the ship's ticket and traveling expenses. Good. Better than hoped. Keyle insisted that I take more along. In the end, I left her seventy-five guldens.

Finally, the day came for me to leave. Uncle Moyshe Loker was traveling to Vienna, so we went to Vienna together. An hour before we were supposed to leave for the train station, the tailor who made Keyle's wedding clothes appeared and said that he was owed another ten guldens that Hirsh Loker did not want to pay. He said that Binyomen should pay. And here came the coach that was to carry us to the train station! In short, I paid him the ten guldens and we got in—Uncle Moyshe, Keyle, and my sister. I said goodbye to everyone and adieu to Kalush.

When someone leaves his native city, he leaves behind so many joys of youth, so many sweet and heartfelt memories, that he brings his memories along with him so that he can recall them joyfully. But what kinds of youthful memories did I bring with me? Kalush gave me nothing. No education. No one bothered with a poor orphan. Many Jewish orphans wandered in the streets in tatters, half naked, and the respectable Jews did not even want to take notice. They were immersed in themselves. And yet, I felt a longing upon leaving my native town.

The train arrived. I said goodbye to my Keyle, and held her tight, thinking, Who knows when I will be able to hold you in my arms again? I said goodbye to my sister, who cried bitterly. I cried along with her. She handed me a package with cookies that she had baked for me. Then Uncle Moyshe and I boarded the train. I saw Keyle and my sister standing and watching the train fly further and further away. My eyes followed them through the window. I thought to myself, Poor sister. Will you be able to get along without me? May God help you.

We arrived in Vienna. Gedalye, Uncle Moyshe's son, was waiting for us at the train. We went to Yankev Fridlender, who was actually an in-law of the Lokers. He was a broker here, in whatever allowed him to earn a gulden. I knew that it was not going very well for him. At dinnertime, I was sitting by the window and they were bringing pierogi with cherries to the table. Everyone in the household sat down around the table and started to eat. They did not invite me to eat with them, so I took out my pack and had a bite. To this day, I cannot explain why they did not invite me to eat with them. Anyway, uncle could not do anything. He was a guest himself. But the Fridlenders were, after all, cultured people. They understood the etiquette very well, of course. Impossible to understand.

Evening. Uncle slept there. I went to a hotel not far away, paid seventy kreuzers, and went to sleep.

The next day we went to the shipping company to buy a ship's ticket for me. At the entrance, I read, "Holland-American Shipping Company." Now I had the ship's ticket in my pocket. That night, I did sleep at the Fridlenders' home. Uncle later told me that he (Fridlender) had gotten a broker's fee of three guldens. The next day, the train took me to Germany and from there to Rotterdam, Holland. I waited a day in Leipzig until I could board a train for the Dutch border.

When I arrived at the border, a tall gendarme boarded the train and shouted, "*Alle heraus,* everyone out!" Well, we all got out. They lined us up. Now another official with polite manners came up to me first. He asked me, "*Wo ist ihre Zeugnis?* Where is your certificate?" My head started to spin. What should I show him? My ship's ticket? He did not ask me for a passport, but for a certificate. He saw from my face that I was scared. He said, very politely, "*Schrecken sie sich nicht.* Don't be afraid. Show me what you have." I took out the envelope with my ship's ticket. With a smile, he took a look and shouted out, "Correct. To the station!" I got back on the train. So, he was the shipping company's person!

In Rotterdam, I waited a day for my ship to depart. It was Sunday, June 30. I boarded the ship. During the first day and part of the second day, I did not feel bad. But later, up to almost the last day on the ship, I was seasick and ate almost nothing.

They brought us to Castle Garden.* I expected that my brother-in-law Motl would come to pick me up. When my turn arrived, the officials asked me how much money I had. I showed the sixty guldens (about twenty-four dollars). They asked me if anyone was coming to pick me up. I said that I expected my brother-in-law to come.

An official turned to an officer and told him to ask me the street and the address. I said, "179 Eldridge Street." He told them to show me where the ferry was and they took me and showed me. I took my suitcase and went out. I saw many people going to the ferry. I followed them. On the ferry I recognized a Jew and asked him how to get to Eldridge Street. He told me that he would put me on the right streetcar himself and wrote on a piece of paper for me to show the conductor. The conductor let me off at Grand Street and showed me which way to go.

Here was Eldridge Street. Then I saw my number, 179 Eldridge Street, second floor. I entered the apartment. My brother-in-law Motl was getting ready to go pick me up at Castle Garden. He had just come from work, where he was a presser of skirts. He had not been able to leave the shop any earlier. I had been traveling on the ship for seventeen days and had been seasick almost until the last day.

I arrived in this blessed country on Tuesday, July 15, 1896. Grover Cleveland was then the president. It was an election year. McKinley was running for the Republicans. Their principle was the protective tariff. The brilliant orator and then liberal, William Jennings Bryan, was running for the Democrats on the issue of free trade and free silver at 16 to 1. And a lively campaign it was![27]

I arrived in New York in the midst of that lively whirl. Motl and I stayed with a *landsman*,* Yitskhok Hammer, and his wife Khanetshe. At home, he had been an inspector for Leybtshe Shpindel, serving as a guard in a distillery. In America, his children had become good tailors in a couple of years and had brought over their parents. They bought him a soda stand on Essex Street, which did not even earn him peanuts. So they kept boarders. Six of us slept in one room. We paid three dollars a month with laundry, and one dollar thirty a week for supper. That's how people lived in those days. Nevertheless, they lived a happy life. People went to the theater, to social gatherings, and to various meetings.

Yes, life then was truly interesting. The first couple of days after my arrival, my brother-in-law Motl took me to street meetings to hear various speakers about the election campaign. Suddenly, I heard a Yiddish speaker speaking from another corner of Suffolk and Rivington streets. A young man was standing on a box and speaking full of enthusiasm. I pushed through the crowd to be closer to the speaker. He was a tall young man, with one eye that looked a little bit upward. It was the first secretary of the United Hebrew Trades, Bernard Weinstein.[28] I had never heard such words in my town: "Worker freedom. . . . You toil bitterly in the sweatshops and your children go naked and barefoot. . . . Social, political, and economic equality and security." He urged the listeners to come to the Socialist club on Ludlow Street in the evening; there would be good speakers there.

It was the first time in my life I had heard the word "Socialist." Excited by the speaker, I went home to sleep. As I lay on my bed, my mind worked over the speech that I had just heard: "Work should be based on justice and right. . . . Your children go around in the street barefoot and naked. . . ." And I began to think about my town, Kalush, and about the leaders of the community. Why didn't they take an interest in the children and build a talmud torah,* or some other social improvement for poor children? They sit over the Gemara and move their lips, and they do not put into effect a single word of what they study. Do they not study in Tractate Nedarim the passage, "*Hizharu bivney aniim shemeyhem teytsey Toroh*"?[29] And, if they do not believe in what they are studying, how can they sit over the Gemara and simply babble on? With these and similar thoughts, I fell asleep.

The next day, I got addresses of tinsmith, sheet metal, and copper-brass shops. I went to Brooklyn, where they took my name in the shops and said that they would let me know. Friday, the third day after my arrival, I went to try my luck in New York, going from one shop to the next.[30] I entered Fulton Street and saw a sign: Lamps and sheet metal work on the third floor. I went up and a sturdily built man in overalls was sitting not far from the entrance. He was a Jew. I asked him if he needed a tinsmith. He asked me where I had worked before, putting me into an uncomfortable position. He awaited my answer. Since I had some addresses from Brooklyn I responded, "On McKibben Street, Brooklyn." He brought me over to the workers, also Jewish, showed me work that they were doing, and asked whether I could do the work. I answered, "Yes."

"But remember, this is very particular work."

"Absolutely," I answered, "I will do the work. You'll see, you'll be happy."

He wrote down my name and told me to come on Monday. I ran home and told Motl that I had gotten work.

In the evening, I went to hear the street meetings. Some of the speakers attacked religion. Even the good-hearted Max Pine threw in a couple words criticizing religion.[31] I did not like that. I thought to myself, mixing anti-religion together with social and economic justice leaves behind the same taste as a slap instead of a Sabbath greeting.

On Monday, I went to work. They put me to work making street lamps with two other workers, each at his bench. The other workers had been there for a couple of years. I noticed that they frequently looked to see how I was doing with my work. Once, I went to the other room for solder and I saw one of them carrying his moldings (that were to be soldered to the lamps). He carried them to my bench, and took mine away! Right away, I thought to myself, better keep quiet. Don't complain about him to the foreman, because I don't want to make any trouble. I began to put together his moldings. They did not fit. Well, I figured out what to do. The places that did not fit were hollow, so I filled them up with solder and nobody could tell. Then the lamps were painted.

Then, both workers started to speed up the work so that I would fall behind. I kept up with them. In short, by six o'clock we had each assembled the same number of lamps. The foreman examined my work. I asked him if it was alright. He responded that, for the first day, I was alright. "You will break yourself in on this."

This was my first day of work in America. Payday arrived. He handed me a small envelope. I took a look: seven dollars. He told me that when I got broken in he would give me a raise. Good, I was happy. At four weeks, I received a raise of one dollar—to eight dollars a week. Not bad for a greenhorn.* I worked for nine weeks and then it was "slack."* I and a couple of other workers were laid off.

Saturday night, we heard that Abraham Cahan was to speak at the hall on Ludlow Street. I was curious to see him and hear him speak. The war with Daniel De Leon was already underway.[32] He spoke about the election between the two capitalist parties. I was so excited by his speech that I kept applauding. With that one speech, he explained more to me than the several speeches I had heard earlier. Above all, I liked his fine and juicy Yiddish. I left the hall with great excitement.

It was slack throughout the country, and hard to get work. It was getting closer to the election, and a president had to be chosen. I read a lot and learned about the customs and laws of the land. I went to radical meetings. I listened to all the various perspectives. At the same time, would I sometimes drop in at the synagogue on Allen and Attorney streets, take a seat, and immerse myself in the Gemara. I traveled uptown to look for work, but I did not get any. I passed 102nd Street and saw a tinsmith's store. I went in and asked if I could get any work. The owner was a Hungarian Jew who had already been in the country for twenty-five years. He also sold metal goods, as well as old stoves that had been fixed and polished. He asked me if I would like the work. I said, "Of course, why not?" He offered me six dollars a week, plus room and board. I asked him how many hours I would have to work. He answered, from eight in the morning to six in the evening, with an hour's rest at lunchtime. I agreed, and the next morning I came to work. On the first day, he told me that he was happy with me and that I could work for him as long as I wanted.

In the morning I would pray, wearing my prayer shawl and *tfilin,* and any family member who came in would find me praying. So one of my boss's cousins said to her husband, "Joe, he must be a holy young man."

After I had worked for him for five weeks, he said to me that all the stoves would soon be fixed. Slack was starting here as well. He told me that he was doing good business with his store and would like to sell it, if I had enough money to buy it. I answered that my wife was in Europe and had money. If he could wait until received an answer from my wife, I would write her that it was a good business. I asked him how much he was asking for the store. He answered that he would take three hundred dollars, without several of the machines. "There, you see these four machines? I want to take them with me."

"Alright," I said, "if you want to wait, I will write a letter to my wife this very evening."

He said, "Yes, write her that it's a golden business."

My boss knew that he was dealing with a greenhorn. But I, the greenhorn, thought, work can't be gotten. It will have to take at least four weeks to receive an answer from my wife. So at least I'll work for another four weeks. Oh, it isn't ethical or nice to lie to him that I have written to my wife. But, you know, it won't hurt him and it will do me good in terms of a living. In any case, I'll be working for my wages, so it is not much of an injustice.

They started to pamper me, but good. He took me to jobs in his customers' homes and introduced me. At the end of the four weeks, I could not make him wait any longer. One morning, I came from lower Manhattan, where my brother-in-law lived, and told him that, unfortunately, my wife had written me not to buy any business until she came over. I worked the day. In the evening he paid me and we parted respectfully.

My Motl moved out of the Hammers' home and in with a certain family Blank. There was room for me, too, and I moved in. Mrs. Blank was a divorcee. There was a brother, Sam Blank, and a sister Zhenya, a girl of nineteen. She worked at millinery. Sam was the operator of a sewing machine making pants and was a learned boy. He was secretary of a Jewish Socialist branch, for which he kept the books in German. I learned a lot from him. (He was Romanian.) A friend of his by the name of Kraytser, a very ardent Socialist and a carpenter by trade, would visit him. One evening, I went to hear Johan Most, the great leader of the Anarchists.[33] His lecture was wonderful. He breathed fire at the present capitalist order. Neither did he spare the Socialists for their principles. He said that if the Socialists came to power, they would be no better, if not worse, than the capitalists. Well, so far I liked the Socialists' principles better. Nevertheless, Most spoke from the depths of his heart.

Election day came and went. McKinley was elected. They said that prosperity would soon begin. I joined the Socialist Party, as the feud among the majority of the Socialists became more and more heated.[34] Our local branch took the name Engels-Forverts Club.[35] The present Judge Panken was still in school.[36] He was chairman of most of the meetings. I still remember now how during meetings he would good-naturedly request that the comrades not talk among themselves while the meeting was going on.

Two weeks after the election, I went to Centre Street to look for a job. I noticed one very large shop that occupied two floors. I saw that they did very fine, fancy brass and copper work. And much of the work was also nickeled. I thought to myself, I'll go up and try; perhaps I will get work here. I went up. A sturdily built man was sitting in the office. I asked him if I might get a job here. He started speaking to me in German. He asked me if I could do the work well. I told him I could and asked him to give me a chance. The company was called Baron and Houchin and Co. Mr. Baron was born Jewish, but he now had very little to do with Judaism, except that his children and grandchildren were circumcised. His partner, Mr. Houchin, was the financier of the business.

On Monday I arrived at work. The boss gave me small four-cornered brass lamps to make. I did the work better than he had hoped for. Payday arrived. I opened the envelope and took a look: ten dollars. Oh, I was on top of the world! And it was easy work too. And I got ten dollars for the first week! What could be better? The only thing that I did not like was the other tinsmith who sat next to me. A German and an anti-Semite, he used to needle me and hide my tools when I needed them.

I worked for seven weeks. One day, a man and a boy came in and spoke with the boss (Baron). The next day, the boy came to work and the boss brought him to me to show him how to make this and that. The boy was Jewish, from Romania. His name was Schwartz. Anyway, the boss then handed me the pay envelope himself and told me that he was laying me off. If it got busy, he would take me on again.

I said to him, "But you just hired the boy!"

He responded, "Yes, I pay him only six dollars a week."

Two days later, I was walking on Forsythe Street when I saw a man working in a large, well-lit cellar at what were then called "bar tanks." These were for behind the bar in the saloons where the glasses were washed. I went down and asked him if he needed help and he answered that he would hire a good tinsmith. I answered that he could try me out. The next day I came to work. At the end of the week, he handed me ten dollars. I worked for three weeks, and then got a letter from Mr. Baron telling me to come to work immediately because it had become busy. I told my boss, Mr. Flitter, that unfortunately I had to quit and showed him the letter.

I returned to work. The boy, Schwartz, was no longer there. Mr. Baron called me into his office and told me that he was going to fire Edward and make me the head of the other three tinsmiths. Well, I told him that I would try my best, and he gave me a raise of two dollars to twelve dollars a week. I could now send a ship's ticket to my wife.

I received a letter from my wife that Efroim, Moyshe Avrom's brother, was also coming to America and wanted to travel with my wife. I was very happy that she would not have to travel alone. I took rooms on the second floor at 141 Eldridge Street. I brought in furniture and necessary things for the house. On July 4, 1897, I picked up my wife and Efroim at Castle Garden. A week later I got Efroim a job at a tinsmith factory.

And so life went on. Ten months later, my wife gave birth to a beautiful boy. We rented three rooms at 153 Orchard Street. One morning, I came to work and heard that Mr. Baron's partner had shot himself. A month later the shop moved over to Brooklyn. I was already getting fifteen dollars a week, considered fine wages at that time. We sent a ship's ticket to Alte, my wife's sister.

I attended meetings and went to lectures. At the same time, when I had an opportunity, I dropped into the synagogue and sat savoring the Gemara. (I still enjoy looking into the Gemara today.) My sister-in-law Alte came from the ship. My brother-in-law Motl (her brother) took her to his shop and taught her to be an operator on skirts. The shop where I worked continually increased its business. I was now getting seventeen dollars a week. Fifteen months later, my wife gave birth to another baby boy. My sister-in-law fell in love with a boy, also a tinsmith, and six months later we married them off. We were very happy that she would not have to languish over the sewing machine in the shops.

Efroim had a cousin named Gedalye Sigel who owned a cigar factory in Pittsburgh. Efroim wrote to his cousin, asking whether he would be able to get work there. The cousin wrote back, yes, he didn't see why not. Efroim went to Pittsburgh. He took a fire pot and several sheets of tin and went to the landlords asking if they had any leaks in their roofs. In that way, he did not earn badly for a while. Then he opened a tinning and roofing shop with a partner, a certain Yoysef Klein. Later, he brought his family out to Pittsburgh.

Seventeen months passed. My wife gave birth to a little girl. At the same time, I got a letter from Mordkhe asking me to send him a ship's ticket. I sent it to him immediately and he came. I got him a job on Grand Street, where they made wash boilers. Two Jews were the bosses. They worked eleven hours a day. I could not take him into my shop because there was only work for the old workers, so he wrote to his uncle Efroim asking whether he could get work in Pittsburgh. Efroim wrote that he should come. Mordkhe went to Pittsburgh and got a job at the Pennsylvania Railroad.

It was winter. Early one morning a fire broke out in the candy store below us and we were awakened by the smoke. The hall was full of smoke. Before long, two policemen entered our rooms and led us, with our three small children, up to the roof, and then over to the next roof to a neighbor's house. My oldest boy caught cold and was sick for several months, until he died. Our sorrow cannot be described. We moved with our two children to Fifth Street, which was then a nicer neighborhood. My wife's sorrow was very great. She could not be comforted. I was afraid for her health. Finally, she told me that she could not stay in New York anymore. Perhaps in another city she would gradually forget about our child's misfortune.

By that time, I was getting twenty dollars a week and had a steady job. I expected to become a foreman soon in my line of work. One does not get that sort of job so easily. Our friends advised us not to do such a thing as leave the city. One might yet regret, God forbid, quitting such a job. But my wife still felt badly, so I wrote to Mordkhe to ask what I should do. He had already gotten married. He told me to come and that I could work with him at the Pennsylvania Railroad and make good money. We shipped the furniture to Pittsburgh and on the eve of Shavuot, 1904, we arrived in Pittsburgh with our beautiful, vibrant two children, a boy and a little girl. We took rooms on Logan Street from a certain Mr. Blumenthal. The rent was seventeen dollars. Before we moved in, an older woman and her daughter had lived in the rooms and they made a mess of the rooms. Mr. Blumenthal kept a mahogany wardrobe in the rooms, and it had become so filthy that the landlord wanted to do us a favor and throw it out.

In the meantime, we were with Mordkhe. We went at the rooms and, yes, also at the wardrobe. My wife and I made a palace of the rooms and the mahogany wardrobe sparkled. When Mr. Blumenthal came into the rooms, he thought he had gotten lost. He asked my wife, "Oh, where did you put the wardrobe?" My wife showed him. "This here is your own wardrobe." His mouth dropped open. The following Monday, he took three dollars off our rent. Though none of his other tenants could get along with him, my wife and I thought that he was a decent man.

I was already working at the railroad in the tinsmiths' shop. It was piecework, but sometimes I got thirty cents an hour for special jobs. We got paid every Monday. In general, I made out the same as in New York, though in New York the work was nicer and more refined. But as long as my wife started to feel better. . . .

Once, the boss sent me to fix a small boiler under a locomotive engine. He gave me the number and said, "But make it fast, because the engine has to leave in twenty minutes." I took my tools and ran to the engine. The engineer was already sitting in the locomotive, ready to drive. He said to me, "Do it on the hurry-up. I don't want to be late."

I went down under the engine, right by the wheels, and started to fix it. We knew that when they wanted to start to drive an engine they rang the bell so that no one would be in the way. But I felt instinctively that I must not trust this Irish engineer and here I was, lying on the tracks under the wheels. First, I put my tools further away from me under the engine so that they would not get in my way if I had to crawl out from under the engine in the blink of an eye. Second, I told the engineer not to start up before he asked me if I was finished. He yelled out, "Yes, yes, Jew. Hurry, hurry." I hurried. I heard a kind of a little squeak. Then a bigger one. And all at once, without a bell, the engine started to move. In the blink of an eye, I dragged myself out from under the engine. I was still on my knees. Should I stand or sit? My eyes were closed, for about a minute. Then I opened my eyes and turned to the left and saw far, very far, off a plume of black and gray smoke snaking its way up from the engine I had been working on. I lifted myself up and glanced at a bunch of workers who were looking at me and laughing. And one of them said, "You can't fool a Jew."

I came to my senses and went up to the shop. I thought I would tell the shop foreman, or "boss," as they used to call him. He was a man of over seventy years of age, who had worked for the company since he was a young boy. He had long been entitled to a pension, but did not want to quit. His son helped him out. Well, with the number of the engine in hand, I set out to see Mr. Hough to tell him what has happened. I took a couple of steps and stopped short, thinking about whether I should even tell him. Would I get any satisfaction if I did? And then again, six of us Jews worked in the shop among many Germans and Irishmen. Would complaining not have a negative effect on us Jews? I thought to myself, let me not make a stir or any noise. And I swallowed hard and, as we Jews say, made quiet. I did tell Mordkhe, but only when we were on our way home from work. He told me that I did right by not complaining to Mr. Hough.

Mordkhe had already sent ship's tickets to a brother and a sister. They arrived and went to work at stogies—a kind of small cigars. Mordkhe's wife was from Podkamen, Galicia. He married a woman who was in no way his equal and she was very, very stingy. She kept six boarders, who ate with her as well. She ran a regular restaurant! Well, they made so much that they bought a house. Two months later, they were offered six hundred dollars profit and sold the house. That was Mordkhe's first step in money-making. Then they lent out several hundred dollars for good interest. Mordkhe and his brother and sister wrote to their father, Moyshe Avrom, telling him to sell the house and come to America.

I worked for another couple of months and then the company laid off several hundred workers in the Pittsburgh district. Mordkhe stayed on, but I thought to myself, I won't go to work at the railroad again. I went to look for a job in my line: tinning, roofing, pipes—just sheet metal work. I went into a shop and met the boss. He was helping the rest of the workers. I understood that it must be busy. The boss was a thin man, not tall, with small, good-natured eyes. He asked me if I was a union man. I answered him, "No, but I want to become a union man." He told me that if I became a union man first, he would give me a trial for two weeks. Within two days, I had joined the union and was given a trial. And from the two-week trial, I ended up working for him for eleven years until I went into business for myself.

When Moyshe Avrom and my sister got a letter saying they should sell their house, they seized the opportunity enthusiastically, because they were not making a living. They had not paid off any of the principal and had to borrow more to pay the interest, so they were paying interest on the interest. It turned out that Yankev the Dairyman bought the house from them. My brother-in-law was left with seven hundred guldens for all his years of drudgery with his houses. And the whole family came to Pittsburgh and all of the children lived together. At first my brother-in-law did small jobs. Later the children brought in enough to live on.

My little boy was already in school. My little girl went to kindergarten. They were beautiful little children. When my wife walked on the street, people would point at her and say, "That's the mother of the two beautiful children." She dressed them very neatly, and combed their hair nicely. And she herself also dressed very neatly. And a delicious feeling radiated from every corner when one came into the house. When we visited my sister, Mordkhe's wife would screw up her nose as if to say, "Who sent for you?" Well, we seldom visited them. She was jealous of my wife.

We lived in what was called the Hill District. It was not so neat or clean in that neighborhood and there was no place for children to play. So we decided to move out of the city to a place called West Pittsburgh where there was green all around and plenty of fresh air. The children simply came to life. Each house stood a block apart from the next one, and sometimes two or three blocks apart. A small school stood on a hill. My little girl went to that school, and her mother, long may she live, would bring a glass of milk up to her twice a day. My little boy used to call the school the "chicken coop." He himself went to school in Elliott, so he had to go first through Sheraden and only then to Elliott. That was over hills and fields, but bad weather never kept him from going to school. Rain or snow, he never complained, nor did he catch cold.

After we had been living there for several months, a new five-room house was completed and we rented the house for seventeen dollars a month. There was plenty of land, so we planted various vegetables. Mother showed the children how to plant, and they planted a couple of packets of seeds themselves. When I came home from work and my wife and children were dressed nicely and every corner smelled of cleanliness and freshness, I thought to myself that the Gemara tractate Yevamot (maybe it was *Sefer ben Sira*) was right when it said, "*Isho tovo matono le-ba'alo.*" A good wife is a precious gift to her husband.[37] Right on the money!

When the sheet metal workers went out on strike, our shop did too. I wanted to stand on the picket line, but the union officials told me that they needed to have someone stronger to picket. They thought that they would settle with the bosses by the end of the week, but several weeks passed and the strike went on. In addition to the five dollars a week in strike benefits that we drew, the union allowed work in the factories— anywhere that did not have to do with the building trades.

Well, I went to look for a job at the National Casket Company. They made wooden caskets, but they had just begun to produce bronze caskets at three prices. The minimum price was 1,100 dollars, followed by 1,700 dollars and 2,300 dollars a casket. I understood that the work had to be very particular. They sent me to the engineer who had actually designed the bronze caskets. He asked me if I could do such work. I answered that I had never worked on a casket, but that I was certain that I would be able to do the work. He set me up to make the moldings on the casket, which was the hardest and finest work. The molding was just over a sixteenth of an inch thick. The miters had to be cut on a fine electric saw, and had to fit to a tee. If they were even a hair smaller or larger, they would not fit and the whole casket would be removed from production. Well, he showed me how to do the first molding. Then I went to work. I thought that I would take my time and that is how it was. I cut the molding and brought it to the casket and soldered it together. The engineer, Frazier by name, examined my work and said that he thought that I would be alright.

He offered me fifteen dollars a week in pay. I said to him, "Mr. Frazier, I expected eighteen dollars a week." He answered that if I did the job more quickly, he would pay me eighteen dollars next week. (I found out that he was partner in the business and received a certain percentage of the profits.) "Alright," I answered him. The next week my work went much more quickly and the molding came out so that there was no way one could tell that there was a seam. It was as if it had been poured out in one piece. Payday arrived: The same fifteen dollars. I asked him again, "Mr. Frazier, you promised that you would give me eighteen dollars if I made more moldings around the bodies. The first week I wasn't experienced. But you see now yourself that this week my work is much faster and better. Why have you given me only fifteen dollars?" He answered me that the work was good but still not fast enough. A worker next to my bench—he had already been working there a long time—told me that it was very hard to get a raise from Frazier.

I joined the newly founded Branch 45 of the Workmen's Circle.* And later my wife joined Women's Branch 104.

Within a few weeks I had adapted to the job so well that I could have put out twice as much work. But I did not do so, because, very simply, I had been a tradesman ever since my youth, so I was more skilled at handwork than the rest of the Christian workers. (I was the only Jew.) And, after all, the strike had to be settled. Why should they have to race their hearts out? So I did my work very slowly, but in such a way that it not draw any attention.

One morning, Mr. Frazier came in and told everyone that some large orders had arrived, that the small stock had been sold, and that we needed to put out the work faster and faster. They were practically snatching the work out of the workers' hands. Well, I knew at first glance that it was some trick on the part of the company. They wanted to test the workers and afterwards give them piecework. This was already the case on the upper floors where the wooden caskets were made only by piecework. And in the end the workers there had to slave to make a living. Yes, the workers were making from nine to twelve dollars a week. So they wanted to institute piecework on the bronze caskets as well, and it surprised me that the other workers did not recognize this. When the superintendent came into the shop and said, "Hurry, hurry," the workers actually hurried! I was afraid to explain to the workers what the bosses were really up to. They were driving me as well, just like everyone else, but I made it seem as if I was hurrying while actually taking my time. And so we worked for the entire week.

On Monday, before we got to work, every worker found a list of prices for his line of work. So piecework it was. For me, too. The price for my work was four dollars a piece. Oh, I probably could have made a piece in one day. But for that, I would have had to work "hurry-up." Well, the workers saw the list and became upset, because, according to the set prices, they would barely be able to make ten or twelve dollars a week, no matter how hard they were forced to work. Two workers quit immediately to look for other jobs. And the rest tried it out for a week to see whether they would be able to make out. They would then go to the office and say that they had tried and it was impossible to work for that price. For my price, I would have been able to make seven dollars a day, but what would have been the result? They would have immediately cut the price. And besides, I did not want the work to be so hard, at least for the worker who would end up doing my job after I left. So I only made one casket molding and made myself the four dollars a day.

In other words, I did well with piecework. (Oh yes, we worked ten hours a day.) This caused an uproar among some of the workers, and one in particular—Bill, he was called, and he was an anti-Semite. "That Jew b—— got the best price." But he did not dare to say this to Mr. Frazier.

So I worked there another month until the strike was won. Before, we received three dollars and twenty cents a day. Now we got four dollars a day for a forty-four hour week. I walked into Mr. Frazier's office and told him that I quit and that he should pay me what I had coming. Then I went back up to the shop. I took a piece of molding in my hand and went up to Bill and said, "You see, Bill, B the Jew set the price at four dollars. I could have made more, but the Jew didn't want to spoil the price and make you have to work hard here. I quit," I continued, "and will return to my work. But from now on, do not hate a Jew." And I took my tools and went to the office for my pay.

We took rooms a little bit up from the center of town. We had lived there for several months, when my wife saw that they were building a new three-room house on the next block with all the new modern fixtures. My wife watched the house almost every day. When the fixtures were about to be finished, she asked who the owner was. She found out that it was a certain man, a lawyer, but that he did not rent to Jews. But my wife said she would try to speak with him and went to see him. She went into his office and told him that she would like to rent the second floor. He answered that the second floor was already rented, but not the first floor. He asked, "Will three rooms be enough for you then, with two children?"

"I'll manage," she responded. "The three rooms and bath will be enough for us."

"Mrs. R.," he continued, "I don't rent to Jews." This was because he had heard that they do not keep the house clean. "There's no telling what bad people will say," she answered. "Give me a trial and you'll see how clean I keep your house." He considered my wife from head to toe, and said to her, "Mrs., you look to be a respectable and clean woman. I'll give you a lease for just thirty days and after the thirty days I'll see how you keep the house. If it is satisfactory, then I will give you a lease for a year." And we moved into the new house.

When the month was up, he came and looked around and liked what he saw. But in his pocket he had a lease for just a month, saying that he wanted to wait another month. Finally, at the end of the second month, he looked around once more and told my wife that he would mail her a yearly lease. He would also never again believe the bad things they say about Jews.

During this time, my sister had a store on Logan Street with cheap goods, like shirts, sweaters, and the like, and made money. They now married off their pretty eldest daughter and a son, Noyekh. All of the children were earners. Moyshe Avrom and Rokhl truly thanked the Holy One, blessed be He, that they were now in this blessed land. They even bought a brick building with two stores. One store they had for themselves and the other they rented out as a confectionary. In general, life treated them well. Moyshe Avrom sat with a long pipe, blowing smoke and contemplating it as it snaked its way up. They lived next door to Mordkhe, who dropped by several times a day.

His parents derived proud pleasure from Mordkhe. What was this pleasure? First of all, he was successful. Mordkhe had long since quit the railroad. He no longer carried his lunch bucket to work. He thought only of making money. And he made money. Mordkhe then already possessed fifty thousand dollars. He bought houses, sold them, and made a profit. Second, he lent several people money as mortgages. Later, he convinced the owners that they should fix up and paint the houses, and install modern fixtures. Naturally, the owners became very excited. What a fine man is Mordkhe! They borrowed more money from him, and Mordkhe saw to it that the best fixtures were installed. When time was up on the mortgage, he refused to renew it. He took the house away from them, together with the bonuses that they gave him for lending them the mortgage, so the people were left at sea. Well, let God worry about it. That is what Mordkhe's wife taught him. She taught him to be so stingy that he would not allow himself to pay the nickel carfare that it cost to go downtown. Instead, he went on foot in the greatest heat and the greatest cold. That is how one makes money.

His boys did not even go to public school. They sent one to sell flowers downtown and the second boy to do some kind of other work. As long as they made money. Yes, money and more money. Heaven and earth and money. The youngest, a very charming little girl, did go to school.

The younger brother, Noyekh, also had a store, like his mother. But he saw how Mordkhe was making money from houses, so he gave up the store and with his mother's help he bought old houses, fixed them up, and rented or sold them. He also profited. Not like Mordkhe, but he was always busy with the houses. Their eldest daughter, Annie, and her husband Louie Kaplan also dealt in houses. But he was American-born, so he did his business in an American business way.

My boy was already in high school. He was an able student. And I began to take part in the movement. I became very active in the Socialist Party and the Workmen's Circle, and took an active part in forming our own Labor Lyceum.[38] I threw myself into the work with religious enthusiasm. My wife also became a member of the Socialist Party. We both understood that the world as it was presently run was not a just one. Society was built on injustice and this had to be abolished. Therefore we had to see to it that Socialist teachings were spread in the Jewish community. At that time, the Socialist Party was flourishing throughout the country.

The Pittsburgh Socialist Party published a weekly newspaper, the *New Era.* Many comrades solicited advertisements for the *New Era,* but it was hard for them to get any. So I took it upon myself to get the advertisements. I set out, first in the Hill District, to all the stores and told them plainly that if they wanted people to patronize them, then the large membership of the Workmen's Circle and of the then-largest Jewish Socialist branch demanded it of them. I needed to say nothing more. For a long time, I got the advertisements. I traveled downtown and got advertisements from many of the department stores as well. I explained to many members of the Workmen's Circle that they should become members of the Socialist Party, and many became party members. I was elected recording secretary and held the office for a couple of years. Then, when I had other business to attend to, I barely was able to convince the comrades to elect someone else instead of me.

It was a pleasure to work with many members of the Socialist Party and the Workmen's Circle. One of them was Friend Leon Arkin, the present manager of the *Forward* in Boston.[39] He worked with all his energy and enthusiasm in all areas of all the branches. He never refused to do any of the routine work. One would see him walking with a man from the billposters' union. With a canvas bag of posters hanging from his left shoulder, Friend Arkin would show the union man where to paste up a poster. One could see him giving out flyers in the street himself. There was not an event in which L. Arkin did not participate. It happens that we were not always in agreement at the meetings. But this was actually a good thing —the exchange of opinions. After 1910, when Leon Arkin married the charming Adele Arkin, Mrs. Arkin would often attend meetings as well. When the *Forward* hired him as manager of its office in Boston, we made a banquet for him in a packed hall before he left. I made a short speech, saying, among other things, the following: "We would be one hundred percent happy if this banquet had been made for Arkin's work for the movement, and we are envious of the Boston comrades and friends that they will have Friend Arkin in their midst."

We bought a building to renovate as a Labor Lyceum. Many committees were elected to raise money. I was one of the "committees." Every Sunday, I went out to collect from morning to late, and every evening as well. Sundays, I had nothing but coffee and a snack for the whole day. I collected over seven hundred dollars from Workmen's Circle members. When people recall their youthful past, they are refreshed by the joy of their sweet youthful years gone by. But I never knew the joys of youth. So this work that I did for the movement was the most beautiful, most inspiring time in my life. This is my best and sweetest memory.

We lived in the three-room apartment for two years and then moved into a four-room house. There was a row of adjoining houses under one roof, each with four rooms and a porch. Each porch was connected to the next house. A couple of party and Workmen's Circle members also moved into the adjoining houses. Almost every evening, we would get together on the porch and debate about the day-to-day outlook and the events that were then taking place in the world. The discussions were very heated and interesting.

Some time later Mordkhe brought in new furniture. Alas, people—just friends of his—reproached him and said that he had to throw out his broken furniture. So, he could not help but buy new things. Well, when one has new furniture, one must throw a party for all one's family and friends. They even invited the politician Squire Frankel.[40] Well, fine for them.

My wife and children and I went. In the front of the house was a store through which one entered. So my wife and children and I sat ourselves down in the store. We did not want to be in the rooms, because it was too noisy. The door opened. Louie, my sister's son, came in with a fat cigar in his mouth, his hat tilted a little to the side, and took a look at everyone. Without a word, without a greeting, he went right on his way into the back rooms where the crowd was gathered—as if he no longer knew us or who we were. My wife was beside herself. Why did he do that? Why did he pretend not to notice us? Had money so corrupted him that he was ashamed of his own flesh and blood for the sole reason that we did not have thousands of dollars? We did not say a word, but we said goodbye to everyone and went home.

My family heard that I wanted to go into business and open a shop. From whom they heard, I do not know. A short time later, they married off their youngest daughter, Khave. She married a fine young man and they rented a store and sold dishes. They did not invite me to the wedding. That was no surprise to me because I already knew them too well. It did not bother me much either, and certainly not my wife.

We found out why they did not invite us to the wedding. The parents and children had gathered together secretly. They had heard that I was looking for a neighborhood in which to rent a shop. Well, if I was going into business, I would certainly need money and would probably come to them to borrow several hundred dollars. What did they need this for? So they all decide—with Mordkhe's wife inciting them further—not to invite me to the wedding and good riddance, so I will finally understand that there is no place for me there. Moyshe Avrom heard the decision and did not say a word. He held his long pipe in his mouth and blew smoke.

The following episode took place some time earlier—more exactly, about three years earlier. Rokhl and the children would often send several dollars to our other sister's son, Moyshe, in Golyn, Galicia. I would send extra each time. In the month of November, 1913, I sent him extra money for Hanukkah. He received the Hanukkah present and nicely thanked me. He also wrote me that his eighteen-year-old boy had some sort of illness and that the doctors advised him to go to Vienna as quickly as possible for an operation.

I brought the letter to Rokhl. She started to say strange things to me. She asked me how much money I had saved up while working for others. She also said that I would never work my way up. She talked so long that I became upset.

I brought the letter to Mordkhe. I found Mordkhe and his wife. I handed him the letter from Moyshe. He read the letter out loud so that his wife could hear. When he finished reading the letter, she stood up from her chair and said to me, "B, don't come to me with such letters. I have my own family in Podkamen (Galicia) to take care of. Why don't you send money to Moyshe yourself. I don't come to you asking you to help me. And do you know why I don't come to you? Because we are in business." And Mordkhe heard what she said and did not say a single word in response.

I think to myself, Good Lord, what is going on here? All one hears from these people is business! Heaven and earth and business! It was simply repulsive to me to hear from them day and night—business and business. So I now responded to Mordkhe's wife with the following words: "If it is a matter of throwing people out of the houses into which they have put their hard-earned cents, and if it comes to gouging huge interest rates– and bonuses on top of that–from poor people, then I prefer to work for someone else and earn my living, fair and square." And I left. So she went right to Rokhl (I do not know whether Mordkhe went along with her), and said such things about me not a single word of which was true.

The next day I got a letter from Rokhl, which surprised me very much. Twenty-nine years have now passed since I received that letter and I keep it to this day.

Six months later I had surgery for appendicitis. I was in the hospital for fourteen days. Rokhl found out that I was in the hospital. On the fourth day after I had come home, the door opened and in came Rokhl—with a request that I forgive her for her letter. Yetta had told her that I had said such things that right on the spot she told someone to write the letter to me. And, again, I should forgive her. I heard her out and paced back and forth across the room. I didn't answer her. My mind worked without stop.

Suddenly, I recalled how when my mother, may she rest in peace, died, and we were coming from the grave, my uncle said to me, "Binyomentshe, see to it that you don't make Rokhl angry." After a moment of silence, I went up to Rokhl and said, "Alright Rokhl, I forgive you."

Right away, she took a fifty out of her pocket and said, "I am giving you fifty dollars. Spend it. Get better and wait a week to go to work. Don't hurry. Take good care of yourself."

I thanked her and said, "Take back the fifty dollars, Rokhl. I don't need it. I have my own money."

She answered, "B, I will feel better if you take the money. Please. Do me a favor and put it in your pocket. You will take better care of yourself."

I answered her that my Keyle already took care of me. After a long struggle, she put the fifty back in her pocket.

After that, we seldom visited them. Three years passed until, as mentioned above, they did not invite me to the wedding, so that when I went into business, I would not come to them to borrow several hundred dollars.

My boy finished high school in three and a half years. In his free time he worked in a shoe store. And my girl went to high school. My boy wanted to go to Carnegie Technological Institute first to study chemical engineering. Then he wanted to go to the University of Pittsburgh. Well, I was happy, as was my wife.

At the same time, I was still active in the movement. We had built a Labor Lyceum. Our Jewish Socialist branch was the largest in the country. Branch 45, Workmen's Circle, was the second largest after Philadelphia Branch 12. The work for the movement was becoming more and more interesting. My wife transferred from Branch 104 to Branch 45, because it was more lively and interesting there.

One Thursday evening, as I was coming from a meeting and walking home on Centre Avenue, I ran into Jacob Benjamin. Also a union man in my trade, he had a shop where he made and fixed automobile fenders, as well as radiators, lamps, and the like. He complained to me that he was sick. He suffered from rheumatism and wanted to sell his shop and go to Mount Clemens to take the baths. "I'm not saying one would make a fortune," he continued, "but one can make a living." I told him I would come to see him in a couple of days to look over the shop.

I came home and told my wife and children. We talked it over seriously: Our boy goes to Carnegie Tech and will soon enter the University of Pittsburgh. And our girl may as well. Well, since our expenses will increase, perhaps it would be a good idea to buy the shop. I looked over the shop. It was in the East End neighborhood, where there was a large population. The rent was cheap, 35 dollars a month. Though it wasn't a big shop, it was enough for me to start. I thought to myself that I would work at my own trade in the shop, namely sheet metal work and furnaces to heat houses. I asked him how much he was asking, and he said 160 dollars. I answered that I would let him know. That was in March.

It was not so easy for me to decide to quit my job. It is worth describing my boss, Charlie Kirk, and his family, an old Scottish American family. He was a likable and a liberal man. The boss's brother, Joe, worked for him since he was a thirteen-year-old boy. He studied sheet metal work at Carnegie Tech and knew drawing and blueprints well. I learned a lot from him and he was eager to show me. That is how all of Kirk's children were. One of them was the bookkeeper. Well, having been with such people for so many years, where everyone liked me and I had steady work, it was no wonder that I could not decide so easily what to do.

So it dragged on until the April 16, 1916. In the evening, I sat down at the table with my wife and my boy to consider the issue seriously. We had to make a decision that day—yes or no. Finally, after a lengthy consultation, we took up our accounts to calculate how much our fortune consisted of. And here it is. On the table lay an old yellow piece of paper. So I pulled it over and started to write the following figures:

Outstanding loan to the Workmen's Circle – $100
In the union bank – $83
In Washington Bank – $35
My boy had saved – $61
So my capital consisted of – $279.

Well, not bad. I thought that I would not pay more than $130 for the shop. So we were left with a balance of

$279
– $130 (shop)
$149 (balance)

Good. I had no doubt in my abilities.

Of course, one cannot know how things will end up, and what accusations might arise. So I took the piece of paper on which we had made the calculation and wrote out a sort of declaration—a "Declaration of Independence"—and my wife, my boy, and I signed it. I still have that piece of paper today. That was April 16, 1916.

Well, easier said than done; it took two months. Mr. Kirk was very busy. Naturally, I would not leave him in the middle of a busy season. I told Kirk that I was going to try a shop for myself. He was uneasy but did not try to stop me. Finally, I bought the shop on July 12 for 130 dollars. On July 14, my last day at Kirk's shop, I said goodbye to everyone. Finally, I said goodbye to Kirk. In the middle of saying goodbye, I broke into tears. I had spent almost eleven years working in that shop. I had raised my children and never known slack. What's more, I had been treated very well. Maybe I had made a mistake by even starting to talk about a shop. When Kirk saw that I was crying, he also started to cry. Then he said to me, "Ben, anytime you need help, tell me. I will help you in any way I can at any time. Or if you want to quit business, then you are welcome at any time to return to the shop." We said goodbye again and everyone wished me luck. As I walked through the door to leave, I took another look at the shop and tears started to pour once again. I came home and said to my wife, "The last pay envelope. Good luck to us." And she and the children embraced and kissed me.

The next morning, I went to the new shop, thinking that I was entering a new field of work. Dear God, *al tastir ponekho mimeni,* do not hide your face from me.[41] A little later, Jack Benjamin came by and said to me, "Come, I will take you to Mr. Glesenkamp. He has a large automobile repair and paint shop, and I do work for him. I repair fenders, lamps, and radiators for him. I will introduce you." I went with him. He introduced me to Mr. Glesenkamp, who said that he had some work for me that very day. I did his job the first day. And work came in from outside as well.

The next day, I had business cards printed up. After I got the cards, I went to the real estate offices. I went into the first real estate office on Highland Avenue. I went up to the desk where I saw a small bronze sign: Mr. Green. I handed him a business card. He took the card and looked at it. Then he looked at me and, for a moment, he was quiet. He got up. I thought to myself, this Mr. Green, with his fine head of white hair and so tall, looked more like a high judge than a real estate man. He said to me a bit gruffly, "Mr. R, I want to ask you something, and you should answer me."

"Yes, Mr. Green," I said.

"Let's say you work for me. Would you like it if the work were taken away from you?"

For a second, I was quiet. I had not expected such a question. But then I answered him quickly. "Mr. Green, you are right. I don't mean to take anyone's work away. But in case your tinsmith is too busy to do a job for you, give me a chance. You'll see, you'll be happy with my work."

He looked at me and after a moment of silence he responded, "Alright, Mr. R, I will let you know."

I went right into another office to a Mr. Sherrer, an even bigger real estate man than Mr. Green. I handed him my business card and he immediately asked me, "Is your work satisfactory?"

I answered him, "Yes, Mr. Sherrer."

He opened up a ledger, wrote out three addresses, gave me the paper with the addresses, and said to me, "Go to these two addresses and do the job immediately. At the third address, examine it and give me a price, because I must first send it to the landlord. When I get an answer from him, I will mail you the order." I thanked him and left the office, a happy man.

My wife came to the shop around ten o'clock to answer the telephone and write out orders. And when my boy or girl came from school, they let their mother go home and they did their homework in the shop. I had enough credit for material, because the salesmen who came to Kirk—like from the Demmler Brothers and Pollensby-McLear—all told me that I could get as much material from them as I wanted. After all, they had known me for a decade. I only ordered as much material as I could use, so that I could discount my bills every tenth of the month for paying on time. And that is how it actually was. Not once, in the whole time I was in business, did I fail to discount my bills—to the last month when I retired from the business.

One day, Kirk came to visit me in the shop. He had a job in my neighborhood and wanted to know how my business was going at the start. I used the opportunity to ask him to transport my material to a couple of jobs. He immediately ordered Dick and Harry, who were with him, to transport the materials. I was very happy, because sometimes I had to wait a couple of hours for an express truck.

Three days later, I came from a job. I took a look and one of Kirk's edge machines was in my shop. My wife told me that Kirk had left the machine for me. I was flabbergasted. True, it was an old machine, but, even so, it was still worth 120 dollars. The machine would really save me a lot of time. I immediately called Kirk and thanked him profusely. He responded, "Don't mention it. Don't make a big deal out of it, Ben."

Agents started to come to me to sell me a truck on installments. I answered them all that I never bought anything on installments and I wouldn't now either. Oh, I have to wait a long time to get a hired truck? Well, I'll wait another few weeks.

Well, what do I do now? I needed people, but I did not want to take anyone on until I could give him steady work. After thinking for a while, a plan came to me. I would go to Efroim, Moyshe Avrom's brother, and would take him as a partner to each job, until I got to the point where I could keep at least one man steady. I went out to him and laid out the plan. Well, he did not need much convincing. He told me that he would do it for my sake, to help me out. Very well.

Now I called a Jewish salesman, Mr. Hochstetter, to come see me about a truck. Three days later, I had a truck for which I paid cash. True it was only a half-ton truck, but it did not matter. It was enough for now. Gradually, I opened checking accounts in the City Deposit Bank (a branch of Mellon's bank), in East End Savings and Trust Co., and a year later also in the Highland National Bank. I thought that there should be a little in three banks in the same neighborhood. Never mind, later I'll get some sort of favor out of it.

Now I took on my first man to work. I thought that at least I would be able to keep one man steadily, in addition to the helper. Besides them, I now had two or three men at work, but only as long as I was busy.

I bought a Remington typewriter. I hired a girl for the office to do estimates and other work that a business requires. I had already saved up several hundred dollars and put it away in the bank, not to be touched. My wife and I still attended meetings. And, in general, I couldn't complain.

Now begins the most interesting part of my story, at least for me and my family. One day, I was out on business. My boy came to the office after school with his books and was studying. A young man in his thirties came into the office and asked my boy where the boss was. My boy answered him that he was the boss's son and asked what he could do for him. The man told him that he was the superintendent of the United Construction and Engineering Co. A year before, he had built a house, and on one end of the gutter, when it rained, it ran onto the next-door neighbor's house. "Tell your father to come as quickly as possible to fix it." His name was Dave M. Everson.

Then Mr. Everson sat himself down next to my boy and they talked for about an hour. Mr. Everson said to him, "The house where I live is too small for me. It is a six-room house. Tell your father that, while he is there, he should take a look around. I think that the house would be good for you. It is not a large house."

"Alright, Mr. Everson," my boy answered him.

When I returned, my boy told me everything. I replied that we should go the next day and do the job so that his neighbor would have no more damage. I went to the job myself. When the job was finished, Mrs. Everson called me inside to show me the rooms. Well, it was wonderful. It goes without saying that it was well built. I came home and told my wife what a nice house it was. But what good did a nice house do me when we were not yet able to afford a house?

I sent Mr. Everson a bill for seventeen dollars. The next day, he came to the office in the late afternoon and asked my boy, "How much of a discount will you give me? I will make you out a check." My boy answered him, "Two percent." So Mr. Everson made out a check for sixteen dollars and sixty-six cents, and said, "Tell your father that I will sell him the house for six thousand dollars, and I will give him the mortgage. Have him come to me this evening with your mother. We will be at home." The boy told us. So my wife said to me, "B, let's go out and see the house. What can you lose? Come, let's take a little trip." Well, when your wife asks for something, you have to oblige her.

And so we came to Mr. Everson's house. He started to speak. "I see that you are honest people. That is why I want to sell you the house, and on easy terms." And he asks me, "Mr. B, how much can you put down on a house?"

I told him, "Mr. Everson, at the moment I don't have enough money to buy your house."

He asked again, "But still, how much could you pay now?"

I said, five hundred dollars.

"Well," he said, "not bad. We can work it out." And he calculated right away, and said, "Two thousand dollars on a three-year mortgage, five hundred cash, equals 2,500 dollars." And I should give him 3,500 dollars when I have it, even if it takes five or six years. I answered him that those really were very easy terms. But, what if it happened that it was slack for a time, and I could not make the payments? He answered me, "It doesn't matter. I'll wait until it gets busy."

We told him that we would talk it over and let him know, and we left.

My wife was struck with fear. "B, we mustn't let such an opportunity go by. There is only one thing to do, and that is buy that nice house. I even think that I should call him myself tomorrow and tell him that we have decided that if he will sell us the house for 5,500 dollars, we will give him a deposit right away." I answered her, "You can try." The next morning she called him at his office. In the end, he told her to come with me to see him at home that evening. After haggling over a compromise for a little while, my wife repeated what we could afford to pay. Well, he said to give him a deposit. I made out a check for two hundred dollars, and he wished us luck and told me to go ahead and tell my lawyer the next day that we would be at his house to make out the deed.

I actually called my lawyer that same evening. His answer was that everything would be ready. And that is how it was. The next evening we both signed the deed. My wife was the happiest woman in the world.

Now I had six or seven people working for me. Business was going very well and the customers were also good. Checks came in on time. I called up Mr. Everson and told him that, if he wanted, I could send him several hundred dollars. He answered me, "Well, I could use it." I sent him five hundred dollars and within a year I had paid him two thousand dollars.

The sheet metal workers' union went out on strike for higher wages. Naturally, I immediately agreed to the union's demand. My workers did not stop working. Two days later, the business agent came to ask that I help win the strike. I asked him, "What can I do? I will do what I can." He said that I should take on as many strikers as I could. I replied that I would look over my orders in the next few days and let him know how many people I could hire. Since the strike had already been going on for almost a week, I was actually getting more work. I called up the union office and told them to send me three people, and the next week another striker. The strike lasted for only about three months and it was lost. But two months later, when the season began, the Master Tinners' Association raised the pay scale itself.

My girl finished high school. She did not want to go to college. She said that she could study privately, and with time she would be just as educated as if she had gone to college. We could not do anything about it. And at the same time, she really did study on her own. She was always reading books. Today she has a pretty good education and a better understanding of various fields than many who have gone to university.

My bookkeeper got married and my girl took over the work. She made the estimates and attended to all the needs of the office. Often when she sent out an estimate, I got the order even though my bid was higher, because the customer liked the way the estimate was laid out.

Once I noticed that I was constantly missing materials. I could not understand who was stealing it. A worker who had worked for me for several years—a good tradesman—told me that he was going to buy the house next to mine. "Alright," I said to him, "good luck." I gave him the truck to move his things into the new house. And everything was fine and dandy. Two months later, my wife looked into his cellar by accident and saw a substantial stock of my materials: tin, brass, copper, etc. She called me right up and told me what she had seen in Joe's cellar. I was flabbergasted that Joe would do such a thing.

Joe came from work. He told me what he had used—materials and hours—on various jobs. Then I asked him, "Joe, how did my materials get into your cellar?" He became white as chalk. Unintelligible words came out of his mouth. I did not ask him anything more, and he left the shop without saying good night. I sat there and thought again: How could Joe do such a thing? The materials did not concern me, only that Joe should turn out to be a thief. Well, what's done is done, and that's it.

The next morning, he did not come to work. My wife called me and said that Joe had left the house in the morning and not come back yet. And so it was every day throughout the week. Suddenly, a moving van came up to his house and they moved out. We told ourselves that he probably was ashamed to be our neighbor because of his stealing, so he moved out. No doubt, he had rented it to someone else. It could not be otherwise.

The next day, my wife called me up with a cry that three black families with very many little children had moved in, and their screaming and shouting could be heard to the high heavens. I left my work and ran home. When I came to the house, it was as if someone had hit me over the head with a hammer. Broken beds, tables and chairs lay around, and torn mattresses were next to my garden, and the stuffing from the torn mattresses and pieces of rug lay on the green grass and flowers. Well, if Joe had sold the house to a clean black, it would have been fine. By all means, two oppressed peoples ought to be good neighbors. Of all people, we Jews are very familiar with the signs at many hotels: "For Gentiles only." We feel great pain when we see that. Because of that, we need to set an example of living in peace with other peoples without regard to color or race. We need to live with our neighbors in a friendly way. But my current three neighbors in one little house, with eight or ten children (no, ten children rather than eight)—and boys are already coming to visit my girl—and with their filth. . . . It can, you know . . . However liberal you are, it is very, very unpleasant.

I told my wife that I would go to a black agent, because no white would buy our house now, of course, and get him to sell the nice house for me. And the very next day, I went to the office of a real estate man of my acquaintance—I did work for him as well—and asked him to sell my house. But, I told him, I wanted cash, no mortgages. He told me that he thought he had just the man who was looking for a house like mine. He was a widower with two grown girls, who wanted to fix up a nice house for his girls. And he had cash. He was the chief cook of the Rittenhouse Hotel. And if I wanted to wait he could call him and arrange a time when he and his girls could come to see the house. "But, Mr. R," he asked me, "how much do you want for the house?" I told him, ten thousand dollars, with five hundred dollars cash down, no bargaining. He called him up and said that he would come out that evening with his daughters.

In the evening, they came with the real estate man. Well, it goes without saying that they liked the house. The girls were simply delighted with it. They looked through every corner of the house with their father, studying all the details. In short, I sold him the house for ten thousand dollars cash. And with great effort, we found five rooms without steam heat for 150 dollars a month, because at that time it was very hard to find rooms.

My son graduated from the university and became an instructor of chemistry at the College of Pharmacy. In the two years that he taught, he also learned pharmacy on his own and from the books, and got a degree in pharmacy. My girl was being visited by a very decent boy, with a good reputation, a graduate of the University of Pittsburgh, well acquainted with Latin, a member of the board of directors of the university, and also a nice and pleasant person. And, with good fortune, they became engaged. I bought a lot and built a house and, before long, I married off my daughter. I invited my sister (an older sister, after all) and brother-in-law and she had a good time until the break of day.

My son became engaged to a girl who had also graduated college, as well as Pittsburgh Musical Institute. My wife and I wanted him to live with us after the wedding, so it would not cost him any rent. He answered that he had already talked it over with his bride, and she preferred to live separately. Since the house was pretty big for us, I sold it and lost several hundred dollars and we bought a duplex. From one apartment we took in rent, 125 dollars. Nice rent, no? But a couple of months later, we found out that the agent had rented it for 130 dollars and was only sending me 120 dollars. Of course, he was already deducting his commission.

Business was going well, but one cannot live from day-to-day work alone. I tried to be as active as possible in the labor movement, which makes life richer in spirit and more interesting than the petty concerns that every person has in his own life. So, from time to time, I went to the meetings. True, not as often as before. And that really grieved me. Also, sometimes I dropped by at a synagogue, somewhere they didn't know me well, and sat myself down over a Gemara and studied enthusiastically. I really did love the Gemara. And, again, I did not see how my social and world outlook conflicted with the great treasures of the Talmud. The Talmud does not only discuss Jewish laws, although they are very just ones, but also social justice, with fairness and understanding for people. Accordingly, they are in full agreement with the spirit of my political, social, and economic outlook.

It is worth noting here that selling the house and losing several hundred dollars may have done me a big favor. I derived a moral from it: one cannot depend on business or on houses to prepare for one's old age. And, indeed, I soon invested in a fund. Even my dear wife did not know about it at first. I even thought that I would be able to make a lot of money. I would not touch the money, and thanks to that step, my wife and I would not have to turn to our children in our old age.

We finished with our duplex and I sold it. We got four thousand dollars in profit, bought a large lot, and built two duplexes and a five-room house for us.

My son got married and everything went satisfactorily. Beginning in 1927, we went to Florida every winter and stayed there until spring. Although I could not depend on the foreman to run the business, I looked the other way, because Florida did us a lot of good. It was characteristic of my workers that, although I used to bring them presents when I returned, they talked among themselves: "Here he goes on vacation every winter and we have to suffer here in the winter cold," and so on.

We also went on short trips during the summer, and people considered me a rich man. For my part, I thought that if paying your bills on time means you are a rich man, then I am certainly rich. And so people live happily with one another thinking that so and so is rich, although they are far from being rich.

My wife and I would visit my sister from time to time, and Mordkhe sometimes as well. Mordkhe was very busy with his houses, buying and remodeling and selling. It would not have been so bad if he had taken on a general contractor when he had to rebuild, or simply build. But he did not do that. He thought he would save the contractor's profit, so he himself hired various workers for the day. And he thought that they could give him more work, but they did not work fast enough. So it continually gnawed at his heart, until he had a heart attack. And after several weeks of lying in bed, he got better and went on with his work as before. My wife and I pleaded with him, "Mordkhe, Mordkhe, look at how you live! You will amass a great fortune and your children will know how to use the money, so enjoy life yourself as well." His answer was that he had his three meals a day, and what else does a person need? To go to the theater or to go on a vacation is a waste of money.

On February 28, 1928, my sister became ill. For one day, I sat beside her bed, hoping that she would get well. Then my family and I went off to Florida. A week later, I got a telegram that she had been taken to the hospital and several days later she died.

In the spring, we came home from Florida and found our house fixed up nice and clean, as usual after an absence of a whole winter. This was the work of our steady maid who had worked for us for several years. But right after we arrived home, she told my wife that she was leaving for Chicago to be with her relatives. Well, we took one girl after another and could not adjust to them. As my wife used to say, they were all dirty women. We had such trouble with them.

My daughter said we should give up the house and save having to deal with servants. Accordingly, she wanted us to move in with her. She had built a big house for herself, and would give us the nicest rooms. My wife and I did not want to hear of it. But one time when she knew that we had gone downtown, she hired a truck, went to our house, and removed all our bedroom furniture and installed it for us in her best bedroom. My wife and I came back and went into the bedroom—and the bedroom was empty. The furniture was gone. Naturally, we understood that it was our daughter's handiwork. So my wife immediately called her up and told her that it would do no good. We went over to her place, and she started lecturing us: She had enough servants and nurses. She said, "Mamma, you have already put in enough housework. And you don't have deal with girls anymore. Sell the house and make your home here." Well, since the furniture was already at her house, we said to her, "Well, we'll try. If we want to return to our house, we will move the furniture back."

So we tried it out for several months. And what do we learn in the first

Torah portion in Genesis? *Va-yare Elohim ki tov.* And God saw that it was good.[42] We realized it was actually not bad. The burden that a house brings with it was off our shoulders. And best of all, my wife did not have to work around the house. She had worked enough already. It was now time for her to relax. So I looked into selling my house.

I would often visit Moyshe Avrom. Sometimes I found him crying. He missed Rokhl very much. And sometimes I found him reciting Psalms. And on November 28, 1929, he died. Naturally, I was at his funeral. He left his children an inheritance of several thousand dollars, over which they had many disagreements until they divided the several dollars among them.

Mordkhe had another heart attack. This time they took him to the hospital in critical condition. One morning, my wife and I visited him in the hospital. The picture we saw was too dreadful and sad to describe. We came into his room. His bed was propped up very high at his head, and he kept his eyes and mouth open. A nurse was standing over him with a dropper, letting drops of water fall into his mouth. But it was wasted work on the nurse's part, because Mordkhe was near death. The rattle in his throat was terrible to hear.

We left the room and went into the hall. The whole family was there. His wife came up to me with a cry, and said, "B, you know how bitterly hard I worked and didn't indulge myself."

I asked her, "Well, what do you want?"

"Now," she said, "take a look at my misfortune and my pain."

So now I asked her, "Just say, Yetta, for example, that you could now begin to lead a new life. Would you go down the same road that you have gone down until now?"

She answered me, "So? Every person makes a mistake in his life."

Mordkhe died the same night. This was in December 1930. My family, my wife, and I already had tickets to leave for Florida. I wanted to stay behind for a couple of days to be at his funeral. But my wife and daughter, and also the grandchildren, insisted that I not stay behind but go with them. We left for Florida the same night. So I wasn't at Mordkhe's funeral. I sat on the train with a heavy heart. In my heart and in my soul, I felt gray and sorrowful. In my mind, I thought it over: Will people learn the lesson of how to live in the world in order to be useful to themselves and their fellow men? Or will they lead the kind of life that Mordkhe led? Working to make money and only for the sake of money. And this sad thought did not give me peace all night until we arrived in Miami Beach.

Sitting by the sea under the bright and warm sun, thinking about what kind of life Mordkhe had led, I suddenly stopped short, and reflected: Is my own life so completely honest and kosher? Do I not also have to reckon with whether I have acted correctly? Here I am at the beach, and every so often I go into the sea to take a dip and come out of the salty water refreshed. And at the same time, people are working for me and they are where it is snowing and the wind is blowing. Is that right? Perhaps I am no better than the others, but in a different way—although I only make a livelihood, and that from my own labor. But still, do I not exploit my workers somewhat?

I soon consoled myself that others in my place lay off most of their workers during the winter, while I keep them on, if not the full week, then at least I give them work most days of the week. Two of my workers, John and Cook, have saved up enough with me to buy a house. And, not only do I not earn anything from them during the winter, but when I go to Florida in the winter I actually lose money. Every spring, when I come home I must withdraw quite a few hundred dollars to cover their wages. That is how my mind was working—until a grandchild came up to me and woke me up from my thoughts, saying, "Grandpa, it is time to go home."

I sold my five-room house and lost five thousand dollars compared to what it had cost me. Still, I was happy that I sold it, because, as time went on, the price of houses fell further. And the rent fell sharply on my two duplexes as well, and they could not be sold. So I held on to them for several years and paid the mortgage, not to have to pay so much interest.

I think that it is worth mentioning that with all the individuals and peoples that I did business with, I had the occasion to deal with all races— with whites, with blacks, with Italians, and, of course, with our brothers, the children of Israel. For the most part, all were good customers. Among the blacks there were such good-hearted people that, even before I finished the job, they would bring the money out of the house for me. And sometimes, the work amounted to more than a little—a hundred or even 150 dollars at once. If it happened that the terms were to pay it off in installments, they would bring it on time. That is how it was with the Italians. With them, I did quite a lot of business. And, naturally, it was the same with our Jews.

When a bad customer did not want to pay, I never sued. Seldom did I use a lawyer. When the bad payer met me in the street, I gave him a hard look right in the eye, so that he would turn away his head in shame. Especially after several such meetings, he would bring me the money that he owed me himself, with the excuse that money had been very tight up to then. This is what happened several times.

There were also several bad payers with whom I resorted to various means to get out of them what was coming to me.

There is a Jewish householder. He is considered a rich man. One of his daughters, about eighteen or nineteen years old, called me up to say that the icebox was leaking and the kitchen was full of water. I sent a man with the truck to fix the icebox. Not only did they fix the icebox, but they also installed a narrow pipe so that if the icebox leaked again the water would run out into the yard and not in the kitchen. I sent a bill to her father, Mr. B, for six dollars and fifty cents. Six or seven weeks passed and I did not receive a check. I called Mr. B and told him that he must have overlooked the bill. He answered me, or better said, he asked me, "Who gave you the order to fix the icebox?"

I answered, "Your daughter."

He answered me back, "I didn't give you any order. So, I won't pay you the bill for six and a half dollars."

"What do you mean, Mr. B . . ."

He hung up the receiver. Well, if someone else had told me such a story about Mr. B I would never have believed it.

It was not the couple of dollars that bothered me. It was only that he brought shame on the name of his sort of person. There is a passage in the Talmud, "*Im ha-rishonim ke-malokhim, onu ke-bney odom, ve-im ha-rishonim ke-bney odom, onu ke-khamorim.* If the ancients were as angels, contemporary people are as human beings, but if the ancients were as human beings, contemporary people are as asses."[43] If we deal so outrageously with our fellows, then there is no question that we are damn asses.

The interesting thing is that I heard that Mr. B is a believer and gives a lot of support to the synagogue. But faith has no meaning for such people, because they do not live according to the principles of their belief. Faith has no influence on their lives, and makes no impression on their relations with other people.

Some time later, a synagogue not far from where I live had a celebration on having completed a reading of the Talmud. I was invited and noticed that on the other side of the table sat Mr. K and Mr. B. Mr. B took a bottle of whiskey out of his breast pocket and poured out glasses of whiskey for everyone. And everyone took the refreshment. I heard the people around saying that it was imported whiskey, that it warmed the soul. I heard this and thought to myself, oh people, you should only know that the one who is warming you up with a glass of whiskey has a heart that is cold as ice—as cold as the icebox for which he does not want to pay.

And now my mind started to work and my thoughts went way back to my childhood years. I remembered how my blessed mother explained the *Ethics of the Fathers* to me and how I listened to her so attentively as a child. Namely, "*Rabi omer, ezohi derekh yeshoro sheyovor lo ho-odom?* Which path in life should a person choose?" And my good-hearted mother answered me, "*Kol shehi tiferes le-oso ve'tiferes lo min ho-odom.*

He who feels in his heart that he is good to people and also does good publicly for people." These golden words should have been asked and answered for Mr. B and Mr. K, who sat at the table. And Mr. B warmed everyone around the table with a glass of whiskey!

Well, I would be finished writing about bad householders if I did not have to tell the following extraordinary and very interesting story of a bad debtor. Listen closely. One day, a contractor walked into my office with a blueprint and asked me to give him a price for my line of work. I looked over the blueprint and gave him a price: 165 dollars. He told me that if I could send people to begin work immediately, he would give me the price that I had asked. I answered that I had the material on hand and that we would get to work the next day. The bookkeeper made out the estimate and Mr. Smith signed it. When the work was done, Mr. Smith was happy. I sent him a bill, and four weeks later I found out that Mr. Smith had gone bankrupt. To bring him to court or to go to a lawyer was out of the question. I would not invest the time nor the money.

I was at my desk, thinking about how I could get my 165 dollars out of him. After thinking it over for a long time, I thought of something, namely, I must shatter his nerves. In the early morning, between two and three o'clock, when people are sleeping quite soundly, I called him on the telephone. He came to the phone and asked, "Who is this calling at such a time?"

I told him, "Don't be scared, Mr. Smith. This is Mr. R. I want you to send me what I have coming."

He answered me, "Mr. R, I have many debts coming to me. As soon as enough money comes in I will send you a check."

I answered him back, "Whether your debts come in or not, I want you to pay me what you owe me." He hung up the receiver.

I thought to myself, I will not leave him alone until he pays me. Early next morning, I called him up again. This time his daughter came to the phone and said, "Mr. B, my father says that you will be the first one to be paid. Please just have a little patience."

I answered her that I would not leave him alone until he paid me. "And tell that to your father."

Early the third morning, his telephone rang and no one answered. The operator told me that there was no answer. I told her that the people must be fast asleep, but they were there. I asked her to please continue ringing. She obliged me and the bell kept ringing without stop. I understood that the nerves of the members of the household there must be shot. Finally, finally, his daughter came to the phone, and said to me, "My father says that in two or three days he will come to your office."

"Alright," I said to her, "but no later."

And two days later a check for $165 arrived for me. But someone else had signed the check, not he. And that is how, with an extraordinarily strange idea, I succeeded in wresting no small note out of a lost debtor. Yes, the human soul is always a riddle in itself.

I understand that people would like to know how it can be good to live with our children. The thing is this. First, financially we are taken care of. And that is, after all, the main thing that can lead to discord. On the contrary, we spare no expense at any time or at any occasion, like birthdays, anniversaries, commencements, and so on. We send the children and grandchildren presents. And of course they appreciate it very, very much. And we are highly regarded by the children. Their love for us is great. Since the children always call me "papa," or "pa," all the grandchildren also became used to calling me "papa" or "pa," ever since they were small. They call their father "daddy."

And they call their grandmother "grandma" with such great love that it cannot be described. Yes, mother is treated with great tenderness by her children. But the following must be said, namely, that the mother, the eternal Jewish mother, sometimes does not want the children's tenderness. To the contrary, she would prefer to treat them tenderly. In one word, the mother had happiness her whole life from making things right for the children, and from preparing many good things for her son-in-law and daughter-in-law when they came to visit. When we lived in our own house, this is what she derived pleasure from. Now she misses that. Instead, they prepare things for her. She talks to me about this sometimes. On the other hand, she knows quite well that it is hard to get help these days. She actually sees this in the case of her daughter and son-in-law, and everywhere actually. So she saves herself the worries.

We received a telegram from my wife's sister that she was terribly sick with an inflammation of the lungs. The next day Alte died, leaving five children. This was a hard blow for my wife. I went away with her for a few days so she could straighten herself out and get a hold of herself.

I began not to feel so well, but the shop kept on working. I wanted to sell my houses and could not. So I tried to remodel them and I invested another two thousand dollars; perhaps I would get a customer. But I did not. They could not be given away for free! Since I did not get better, I gave up the shop and turned it over to my two oldest workers for a very small sum. I had installed new machines just a short time before. I told them that I would help them in any way I could. There was only one thing that they should not ask me for, and that was credit, because I would not be a guarantor for them. "Begin as I began—small and not all at once. The main thing is that I am leaving you a ready-made shop, with material and with ready-made customers. It is up to you to make it good." In a few weeks, after I got them established, I went to Florida with my wife and family.

In Miami Beach, I would always go to the second service on Friday nights. I liked very much to hear the young cantor sing. It was a pleasure to hear him, and while the congregation was greeting the Sabbath (if one can call it that), I sat in a corner looking into a Gemara or some other holy book.

One Friday evening, a Gemara lies on the table. It is tractate Bava Batra. I open the Gemara to no other chapter than to the one on "a presumptive title to houses." I take a glance at it. "*Omar Robo,* Rabba said, *shato komayso mokhil inish.*" And here I fall into a dream, leaning my head on my left elbow. And I see here before me my teacher, Meshel, dozing lightly off, with me sitting opposite him at the table memorizing the Gemara. And Zekharye, the innkeeper's son, says, "*Shato,* he drank." And the rebbe wakes up with a start and says to Zekharye, "Repeat, '*Mokhil,* he lay in the mud.'" Zekharye repeats. The teacher goes on, "*Inish,* he made a *tsimes.*" And now Zekharye understands that it is a ridiculous interpretation and he falls silent. And I burst out with a loud laugh. And the teacher says to me, "Binyomen, why do you laugh. You say it. Let's hear you out." And I say to him, "*Shato komayso mokhil inish, sartey mokhil, slos lo mokhil.* For the first year a man will forgo [his rights], for two years a man will forgo [his rights], but for a third year no man will forgo his rights."[44]

And still I sit with my head bent over and I slowly come to. And several tears roll down over the Gemara as I think to myself, oh you bittersweet years of childhood, how far away you have flown. I probably would have remained sitting hunched over like that if the beautiful, sweet singing of the cantor—*mizmor shir la-yom ha-shabos,* a psalm, a song for the Sabbath day[45]—had not awakened me.

We came home in the month of July. I went to see if my former workers were doing good business. I came into the shop and I asked how the business was going. They answered me, "Alright, boss. We have no kick."[46] And they tell me that the have bought automobiles and radios for themselves. Well, I think to myself, so they have bought things for themselves. That's their business. And I asked them, "For cash?" No, they answer me, on installments.

"Oh, you bought on installments."

"Oh yes."

They kept the business for a year and a half, and then John became an insurance agent and the other went off to work somewhere else. And the landlord took everything from the shop, because he was owed rent.

Finally, finally, I sold my houses. I got even less for them than a third of what they had cost me. But we were happy to get rid of them. An unnecessary burden was off our backs. And in 1939, we took a trip to the far west. We traveled to Los Angeles, California. We wanted to take an apartment for a certain amount of time and, since we wanted to get to know the neighborhoods, we stayed in a hotel at first. But about four or five days later, our old Pittsburgh friends found out that we were there, and they took us to stay with them for several days. At the same time, they picked out an appropriate apartment for us between Wilshire and Hollywood Boulevard.

We received a letter from our son that his boy's bar mitzvah* would take place soon. Well, when our grandson becomes bar mitzvah, we must go home. We were in Los Angeles for over six months and had spent a lot of money. We had intended to stay there for at least a year, if it had not been for the bar mitzvah. Well, we came back for the bar mitzvah. But to tell the truth, we had more pleasure from the *bar,* the son, than from the *mitzvah.* A dear boy, a good boy. After his bar mitzvah, he went to Hebrew school for another year, mainly because my daughter-in-law is very active there. She has also been president of the ladies' auxiliary for two years as well as president of Hadassah.* She also belongs to a musical art club and gives free concerts on the piano for various philanthropic purposes. My son is also very beloved and is well regarded by everyone who speaks with him for even a short time. He is respected by everyone.

My daughter is also active in Zionist organizations, especially in Hadassah. She also held office for two years. The same is true of my son-in-law. All my family members are liberal people, even our grandchildren. When there is a debate or a discussion in school, they always take the liberal side. My daughter's boy and a girl finished high school in three years and now go to college. Another girl goes to high school, and has already won several prizes for art painting. All are dear grandchildren. They honor and dearly love their grandma and grandpa, and we truly have pleasure from all of them.

I mention the word "pleasure," even though at the present unhappy time it is hard for the tongue to say that one has "pleasure"—while the world is burning and being destroyed, and our Jewish brothers are being persecuted and murdered. But let us hope that the current horrible destruction—which eats at everyone's heart and soul—and all the troubles of the present time are the birth pangs of a new and better world.

I recently met an old friend of mine. After we had chatted about old times he came out and asked me if I still adhere to my old ideal of social democracy. I responded, certainly, even more than in earlier times. If someone came to me and convinced me that he had a better system for humanity, then I would be willing to accept his new system. But as long as I do not see any better way than people living in peace I think that, in the beginning at least, the social democratic principle is best for humanity. I would also like to see, if possible, a Jewish home in Palestine. And I want to hope that after the current bitter war, it will really happen, and the Jews will be liberated together with the rest of the peoples. And it will bring salvation for the whole world. *Sholom al yisroel,* peace on Israel.

NOTES

1. Stanislav is also known as Ivano Frankovsk.

2. Leviticus 1:1. All Bible translations are from the *Jewish Publication Society Hebrew-English Tanakh,* 2d ed. (Philadelphia: Jewish Publication Society, 1999).

3. A fur-trimmed hat worn on the Sabbath and on holidays.

4. See Jeremiah 31:15.

5. "Rabbi said, which is the right way that a man should choose unto himself? One which is [itself] an honor to the person adopting it, and [on account of which] honor [accrues] to him from men." Tractate Avot, chapter 2, mishna 1. Translation from *The Babylonian Talmud: Seder Nizikin,* vol. 4, trans. and ed. I.

Epstein (London: Soncino, 1935). A tractate of the Talmud, *Ethics of the Fathers* deals with ethical issues.

6. Especially in small towns, it was common to call someone after a parent, spouse, or other relative, using the possessive form of the relative's name.

7. According to Jewish custom, the corpse is laid on the floor, with the feet toward the door. Mourners sit on small benches, crates, or stools. The body must be buried as quickly as possible, but not on the Sabbath.

8. Ketubot, Gitin, and Kidushin are all tractates of the order *Nashim* (Women), dealing with such issues as marriage contracts, relations between husbands and wives, rape and seduction, divorce, and betrothal. Bava Kama (Aramaic, "The First Gate") is the first tractate in the talmudic order Nezikin (Damages), dealing with issues of civil damages, assault and battery, and theft. Bava Metsia (Aramaic, "The Middle Gate") is the second tractate of the Nezikin order, dealing with issues of lost property, business dealings, interest, hiring of laborers, and other matters.

9. Third chapter of tractate Bava Batra, folio 28a.

10. Bava Batra, folio 61a.

11. Bava Batra, folio 29a. The full passage reads: "Rabba said, for the first year a man will forgo [his rights to the produce], for two years a man will forgo [his rights], but for a third year no man will forgo his rights." When Zekharye mistranslated *shato*, "year," as "he drank," the teacher started leading him to ever greater absurdities. Translation from *The Babylonian Talmud: Seder Nizikin*, vol. 2, trans. and ed. I. Epstein (London: Soncino, 1935), 142.

12. In *heder*, Reisman had learned to read Hebrew and Aramaic, but not to write. He had not learned to read Polish, which is written in the Latin alphabet.

13. Genesis 37:1.

14. Translation from *Pentateuch with Targum Onkelos, Haphtaroth and Rashi's Commentary*, trans. and annotated by M. Rosenbaum and A. M. Silberman, in collaboration with A. Blashki and L. Joseph (New York: Hebrew Publishing Company, n.d.), 179-81.

15. The Belzer rebbe, Yehoshua Rokeah (1825–1894), was one of the leading lights of Galician Hasidism. He fiercely opposed the Haskalah and any innovation in traditional Judaism. He was succeeded by his son, Issakhar Dov (1854–1927). The Chortkover rebbe at the time was Dovid Moyshe Fridman (1826/27–1903).

16. Reisman worried that spending the extra money on train fare would mean that there was not enough left over for the necessary supplies for the festive Sabbath meal.

17. A song for the end of the Sabbath.

18. Two-day, late spring holiday commemorating the giving of the Torah at Mount Sinai. Customs include eating dairy foods, reading the Book of Ruth, and maintaining an all-night vigil to study Torah.

19. In Jewish tradition, the Sabbath is described as a queen.

20. The "sufferers," as Reisman calls them, were apparently practicing forms of self-abnegation, not sleeping or, perhaps, eating in the hope of rendering themselves unfit for military service.

21. Most likely, the *Yalkut Shimoni*, an anthology of midrashim and rabbinic sayings probably compiled in the thirteenth century by Simeon ha-Darshan (The Preacher).

22. "Turn away thy eyes from [thy neighbor's] charming wife lest thou be caught in her net." Yevamot, folio 63b. Translation from *The Babylonian Talmud: Seder Nashim*, vol. 1, Yebamoth, trans. and ed. I. Epstein (London: Soncino, 1936), p. 426.

23. A diminutive or endearing form of Binyomen.

24. Exodus 30:11–34:35. Adar corresponds to February or March.

25. Nisan falls between the middle of March and the middle of May.

26. An honorary dance with the bride reserved for an older male relative.

27. Grover Cleveland (1837–1908) was the twenty-second and twenty-fourth president of the United States (1885–1889, 1893–1897). A Democrat, he championed civil service reform and low tariffs. William McKinley (1843–1901) was the twenty-fifth president of the United States (1897-1901). A Republican, he supported high protective tariffs and the gold standard and presided over the Spanish-American War. He was assassinated just months into his second term. William Jennings Bryan (1860–1925) was a leader of the radical, pro-silver, anti-imperialist wing of the Democratic Party; he was the party's presidential nominee in 1896, 1900, and 1908.

28. The United Hebrew Trades, founded in 1888, was a federation of predominantly Jewish trade unions in New York. Bernard Weinstein (1866–1946) was a pioneer of the Jewish labor and Socialist movements in New York and secretary of the United Hebrew Trades.

29. "Be heedful of the children of the poor, for from them Torah goeth forth." Tractate Nedarim, folio 81b.

30. At the time, Brooklyn and New York were separate cities.

31. Socialist and labor leader Max Pine (1866–1928) served, among other things, as secretary of the United Hebrew Trades and Socialist candidate for a number of public offices.

32. Abraham Cahan (1860–1951) was a Russian-born Socialist journalist, writer, and lecturer in Yiddish, English, and Russian. As editor of the *Forward* in 1897, 1902, and from 1903 until his death, he guided the newspaper to its preeminent position among Yiddish dailies. Daniel De Leon (1852–1914) was the brilliant but rigidly doctrinaire leader of the Socialist Labor Party (SLP), founded in 1876. Dissidents within the party feuded with him in the 1890s and eventually left. In 1901, they helped form the Socialist Party, which soon overshadowed the SLP.

33. Renowned for his fiery oratory, Johan Most (1846–1906) was the leading American proponent of Anarchism at the end of the nineteenth century.

34. In fact, the Socialist Party had not yet been formed, and Reisman probably means the Socialist Labor Party.

35. German social philosopher Friedrich Engels (1820–1895) was a close collaborator with Karl Marx. The second half of the club's name, Forverts, referred either to the German Socialist daily *Vorwärts,* which was widely admired by Socialists around the world, or to the New York Yiddish Socialist daily *Forverts* (Forward), which was officially founded at the end of January 1897.

36. Labor lawyer Jacob Panken (1879–1968) was elected to the municipal court on the Socialist ticket in 1917. He later served on the family court.

37. Tractate Yevamot, folio 63b. The Gemara quotes *Sefer ben Sira,* an apocryphal book of poems and aphorisms promoting wisdom and virtue.

38. Labor Lyceums were Socialist community centers, often sponsored by the Workmen's Circle branches. The Pittsburgh Labor Lyceum was dedicated in 1916, but fundraising for its construction began as early as 1907. A broad array of Pittsburgh's Jewish leftist and labor organizations used the Labor Lyceum until the building was closed in 1930.

39. Members of the Workmen's Circle addressed each other as "friend." Leon Arkin (1888-1953) managed the Boston office of the *Forward* from 1922 to 1949. He also served as president of the Workmen's Circle.

40. Samuel Frankel was a Pittsburgh alderman. "Squire" may have been a nickname.

41. See Psalm 27:9.

42. See Genesis 1:4, 1:10, 1:12, 1:18, 1:21, 1:25.

43. Tractate Shabbat, folio 112b.

44. Bava Batra, folio 29a.

45. From Psalm 92, part of the Friday evening service for welcoming the Sabbath.

46. "We have no kick": Slang expression meaning, "We can't complain."

Chapter 3

I Have Nothing to Complain About

Shmuel Krone

b. 1868, Verkhovichi, Belarus
To U.S.: 1903; settled in Denver, Colo.

The most important theme of Shmuel Krone's story is his triumphant struggle to remain a religious Jew despite many obstacles, including service in the Russian army in the 1890s. Upon his arrival in Chicago in 1903, Krone (fig. 6) left the home of relatives when he discovered that they did not keep kosher. He relates his attempt to find employment that would not require him to break the Sabbath, a futile search during which he feared that he and his family might starve. Krone experienced mixed success in various business endeavors before becoming a ritual slaughterer at a sanitarium for tuberculosis patients near Denver, Colorado. He also describes a failed attempt at homesteading in Wyoming with frustrated if amused irony.

Written with God's help, Friday, the week of the Torah* portion that begins, "Korakh, the son of Izhar," 5702, Denver, Colorado.[1]

I, Shmuel Pinkhes, son of Mordecai Krasnitske of blessed memory, known by the name of Krone, was born to poor parents in the year 1869 in a small town, Verkhovichi, Grodno Province, District of Brest. My father was a sexton and a traditional teacher, a Kobriner Hasid* who believed that, as it states in the Gemara*: "Hanina . . . has to subsist on a kab of carobs from one week end to the next."[2] That means, one day we had bread and small potatoes with their skins, the next day no bread. We were a family of an even ten—six daughters, two sons, a father and a mother, may they rest in peace. If my mother, may she rest in peace, had not contributed to the family livelihood we might have perished from hunger. She sold kerchiefs and beads to the peasant women in the coun-

Fig. 6. Shmuel Krone in the kitchen of the Jewish Consumptives Relief Society sanitarium in Denver, where he served as ritual slaughterer and *kashrut* supervisor for more than twenty years. Courtesy of the Beck Archives, Special Collections, University of Denver

tryside, and the peasant women would give her a little bit of rye or wheat or eggs.

One time she met a peasant woman whose husband had gone to the forest and brought back wood. The peasant woman prepared an exact measure of four Russian pounds for her, and my poor mother heaved the wood on her shoulders and ran the two *versts** home, fearing the return of the peasant woman's husband.[3] When she got to the house, she collapsed and fell ill. She lay in bed for two months.

Later, things got much better for us. As poor as we were, my parents did not a allow any of the girls to serve in a rich man's home. It was shameful to be a servant girl, though there was no other work in our town. How would it look when the time came to make a match and people said that the prospective bride was a servant? And here there were six girls in the house. You can imagine what fun that was! But as poor as we were, my father, of blessed memory, sought capable scholars as sons-in-law, and he succeeded. When the matchmaker came to discuss matters, my father said he had a hundred rubles of the dowry demanded for his first daughter and that God would take care of the rest. He went on foot to Reb* Nosn, of blessed memory, in Kobrin, who told him to make the match.[4] And, with good fortune, he made the match.

I remember when he had to make a match for his second daughter. I was eight years old. The future in-laws were due to arrive from Brest. But we lived in a house that was a threat to our lives. How could we invite in-laws—in-laws from Brest no less—into such a house? Once again, my father walked to Kobrin to Reb Nosn, of blessed memory, five Russian miles away and returned in a joyful mood. The rebbe had told him to build a new house. He did not tarry but set to work immediately. Two months later the house was ready and nice enough to welcome the future in-laws: a fine groom, indeed, and a fine family. The prospective father-in-law was a Gerer Hasid, and, with good fortune, it was decided to make the match. In this way, my father, of blessed memory, married four daughters to good sons-in-law. He did not survive to marry the last two daughters. He died at the age of sixty-three. My mother was eighty-five years old when she died. They both died in Europe.

Now I will write about myself. I started studying Gemara at the age of eight. In our town, there was no Gemara teacher, so we hired a teacher from somewhere else. There were six young children in town. Four of them were rich. I and another boy, we were the poor ones. My father tried to pay tuition for me, as the wealthy did. A teacher from Sokolke by the name of Reb Shimen, of blessed memory, was brought in. He had been a great scholar and a teacher in our town before I was born. All who had studied with him became scholars, so they hired him again. The fathers and mothers were overjoyed. Each term, he received room and board with each family for three weeks. He was paid eighteen rubles per child for the first term and twenty rubles per child for the second term. In this way, he received a raise every term, until he received thirty rubles per child for each of the last four terms. I studied with him for four years. During the final year, we learned three pages of Gemara a week, along with *Tosefos** with Maharsha.[5] On Friday mornings, we had to go to the study house, where the teacher slept, to wake him up and recite our lessons and all the commentaries by heart. If someone failed, God forbid, and did not know the week's lesson, the teacher made him fast all day and did not allow him to go home until after the first service of the Sabbath that evening. Back at home, they said, "Good for him, he didn't know his lessons, damn him." Every summer, during the week we recite the Torah portion that begins "This is the statute of the Law," the Visoker Rov, Reb Leybele the Sharp One, also called the Kaidoner prodigy, would come to town.[6] On the Sabbath, he would give a sermon, and, when he finished, he would take a stroll with me on one arm and the ritual slaughterer's boy on the other, and we recited our lessons for him by heart. The entire town watched us and considered me greater than the Russian tsar, may his name be erased —not to mention my parents, who were in seventh heaven that I remembered everything.

But I did not want the honor and I did not want any part of our teacher. He was a murderer; he would beat us to death. I spit blood from his slaps. In the end, he left and the whole Torah went with him. I did not remember a word of his teaching.

When he left, I was eleven years old. I was sent to yeshiva* in Kamenets. The head of the yeshiva was Reb Sholem Leyb, of blessed memory. I now started to get a taste of "eating-days."* Though I had a grandmother in Kamenets and two uncles, one of whom had no children, still, I had to eat days. But one uncle did me a favor. He let me sleep on the oven at his house! I studied for a year until I turned twelve years old, and then went home for the holidays. I had intended to go to the yeshiva in Mir after the holidays, but I was too shabby. My overcoat had two holes in the back. (This was the style. It showed that you had worn it out, sitting by the oven and studying.) So my parents told me to become a teacher in a village for a term, so I could earn a few rubles for clothing.[7]

In fact, I went to a village not far from town. A village Jew wanted to teach his two daughters Yiddish so he hired me at fifteen rubles a term. I was a good enough teacher to last two terms and earn thirty rubles, but I could only have an overcoat made because with the rest of the money we had to pay the builder who had built our new house; we still owed him money. I could no longer return to the yeshiva. My parents, may they rest in peace, saw that they had gotten a house out of me, so they wouldn't allow me to leave home. I now traveled with my mother, may she rest in peace, to the villages, helping her carry the eggs which she had started buying and selling. I could carry baskets of eggs on both arms. Sometimes, my brother-in-law would teach me. In this way, time passed and I had no further education until I turned sixteen years old.

I began to think about what would become of me. By now, I had forgotten everything I had learned. So one fine day—it was just after

Passover*—I packed everything I had, my two shirts, my *tfilin*,* and a small prayer book, and fled to Orlya. I had heard that this was a place of Torah, that people studied intensively there, and I was not mistaken. I traveled the distance of four Russian miles throughout the day and arrived in Orlya during afternoon prayers. I went straight to the old study house and found people studying, including a man from my town who was living in Orlya. I told him that I had come to study and stayed the night with him. He also found eating days for me and proved himself to be a good friend. We savored our learning together for a year's time. After that, we set out for the yeshiva in Łomża.

On the way, we had to go through Ciechanowiec, so we stayed for the night. In the morning, on our way to pray, the sexton came out and asked us where we were going, so we told him we were going to pray. So he told us to come to his place, also a study house. They had just finished building it, and it was quite nice. He told us that the leaders of the old study house laughed at them and said they had built a train depot—a beautiful one, but not a place where people studied.

We went in. The moment we entered, a group of well-off Jews with big bellies, quite the aristocrats, came at us. These were the wealthiest and most aristocratic Jews of Ciechanowiec. They asked us, "Where are you going, children?" We said that we were going to the yeshiva in Łomża. They said to us, "Why should you go to Łomża and starve before you get eating days? Stay here with us and you won't have to worry about where your next meal is coming from. The sexton will show you where to eat every day, and we'll give you fifty kopeks a week spending money. Our *maggid*,*8 Moyshe Holer, can give you your daily lesson."

Moyshe Holer was truly a great scholar and a *maskil*,* a follower of the Jewish Enlightenment. We knew him from Orlya, and now he was sitting here and studying. We figured that their offer was a good one. Why did we need to starve when we could have everything we wanted without worry? So we stayed and every day the sexton indicated where we should go to eat.

Everything seemed to be fine and dandy, but it did not work out. First of all, on Fridays and on the Sabbath, I ate at the home of a rich man, the owner of a wholesale liquor business, who desecrated the holiness of the day. Friday mornings, the woman of the house would give me a fat soup broth with a warm roll for breakfast and I would immediately get diarrhea. I could barely make it to the study house. I would not get back to normal until Wednesday, but the same thing would happen again the next

Friday. I suffered like this for two years, but I studied well and with gusto. I started to learn the laws of ritual slaughtering.

Suddenly, I received a letter from my parents, may they rest in peace, asking me to come home because I needed to get a certificate of registration for the draft, for which I would soon have to present myself. So I went home and then traveled to Shereshovo to get my certificate, because we were registered in Shereshovo. Upon my arrival at home, my parents said to me, "You will soon need to present yourself for the draft. You have neither a deferment nor any money. So you must do something to save yourself." I agreed, so I became a teacher again. I went to a town ten *versts* from home and became a teacher for ten rubles a term, a large amount of money. I taught until the time came for me to serve. In the meantime, I went home for every holiday and gave my salary to my parents. They made a match for one of the girls and gave my money away as dowry! When the time came for me to serve, I did not have a penny—and I was snatched up into the army just like that!

A new chapter of hardship now began, one which made me unhappy for the rest of my life. I became a soldier. I had no money. As is well known, nothing gets done under the tsar if you don't offer bribes. One had to pay off the head of the company and the head of the battalion and I could not afford to. They harassed me to the point where it was impossible to endure. I suffered in this way until Purim* and—while people were reciting the Megillah, the Book of Esther—I fled to Brest. I had friends there who started thinking about what to do with me. I had no money to help me get to America, so they sought to match me with someone who also wanted to go. She would have to know that I had run away from the army.

Seek and you shall find. They found a young woman with a two-year-old daughter. Before long, we married and began discussions with an agent who would smuggle us over the border. At that time, however, there was a cholera epidemic in Hamburg, the only port from which one could depart. Nor did the adventurers want to take responsibility for a deserting soldier. I was extremely bitter. I had hooked up with a young wife and a little girl, but if I could not get to America, why did I need the whole business? Luckily, she was a dressmaker and supported herself, because I could not do a thing for her. We suffered, until we ate up 125 rubles, everything she had. There is nothing to say about what I experienced during that time, the fear and hardship, until I decided to return to the army. Whatever will become of me, will be!

I went to Chelm, to the regimental commander's house, and told him my whole story. I submitted myself honorably, admitting that I had fled from the Fourth Company of the year 1892. The colonel was not at home, but his orderly said to me, "Go to the barracks, but do not run off again." The commander lived near the train depot on one side of town and the barracks were on the other side of town, so I set off. The orderly said to me, "Wait, I'm going into town too. We can go together," so we both went. We walked four blocks before the colonel arrived from town unexpectedly. The orderly told him who I was. I repeated the whole story, to which he replied, "Go to the barracks, and tomorrow we'll figure out what to do with you."

Eight weeks passed and I did not hear anything, until one fine morning they brought my marching orders. The sergeant major called me into his office and told me to get ready to go to the regimental headquarters at ten o'clock for my trial. They were going to try me for fleeing.

I arrived at headquarters. Three officers, a subcommander, and a priest sat in judgment. I was told that I was guilty and that they were going to prosecute me. They then told me to leave the room. About fifteen minutes passed before they called me in and read the sentence: six weeks in the military prison in Warsaw, and if there was no room in the prison, they would give me three weeks in the dungeon on bread and water. They ordered me to return to the company after serving my sentence. Two weeks passed and I did not hear anything.

On the eighth day of Hanukkah,* in the morning, two soldiers with rifles arrived. They told me to get dressed and come with them to the train depot. They were sending me to prison in Warsaw. They told me to go, so I went. We arrived at the depot. I sat down, and the soldiers stood on either side of me with rifles in their hands. We had to wait two hours until the train arrived. Every civilian stopped to look at the arrested soldier, probably thinking I surely must have killed a man. The shame was horrible for me to endure. When the train arrived and they led me to the prisoners' car, four convoys came out with swords drawn. The car was full of prisoners. As we approached Warsaw, they shackled everyone but me. I thought I would die of fear. When we arrived in Warsaw and started to disembark we were given a fine reception—an entire company of Cossacks bearing torches with their swords drawn. It was two in the morning and we had to walk for about a mile, as the train did not go to the central train station. The chains clanked. I thought, if the people from my town saw this, they would think I was being led to the gallows. They took me to the military authority and led the rest of the prisoners away to the city prison.

I could write fifty pages about the period from the moment I got to the commander until they led me to my cell in the prison, but it is very difficult for me to write of it. I can only give you a shred of information about the "friendly" reception they gave me. I was very tired when I entered the prison room since I had not slept for three nights. I sat down and fell asleep. But it is forbidden to sleep until they tell you to sleep, so the guard came in and slapped me across the face. My face was now turned to one side, so he gave me another slap on the other side to even things out. These are just some aspects of what I experienced on the way from Chelm to Warsaw. To write everything that occurred until I got out of prison would take much time. It is very tragic!

When I got back to my company, all the soldiers told me that I would not be able to serve out my time under the captain of the Fourth Company. He was the worst of the whole regiment; he was very independent. The colonel feared him, because his company had the best marksmen. When a general came to inspect, they would call out the Fourth Company. But as they say, even a broom can shoot if God helps. I happened in fact to be a good marksman. I do not know how it happened, but every time I took a shot, the captain would give me two pieces of sugar. In his eyes, I was the top of the heap. He let me go home four times. Thank God, I served out my time and came home in one piece!

Now a new question arose: what to do for a living. There was no other choice but for me to become a teacher once again. I took on six children in town for ten rubles a child per term, sixty rubles a term for myself, my wife, and two children. That was great fun! I toiled in this way to make a meager living, until Russia started to fight Japan in 1903.[9] I was about to leave again and give my life to the tsar, may his name be erased. But then I thought, no, I had to go to America. Where would I get the money? Another miracle occurred. My mother-in-law had a son and a daughter in America. Her only son missed his mother terribly, and she missed him. The son had sent a ship's ticket to his mother, so that she could come to America. But she was a woman in her seventies and afraid to travel alone, so she gave me money to go with her.

Though she was one of those women who kept complaining that she did not have any money, she had a few hundred rubles. When we arrived safely at the port of Baltimore and had to show that we had money, she told me that she would give me some rubles to present when we got to the office.[10] It turned out that she was the tenth person behind me in the line going to the office. Now what should I do? I went ahead. I looked so afraid, I thought they might send me back. I went over to the desk and the officer asked in German if I had money. I answered, yes, I had ten rubles. I moved to put my hand in my pocket, but before I did so, the officer said to me, "Go in God's name. Do good business." When my mother-in-law got to the desk and he asked her if she had money, she said she did not. They immediately detained her. I, however, left right away for Chicago, while she remained in Baltimore for ten days until they found her son.

When I got to Chicago, people came to the depot to pick up those who had arrived, but no one came for me. I was left standing by the grating looking out, with nobody to pick me up. A Jew came over and asked me my name. I told him. He went to a policeman and then called me over. I had a Chicago address since my mother-in-law's son and daughter lived there. The man led me to an express man[11] who told me to get in the wagon. It was Friday evening. The express man got on his way. My heart skipped a beat. How could I travel on the Sabbath? But how could I help it? So I traveled. My address was the first stop on Jefferson Street. The express man got off the wagon and took a look around. He returned and told me that the people had moved quite far from there. So, he continued on his way. He dropped off all his passengers and went home to where he lived on Jefferson Street. Since the time was now two o'clock in the morning, the express man told me to get out of the wagon.

"Wait here. This is a Jewish street and Jews will soon start making their way to synagogue to pray and they'll take you to the synagogue."

"Why won't you take me to your house?" I asked him.

"I have nowhere to sleep," he said.

"I won't get out of the wagon and, if you want to throw me out, I'll cry for help."

He asked if I might have another address, to which I replied that a woman who had been traveling to her husband had given me the address where her husband was staying. In fact, it was not too far, Twelfth Street near Loomis, so he took me there. It was a fish store and a boy was sitting in the store. It was August 22, and so hot that people could not sleep. The express man said something to the boy in English and the boy told me to get out of the wagon. He led me upstairs where he lived with his family above the fish store.

I entered the house. The light came to my eyes and a joy to my heart, seeing the electric lights burning and the table covered with a white table-

cloth. A beautiful silver lantern stood on the table with pieces of hallah*
left over from supper. I felt joy. The boy gave me something to eat, what I
don't recall, only that it simply refreshed me. I was hungry and exhausted.
When I finished eating, he took me into the husband's room (the man
whose wife I had met). I lay down and slept until it was time to pray. The
boy came to wake me up and gave me coffee. The father, a Mr. Pakcherski,
said to me, "I'm going to synagogue, but you can go with my boy to a
*minyan** in the next courtyard. You can pray there. They'll give you an
*aliyah,** and you can say the blessing for surviving a perilous journey. It's
too expensive for you to buy an *aliyah* at the synagogue."

When we all returned from services, a beautiful table was prepared and
we made *kiddush.** Mrs. Pakcherski passed me a delicious European-style
*tsholnt** and I was very happy. During the meal, a man by the name of Mr.
Becker came with the message that his wife and children had arrived. He
introduced his family to the full house of people, and I introduced myself
to him. Throughout the Sabbath, guests arrived all day to take a look at
the greenhorn* wife, and it heartened me.

The next morning, Sunday, the boy went with me to look for my
brother- and sister-in-law's place, which he found at Forty-eighth Avenue
and Madison Street. The boy went home and I stayed with my brother-in-
law. I saw right away, however, that there was no room for me. He had a
dry goods store and they lived in the back room, one room for a family
with six children! My sister-in-law went to make food for me. She started
frying eggs in butter and I smelled something in it that made me think I
might get angry. I realized that they were living in a *treyf** house. When
they saw that I was leaving and that my underwear was falling apart, they
did even not give me a shirt to change into. I realized that I was in big
trouble, that my bad luck had come running after me to America. I asked
them to take me back to the place I had just come from, but they did not
want to, so I stole out and started walking.

It was about fifteen miles from Forty-eighth Avenue to Twelfth Street
and Loomis. I walked all day and into the night, because I did not know
the way. I thought I would collapse. Luckily, I saw a sign for a yeshiva,
Yeshivath Etz Chaim, so I sat down to rest.[12] Seeing a greenhorn sitting
there, a teacher came over and greeted me. We got to talking and I told
him of my troubles. He took me to a grocery across the street. He went to
the president of the yeshiva and convinced him to let me sleep at the
yeshiva. Thank God, I had a place to lay my head. At the grocery, I bought
some bread and buttermilk and paid five cents—three cents for the bread

and two cents for the buttermilk. I went to the yeshiva and went to sleep, not knowing where the night went. In the morning, I finished my prayers and once again went to the grocery, and used up another five cents—three cents for the bread and two cents for the buttermilk. And I went out to search. Perhaps I would find a familiar face.

Indeed, I met a man from Bialystok, a very fine man. I told him of my sad situation and he said, "Don't worry. You'll be alright yet. Every green-horn has to undergo the birth pains of greenness." He said he had an empty bedroom at his house. I could move in with him for three dollars a month. I told him that I could not pay, to which he replied, "When you start earning, you can pay. I am sure that you will earn good money. You'll find something."

He taught me the first lesson a greenhorn had to learn: peddling brooms. I still had four rubles. A broom peddler lived next door, so the man from Bialystok asked him to take me with him when he went to the wholesaler, where I bought six brooms for sixteen cents a piece. I asked the broom peddler how to peddle. He told me to walk along the street selling the brooms for thirty cents each. Good. I would make ninety cents a day to live on, which meant a ruble and eighty kopeks. It was better than being a teacher in the Old Country.

So I took the six brooms on my shoulders and walked straight to Twelfth Street, over to the downtown area to Michigan Avenue. I held up my head and looked into the windows to see if people were calling me in so they could buy a broom. I sensed that people thought I was harassing them, since I seemed to be holding my head up in a haughty way. I looked around and saw a policeman. He stopped me and spoke to me, but I did not understand a word he said. He led me to Wabash Avenue, and I understood that he meant to say that I could peddle there. It was easy to understand this cop.

I started walking along Wabash Avenue to Eighteenth Street. I walked west along Eighteenth Street to Albany Avenue. I was happy when I saw a Yiddish sign for an old-age home across the street from Douglas Park. I threw myself down on the grass, laid all six brooms at my head and slept a bit. I had not sold a single broom and it was already three o'clock. I thought, it's already time to go home! I took my six "friends" and walked home with them. Upon my arrival, I threw down the brooms and stood paralyzed, unable to make a move. With great difficulty, I sat down. I fell asleep sitting there and slept through the entire night. In the morning, I solicited my grocery man and he bought all six brooms for the price I had paid for them.

Well, what would I do now? My landlord told me I should look in the local Yiddish newspaper, the *Jewish Courier,* where I could read about who needed workers.[13] So I bought a *Courier* and took a look. It said that someone needed a man to cut leather strips for mattresses right on Twelfth Street, a half a block from my house. I went in and the boss hired me for fifteen cents an hour. I worked for six hours and he paid me ninety cents, but I could not move my right hand. It had swelled up and I had to rest again until it got better. But I was happy with the ninety cents. With that, I could live for two weeks. Again, I started to search for work in the paper, but I found only work that interfered with my observance of the Sabbath. I had resolved that I would not desecrate the Sabbath or any part of Judaism. I would rather die of hunger than lose my Judaism. "If he comes to purify himself, he is helped."[14]

The only choice remaining to me was to become a teacher again. It seems that teaching had traveled with me here under my seat without a ticket, chasing after me. Well, it was no use. It had to be this way. I started to look for students and found students the first week; this brought in three dollars a week. That was six Russian rubles. When had I ever made so much in Russia? Good. I was content. I spent a dollar fifty a week and sent a dollar fifty home, so my wife could live like a noblewoman on three rubles a week. Two months passed and I made ten dollars a week. I sent four dollars home, kept six dollars for myself, and started to save money. Six months passed. I brought over my stepdaughter. The girl was now fourteen years old. My wife remained with one child, living very frugally. It took a year and a half before I received a letter from her saying that she was now in Hamburg and on her way to America and that I should wait for her at the depot.

After her arrival, my wife was a dressmaker. The girl became an operator on overalls and in the evenings she went to school. We settled into life quite nicely. Two years passed and we saved five hundred dollars. During that time, a talmud torah* was founded on Grand Avenue, and I had the privilege of becoming a teacher there. I received eighteen dollars a week, excellent wages! I had taught there for about five months when the president of the talmud torah, Mr. Kohn, approached me—he was from Kurland, a fine man, the owner of a dry goods store. He said to me, "Mr. Krone, I feel for you, such a young man as you working as a teacher in America. You are too talented to be a teacher."

"So what should I do?"

"Open a dry goods store like mine!"

"First, I have no experience," I say to him. "Second, I don't have enough money. And the main thing, what would I do on the Holy Sabbath?"

"You'll keep the Sabbath just as I keep the Sabbath," he answered. "As for experience, I can teach you. Since you have five hundred dollars I'll go with you to my creditors. With your five hundred dollars, I'll get you fifteen hundred dollars to buy goods—very nice, starting off with fifteen hundred dollars. There's a store standing empty a block from my store. I think you can get that store for twenty dollars a month. That will pay for rooms in the back of the store, you know, as many as you need."

Mr. Kohn went with me to a secondhand furniture store and purchased the fixtures for me. Then he went with me to Mr. Phillipson, a dry goods wholesaler, and told him that I would give him five hundred dollars and he should give me a thousand dollars in credit. Mr. Phillipson, may he rest in peace, said it would be all right and they fixed up a beautiful store for me.

It did not go badly—but then the Sabbath business started. My wife could not resist the temptation to break the Sabbath. I would go to synagogue to pray and she would open the store. When I got home from synagogue and found customers in the store, I could not tolerate it. We started to fight and tore at each other like cats. We came close to separating, until we gave up the store. I tried moving to a Jewish neighborhood, but it did not help at all. My wife wanted to break me down, but I did not let her. We had to give up the store, in which I had labored for several years.

I no longer wanted to be a teacher, so I took up the ritual slaughter of poultry. Not only that, I got myself a synagogue where I served in every way. I also supervised *kashrut** in two butcher shops. I had once again gotten off to a good start. During that time, we found a boy and married off our daughter, giving her a dowry of a thousand dollars. I also sent a good bit of money to my sisters and my two nephews, both rabbis, as well as to my mother, may she rest in peace. From month to month, I hardly noticed how much she needed from me and everything was fine and dandy!

But an evil spirit meddled in the midst of this and turned everything upside-down once more. A cousin of my wife came to visit—he had a homestead in Wyoming State—and told her some story about how his community needed a ritual slaughterer and a teacher, who would get a homestead as well.[15] They would till and sow the field for me and get everything ready. What is more, he told her a story about how he had found gold when he dug his cellar. In reality, he needed a few horses, he knew that we had a few dollars, and he thought he could get them out of me. My wife started to work on me about the homestead. Her cousin had to go home right after Passover to work in the field. I told my wife that she should go with her cousin to see if there was any truth in his talk about his fortunes, and then write me whether to come. I could not go immediately because my older boy had to finish public school in July, and I had to wait for him. So she went by herself with the baby.

In the first letter she sent me after her arrival in Goshen County, Wyoming State, she wrote me that it was a regular Garden of Eden. The birds sang such divine melodies; she had never heard such beautiful melodies. In the second letter, she wrote me not to rush, because the heat was terrible. So it went until July. One week she wrote "come." The next week she wrote "don't come." Meanwhile, we had given up the house when my wife left, and I grew tired of moving around and staying with other people. So, right after my child finished school, on July 12, I picked up and left for the homestead in Wyoming.

As soon as I arrived at the homestead, my spirits fell. Just mountains and valleys. I saw no green grass, no trees. Everything looked as drab as in winter. The "palace" where the cousin lived was ten by twelve feet, and he had a wife and three children. There was simply nowhere to sit down and we were now two families—nine people. It was fortunate that we had brought two beds. We set them up in the road and slept there. At night, coyotes came out with such cries that we thought they would eat us up. Fifty feet from the house, there was a mountain they called Rattlesnake Mountain, full of snakes. Christian farmers came on Sundays with rifles to fight the snakes—a regular Garden of Eden!

I arrived on a Thursday, and I resolved that we would stay over for the Sabbath and leave on Sunday for Chicago. But a voice from heaven told me that I would not go to Chicago, that it was my fate to go to Denver. That Sunday morning, my older boy woke up and said that he did not feel well. Then he passed out so that he could barely be roused. Then he kept sleeping. It is too much to write what we went through, but we had to remain until after Sukkot.* Right after the final blessings of Sukkot, we went to Denver. I was ashamed to return to Chicago, because everyone had warned me not to go to a homestead. So we went to Denver.

In Denver I became a fresh greenhorn again—no one's friend, no one's acquaintance. There was simply nowhere to stay overnight. Everyone thought that we had come for health reasons and were afraid to let us in.[16] Thank God, we found a man who had three empty rooms in his house. He rented them to me for three dollars a month, so we had a place to sleep. In the morning, I went to synagogue and told people there that I had not come for my health, but had accidentally ended up Denver. I said that I was a ritual slaughterer and asked if perhaps I could get a position. People told me that a wanton fellow from the East could not be a ritual slaughterer in Denver, especially at this time. A quarrel was going on between a Hasidic rabbi and a Lithuanian rabbi who had recently arrived. No one was interested in questions of ritual slaughtering! Now what would I do? I had to look for work to make a living.

They gave me the name of a Jew called Grimes, the richest Jew in Denver. He sold newspapers and hired men to make the bundles—and he closed on the Sabbath. I went to him and told him of my sad situation and that I was a ritual slaughterer. He took pity on me, wondering how such a Jew had come to his kind of work, but he did not want to hire me. I begged and explained to him that, because I was a man of conviction, I would have to die of hunger. So he did me a favor. He told me to come to work at the newspaper for a dollar fifty a day. I worked for a week and was more dead than alive! I thought to myself that after fifteen years in America, having already worked my way up and made a nice living, I would now have to repeat my "green" years once again. I decided to return to Chicago. As they say, better shame-faced than heartache. I made my decision to return to Chicago. I would go myself for the time being, and, after working my way up a bit, I would bring over my family.

Just as I was ready to go to the depot, a man came to me, telling me that he had come from Boulder, Colorado. Someone had told him that I was a ritual slaughterer and that I wanted to return to Chicago because I had nothing to do here. His community needed a ritual slaughterer and a teacher, and I could open a grocery business as well. I would live well. I asked what he did on the Sabbath. He said that since all the people in Boulder were Sabbatarians—they kept the Sabbath—they would buy everything from me. Everything would be fine and dandy! As he had come with his own horse and wagon, he asked me to return with him. I could speak to the other Jews in Boulder to ensure that he was not deceiving me. I thought, what will be will be. What did I have to lose? I went with him.

I arrived in Boulder, a very beautiful city, and met with a few more Jews who told me the same thing. The first man, Liberman, walked around with me and helped me look for a store on the main street. We found two empty stores. I rented one of the stores and gave my deposit. I had to move in three weeks later. In the meantime, I bought some grocery stock.

It was dark at two o'clock in the morning when we arrived in Boulder. But when I got up in the morning and went out, I saw that the store next door to mine was a grocery with a butcher shop, so a grocery store was now out of the question. I went to find out what was happening with the position of teacher and ritual slaughterer, but as the saying goes, "There were no bears and no forest." Now what would I do with the grocery stock I had purchased in Denver? I persuaded the Jewish grocery man to buy some and kept some for me and my family.

What to do now? I still had four hundred dollars in my possession. A certain Berman, a truly honest man, lived in Boulder. He came to me and said, "Don't be so crestfallen. No Jew has yet died of hunger in Boulder and neither will you. You see, that little Jew Liberman, the one who led you here, came to Boulder four years ago. They took up a collection for him and now he's worth thousands of dollars. And you're brighter than he is. He still doesn't speak a word of English and yet he does business."

"What does he do?" I asked

"He has a junkyard. You could do the same."

"I don't know how to handle a horse," I said.

"I can teach you," he said. He bought me a horse and wagon, harnessed it, and traveled around with me for three days, showing me how to buy goods. On the fourth day, I went by myself, dragging as much merchandise as I could into the wagon. I started doing such good business that Liberman had to flee from Boulder. He came to me and said, "No one injures a man as much as he injures himself. Why did I have to bring you to Boulder? Now I have to leave. I can't make a living!"

I started to send loads of merchandise to Denver. I got to know people, including the Lithuanian rabbi, and earned a very good reputation since I dealt very honestly.

I lived in Boulder for five years, during which time my older boy finished college. He is now a public accountant! I did not make a great fortune because, during the best of times, when people were making good money, I was still green at the business. When I figured out how to sell the merchandise, when I finally had experience and started to do business, everything had gotten too inexpensive. It was a year after the First World War and everything was so inexpensive that there was no market for sellers at any price. I just had too much merchandise. All of my capital was in the merchandise, which was impossible to sell, and I had no money to continue.

Fig. 7. The grounds of the Jewish Consumptives Relief Society sanitarium in Denver. Courtesy of the YIVO Institute for Jewish Research

The Lithuanian rabbi knew of my situation. The *kashrut* supervisor of the Denver Sanitarium (fig. 7) had died and the Denver rabbi came to me in Boulder with a member of the board of directors, asking me to accept the position of ritual slaughterer and *kashrut* supervisor at the sanitarium, and I accepted. In September, I will have held the position for twenty years.[17] Thank God, I lead a quiet, peaceful life. I have nothing to complain about in America. Both of my sons are married to fine Jewish women. They live in Chicago and make good livings. They know how to pray well, but they do not do so. My younger son writes beautiful Yiddish and can recite the Haftorah well on any Sabbath. This is scholarship in America, may they be well.[18] May Hitler be erased from the world, so there will be peace for the people of Israel.

NOTES

1. Following traditional custom, Krone dates his manuscript by using the first line of the portion of the Torah (Numbers 16:1) to be chanted that week in the synagogue.

2. Tractate Brachot, folio 17b. Translation from I. Epstein, ed. and trans., *The Babylonian Talmud: Seder Zera'im* (London: Soncino, 1948), 104.

3. A Russian pound is a little more than nine-tenths of the avoirdupois pound used in the United States.

4. Perhaps a reference to Reb Menachem Nachum Rabinowitch, the Kobriner rebbe from 1846 to 1878.

5. Acronym of Rabbi Shmuel Eliezer Edels (1555–1631), a talmudic commentator. Most editions of the Talmud were printed with his commentaries, and a mastery of these was considered part of a basic talmudic education.

6. Leybele Harif (d. 1885) was a rabbi of Vysokoye, Belarus. The Torah portion referred to begins at Numbers 19:1.

7. It was common for village Jews, who were isolated from the Jewish communities in the towns, to hire young yeshiva students, or even advanced *heder* students, to come teach their children the rudiments of Jewish learning.

8. *Maggid* is a Hebrew and Yiddish term meaning "preacher." Some *maggidim* had official communal positions, while others were itinerant.

9. See "Russo-Japanese War" in the Glossary.

10. Immigrants were required to show that they had some money to prove that they were not "likely to become a public charge," which was grounds for exclusion under the Immigration Act of 1882.

11. The owner or driver of a wagon used to move freight.

12. Yeshivath Etz Chaim, founded in 1902, later merged with Beth Hamedrash La Rabonim to form the Hebrew Theological College.

13. *The Jewish Courier* (Der yiddisher kurier, 1877–1944) was a Chicago Yiddish daily with an Orthodox religious and conservative political orientation.

14. Tractate Yoma, folio 38b. Translation from I. Epstein, ed. and trans., *The Babylonian Talmud: Seder Mo'ed* (London: Soncino, 1938), 181.

15. Under the Homesteading Act of 1862 individuals could claim up to 160 acres of land for nearly no payment. They secured full ownership by building a house and farming the land continuously for five years. To finalize their claim, homesteaders needed to be citizens or to have filed a declaration of intent to become a citizen.

16. Denver was the site of several Jewish hospitals and sanitariums for tuberculosis patients.

17. Krone was the slaughterer and *kashrut* supervisor at the Jewish Consumptives' Relief Society.

18. Krone is being slightly sarcastic, since being able to chant the Haftorah, a selection of the prophetic books of the Bible, is not traditionally considered a very advanced skill.

Chapter 4

Why I Left My Old Home and What I Have Accomplished in America

Aaron Domnitz (Aba Beitani)

b. 1884, Romanovo, Belarus
To U.S.: 1906; settled in Baltimore, Md.

The autobiography of Aaron Domnitz is the purest example of the maskil *type in this collection. A deeply pious and zealous student of Gemara as a child and youth, he was drawn to the study of Hebrew literature and secular subjects as a yeshiva student. Influenced by the revolutionary fervor surrounding him, Domnitz romanticized workers and industrial labor but lasted only a brief time in the "shop" when he arrived in the United States. Domnitz describes his experiences as a member of the literary and intellectual circle known as "Di Yunge," the Young Ones, while living in the Bronx in the first decades of the twentieth century. An ideal informant, the writer has a knack for keen observation, evoking his surroundings with a sharp eye and close detail, always placing the phenomena he describes vividly in their historical contexts.*

Introduction

I want to make use of the autobiographical form, so I will skip many, many things that have occurred in my life. I will record only those details of my childhood that have in my consciousness some connection with my later urge to travel somewhere. Ruminating over my past has renewed in my memory several details that at one time made a strong impression on me, and I portray them here. These too would be interesting for a historian who might sometime ruminate over old documents and want to form a complete picture of the people who took part in the great Jewish immigration at the beginning of the century.

I was born in the year 1884 in a little village called Shalovitsi, near the town of Romanovo in the District of Slutsk, Minsk Province, Russia. I was raised in Romanovo. My mother's parents in Shalovitsi were, like all their children, true country folk. My grandfather was a tailor and also had land, fields, and gardens. As a boy, I would come from town to help him sharpen plows, dig potatoes, and cut hay. My mother did all kinds of fieldwork and knew her way around livestock. My uncles also kept gardens and orchards. I used to help them harvest fruit, pick cherries, gather gooseberries, and guard the orchards at night.

My father's father lived in Starobin, on the other side of Slutsk where the Polesia region[1] begins. He was a peddler. (In our area this was called a "traveler.") He was a quiet man and a hard worker with no education. He would fall asleep during the recitation of the first chapter of the Psalms. My father's brother had a similar occupation. He traveled farther into the surrounding villages, however, where he bought grain from the peasants to sell to merchants in the city.

My father was a traditional teacher in Romanovo. He raised me and taught me from my earliest years. He himself had learned the entire Tanakh,* Gemara,* and Hebrew grammar. I recall that he read the *Ha-Melits* and *Ha-Tsfira* newspapers[2] in town, though he didn't subscribe. He would go to the grocer, who received the newspapers wrapped around his goods from Slutsk. After unpacking, the grocer smoothed out the papers and put them together more or less according to date, so people had reading material for several weeks. In synagogue after prayers or on the Sabbath, strolling in the orchards, my father would discuss with his friends events described in the paper that had happened long before, though Zalman the Storekeeper had just brought the news to town. Mostly people marveled at the language used in the newspapers.

I was a "good boy." I knew everything that people taught me. The teacher praised me. My father enjoyed that. The "neighbors" who stood next to my father in synagogue would ask me questions, smiling to my father and pinching my cheek with the back side of their middle fingers.

I had a little trouble with some boys in *heder,** however. They hated me. On Fridays, when we had to read from the Khumesh* by ourselves, I always knew the lesson and they didn't. As was the teacher's custom, I had to slap them. Outside, they would return the slaps.

I quickly parted from my friends. I skipped a grade and went to a more advanced teacher. At eight years of age, I was already learning Gemara. The boys at that *heder* were older than me, and, once again, they made me suffer. They avoided me and didn't let me in on their games, so the result was that I spent time by myself, immersed in thought. I grew accustomed to spending a lot of time by the cabinet of religious books in the study house, looking at the title pages with their strange letters and counting the chapters of the Gemara. I quickly learned to read the pages of Gemara by myself. Soon I attended my father's *heder* but could not remain there for long. In small towns, parents were not happy when a teacher kept his own child in his *heder*. If the teacher's boy was good, then they had reason to complain that the teacher was focusing all his learning on his own child. So my father hired a scholarly Jew, not a teacher by profession, to study Gemara with me. Early before prayers and all day long, I studied by myself in the study house. Thus I was once again on my own, lonely and without friends.

The scholar, Reb* Ayzik, with his beard matted from constantly kneading it with his fingers, didn't charge much for his lessons. He said he enjoyed studying with a fluent and capable person. I recall that he would often immerse himself in a question without regard to me, but I followed along with him. Many times he would get confused at a difficult place. He would wrinkle his brow, knead his beard, and his face became serious and fretful. With childlike simplicity, I would then steer him toward a different question on a similar matter and help him extricate himself. Because of this, I received a reputation as a prodigy.

One winter, a small yeshiva* was established for the better Talmud* students in town. My father enrolled me. There we studied like adults. After the Talmud lesson from the head of the yeshiva, everyone would study at their own lectern. We also chanted like adults as we studied. Singing occupied an important place in our studies. Without it, we could not savor our studies properly. Little boys in *heder* didn't sing, but those who studied partly on their own in the study house had to sing. Common people didn't sing either when they studied the *Ein Ya'akov*.* They just read it. Neither did one sing while studying the legends in the Talmud; it was easy to rush through them. But when studying talmudic law, one had to sing if one wanted to go deeply and understand. We could often identify the student by his singing.

In the evenings, everyone studied by a candle on his lectern. We never bought the candles. We "stole" them. This was an old custom in the small towns, sneaking candles from the sexton to study by after evening prayers. The sexton took good care, but the boys were very adept at swiping *yortsayt** candles from under his nose, and then using them up singing the Gemara.

That winter I became a zealot. I made an agreement with a friend to get up early before dawn to go study at the study house. We undertook to learn an entire tractate of the Talmud by ourselves, without the help of the head of the yeshiva. This was a secret. Our parents didn't need to know how early we got up and quietly shuffled out of the house in the dark. Since we had no watches, it often happened that one of us would arise in the middle of the night around two or three in the morning and quietly leave his house for the synagogue. I was ten years old at the time. My friend Zalman Itshe-Gite's (now Sam Parton, somewhere in Belfast, Maine) was twelve years old and lived quite a distance from synagogue. Still, we kept this up for two winters in a row.

To enter the study house, one had to walk by the cold synagogue, from which it was said that "the dead called out at night," and the shed in the cemetery, with its broken windows, where they prepared bodies for burial. The stretcher on which the dead were carried was kept there. We turned up our collars so as not to look "over there" and ran by quickly. Inside, we turned up the fire in the hanging lamp that always burned over the table next to the oven and sat down to study.

Studying at night had a completely different feel. Our thoughts were clear and fresh and undisturbed. The accompaniment to our learning, our singing, also had a different sound and a different effect. The house of study was empty and dark. The posts on the *bimah,* the platform from which the Torah was read during services, cast long shadows. The lecterns looked like thin men sleeping while standing up. Outside the wind howled in the windows. The hanging lamp swayed, and the shadows of the tall posts and outstretched lecterns swayed with it. It blended with the melody and filled our hearts with bittersweet feelings of zeal, persistence, and sacred calling.

I recall that sometimes it was difficult to get the right mood from the surroundings, especially when it turned out that one of us was alone because he had gotten there first. The shadows appeared fearful; the great clock on the western wall of the synagogue beat out its slow, ceaseless tick-tock, tick-tock. A gust of wind suddenly blew through the windows. Uneasy voices seemed to come from the women's section. I am lonely—a fear seizes me—but I must be strong! The melody begins: It rings louder and more resounding. My learning grows stronger and surer. The words run faster, lines chase after each other, page after page. The melody charges forward, like a protector. My thoughts follow and—we are triumphant! My fear has disappeared and I've sung through another two or three pages of Gemara.

We weren't alone every night. Once a month, Itshe the Preacher, an old ashen Jew, would come in from a nearby prayer house where he had his bed, to study and pray at midnight according to custom. By the glow of the candle melted to the bench along the far eastern wall, he would sit in a little chair on the ground and mourn the destruction of the Temple. On those nights, the synagogue looked different. The moan of the blizzard outside accompanied the quiet inner lament of the matriarch Rachel weeping for her children.[3] The lament moistened the air and it grew stiller. The clock's tick-tock became more reticent and muted. We would stop studying, as if the moment were too sacred for studying, but the words of the Gemara began to draw us in again, and again the lines spread themselves out before us. Our eyes were drawn to the eastern shadows. Only one thing quietly persisted—the melody. A light melody, without words, fluttered modestly over the Gemara, as if it did not want to sever entirely its connection to the surroundings. Those were our nights of midnight study and prayer.

When I had gone as far as I could go with my studies in my town, my father sent me away to Reb Nekhemie's yeshiva in Slutsk. He immediately took me into the "big table," the upper class. Nekhemie was known as a strict yeshiva head. He spoke little outside his lessons. He led the yeshiva with the look of his eye. Walking around the *bimah,* hands clasped behind him and a pinch of snuff between his fingers, he observed every boy at his place. If someone wasn't behaving himself properly, Reb Nekhemie gave him a look. That was enough. We studied there enthusiastically and had great respect for the head of the yeshiva, his scholarship and strong discipline.

I recall a few incidents from that time.

One day, we caught a thief in the courtyard. The yeshiva students had started to miss things, so they searched for a thief and caught him. He was a tall boy, not from that neighborhood. The students grabbed him by the arm, dragged him out into the yard and executed his sentence "Russian-style": they beat him. I arrived in the middle of the action and saw how the thief bawled and the crowd pummeled him. I intervened and told them to leave him alone. The thief got up from the ground. Our eyes met and we recognized each other. It was the smith's son from my town, a former friend from my earliest *heder* years. He was the one I had to punch every Friday for not knowing the Khumesh with Rashi's* commentaries. Our paths had parted long ago. Now we had coincidentally met away from home, I as a student at Nekhemie's big table and he as a thief of young men's wallets. I was embarrassed meeting him in such a state. He cast an angry look at me and quickly escaped. It turned out that I encountered him again, but under entirely different circumstances.

I Get Slapped for Studying Tanakh

The story goes like this. My father ordered me to write my letters in Hebrew, but where would I get Hebrew, having spent so little time in *heder* and having studied only Gemara in Aramaic? I wrote to him with mistakes, so he sent back my letters with corrections and ordered me, for God's sake, to take a look at the Tanakh for half an hour a day between afternoon and evening prayers. So one day, I sat down with a Tanakh and took a look. A respected Jew from Iserke's synagogue—that's where Reb Nekhemie's yeshiva was located—walked by and, seeing what I was looking at, slapped me in the face.

"That will lead to heresy. Here we study Gemara, not the twenty-four books of the Tanakh!"[4]

That slap immediately got good results. A little later the respected Jew's son came to me, a young man a few years older than me, and suggested that I study Tanakh and Hebrew with him. He brought me to his friend. In a room full of books, they gave me a book from which to read. I did not understand a single word. The short lines with punctuation seemed mysteriously drawn out to me, like the tall young man in the room who took me in so sympathetically. I started to study diligently for a few hours a week.

The Jew who slapped me for looking at the Tanakh was called Lipshits. His son, who led me to Hebrew, was called Faytel. At that time, he had already begun to send correspondence to *Ha-Melits*. Later he participated in *Ha-Dor* and *Ha-Shiloah*.[5] In the latter, he wrote a series of articles about political economy in the years 1904–5. Later, he became a teacher in a Swiss institute.

After attending Nekhemie's yeshiva, I remained in Slutsk for a few

years, studying on my own in various study houses, "eating days,"* sleeping in the study house, and paying expenses from the usual occupations of
an independent scholar such as myself: helping to make up a *minyan** to
pray for the dead, writing letters for wives to their husbands in America,
and the like. For a time, I helped the Slutsker Rov, the famous Ridbaz,
copy the manuscript of his great interpretation of the Jerusalem Talmud.[6]

My parents were very poor at that time. That summer, a fire took place
in Romanovo, and the fire consumed my father's teaching post as well.
They moved to Starobin, the town where my father was born. There were
still five children at home, two older sisters and three younger brothers.
My father wanted to put together a *heder,* but the other teachers in town
prevented this. Teachers had a strict guild in that region, although without
a written charter. The regulations were moral. A teacher was forbidden "to
ask" parents for a boy; he had to wait until the father offered. It was not
allowed to take a boy out of *heder* in the middle of the term. A boy had to
study with a teacher for a certain time, about a year, to complete his entire course, along with the rest of the children who had started with him.
In this way, whole classes passed from a lower teacher to a higher one.
Because the whole educational system was organized by a group of teachers in town, it was difficult for a new person to get into the field. Sometimes an individual child would fall out of the system: the slow learners or
the badly behaved who fell behind, or those students the teachers didn't
want to take on because they didn't pay. These "damaged goods" were
what was left for a new teacher. So we went hungry at home.

My sisters started to earn a bit, one with sewing, the other by helping
out in a store. As a supplement to his teaching, my father also started to
engage in a trade. He worked wiring pots. As he now tells me, my father
had learned this in his youth when he was a teacher in a village.[7] Besides
teaching the villager's children Hebrew, he had to help the villager out
with his work. The craft consisted of putting together broken clay pots,
tightening them with rings of thick wire on two sides, and then drawing
thinner wire through in a box shape "cross-wise" to hold the pot together
for a long time. Payment for the work was three to five kopeks, depending
on the size of the pot. Peasant women paid with produce—eggs, potatoes,
cereal. This helped a little, but really only a little.

When I finally went home for the holidays, my parents immediately
started in with the question of what I would do now. When my father
insisted on apprenticing me in a trade, my mother burst into tears. My
mother, who was raised in the country almost like a peasant woman and

could barely crawl through a few short lines of prayer in a *siddur** or *tekhinah,** wanted me to become a rabbi. For his part, my father, a scholar and Hebrew grammar expert, spoke constantly in praise of work. He cited every saying from the Gemara about the importance of the trades and the talmudic maxim of earning a living by one's own hand. He often mentioned the talmudic sages Yokhanan the Shoemaker and Yitskhok the Blacksmith.[8]

He later fulfilled this image of work with my younger brothers. Although they were also good students, he apprenticed one as a gaiter stitcher and set up the other as a smith. They have remained intellectual workers to this day. The gaiter stitcher is a leather goods maker here in America. He knows Hebrew well and has recently begun publishing poems in provincial newspapers and journals. The smith is now in labor circles in the Land of Israel and also publishes in the press there sometimes.

At that time, however, it was not my fate to become a worker. I had already gone too far with my studies. It was suggested that I "travel under a contract," in other words, become an instructor in a village.

Our town was at that time a major provider of teachers for a large number of villages in the region, all the way to Pinsk and Mozyr. Starobin was the center for the agents who would provide the peasants with all their needs from the city in exchange for their produce from the countryside. These same agents provided teachers for the Jewish families in far-off villages. Between school terms, Starobin was like a fair. Besides the significant number of local teachers, "goods" (teachers) were brought from yeshivas in Slutsk. Starobin hawkers sorted them according to which teachers were appropriate for which villages and led them away. The villagers from far away villages had no opportunity at all to inspect "the goods" beforehand. They depended on the brokers to follow their instructions. One village Jew wanted a younger teacher for a beginning student; someone else needed an older teacher who could also help out in the granary; yet another wanted a good-looking lad, perhaps to strike a match with an older daughter. Rarely did a village desire a Gemara teacher. The most important attributes were a nice handwriting, a little Russian, and arithmetic. That is how Jewish children in the villages of Polesia got their education: from hawkers who received brokers' fees from both sides.

Fate carried me away to a far-off village near Mozyr. I was then thirteen and a half years old, stuffed with Torah, with an inkling of Enlightenment, but utterly without common practical knowledge. Moreover, I was shy and

didn't know how to talk to a person, not to mention how to handle children. Two of the boys I was supposed to teach were my age; one girl was a
bit older than me. I felt lost when she looked at me. How could I be their
teacher?

It was a bad situation indeed. The coachman let me off in the village
and left. The housewife, who was from the city, was an excellent judge of
character and saw right away that I wasn't right for them. They still let me
stay: It was too late to change and an agreement is an agreement. I got
used to teaching the students Khumesh and Tanakh, but discipline was
bad. I had no influence on them. The villager would need to come into the
room, take off his belt, and restore order. My spiritual emptiness was indescribable. I thought of fleeing but I had no money. The villager apparently
suspected my intentions and didn't trust me with any cash. I lived in that
hell for six months.

I remember that I got more pious that winter. I prayed mournfully
every morning. God was very close to me. I asked him personally to help
me as one asks a powerful protector.

When winter was over, the same agent came and released me. To my
great astonishment, the villager paid me the entire sum of forty rubles as
we had agreed, and I was free. The joy at home was no smaller than my
own. We drove away the poverty from the house for a little while. We got
some clothes for ourselves, and celebrated Passover.

After the holiday, I went to Minsk. My father wanted me to go to
yeshiva and study for rabbinic ordination. Now I wanted to "educate myself," as we called learning secular subjects, even though I had become very
pious while in the country. But afterwards I liberated myself from the fear
of God and continued on my way in a new direction.

In Minsk, I got into a little yeshiva on Romanover Street. I had information that there were fewer obstacles there if one wanted to read books
on secular subjects. I had no sustenance besides the yeshiva. The head of
the yeshiva supported the students with bread and some change. He got
support for his yeshiva from two wealthy men in the city, Rappaport and
Luria. By the second week, I had already found the way to Nofakh's library
and threw myself at Hebrew literature like a thirsty man at water.[9] I also
encouraged the other fellows to read. I started to give them lessons in
grammar. The Romanover synagogue became a place of knowledge and
enlightenment.

The head of the yeshiva, Reb Menakhem, discovering that I was too
involved with books instead of Gemara, feared that his yeshiva would get a

bad name again—as had happen a few years before I arrived—and forfeit the support of the wealthy class. So he had a little talk with us and asked us not to do anything improper in public. This shocked me. I saw the beginning of the breakdown of the old orthodoxy. He knew what we were doing, but looked the other way.

Not long after that, I was no longer completely dependent on the yeshiva. I took a job giving private lessons and got by, as it were. It was a strange time, when material life held little interest for me and my friends. For us, there were more important matters. We were nearing a transitional period, as boys and as people. New influences and aspirations emerged: a thirst for knowledge, the desire to get to the truth about God and the world, about people and society. This came together with a period of *Sturm und Drang* in Jewish social life. Minsk was at that time the cradle of many movements in Jewish society—Zionism,* Bundism,* Labor Zionism, religious Zionism, Socialism of all shades. Even the unsuccessful "independent" movement had its root in Minsk.[10] We young people—formerly in yeshiva, now pretending to study for *gymnasium**—lived intensely with the times, read, discussed, joined one political "tendency" or another, flocked to secret gatherings, carried illegal literature around with us, destroyed worlds and built new ones in our imaginations—all the while neglecting ourselves entirely.

Our circle stuck together, sharing bread and tea. We had left our homes in the small towns, forgetting the severity of our fathers and the devotion of our mothers. Without brothers and sisters, without cousins, we lived in a world of abstract ideas like shabby ascetics, emaciated and ragged. We forbade ourselves to think of practical ends. That would have meant weakening! Sometimes someone from home mentioned them in a letter, but we —modern, enlightened—ignored it with a smile. We experienced uplifted emotions from one book, derived honest aesthetic enjoyment from another, and became intellectual paupers—although we didn't see this in ourselves.

This sort of life began to affect the health of several of us. Someone started to spit blood. Another became melancholy and later ended up going mad. One of us then revolted and went back to the study house, started studying Talmud again, and later became a rabbi. It was then I thought for the first time of leaving Russia.

At that time, I had coincidentally come into contact with the problem of Jewish emigration. I worked for an agent who helped lead emigrants over the border. His partners lived in border towns, and he delivered

customers from the Minsk region. Because he didn't want the correspondence in his handwriting, I wrote his letters and someone else wrote the
addresses. The language was also disguised: instead of men, women, and
children, he talked of oxen, cows, and calves. It was often very painful to
read the telegrams from his partners saying that they had taken so many
"cows and calves over the pasture," or similar things. Most of the emigrants didn't need to cross the border illegally at all. They could easily have
gotten legal passes and traveled like human beings, but they were ignorant
and there wasn't anybody to enlighten them. Though it was discussed in
the press, it never reached the masses. No committee existed among the
people to enlighten them. There was absolutely no one around who would
take up that task. The intelligentsia was busy with "rebuilding" the world.
Common work with the people was considered almost dishonorable.[11]

I started to feel discontent with Russia and its customs and alienated
from its movements and activities. Together with their revolutionary high-
mindedness, I found among my Jewish Socialist acquaintances the inferiority complex of the assimilated. As soon as one of them started to read
Russian books, he derived great sadistic enjoyment tearing asunder everything that was Jewish. I felt spiritually constricted in a voracious Russian
culture that tore away and devoured more and more parts of my Socialist nationalist circle. My desire to leave and go "somewhere" grew quite
strong. It wasn't clear where I would go. My first thought was Germany or
the Land of Israel.

Meanwhile, I went home. I had been in Minsk for four full years. I was
very gaunt. My mother tried to make me healthy by feeding me milk and
fresh eggs. I had already forgotten what a mother's gentleness is. I was revived and decided to stay at home for a time.

My father had settled into teaching a bit but made a very poor living.
He still repaired pots. My brother, who had been with me for a year in
Minsk, was now working as a gaiter stitcher. And what should I do?

The town leadership gave me an answer only after I had conceived of it
myself. My long Hebrew letters that I occasionally wrote to my father had
probably been passed from hand to hand, and I had become famous as a
person of knowledge. So they invited me to open a modern *heder* for the
more advanced children who had nothing more to study with their previous teachers.

I took on the project and remained in town for two years. The work
was pleasant. My students, not much younger than me, studied Hebrew

literature diligently. They practiced expressing themselves in writing in a fluid and appropriate way. I helped to educate them in the spirit of progressive Jewishness. I was also active in other cultural areas. I opened a library. Together with my younger brother, we organized the children who worked for tailors and shoemakers. I founded a Labor Zionist association and worked to enlighten young and old.

At the end of two years, I was again overcome by restlessness. The small town felt narrow to me, and I wanted to go somewhere else. I was drawn to a large urban center. There could be no discussion of going to a big city in Russia. It was 1905, the year of revolution and unrest. Even my parents asked me to go abroad. The mood in town in general was to emigrate, although no one was forced to do so by the economic situation. No one was idle. Starobin had gradually developed as an important commercial center for its size. The town had a canal to the Berezina River, which flowed into the Dniepr. People transported railroad ties, pig bristles, skins, grain—all gathered from the villages—to Pinsk, Kiev, and Koenigsberg.[12] Jews kept watermills and windmills, resin works, gardens and orchards, and maintained livestock and estates. In short, Jews were a necessary economic element. Capable young people had the same opportunities as young people in other normal countries. There was no friction with non-Jews in our town. It remained peaceful there, even in the later years of great unrest, and yet the youth continued to make their own way. The general mood, the new social ideas, created a feeling of discontent with their parents' livelihoods and a desire for change through emigration.

I was apparently also overcome by the same "psychosis." I began to prepare to go abroad. I spent the last few months before my departure in Slutsk, which had changed much in five or six years. The formerly quiet, pious Slutsk buzzed with political parties and sub-parties, *birzhes** and gatherings, as in the larger cities. I noticed a new trait, or phenomenon: the use of force. Too often, party members used their fists, not against the enemies of the working class, but against their own people from another political tendency.

Groups organized for self-defense. There were rumors about Black Hundreds agitators from Bobruysk, and it was before the fair.[13] Two parties took the lead, the Bund and S.S., the Socialist-Territorialists.[14] As a Labor Zionist I opposed the Bund, but I had even less love for the S.S., so I joined the Bundist self-defense group. At our nightly meetings, people said nothing about our own problems or about Socialism. All they did was throw dirt on others, particularly Zionists, making false assertions, ascribing to Zionist leaders claims that they never made. Protesting against these falsifications did not help. One only got cursed out, but good.

One night, we had one meeting in the large study house. As was the custom, we appropriated the place. The head sexton of the synagogue knew about the meeting, however, and also came in the middle of the night to see what was taking place. We detained him inside and forced him to be quiet until the meeting was over. The frightened sexton sat gaping under the watch of a revolutionary. He couldn't believe his eyes: Here were the children of the town leaders who had always been outwardly dignified.

Then something happened. One speaker took off his hat as he went up onto the small platform next to the Ark. The old, respected sexton could no longer restrain himself. He jumped up and shouted, "Kill me, shoot me, but this I will not allow!" Those around him endeavored to quiet him down. Someone pushed through the crowded mass of people and took aim at the sexton with a club. I grabbed the guy by the arm to stop him. Meanwhile, the chair of the meeting restored order and convinced people not to use force this time. The disappointed guy turned to see who had held him back. Our eyes met and we recognized each other once again. Yes, it was my one-time friend from *heder,* the smith's son, who I had to slap every Friday for not knowing Khumesh, and who I later encountered in the schoolyard as a thief. Again we met, for the third time, under completely different circumstances. He was a rank-and-file Bundist, a guy with a vulgar face and robust muscles. He served the movement by fulfilling "certain functions," when they needed to have a strong arm with a club. And I—the former prodigy, the zealot for study, who later suffered through Socialist theory and who had dreamed up a Socialist worldview —stood there before him, that same moralist holding back the club.

He threw a contemptuous sidelong glance at me and sauntered off arrogantly in another direction.

I think sometimes that it was a good thing that I didn't happen to encounter him for a fourth—and final—time a few years later, wearing a leather jacket and high boots and strolling through the chambers of the Secret Police, guarding the purity of the Bolshevik Revolution, while I, an arrested "intellectual" and counterrevolutionary, sat below in the cellar.

Before departing, I wanted to cross the threshold of Iserke's synagogue, where I spent a few years of my childhood in Nekhemie's yeshiva. From the outside, everything appeared as it had been. Boys rocked over their lecterns. The familiar scholar's melody resounded over the Gemara. Reb Nekhemie walked around as before, his hands behind him, snuff between his two fingers, with one eye on the students. When I entered, I remained standing, removed to the side. He noticed me, walked by me and stopped. He had a reputation as an acute observer, and he recognized me, calling me "the Romanover," by name.

He asked, "So, where do you stand? Have you received rabbinic ordination already?"

I was embarrassed. When he heard my candid reply that I had given up my studies, he looked at me quietly, turned his eyes to the window and slowly and silently left. I was left standing there in the gloom. I knew what he felt in his heart at that time. He didn't say anything, but the poet sang for Nekhemie, *Kulam nasa ha-ruah, kulam sahaf ha-or.* "The wind carried them all away, the light swept them all away."[15]

I left Russia at the beginning of 1906. I went through Virbalis. The German border officials wanted to take me out of second-class where I belonged, as my ticket stated, and put me in the special car for emigrants traveling through Germany that would take them first to the baths and then straight to Hamburg. But I outwitted them. I insisted that I was going only to Germany. Where? To whom? I gave them the address of a Dr. Simon Bernfeld in Berlin.[16] At that time, one could still make the Germans believe something. That is how I managed to travel in a railroad car like a human being.

Quite early in the morning, I arrived at Friedrichstrasse Station in Berlin. A Jew came over to me, introduced himself as a representative of the aid society, and asked me the same question the border officials had asked me, whether I was going to America. I wanted to get rid of him as well, but he explained to me that there were new laws in Prussia about Russian immigrants, and he would prefer that I not have to deal with the police. Rather, I should go straight to the aid society. So I went with him.

At the aid society, they advised me not to remain in Germany, as I had planned. They gave me precise information about the situation in America, about the circumstances of working and studying there, and I complied.

Being in the office for a day, I made myself useful by translating Hebrew letters of inquiry from Russia for the officials. My impression was that the aid society did useful work. Besides providing information, they really helped those who were traveling through, as well as the many who decided to stay in Germany. If only there had been such a committee in Russia to help with emigration expenses, it would have saved the Jewish wanderers much money. I also found an aid society in Hamburg that was concerned with those in the immigrant dormitories and helped out. After a month of tossing and turning over the Atlantic, we arrived in the land for which we had yearned.

My First Impressions of America

My first contact with my new country was the brief conversation between me and the immigration officials. We were put into short lines as we entered the large buildings at Ellis Island* (fig. 8). Each line had to go by a small table next to which officials sat who questioned each immigrant in his language. The new immigrant felt right at home. My line spoke Yiddish. Hence, a big, strange country recognized my language that I had brought here with me from abroad as an official language. In Russia and Germany, I did not receive any such privilege.

One official asked me what I would do in America. I told him that until then I had been a Hebrew teacher. He smiled, "A rebbe*?"

"No," I said, "A teacher!"

Fig. 8. Ellis Island, the busiest immigration station in the United States from its opening in 1892. Courtesy of the YIVO Institute for Jewish Research

Fig. 9. Headquarters of the Hebrew Immigrant Sheltering and Aid Society (HIAS) on East Broadway, the Lower East Side of New York, c. 1920. Courtesy of the YIVO Institute for Jewish Research

A second official called out, "What's the difference?" I explained that a "rebbe" is Hasidic.* They laughed at me. "Go, go," they said, "you'll be a great rebbe in America," and pushed me aside.[17] I looked around. Here I am on the other side of the railing, among those who have been let in. But why did they laugh at me? It's nothing. People are good-natured here and they were joking. I liked the reception.

I was to go to a cousin. He was late arriving to meet me, but they trusted me and let me leave without him. A representative of the Hakhnoses Orkhim* (now the Hebrew Immigrant Aid Society*; fig. 9) took me to my cousin's house in Brownsville. He offered me his help. I wanted to reward him for the trouble, but he wouldn't take it. I had only been here for an hour and I saw only politeness around me. When I later came into contact with everyday reality, I found other kinds of relationships too, but it was pleasant for someone who had just arrived in a new world.

My cousin, I.L. from Shalovitsi, was almost the first person from our family on either side who had gone to America. I say "almost" because when I got here, I.L. surprised me with a story about how he met here, right in Brownsville, an old uncle, a younger brother of my grandfather Yermiyahu from Shalovitsi. Back home nobody had ever spoken of it. They only said that in the 1880s, a boy disappeared somewhere. What drove a boy from Kopyl to emigrate to far-off places in those years I never could figure out. I only saw him once. His wife was very unfriendly. She considered every greenhorn* an animal. I soon lost track of them.

I.L. was the first to come here during my time. He left the village quite young. In Russia he had lived in larger cities, and he knew languages. He had married and gone to America to accomplish something. For a while, his wife and child remained in Staryye Dorogi, a town near Mir. I.L. was a Hebrew teacher and very discontent in America. He discouraged me considerably in my first days here.

The people in the house where I.L. lived were simple workers. They lived better here than in the Old Country. They were content and assured me that "it will be 'alright' if I work." They emphasized the point about work a little too often. I heard no other discussion among them or their many acquaintances who came to the house. Nearly everyone had a greenhorn guest or expected to get one soon. They were always occupied with looking for work for new arrivals, and the conversation among them was only about work.

I remember, however, that everyone felt a joy with the arrival of every greenhorn. Everyone felt that it was his duty to teach and instruct the greenhorn about how to stand and how to sit and what to say. One of my first teachers in the laws of immigration was a young man from Vilna, also a teacher in a Brownsville talmud torah,* whom I got to know on the second day. He was also discontent with America, meaning Brownsville America. The teacher, by the name of Shteynbok, suffered from a mania of exaggerated Americanization. He felt very unhappy because he would never be a genuine American. He had learned English, but he knew that he would never lose his greenhorn accent. He actually cursed Vilna one time, because he was born there and so would never pronounce the English "th" properly.

I immediately struck up a debate with him about national autonomy and the like. I argued that even we have a right to live with our own pronunciation. He was unmoved. He was very embittered about his past, against Jews and Jewishness. He saw the greatest happiness in completely removing his "greenness" from himself and becoming American.

He had another ideal along with Americanization: practicality. He preached fire and brimstone against idealism. He considered it a great misfortune that people—mostly greenhorns—talked about idealism. It was against Americanism. "You have to be practical here!" I found an echo of such opinions in many circles at that time. Greenhorns took to the American dollar and to the easy life here and made a religion out of them, a cult of practicality. For Shteynbok, this had taken on the form of a fixation. Years later, there was a sensation about him in the Yiddish press when this very Shteynbok hurled away his *siddur* and his talmud torah and converted to Christianity. He became a missionary and I think he still has his mission house somewhere in Brooklyn.

On the third day after my arrival in America, I got my first job. My cousin had an acquaintance, a plumber, who took me on as an apprentice. My plan was to learn a trade, work and be independent, to learn English over time, and leave the rest for later. If I liked the work, I would remain a worker. This was in keeping with my idealization of work and workers.

I was then over twenty-one years old. In Russia, at that time, it would have been impossible to become an apprentice in a workshop. Here it was a common phenomenon that older people would begin learning a trade, so I became a plumber. I was even a little happy for the opportunity to learn that trade, and not tailoring like everyone else—as if we were all a nation of tailors.

The shop was on Centre Street near Canal, in a cellar. There was another worker, a Romanian Jew. He showed me what to do and I helped him out. This was the first time in my life that I had held a tool in my hand, a metal tool working on metal. I felt proud. I felt reborn, no more the abstract thinker and dreamer. I made screws and sawed iron, I poured molten lead—I created! This was America: work.

And America was another thing: noise. Sounds from outside always drifted into the shop. Centre Street, an industrial street with all kinds of factories and shops, was at that time paved with rough, uneven stones, so the constant clopping of horse hooves and the hard wheels of freight wagons drifted overhead. It hummed, whistled, and clamored. Boss and workers spoke little, and what they did say I didn't understand. So I was, for the most part, by myself with my own thoughts once again. I did what people told me to do and wondered, is this America?

I didn't get to enjoy the work or my thoughts for very long. At the end of the week, I was fired. Weeks later, I found out the reason from my cousin. The last few days, when my silence got tedious, I struck up a conversation with the Romanian. He asked me about Russia. I told him what was going on there with the working class, and so on. He immediately passed the word to the boss that I was a Socialist. So I was no longer a plumber.

I tried to get a job with another plumber but without success. The trade was completely closed to outsiders who wanted to get in. An opportunity presented itself very rarely.

I started to look for work in other metal factories that advertised in the newspapers that they were looking for hands. I quickly lost my greenness and knew how and where to look. Within a period of about three months, I underwent various experiences in large metal factories. People turned over every other day. At one place, where they polished brass beds, the work was tremendously difficult. I saw several people fainting as they worked. They paid six dollars a week, but it was hard to endure more than a few weeks. At another place, it was easy but very uninteresting. One stood all day next to a machine that spewed out ready-made articles like nails, screws, parts of locks, and the like. One had to move up the bin, and when it filled up, move it away and move up the next. The machine did the work and the greenhorn stood there like an idiot and helped it along. The machine "thought" much more than the greenhorn worker. The machine wasn't berated and humiliated all the while and it wasn't paid three dollars a week.

I started to look for work in other trades—as long as it wasn't tailoring —but it didn't work. One time, I went into a bakery where a sign hung— "Worker needed; no experience necessary"—and offered myself. The woman sized me up with a condescending look and casually rejected me: "You, a worker? You're a rabbi, not a worker!" What an insult!

I got tired of constantly changing jobs and looking for work. I felt the need to have stable employment with a more or less secure income. My relatives and landslayt* lectured me that it was now time to settle down and do what everyone else did—become a tailor.

I became a tailor.

Over time several more of my relatives arrived here. Cousins joined their husbands who were already here. They were all tailors. I made my home with one of them. This cousin was a women's tailor back home and worked here as a cloak maker. People considered him a good earner. In season, he made about fifteen dollars a week, a more than sufficient sum for that time. Most worker families ended up with ten dollars a week. He lived in an apartment of three rooms and a kitchen on Cherry Street. The family—husband, wife, and two small children—slept in one room. In a second room, two boarders slept in one bed. At night, the kitchen was also transformed into a bedroom for a third boarder. One room, the parlor, was not used. Large pieces of furniture were set up in that room, a big round table with chairs and a cabinet with a mirror. In the cabinet stood a platter with a set of six large glasses with colored edges that they never used. On the table was a large lamp that they never turned on. One could barely push one's way through all the furniture set up in there. That was the fashion in those days in immigrant homes.

The main room was the kitchen. We spent our time and received guests there. The only sink was in the kitchen, where everyone washed and the landlady washed the family's and boarders' laundry. The toilet was in the hall, one for four families who lived on the same floor. The landlady also cooked meals for the all the boarders. I remember that, at that time, I earned around four dollars a week, enough for all my needs, including extraneous expenses.

The main meal in the evening always consisted of the same courses, namely a piece of herring or chopped liver, pea or barley soup, cooked meat, and cooked plums, always accompanied by a pickle and a glass of beer. This sort of menu became so standard in Lithuanian and Belarussian Jewish workers' homes that many called this a "Jewish" meal.

The friends and *landslayt* who would come and fill up the kitchen almost every night were all from the towns and villages around Slutsk: Timkovichi, Nesvizh, Kapyl, Romanovo. A person from a completely different region was considered a foreigner. It was as if a Jew from Poland or Galicia was from a different people.

The themes of the conversations were news from the Old Country, greenhorns, and work. When a letter arrived for one person, everyone read it. Letters were received at the address of Max Kobre's bank on Canal Street. Kobre was like an older brother to all the Slutsker *landslayt*. As with the man of wealth in a town back home, every one deposited their money with him. We also paid Kobre weekly installments for the ship's tickets with which we ourselves had come and which we sent to relatives and family. Kobre's was the "clearing house" where we exchanged news from the entire region.[18]

Work was always on the agenda of conversation. We discussed the situation in every shop, prices, grade of material, and the like—not at the union, but in Elie Abramovitsh's kitchen. We knew which *landsman*** was looking for a new place and who could take someone in to work. To take someone into your shop was considered the greatest good deed, almost the only good deed, that the greenhorns performed in their new country.

We mainly devoted ourselves to greenhorns. Before bringing one here, we bought a ship's ticket from Kobre on the installment plan. When the greenhorn got here, he made payments on it himself. After his arrival, we clothed him: *Landslayt* would go with the greenhorn to Canal Street to purchase a suit, a hat, and shoes. Everything had to be American. Clothes from home were defective, even if they were of good quality and well sewn. Going to the stores with the greenhorn on Canal Street was a joyful procedure, like a Jew back home picking out an *esrog*.[19]

The friendship toward *landslayt* often extended to Gentiles, to the Russians from our villages who began to emigrate to America. They clung like mad to their Jewish acquaintances and were under their protection. The Jews helped them out with the language and with getting jobs. The Russians went into the needle trades in the smaller Jewish shops and worked as pressers.

With respect to befriending our peasant *landslayt*, who felt so lonely and lost without the Jews, my cousin Peysakh Mayzl distinguished himself. He had made friends only with Gentiles in his home village of Shalovitsi. Here he was a presser, worked hard, headed the entire department in his area of the shop, and employed the *landslayt* from his village as errand boys. He treated them like brothers, and his name was respected in his village back home.

Here is a scene from that time: One day there appeared in Hester Street Park a Russian just off the boat. Standing amid a circle of Jews and looking lost, he wondered aloud in Russian: "Where does Peysakh Falkova live?" So several Russian Jews were found who enquired of him: Who and where? But the Gentile knew only one thing, that Peysakh Falkova lived "in New York." When they found out that the greenhorn came from Slutsk, they brought him to Max Kobre at the bank. There, people quickly found out who Peysakh was and brought the *landsman* to him. Here is not the place to describe the joy of those two when they met each other. They embraced and kissed. The newcomer delivered greetings from all the Gentiles in the village: "How's the young pony?" "Do you remember the calf with the red stripe over the eyes? She is now a full-fledged cow and has already had grandchildren." Peysakh showed him around for a day, got him settled in, and took him to work. I related this scene at that time to Y. D. Berkowitz[20] to use as a scene in a skit. He later expanded it for other purposes in his drama *Landslayt*.

For the first year and a half, I lived with relatives. I took their advice and became a tailor. For twenty dollars, I learned to sew with a machine. When I could stitch a piece of material on a sewing machine in a straight line, not stretched-out and not wrinkled, I went looking for a job and found one. Even a greenhorn feels at home in a tailor shop. I felt a bit surer of the work and that people would treat me like a human being. I had various experiences in the shops where I worked sewing men's clothes. The trade was just starting to organize. It had started to migrate to new buildings uptown from the small, neglected little shops on Cherry, Forsythe, and Lispenard Streets. The migration brought with it small social transformations. In the old shops, people worked on Sundays. In the new ones, where the building had to be closed on Sundays, people started to work on the Sabbath. This caused something of a stir among workers and bosses alike. Both were "Jewish" Jews and lived in a Jewish way. (I'm speaking here about the men's clothing trade.) The new shops started to employ foremen. They also installed electric sewing machines. The old-fashioned operators were afraid of the machines and clung to the old, smaller shops.

After wandering about in various shops, a week here and a week there, I got a place in a shop on Cherry Street that I will describe a bit, because it was characteristic of the others.

It was a small shop, old-fashioned and not very clean. It had eight machines for the operators, three or four presses, and a few finishers (who pulled out the basting). We sewed men's jackets. The operators had the prestige in the shop, but not everyone at the same level. It depended on what sort of operation he performed. The first in line was the one who sewed the collar and the sleeve. The rest did various parts and had to see to it that they passed their work to the head operator. The last and least important was the sleeve maker. He had to stitch both edges of the sleeve, the inner and outer lining. This had to be done fast. One had to make at least three hundred a day. (We worked for ten hours a day.) The first step in making a jacket, they set a greenhorn to this task. That was my work.

The two bosses also worked. One cut the linings. (A specialist cut the cloth for the outer lining.) The bosses were not bad people. They came from a small town around Slutsk—*landslayt*. They had not been at this undertaking for long and were just learning to be bosses. They sometimes shouted at a worker. But their shouts lacked the true authority of an employer, and the worker often shouted back. This was not the protest of the union man but the sound of a worker back home arguing with his boss. At lunchtime, one could see both boss and worker sitting at the high table, chewing their wrapped-up bits, drinking beer from the same dipper, only each wiped his mouth with his own sleeve.

There were curious types among the operators. One had been a prayer leader back home. He serenaded us with melodies from the High Holidays,* the most melancholy ones. The chief operator, the collar sewer, was an older, depressed family man. He spoke little, feared the union and the new shops "with electra." Another was a tall fellow, Pinye. Not Sam, Benny, Hymie, but Pinye, although he had been in the country for a long time. He often mentioned the fact that he had worked with Kaspe at one time, "the very Doctor Kaspe, of the *Forward*," and with Morris Rosenfeld, when they were still sewing shirts.[21] Pinye was very sensitive if someone hinted indirectly that he was old and past his prime. When the boss got angry during the season when the work was urgent and he thought that we were working too slowly and not passing it along quickly enough, Pinye would stand up, spit artistically toward the ceiling, make a "Russian blessing,*" sit down, and drive his "Katerinka," his machine, so hard that those behind him had to catch up in order to pass the work on to him. Then he would say: "Yep, Pinye is still Pinye!"

I caught Pinye's fancy from the beginning of the season. He wanted to know why I was always so quiet and who I really was back home. "A rabbi or a horse thief, something must be wrong with that greenhorn." At lunch, I ate in a corner and looked at an English book while eating. One time, he grabbed me by the arm. "Aha! Now I see," he cried out, and sunk into thought. "You can't fool me," he confided quietly to his colleagues. "I recognize this. I once worked with Kaspe and Morris at the same time. That one"—pointing at me—"doesn't belong to us."

From then on, Pinye became very polite to me, stopped ordering me around as was the custom with greenhorn sleeve makers. Once he even suggested that I come in early Saturday morning and he would teach me how to sew in a pocket. This was a high-level task for an operator, and the bosses, "damn them," would give me a raise next season.

Through the season, we all became close to each other. In the fall, work slowed down. We went into the shop—we had to come in if we wanted to keep our jobs—but there was nothing to do. The bosses didn't need to make concessions to the workers now, so they became arrogant and put on airs. A boss is a boss, and the season was now over.

One day, the head worker arrived a little late. Although there was no work that day, the bosses grumbled, "Aha, you went somewhere to look for another job?"

The disheartened workman justified himself. No, he had had a party the previous night. His daughter had gotten engaged.

"So congratulations," the boss-cutter grumbled, straining an expression of a benevolent manager.

When the group of workers heard of the party, they immediately suggested that someone should bring in some liquor. Said and done. Apparently the bosses had argued between themselves and were not in a good mood, so they forbade us to celebrate in the shop. The workers felt insulted. They recognized that they were now extraneous; the friendship was over after the season. So they left with their bottle of liquor to the house of the guest of honor. He didn't live far, on Scammel Street, near Monroe. There, everyone partook slowly, made toasts and amused themselves. Several sang songs. The cantor sang the entire High Holiday prayer, *Unsaneh toykef*.[22] I honored them with a few Russian revolutionary songs. Here on Scammel Street, they sounded foreign. The workers, although all Russian, knew little of what was taking place there, but the Russian words reminded everyone of the Old Country, and we grew more intimate. The words removed the barrier between edge-stitcher and sleeve maker. Gradually, we all forgot about the autumn, the approaching "slack,"* and the bosses.

But it was apparently our fate that our intimate friendship would be disrupted again. The door opened and the operator's daughter, the bride, entered. Instead of greeting us, she twisted her nose and hurled a reproach at her father in English, why did he bring drunks in the house? The father, who always looked depressed, looked even more debased and submissive here in his own house. He wanted to say something but couldn't find the words, so he smiled stupidly and helplessly. We saw that his American daughter respected her greenhorn father precious little, and that he felt completely foreign among his grown children.

Our "drunkenness" quickly wore off and we left the house in embarrassment. There wasn't anywhere to go. Our spirits fell. We felt even more lonely and homeless, so, keeping ourselves together, we went to Jackson Park nearby, leaned against the fence and looked at the East River. The water, like the sky, was dreary, autumnal. A ship whistled from afar. Through the mist, we saw the silhouette of the Statue of Liberty. Behind her, the ocean spread out far and wide, and across the ocean somewhere were the shores of the Old Country. We were silent.

Soon afterward, I left that shop and became a Hebrew teacher. A friend of mine from Mefitsei Sefat Ever, "The Promoters of the Hebrew Language," begged me to accept a position at a newly founded talmud torah in a new neighborhood in the Bronx.[23]

I had studied a little English for about a year and a half. At the beginning, I went to evening school at the Educational Alliance,[24] for the first summer. After that, I studied in the small preparatory school of Khaym Faynman and A. S. Valdshteyn, then two Columbia students.[25] I recall that they did not want to accept any tuition from me. I could swear that they were not wealthy men and it seems they never became wealthy men, and yet . . . practical Americans!

I remember the Educational Alliance well. Without that institution, it would have been impossible to exist in crowded and noisy downtown. There wasn't even space in the narrow dwellings to write a letter, not to mention to read, study, think, or do what one's heart desired. In the large reading room, one leafed through the Hebrew and Yiddish newspapers from Russia, read a book, rested, heard a lecture, drank fresh milk for a penny a glass, and learned English. It was refreshing.

Gatherings of various societies were held in the same building in clean, illuminated rooms in a civilized environment. They did not charge rent. Every Sunday evening, the followers of Hebrew held meetings of the historic society, Mefitsei Sefat Ever. The members were students, teachers, workers, merchants, professionals, peddlers. Devoted, friendly relations prevailed among them in those years. Many remained friends for their entire lives. For people like me, who were slaves all week in factories, the Sunday meetings of Mefitsei Sefat Ever were truly refreshing.

I want to mention one more detail about the Educational Alliance. At the end of the summer English course for beginners, the manager—a Blaustein I think—offered to help us take out our citizenship papers.[26] In connection with that, he also advised us to polish off our Russian names. He sat down, called out each person, analyzed his name philologically and translated it into English. In other cases, he made due with only cutting and shortening. Although the idea itself was not a bad one, the procedure of entirely converting names scandalized me. When he got to me, I explained firmly that my name was dear to me the way it was, and that

I would not change it. The manager did not like this. He immediately, however, found a rationale: "America is a free country." I had a right. He immediately stopped the name operation and a substantial number of greenhorns were left with their "ski's" and "off's" on their names because of my impertinence, poor things.

In the Bronx

In 1907–08, the neighborhood in the Bronx where my talmud torah was located was a new territory for Jews. This was the neighborhood between Wendover Avenue (now Claremont Parkway) and Tremont Avenue and between Crotona Park and Claremont Park. Settled Americans lived there. The streets of Bathgate and Washington still had small private houses situated on the tall green hills. One by one, as Jews started to open stores and Gentiles started to move to West Tremont, more Jews moved into their empty houses and the neighborhood became Jewish. As the Gentiles left, the grass on the hills, the bushes, plants, and flowers gradually disappeared. More stores and tenement houses grew up in their place.

At the beginning, one didn't yet see any "kosher*" signs in the store windows. Pious Jews brought kosher meat and Jewish food from Harlem. We, however, young immigrants in the Bronx, knew that in two restaurants owned by Jews, you could get a piece of herring, borsht* like from home, and Jewish bread, if you asked. Gradually, Jewishness was revealed in the windows of the butcher stores, on the shelves of the bakery stores. Here and there, a candy store now sold a Yiddish newspaper. Only a talmud torah was missing. But there were two stubborn Jews by the names of Becker and Meltzer, and they founded—and with great effort maintained —the Bronx Tremont Hebrew School, then on a beautiful high hill among the trees on the corner of 173rd Street and Washington Avenue. There had once been a private school in that house, before the public school system had expanded to all corners of the city. When the Gentiles fled, the Jews took it over.

Bronx was then quiet and peaceful. One still found places between the houses where a human foot had not tread since the first days of creation. On the hill in Claremont Park, snakes still crept amicably. And how quiet and peaceful and clean it was in the small branch of the city library on Tremont Avenue! The books were complete in their beautiful bindings; there was no one to tear them. Later, when our people started to arrive, the library also took on a new appearance. The old librarian no longer napped; he had to enlist another girl to help. Instead of peaceful stories of colonial times, translations of European literature appeared on the shelves, mainly Ibsen and de Maupassant.[27] Books with social content arrived. The Bronx was now a city.

During the time that I worked at the school, various teachers passed through who later took part in various Jewish activities, and I want to draft a few sketches of their physiognomy from when they first started to sprout forth. The first two teachers were a pair of young boys, one from Plotsk, Shmuel Fuks, and another from around Kovno, Tuvye-Zisl Miller.[28] For a long time, Fuks's parents sent him financial support from Poland, so he wouldn't have to work here. His coming here was connected with a little history. A member of a secret organization, Poalei Zion,[29] he had made an agreement with two of his friends to flee to the Land of Israel. They "withdrew" money from their parents and fled. Fuks's parents were people of influence. They sent a courier who caught up with them in Berlin and tried to trick them into coming home. Because of his mother, Fuks found a compromise by going to America, rather than the Land of Israel. His friends continued on their journey. One is now the manager of the experimental agricultural station in Rechovot, as well as an essayist and novelist. The other is the current David Ben-Gurion.[30] Fuks is now Dr. S. Fox, a dentist on Charlotte Avenue in the Bronx and active in Jewish cultural circles.

At a very young age, Miller left his home and strict father and went to South Africa, where he worked with "Kaffirs" in the mines. After a few years, he came to America with the few hundred pounds he had saved and a deep familiarity with classic English literature. He had also maintained his connection to Hebrew and wanted to study for the rabbinate. He was, however, a dreamer and philosopher and couldn't easily concentrate on the elementary studies. We used to go for walks and talk a lot, discussing the problem of the Jewish future. Then we founded a pioneering[31] society, in fact the first of its kind in America. No great emigration began because of that society, but three people left for the Land of Israel. Miller was one of them. He settled in Rechovot and became a big orange planter. He is an important moral force in the Yishuv, the Jewish community in Palestine, beloved and respected among all classes, laborers and employers. He also co-edited *Bustanai* with Moshe Smilansky.[32]

After Miller's departure, I advised the school committee on the hiring of new teachers. At various times, Dr. Valdshteyn, the writer and leader of

Poalei Zion, worked there. Other teachers included Meyer Waxman, now at an institution of higher learning in Chicago, author of a great work in English about the history of Jewish literature; Bloch, now the librarian at the Semitics Department at the New York Central Library; and Dr. Fefer, now a medical doctor and activist in Hebrew cultural circles in the midwestern states.[33]

I also wish to include my friend I. J. Schwartz.[34] He lived in Brownsville. He wanted to liberate himself from the suffocating atmosphere there and was drawn to the Bronx. A man of many moods, in the classroom as well—often seriously sad and sometimes humorously mischievous—he used to love sending funny little notes to the teachers written in Hebrew, Yiddish, Aramaic, and his own made-up words. In the evenings in the park, he would recite entire chapters of the prophets Isaiah and Amos or the poems of Judah Ha-Levi by heart.[35] Apparently, the stones of Crotona Park and the brown-haired Jewish women understood him well. That was the beginning of his great work of translating into Yiddish parts of the old Hebrew literature. The Bronx indeed got more Jewish at that time. Schwartz's presence drew the young literati and friends of the Yiddish word to the Bronx. Circles started to form. People would go for walks and sit in the park in the evenings dreaming and scheming about how to build a new Yiddish literature. The Literature Society was created from those circles that began to publish anthologies under its name.[36] New talents could be found in the Bronx. We looked up to each other and put out for each other, creating an atmosphere of creativity.

In the house where I lived, in the room one story directly above mine, lived a fellow from Mlawa, Poland, Yoysef Opatovski. The year before, we had studied English together in Faynman and Valdshteyn's School. When I came to the Bronx as a teacher, he earned his livelihood delivering newspapers. He worked for a man, Dillon, the father of the poet A. M. Dillon. Opatovski was then a student of engineering at Cooper Union. He was an industrious student and very rarely "tramped about" with the teachers and idlers in the parks. But one time, he confided to me the secret that he too wrote. Quite early in the morning, when he would get ready for his newspaper work, he would often come into my room through the fire escape, bringing with him a bottle of milk and fresh rolls—God knows where he got them—and leave something of his that he had scribbled.

I used to help him out with the rolls and milk, but we did not completely agree on his scribbles. I demanded content from him, themes addressing painful Jewish questions, just like Brenner, for example.[37] He would get angry at me and not show me anything for a time. Until early another morning, he would come in once again through the fire escape with fresh rolls and new scribbles. He threatened to scribble something that I would have to acknowledge. He followed through with his threat.

I later helped him become a teacher and took him into the talmud torah. His class was for beginners, the alphabet and basic Hebrew. He did not take his work lightly. His artistic eye did not abandon him in the class-room either. Every boy in his class had a nickname, for his nose or for the way a boy shrieked and shouted "ouch!" when he got something over his fingers from the rebbe.

In our first anthology, *Literatur,* we accepted his first story "Shar-manchikes," Organ Grinders. He changed his name a bit to Opatoshu, and it has remained so in literature.[38] The literary set hung around the teachers of the Bronx Tremont Hebrew School. I want to recall some of them. Avrom-Moyshe Dillon, the poet who died before his time, who had just begun to write his difficult, tortured lines about sadness and terror, con-tributed much to the literary mood.[39] No man of means himself, he en-dowed others with the power of creativity, and he inspired and demanded. He possessed much inner beauty which unfortunately found no expres-sion in his own poems. His enthusiasm, however, infected others. When a new volume by Shneur or an article by some thinker arrived, one immedi-ately saw Avrom-Moyshe running from one person to the next expressing his enthusiasm.[40] He was a bohemian in a certain sense. He had no ground under his feet, but neither did he have the proper bohemian atmosphere around him. This explains perhaps the limited extent of his creativity.

As in a theater ensemble, every character plays his role, and so the beginner Yitskhok Bloom played a peculiar role among us. He had a tailor shop in that neighborhood. He would come into the same small restau-rant, Lederman's, where we would have our fill, a tomato herring with a piece of black bread and butter for seven cents. (If you let yourself splurge, you spent another two cents for a glass of coffee.) Bloom was a true worker, a tailor from the Old Country. He was a little lonely and had "moods." Listening to us while he ate, he once pressed himself close and revealed to us that he was also interested in such things. Such as? He'd show us. So he invited us to his cleaning and pressing store. On the thick yellow wrapping paper there were little rhyming lines.

Bloom was then very raw and primitive in the so-called creative proc-ess. Besides Shomer* and Dineson,* he hadn't read any literature, not to mention history and the like. Because of his moods, he strove to express himself, but the poetic form fettered him. He had ambition and was something of a stubborn man, familiar qualities of a person with promise. When we showed him that his lines didn't harmonize, he grabbed a pair of scissors and read the lines himself, banging on is tailor's table with the big scissors and stamping with his feet in time. To him it fit together. He rarely allowed anyone to correct anything besides his conclusions, and for our trouble we got our pants pressed for free.

We considered it a joke, but one day Bloom felt as if he were in seventh heaven. In *Di fraye arbeter shtime* the editor had answered a letter of his.[41] That was his first victory. From then on, he redoubled his efforts. Wherever he found a piece of paper in the store, he wrote on it, until he achieved his end: He started to get published. Today, he has a few volumes of prose and poetry. In this way, a folk-writer saw the light of day right before our eyes.

I want to return to my story. You probably want to know what became of the greenhorn who began with plumbing, changed to tailoring and then to teaching.

At the age of around twenty-eight years old, married, and the father of a one-year-old daughter, I still wanted to study. I sensed that I lacked much knowledge. I did not even begin to know anything. I needed to go through an entire course from A to Z. In Russia, this would have been impossible for me. Here in America, it was a simple matter. I enrolled in a good preparatory school and began to study the lessons systematically in the evenings and on my own in the early morning hours. The hours of work at the talmud torah were from four to eight. I got back my former zeal for learning and went through the entire high school course in a year and a half, and passed the New York state exam with distinction. One winter, I spent the evenings at Cooper Union studying chemistry. I was ready to go to university.

I wanted to study medicine. At the last minute, however, financial difficulties occurred, and I had to change my plan and go to dental college. That's how I became a dentist. Here, as with tailoring, I was forced by the circumstances to do what all people do and follow the well-trodden path. There is more than one man among Jewish dentists whose true calling was to be a geologist or a shoemaker, but became a dentist because—a dentist is *also* a doctor!

What happened next? The usual thing. I studied in New York and Baltimore, practiced in Baltimore among Jews and Gentiles, made a living, was active in communal affairs among my own people, got involved in real estate nonsense and lost every cent, traveled to the Land of Israel and came back.

And so I will soon conclude.

I educated my daughter more or less in my own spirit. This was not easy; here it means going against the mainstream and against the laws of physics. The young generation is everywhere demonically rebellious against the old. That is the way of the world. It is a fact that a Jewish education draws the youth backwards. Youth however are drawn forward, so one needs to rack one's brains constantly to outwit the laws of nature. One needs to create around the child the kind of Jewish atmosphere where the past and future, the new and the old blend together harmoniously. A crown of exaltation and esthetics—things that attract Jewish youth like a magnet—must hover over Jewishness. Then the American child will be fascinated by the beauty of Jewish life and strive to rescue it. The Land of Israel is very helpful in this process. The pioneering movement is a refreshing spring for our weakening children. It has until now guarded my child from the dangers of assimilation.

My daughter knows Hebrew and Yiddish, and graduated from college in languages and social science. She is married to one of her equals in education, someone not born in the area, who works for the government in Washington as an economist. Both belong to the Zionist-Socialist movement. They have a set of friends with varying degrees of education and from different social classes, but who are all in the same movement. When I find myself among them—when they sit at dusk in a circle and sing the sad, gentle song with the enchanting melody, "V'ulai," by Rachel, when they sit by the Potomac and sing of "Kineret sheli," my Kinneret—I know the tunes themselves will do for them what the Gemara tunes once did for me on those wintry nights mourning the destruction of the Temple, and I feel more secure.[42]

I want to relate an incident my daughter told to me because it is instructive. An acquaintance of hers in Washington, a Communist-leaning woman who lives in a non-Jewish neighborhood, noticed that her twelve-year-old boy avoids the company of the neighborhood children and feels lonely in his leisure time. Upon questioning him, the mother found out that he is overwhelmed by fear because he is a Jew. He feels inferior to the others, the "aryans" in the street. His mother came to the decision that her boy needs to learn some Jewishness to prevent the further development of feelings of inferiority. My daughter, who has taught high school, has undertaken to teach him Yiddish and Jewish history. They're making a beginning. He already reads short paragraphs—in the *Forward*!

I will end with a few lines about the rest of the members of our family from Starobin of long ago.

One of my sisters and two brothers came here before the First World War. My sister came to join her husband whom she had married in Starobin. He was a smith there, a presser here. He still remembers what he once learned in *heder*. Besides work, he occupies himself with quite important communal work among his *landslayt* in Brownsville. He organizes and leads his society. He helps, and makes others help, every *landsman* who needs a job or a loan. In Starobin, he was from the "edge of town." Like his father, also a smith, he was not connected to the town elite. Here, under different circumstances, the powers of virtuous communal activism were revealed in him, which is admirable.

One of my brothers, a leatherworker, is active in unions and in cultural circles. The other brother, the youngest, who was a clerk back home and a worker during his first years here, is now in business in San Diego, California. He is active in the Workmen's Circle and in Zionist work through the branch in his city. (That's how it is in San Diego. The Workmen's Circle is active in raising money for the Gewerkschaften Campaign for the Jewish National Fund.[43])

Another brother, who apprenticed as a smith back home, is in the Land of Israel, and another sister remains in Russia. Where she is today, we do not know.

We brought our parents here after the First World War. Our mother is no longer alive. Our father lives with our sister in Brownsville. She is very pious, and her house is strictly kosher. She and her husband fulfill the commandment to honor thy father in the most beautiful way.

My father no longer wires pots, but he still studies, by himself and with others, to fulfill the commandment. His grandchildren, my sister's children and mine, are beloved to him. It gives me great joy to see such love from grandchildren to a grandfather. They love his cheerfulness and erudition. At the age of eighty-five, he still sits by a table every day in synagogue, his "boys"—sixty- and seventy-year-old Jews—around him, and gives them a Gemara lesson. He doesn't hear very well, but he recites and they repeat.

When he speaks of money and livelihood, my father still likes to throw in the old-time saying that the most important thing is not wealth, but living an honest life by one's own hand. We children and grandchildren sit around him and understand each other, although our language varies a little. For my father, a good life means living "by one's own hand." In our time, we called it "proletarianization," and the grandchildren call it "*dat ha-avodah,*" the "religion of labor," or "pioneering." On the inside, they are the same. From grandfather to grandchildren there is continuity, the links of one chain.

May the chain not be broken.

NOTES

1. Polesia is a lowland region encompassing southern Belarus, northern Ukraine, and eastern Poland.

2. *Ha-Melits* (Hebrew, "The Advocate") was the first Hebrew newspaper in Russia. Founded in Odessa in 1860, it was later moved to St. Petersburg. It appeared first as a weekly, then as a semiweekly, and, finally, as a daily. An important mouthpiece for the Haskalah, *Ha-Melits* advocated Zionism in its later years. *Ha-Tsfira* (Hebrew, "The Dawn") was a Hebrew newspaper founded in Warsaw in 1862. At first dedicated primarily to scientific articles, it later focused more on current events and eventually became an organ for Zionism. It appeared, with a number of interruptions, until 1931. These newspapers pioneered the use of Hebrew as a modern journalistic and literary language.

3. See Jeremiah 31:15.

4. In many traditional circles, an active knowledge of Hebrew grammar was considered dangerous since it might enable a person to formulate independent thoughts and modern ideas in conflict with accepted interpretations of the sacred texts.

5. *Ha-Dor* was a short-lived Hebrew intellectual weekly in the first years of the twentieth century. *Ha-Shiloah* was a Hebrew monthly published in Berlin, Cracow, Odessa, and Jerusalem from 1896 to 1926.

6. Rabbi Jacob David ben Ze'ev Willowsky (known by the Hebrew acronym of his name, Ridbaz, 1845–1913) was the founder of famous yeshivas in Slutsk and, later, in Safed, Palestine. His commentaries on the Jerusalem Talmud appeared between 1898 and 1900.

7. Jews who lived in rural villages were isolated from Jewish life in the towns. They often hired young yeshiva students, and sometimes even students in advanced *heders,* to teach their children the rudiments of Jewish literacy.

8. Yokhanan was a *tanna,* a Palestinian sage of the first two centuries of the Common Era whose views appear in the Mishna. Yitskhok was an *amora,* a sage of the third to fifth centuries, who contributed to the Gemara.

9. Yehudah Ze'ev Nofakh (1848–1921) was a Russian teacher and Socialist who

converted to Zionism after the pogroms of 1881 and 1882. He founded a trade school in Minsk and was very influential among the city's youth.

10. The Jewish Independent Workers' Party (1901–3) sought to counter the growing influence of the Bund and to defend workers' economic interests without getting involved in political questions. It operated legally with police support and disbanded when that support ended.

11. Most people could leave Russia legally, but acquiring a passport entailed much expense and trouble. Young men of draft age, however, were forbidden to leave. Many Jewish emigrants therefore crossed the border illegally, and smuggling was a big business.

12. Koenigsberg was later renamed Kaliningrad by the Soviets.

13. "Black Hundreds" was the general term for various virulently anti-Semitic groups that often perpetrated pogroms. On market days, many strangers came to town, and the excited atmosphere was conducive to the outbreak of violence.

14. The Zionist Socialist Workers' Party (called S.S. after its Russian initials), founded in 1905 in Odessa, was "territorialist," arguing that the Jews needed their own territory, but that this territory did not necessarily have to be in the Jews' ancient homeland. Strongly Yiddishist, the S.S. joined with other groups in 1917 to form the United Jewish Socialist Workers Party.

15. The first line of a poem "Levadi" (Alone), by Chayim Nakhman Bialik (1873–1934), the great pioneer of modern Hebrew poetry. The poem refers to the Divine Presence, abandoned in the House of Study by young scholars drawn to the ideals of the Enlightenment.

16. Dr. Simon Bernfeld (1860–1940) was a rabbi who wrote in Hebrew and German on Jewish history and philosophy.

17. The leader of a Hasidic sect is called a *rebbe,* but so is an old-fashioned teacher in a traditional *heder.* By using the word "teacher" Domnitz is emphasizing that he is a modern secular teacher of Hebrew. The officials either do not understand the distinction at all or believe that he will end up teaching traditional subjects anyway in order to make a living.

18. Kobre's bank was one of a number of immigrant Jewish banks. On the eve of World War I, a catastrophic run on these banks led to the collapse of several, including that of Kobre. Kobre pledged to make good on his debts to depositors, but he committed suicide in 1916.

19. For the holiday of Sukkot Jews buy an *esrog,* a citron, to keep for the week and say a blessing over. The *esrog* should be as perfect as possible, without blemishes, so carefully inspecting each *esrog* is an important part of the process of buying one.

20. Yitskhok Dov Berkowitz (1885–1967) was a novelist and editor of Hebrew- and Yiddish-language publications. He was the son-in-law of Sholem Aleichem, whose Yiddish works he translated into Hebrew.

21. Avraham Kaspe (1861–1929) was a Socialist, doctor, educator, and writer of popular books on science. Morris Rosenfeld (1862–1923) was a pioneer of modern Yiddish poetry known for his poems on the plight of the sweatshop workers.

22. The *Unsanah toykef* prayer, so called for the first words of its opening line, "Let us tell how utterly holy this day is," is one of the most solemn prayers of the High Holiday services.

23. Mefitsei Sefat Ever Vesifrutah (Promoters of the Hebrew Language and its Literature) was a Hebraist organization, founded 1902.

24. Community center in Manhattan's Lower East Side. Founded as the Hebrew Institute in 1889, it became the Educational Alliance in 1893. It promoted Americanization and provided athletic facilities, a library, meeting rooms, lectures and classes, and other services to local residents.

25. Avrom Shloyme Valdshteyn (1874–1932) was a scholar and Labor Zionist leader. He earned a doctorate from Columbia University.

26. David Blaustein (1866–1912) was director of the Educational Alliance from 1898 to 1908. An immigrant himself, he became a widely acknowledged expert on issues concerning immigration and Americanization.

27. The works of the Norwegian playwright Henrik Ibsen (1828–1906) and the French short-story writer Guy de Maupassant (1850–1889) were very popular in Yiddish translation.

28. Tuvye Ziskind Miller (1888–1962) was editor of *Bustanai* (Gardener), the organ of the Farmers' Union in Palestine. He lived in New York from 1904 to 1909.

29. Poalei Zion was a Socialist Zionist party whose name means "Workers of Zion." Local Poalei Zion groups sprang up in Russia in the first years of the twentieth century, and a unified party was formed in 1906. Poalei Zion was active in the United States beginning in 1903.

30. David Ben-Gurion (born Dovid Grin, 1886–1973) was a Labor Zionist leader and the first prime minister of the State of Israel (1948–1953, 1955–1963). In 1942 he was chair of the executive committee of the Jewish Agency.

31. Those who settled on the land in Palestine, especially Labor Zionist activists who joined collective farms, were known in the movement as "pioneers" (*halutsim* in Hebrew).

32. Moshe Smilansky (1874–1953) was a Hebrew writer and leader of the agricultural movement in Palestine. He edited *Bustanai* from 1929 to 1939.

33. Meyer Waxman (1887–1969), a rabbi and historian of Jewish literature, joined the faculty of the Hebrew Theological College in Chicago in 1924. Dr. Joshua Bloch (1890-1957) became head librarian of the New York Public Library's Jewish Division in 1923.

34. Israel Jacob Schwartz (1885–1971) was a Yiddish poet and translator known for combining Jewish and nature themes. His most famous work, *Kentucky,* is an epic poem describing Jewish pioneer life in that state.

35. Judah Ha-Levi (d. 1141) was a medieval Spanish Hebrew poet and philosopher.

36. A reference to the immigrant literary movement known as Di yunge, or The Young Ones. Di yunge was made up of young immigrant writers whose literary expression centered first around the periodical *Jugend* (Youth) and then the anthologies *Literatur* (1910) and *Shriftn* (1912–26).

37. Joseph Chayim Brenner (1881–1921) was a key figure of the modern Hebrew literary movement and an adherent of the "psychological" approach to literature.

38. Joseph Opatoshu (born Yoysef-Mayer Opatovski, 1886–1954) was a Yiddish novelist and short-story writer. He trained as an engineer at Cooper Union. Domnitz is slightly mistaken. Opatoshu's first published work was "Oyf yener zayt brik" (On the Other Side of the Bridge). It appeared in *Literatur* 2 (1910).

39. A. M. Dillon (born Avrom Moyshe Zhuravitski, 1883–1934) was a Yiddish poet who made his debut in *Literatur* in 1910.

40. Zalman Shneur (1887–1959) was an important Yiddish and Hebrew poet.

41. *Di fraye arbeter shtime* (The Free Voice of Labor, 1890–1892, 1899–1977) was the leading Yiddish anarchist newspaper in the United States, known for its high literary standards.

42. Rachel (Rachel Blaustein, 1890–1931) was a Hebrew poet, translator, and agricultural colonist in Palestine. Many of her poems, including the well-known "V'ulai" (And Perhaps) and "Kineret," were put to music and sung in the Zionist movement.

43. The Gewerkschaften Campaign was founded 1924 to raise money from the affiliates and members of the United Hebrew Trades, or Gewerkschaften (more properly: Geverkshaftn), a federation of predominantly Jewish trade unions in the United States, for the Histadrut, the central labor organization in Palestine and, later, the state of Israel. Founded in 1901, the Jewish National Fund was the fundraising arm of the Zionist movement.

Chapter 5

What Drove Me to America and
My Experiences in Europe and America

Rose Schoenfeld (R.S.)

b. 1884, Drogobych, Galicia
To U.S.: 1912, New York

Rose Schoenfeld's story illustrates, among other things, the power that the printed word held for her generation. As a young woman, with her husband in America, Schoenfeld (fig. 10) fell into a deep depression. Advised by a doctor to take up reading, Schoenfeld went one step further by composing stories herself. Eventually, her work appeared in a number of periodicals in Galicia and the United States. Her literary interests led her to the Zionist movement and local politics. She proudly tells of how she engineered her family's move to America against the wishes of her husband and her parents. A visit to her hometown in 1932 and the outbreak of World War II both confirmed the wisdom of her decision. Perhaps as further validation of her move, Schoenfeld's upbeat account of her voyage and arrival differs drastically from the usual immigrant saga of hardship.

It was not one thing but several that drove me to America, as I will relate.

I was born on the first of the month of Kislev,[1] 1884, in Drogobych, Galicia (fig. 11). My father, Yehude Shrayer, was a great Talmudist.* He studied until his wedding at the age of sixteen, when he married my mother. He was descended on his father's side from the aristocracy of Drogobych. The Shrayers were the richest family and all of the town's industry lay in their hands. On his mother's side, he was descended from rabbis, assistant rabbis, and ritual slaughterers. His mother's father, especially, was a very righteous man. People considered him a *lamed-vovnik,* one of the legendary thirty-six righteous men in the world. My father

Fig. 10. Rose Schoenfeld with her American-born daughters, Sylvia and Hannah, c. 1915. Courtesy of Betty Weissbecker

prided himself more on his mother's family than on the rich Shrayers. Above all, he sought all his years to be at least a little bit like his grandfather, Reb* Yehude Stoyler, after whom he was named. My father had been a soldier for Emperor Franz Josef[2] for three years, during which time he did not eat non-kosher* food for even one meal!

My father was an unusually honest businessman. He could get the highest credit solely on his word, without a dip of the pen. He never went to court in his life. Many times, he paid money that he knew he did not owe, just because he did not want to go to court and have to swear an

Fig. 11. The marketplace in Drogobych, Rose Schoenfeld's hometown, in a rendering by artist E. M. Lilien. Courtesy of the YIVO Institute for Jewish Research

oath. He preferred to pay as long as he did not have to go swear an oath, even about something that was true.[3] When my father died, all the businesspeople closed their businesses and went to his funeral. He used to keep a strict accounting of his business and, when he died, he did not owe anyone a cent.

My mother, may she rest in peace, was a very righteous woman. She was descended from rabbis. The *tsadik* of Zhidachov, of blessed memory, the rebbe* Reb Ayzikl, was her cousin by blood.[4] She was very proud of her relationship to him. The Zhidachover rebbe's children would often come to visit and she would receive them very obligingly. Above all, her task was to marry off poor orphans and aging girls so they would not remain old maids. Not far from their house in Drogobych, there was a Christian hospital. She would cook food for the Jewish patients and bring it to them, because they were hungry and did not want to eat any non-kosher food. Later she saw to it that a kosher kitchen was founded for the Jewish patients. She lived for ninety-two years. In her last years, she could no longer see, so she recited all of the psalms from memory, each morning and evening.

In their youth my parents suffered terribly from want and poverty.

My father was sixteen years old when he married my mother. Actually, by then it was already forbidden to marry until one was classified for the draft. But among pious Jews, it was hoped that by the time one had to report for the draft the Messiah would have come. But the Messiah did not come and they suffered much because of that.

They had a little money from their dowry, so my father opened a business. He established a mill. My father's father used to operate mills; one of my father's brothers operated mills. So my father also leased a mill. They bought horses and cows and kept the livestock hard at work, and things went well. They made a good living.

When my father turned seventeen, I was born. My mother was a great housekeeper and very beautiful, so for a short time they were happy. They loved each other very much. I remember that when I was older, they still loved each other. By the time my father had to report to the military, when he was twenty years old, there were already three children, all girls.

My father had grown into a fine, robust young man. Now they became scared. Who knew what would happen? And here he was, already the father of three children. So they thought that they would buy his way out with money, as was often done in those years. They made many inquiries. The commission was not a bad one, and they hoped that money would get him out.[5] They paid off everyone that they had to, and waited and hoped. But it was just his luck that someone informed on the commission. So on the last day on which he had to report, a new commission arrived. As soon as he went in they drafted him. And all the money that had been passed to the other commission was lost.

There was a great commotion. My mother fainted. She wailed and cried. My father's rich family even interceded. They ran to big shots to rescue him, but to no avail. He was too good-looking and completely healthy, so they did not want to free him and he had to serve. My father did not want to eat any of the "mess," the non-kosher food, that they gave the soldiers, so his family succeeded in getting him permission to go to eat in a kosher canteen, and they paid for that. This cost them the last *groshn** that they owned. They sold everything, lost it, and were left as after a fire. And so for his entire three years of service he ate no non-kosher food, not even for one meal.

My mother took the three children and went to her father in a village where my grandfather leased a tavern.

As one can imagine, my youth did not start out at all happily. If it were not for my father's brother, who had a mill in Borislav and who every week would send my mother two bags of flour for hallah* and regular bread . . . My grandfather, may he rest in peace, was not wealthy enough to support us because there were other children in the house who could not earn anything. So we suffered terribly. The house was small, so we did not even have enough room to live. Sleeping was a great hardship. No one could sleep in the big room where the tavern was, and the younger children slept in the alcove. We slept on bundles of straw under the table, on the table, and wherever else there was a niche. In my grandfather's hall, there was a broken stall, so my mother had a little room made out of the stall and we lived in that little room for quite a few years.

When my father returned home from the military he had no work, so he went to our rich cousins, the Shrayers, and they gave him a little job with a very small salary. The job was in Borislav, where they had oil wells. My father had to supervise the whole little factory and send the oil to the factory where it was made into kerosene and other things, like grease for wagons and polish for shoes. They did not yet know how to make more important products from oil. For his work, my father received four guldens* a week. Naturally, those were starvation wages. My father could not afford a bit of butter for his bread, so he used to eat bread with *povidle,* plum butter, and for dinner a woman used to cook a quarter pound of meat with beans mixed with rice. That was his life of poverty for several years.

My mother started to earn something by sewing linens for the priest's wife. The priest's wife was not a bad woman, and she liked my mother's work, so she gave her vegetables from the garden and even a couple of beds in the garden to plant a few potatoes. Naturally, with small children, she did not have enough time to do the sewing during the day so she would sit by a kerosene lamp all night and sew—anything to help out.

My father seldom came home, except for an important Sabbath or a holiday. We would be very happy when father came home, because he never came with empty hands. My mother would be happy when he came and the whole family respected him very much. My grandfather used to honor him greatly for his piety and honesty. My father would not bother with anyone else in the village besides his children. And the rest of the time he would sit and study. In the factory he had his own office, so, even there, when he finished his work he would study on the spot. Our cousins, the Shrayers, respected him, but they were not happy that he was not starting to do something extra so he could earn more. They considered him an impractical man and said that he would never work his way up, that he would remain a pauper.

Nevertheless, more children were born, so my mother had six girls. But unfortunately, not all survived. Of the six, only three survived.

Since my mother did not have any boys, my younger sisters and I were kept in *heder** just like the boys. We studied Khumesh* and everything else that the boys studied. I often used to get in trouble with the teacher, because, while we were studying, I would quietly prompt the boys on what I knew and they did not.

My mother was mortified that she did not have a boy. They wanted to have someone to say *Kaddish** after them. So my mother used to go to Hasidic* rebbes to have them bless her with a son. I was already twelve years old when, with God's help, my mother had a boy. The joy was mixed with sorrow, because a couple of days earlier a pretty girl of five years died in our family. I am certain that if we had lived in a city the children would not have died, because by the time they brought a doctor from the city, it was always too late. . . .

The little boy was like a god to my parents. My mother gave up her sewing for the boy's sake. The little boy was pretty, but very delicate and pale, because my mother had slaved away at her work during her pregnancy. So she gave up everything and devoted herself to the little boy to keep him alive. When my little brother was a year old and could not yet stand on his feet because he was too weak, my mother would not put him down.

I was already a big girl, already twelve years old. I was the oldest, and the entire burden of work fell into my hands.

In our village, there was a sawmill where they cut boards. The workers used to give me the waste material to use for heating. I would carry the wood to heat the entire house, for us and for my grandmother. We now had a cow, so I would haul large bundles of grass to feed the cow. Because of the hard work, I actually did not grow, so they used to call me a dwarf. Only later did I get bigger.

It was a hot summer's day, Tishah be-Av,[6] and I wanted to fast. It was my first fast. It was hot, so I prepared myself to get through the entire fast. But suddenly there was a problem: I fainted in the middle of the day. And this is what happened. My mother had a brother who came back from the military, where he had served for three years. When he came home, he starting fighting with my mother, saying she should move out of the little room and give it to him and his family. She had nowhere else where she could live, because in that village one could not rent a place to live, and she did not have the means to live in town. But her brother became brutal. He would not listen to reason. He took my mother's things and threw them out in the garbage. When I saw that, it gripped my heart and I fainted. I could never forget that incident, even many years later. When I was already here in America I used to send money to help my family and my husband's. But when my uncle turned to me for help, I could not forget what he had done and did not help, because I could not forgive him. Maybe I did not act correctly, but it is the pure truth. I could not forget my mother's despair when he threw her out.

In the New House

When it comes to seeing into the future, human beings are so blind that often, when we meet with trouble, we despair. It seems to us that our world is coming to an end. Then it turns out that from the bad that others do to us comes good, as you will see.

My mother had to leave the weak, delicate child and go to another village to look for a place to live. In that village, called Dole,[7] she found a residence that had also been made from a stall. The ceiling was right over one's head; you could touch it with your hand. It was so small that only one bed fit into it, with a small table and one chair. But, as if in compensation, there was a large oven that served as a bed for us children.

The room belonged to an old widow who had a large hump on her shoulders. Everyone considered her a witch and the people in the village were afraid that she might harm them with her magic. So when my mother took the place from her, everyone felt badly, because many of the Jews in Dole were my mother's relatives. My mother knew about the woman, but she could not help it; there were no other places to live to be had. But we children did not know about the woman's magic. We were simply afraid of the hunchbacked old Jewess with the many warts on her face, with a beard practically growing on every wart. But later we grew accustomed to her and got along very well with her. She liked me, because I pitied her and often helped her out with work around her house.

The old widow was raising a grandchild, a boy who was an orphan. His mother had died during his birth. The grandmother raised him as a son to say *Kaddish* after her, because she only had daughters, but no son. She also put everything she owned in his name and it was thought that she had a nice fortune. Meyer was sixteen years old when we moved in. He was a tall, thin boy with light blond sidelocks who went barefoot in a shirt with long, broad sleeves, with the ritual fringes worn on top.[8] He had intelligent, good-natured eyes. This Meyer later played something of a role in my life.

Meyer formed an elementary *heder,* teaching small children because he himself did not know very much. He wanted me to be his pupil as well, but I already knew more than he did and this bothered him. Meyer would bring me the best fruits from the priest's garden. He grew accustomed to me as if he were my own brother. More than that I could not feel for him.

We lived there for one year and then my mother bought an old hut not far away. The hut stood right next to the banks of the river, which was called the Trie,[9] which raged every time the ice melted before Passover.* Each time, it tore off a piece of our garden, so that later the hut hung over the water. Every time the water rose a little after a rain, we would have to flee the house for fear that the water would carry us away, along with the hut. Nevertheless, we lived there for four years, until an opportunity arose and my parents became prosperous because of that hut, as I will relate later.

I was a great lover of reading books. My father used to bring books from the city and I was delighted with them. But it did not satisfy me, because he could not bring me many. I found out that on the other side of the stream lived an estate owner who had a fine, though not very large, library. So I borrowed the books and read them, until soon I finished them all. I took to writing little sketches and poems, but I did not show them to anyone. I was simply too shy. I did not want anyone to laugh at me for making a fool of myself. And what's more, I did not have anyone to show them to. The Christian public school teacher did know something about my writing and, when he asked, I told him that there was nothing to see, that I was just making a fool of myself. In that village, there was no more than a public school, so I had to study privately with a tutor. But we had no good teachers either, so I had to get along with whatever I could.

By the age of sixteen, I had grown into a pretty girl. Everyone considered me an ideal girl—I had a little knowledge and was no fool—so there was no lack of matchmakers. Everyone in the area wanted to make a match with me. Meyer's grandmother also sent a matchmaker.

In the meantime, Meyer had grown up to be quite a handsome young man and he was already a merchant. He always visited us at home, and people started to talk of how the witch's grandson was matching himself up with me—and they did not want to allow that. My father did not want to hear of the match. Meyer suffered terribly over this, because he was very much in love with me. But I was apathetic, though I did not hate him. I aspired to escape from the village, and I knew that Meyer could not leave the village because of his grandmother's estate, to which she had made him heir.

Once Meyer came and told me that a female cousin of his wanted to become his bride. I already knew the girl and liked her. She was a simple village girl, but pretty and full of life.

"Why don't you like your cousin? She is a pretty girl and no fool, and she has the same family background as you. Why do you resist?" I asked him.

"And are you, Reyzele, telling me to become engaged to another girl?"

"Why not?"

"And it won't bother you at all?" he asked, looking into my eyes with regret.

"Why should it bother me?" I asked him back.

"Oh, Reyzele, you are already a big girl, but you are still a child. Don't you understand what is happening with you? Do you want to hide what is happening in your heart? Do you want to deceive me and yourself? You can't fool me that you don't love me. I know that a time will come when you'll regret it, but it will be too late . . ."

I saw tears in his eyes. When I saw his tears it gripped my heart and I almost cried out: "Meyer, I can't bear to see you cry!"

But I controlled myself and with a little laugh I called out, "Go on, Meyer, don't be foolish! Go get engaged! And good luck!" Meyer left with a bowed head, seeing that he had lost me. And that very Sabbath he became engaged to his cousin Malke.

I came to congratulate the bride and groom and was merry just like everyone else. I saw that Meyer was suffering. He went around with his head lowered, not merry like a groom should be. It cost me enough health seeing how he suffered. I still had time to say the word and that would put an end to their engagement. But I controlled myself, calculating the consequences of such a match for me. No, I was striving for something bigger, better. The main thing was that I wanted to go to the city, to become something, though I still did not know what.

I went to Meyer's wedding. I danced and celebrated, but I did not enjoy it. I saw Meyer sitting at the table and he was gloomy with sorrow. That gripped my heart and I almost fainted. When Meyer saw that I too was suffering, he came out from behind the table and came up to me and asked, "Reyzele, what's the matter?"

"Nothing, nothing. Go back to your table. See how people are looking at us!"

"Let them look! I see how you are suffering. Say one word and I won't go under the wedding canopy! Just one word. There is still time, dear," he pleaded with tears in his eyes.

"What are you saying, Meyer?" I was afraid of a scandal. "What do you want to do, make a scandal? With you at your wedding before the ceremony?"

"What good does the ceremony do me when we are both miserable?" he asked with pain in his heart.

The crowd had actually started to move closer to us to hear what we were saying.

"Meyer, for my sake, don't make a fool of yourself! Go to the table. You will be happy!"

And I moved out of the room, leaving Meyer in deep sorrow. Meyer had a premonition of his bitter life with his wanton cousin. She was later unfaithful to him.

Nevertheless, they went through with the ceremony and celebrated as is customary at a Jewish wedding. When I came home from the wedding, I did not want to stay in that village any longer. I felt broken up and ran away so I would not meet up with Meyer and see how he suffered.

I ran off to my father in Borislav. I could sew cheap dresses, so I set up a tailor shop and started to earn money, which was a big help to my family. I was a help to myself as well. I could get fresh books to read there, so I used to spend the Sabbath reading books. I also got a good teacher and wanted to study German literature again.

Being in Borislav, I acquired many girlfriends who used to have me sew their dresses and thought very highly of me. One friend introduced me to a cousin of hers who had just come from America. This cousin was a handsome, rich young man who had worked his way up in America. He had a large wholesale meat market in Chicago. His whole family prided themselves in the rich, young man who had brought them expensive gifts of fine jewelry and other fine things. They spoke of him with pride and enthusiasm—how rich he was and what an aristocrat he was. My friend told me that he had come home to look for a girl to marry and return with to America.

"Oh, if only he wanted me," the girl said, but she knew that a girl like her would never appeal to him, because she was short and fat as a barrel. "The girl who gets him will be lucky," she said. She introduced me to the young American when I was at their house. The young man soon asked me to go for a walk with him. We talked about various things. He told me with enthusiasm about American life and said that America was a paradise compared to the poor life in Galicia. He would no longer be able to exist here. He hoped to escape from home and return to his business as quickly as possible. He told me that four hundred people worked for him in his business, and although he was still alone he already had his own rich house with all the finest fixtures—like those of a count.

We went walking a couple of times, and people started to talk that the American had cast his eye on Shrayer's girl and that there would certainly be an engagement. All the girls now envied me that the handsome, rich American young man was in love with me. However many other girls from fine, respectable homes he was introduced to, he did not want them. People were certain that my parents would be happy with their good fortune. But that is not how it was with my parents.

When my parents found out, they became frightened that I would be cast away into *treyfene,** impious, America. They started to watch me to keep me from meeting with the young American. My mother ran to a Hasidic rebbe, crying and wailing for him to wish her the right match, one with the right pedigree, fitting for the family, and for me not to disappear and be lost to them, as if I had died. At one rebbe's place my mother met up with my husband's father, who had also come to get the rebbe's wish for the right match for his son, his youngest.

So the rebbe proposed that my mother make a match with Reb Hersh Meylekh Schoenfeld, who was already my mother's in-law because one of my mother's sisters was Hersh Meylekh's daughter-in-law. My mother immediately liked the match. Yes, they had a grand pedigree that was appropriate to her, as it had been appropriate to her sister. My husband's father had a reputation. He was an ordained rabbi but had never wanted to accept a rabbinical position, arguing that it was forbidden to sell the Torah for money. He used to sit and study and did not want to know what was going on in the outside world.

My mother immediately agreed to the match, especially since the rebbe, Reb Urele of Sambor, was the matchmaker—and that was certainly a good thing.[10] My mother came home from the rebbe on Sunday, and on Tuesday the engagement was concluded, without anyone asking me if I wanted the groom. I had only seen him once and he did not appeal to me very much, but my mother said that it was a piece of good fortune.

This was how European parents could act, with only their own happiness in mind. As long as the pedigree seemed appropriate to them, everything was right. When the American found out that I had already become engaged, he packed his things and left to return to America without a bride.

My husband was a very handsome young man, but not nearly as handsome as the American. But my protests did no good and I had to be satisfied with what they had done. My husband was a good earner and they told me that I would lack for nothing with him. And in addition, he had inherited from his father a house that was considered valuable.

My father was not very enthusiastic about the match. Something gnawed at him, but they did not tell me what. It was because I would have to live together with my father- and mother-in-law, because my husband had already been supporting them for many years. That was the reason that his father had turned the house over to him in a timely way, while he was still alive, so that the other children who never wanted to help would not later want a share of the inheritance. My husband also had a sister, a widow with two children, who depended on him. I did not know about any of this. I only found out later when it was too late to protest. With an embittered heart, I went to the wedding canopy. Then I recalled Meyer and felt as he had felt on the day of his wedding.

My father-in-law, of blessed memory, passed away six weeks before our wedding. My mother-in-law was embittered and broken up. Right away, the day after our wedding, she got into bed sick and I had to be her nurse and attend to her. That was my honeymoon. She did not like the way I cooked or baked. Nothing was any good. But she did not pester me for too long. Six weeks after the wedding, she also died. As my grocery man put it then, I was lucky that I did not have to suffer with a mother-in-law for long. But my sister-in-law and her two children remained with me and they gave me enough headaches.

Yes, I forgot: The first week after my wedding an official came and took my bedding for taxes due on the house. The house was deep in debt. We tried with all our hearts to pay, but we could not, because my husband lost his job the week after the wedding. We did not know what to do or how to manage. His brother, who was my uncle, had a good laugh. He hoped that they would take the house away from us, so we would have nothing from the inheritance, just like all the other children.

I took up sewing dresses again in order to earn something for food. But I could not sew for long because I became sick from all the aggravation. And so we suffered in want and in poverty for several years. We rented out all of the rooms, leaving only a tiny little room for ourselves. And we suffered until, finally, God came to our aid and it seemed to us that we were now the lucky ones.

As is well known, Borislav is a place of oil wells and waxworks. Suddenly there was a boom in tearing down houses and building oil wells in their place.

On our street stood two rows of houses with old landlords, fine Hasidic "Jewish" Jews. Children and grandchildren were born there and everyone lived happily. In Borislav, everyone made a living, everyone had work. Some made more, some less, but they did not worry. They were like family. Every holiday was a grand, joyful experience, being together in the synagogue and in the Hasidic prayer house. Those who were not so pious would get together on the porches and tell jokes, anecdotes, and whatever anyone knew that would help them be merry. My father-in-law, of blessed memory, Reb Hersh Meylekh, was never seen on the porches. He used to spend his whole life in his alcove by the Gemara* or somewhere with a rebbe. Everyone had the greatest respect for him and they honored him greatly.

When I married my husband, they took me into their community and they loved me because they loved my husband, who would also spend time with them. So we would spend time together, like a family. They often used to speak of Reb Hirsh Meylekh and of what a great Jew he was. With time, children were born to us and everyone used to come with the greatest happiness to celebrate our joy. And so twelve whole years passed.

As is well known, Borislav is to this day the site of oil wells and waxworks. In those years, many wells were still in the hands of Jews who were called "the lords." They were very rich and they kept their children in the big cities and gave them an education. Their wives stayed at the most expensive spas and lived in a rich style.

Suddenly, salvation came for the poor Jews as well. Large companies arrived and a boom took place. They bought up the houses from the poor Jews and set themselves up to drill for oil. Every poor man with just a little house became rich overnight. Our street was bought up and all of the neighbors dispersed to the big cities with money and bought themselves large masonry houses. The whole street became like a cemetery and, for monuments, they set up tall towers and drilled for oil. We too were among the fortunate. They bought our old, broken-down house as well. They gave us a couple hundred guldens as a down payment, plus four percent of the income that would come from any oil that was found.

But fortune did not favor everyone. For us, it was fortune—and misfortune. For us, there were brand new troubles. All seven brothers and sisters, who had never wanted to acknowledge their old, sick parents, suddenly became their children and demanded their inheritance. So my husband promised them all that he would give to everyone, just as soon as oil was struck and there was an income. But they did not want to wait. They wanted their share of the inheritance. So when one sister married off a child, we had to provide the dowry. They wheedled my husband into signing notes for hundreds of guldens.

Another sister played a little joke. She brought me with her to the store to get clothing for her daughter's wedding, because I was an expert judge of merchandise. So I had no choice but to leave everything behind, including the children, and go with her. They knew me in the store. And they knew that I was to become rich at any moment, so I had a lot of credit. They cut yard after yard of goods for various dresses for the bride and for the whole family. And when they had piled up a mountain of merchandise for us, the storekeeper brought me the bill, together with a promissory note to sign. If I did not, he would not release the merchandise. I knew what this meant, but I could not help it. I signed a note for six hundred guldens. And so it went, from one sister to the other, and from brother to brother, and they dragged us deep into debt.

My family did not give me much pleasure either. They also knew that I, their daughter, was to become rich—and they were poor. So I also had to help them. When one of my sisters got married, I had to pay for everything.

Oh yes, I forgot to tell this.

With a couple hundred guldens my husband leased a tavern in the only house that was left on that street, which was in the heart of the oil field. We did not make out badly in that business. We worked hard. We kept servants, but the servants stole from us, so there was success without its blessings. And then my husband's sister would come all the time and demand more and more money. No matter how much we gave her it was not enough. My husband is good-natured, so he used to give away everything the business had made. Then he did not have enough to pay the rent.

We had credit because soon, within a couple of weeks, the well would strike oil and we would become rich and be able to pay it back. And there would be enough left over for us. It was estimated that the oil would give a thousand guldens a week income when it was struck.

My Brother Runs Away to the Yeshiva

I have already related that my little brother studied with the rabbi of Borislav, Reb Meshulem.[11] When he reached bar mitzvah* age, the rabbi told my father that he could no longer instruct the boy. My brother needed to be in a yeshiva* in order to amount to anything. He could become a great and learned rabbi if he were sent to yeshiva. This vexed my father very much because he could not afford to send him. It involved great expenses and he did not have the money. The boy heard this and became very upset, because he wanted to study further and he did not have a place to do so. So the little boy thought it over and disappeared. He ran away from home to find a yeshiva. Meanwhile, my father still lived in the village.

What took place then is hard to describe. My parents were afraid because they thought that the boy had taken his life, because they could not send him to yeshiva. The whole village was on its feet looking for him in the woods, in the fields, and in the water. But they did not find them. Two days later a telegram arrived from a rabbi in the town of Skole. The rabbi informed us that the boy was with him, and he, the rabbi, who happened to be a cousin of my father, wrote that he was sending the boy to the Khust yeshiva, but that they should send money for the travel expenses.[12] My mother sold her only cow and sent twenty-five guldens to the rabbi, and the rabbi sent him off to the Khust yeshiva equipped with a long letter. The head of the yeshiva happened to be an in-law of a relative of my mother's, and when my brother arrived there, the head of the yeshiva received him nicely. He did not let him to "eat days"* with local householders like the other yeshiva boys. Instead, he got room and board from the son of the head of the yeshiva for the entire four years that he studied there. I used to send my brother a monthly allowance for clothes and other things for which he needed money.

My Father Becomes Successful

With God's help, the government extended a stretch of the freight railroad through the village where my father had the hut by the water—where they expected that another flood would come and wash away the hut—and the hut stood right on the line. So the government bought it and my father was paid well for it. So he went off to his former hometown, Drogobych, where he had striven all his years to buy a fine house. There he established a business and made an honorable living. Everyone who did business with him had the greatest respect for his honesty. His word was like a written promissory note to them.

When my brother came home after having been in the Khust yeshiva for four years, no one could get over how the delicate, pale boy had become a handsome grown-up youth, elegant and well dressed, with a pressed shirt and gold cufflinks in his cuffs. He was not, as they had expected to see, a backward-looking religious fanatic like the other Hasidic youths who sat in the synagogue and studied. He was a trained rabbi with ordination and, at the same time, he studied world literature and also had an open view of the world and a social sense. Before long, he married a rich girl from Drogobych. But he did not become a rabbi; he did not aspire to the rabbinate. He became a merchant in his father-in-law's businesses. Nevertheless, the rabbis of Drogobych drew him into the rabbinate and he played an important role in all the affairs of Jewish life in the city.

Our Great Fortune Gets Washed Away

Fortune was within our grasp, but if it is not fated there is nothing we can do about it.

Our shaft had begun to strike oil. We were already getting a hundred guldens a week from our oil well. They still had to drill ten meters deeper to reach the real source of the oil. We were already making plans to leave and settle somewhere in a big city like the other parvenu Jews from our area. Many settled in Vienna, in Lemberg, and even in Berlin, where they bought stone houses and led the life of the wealthy class. We too wanted to settle elsewhere, at least in Lemberg. Our children were growing up and we had to educate them as others were doing. A company came and wanted to buy our shares; it wanted to give us many thousands of dollars. The company was from England and they paid in American dollars. By that time, we already were talking about dollars; crowns and guldens had lost their charm. But we did not want to sell. We wanted to feel what it was like to receive a check each month as others had received. And people estimated that we would receive a thousand dollars a month. So we did not sell, but waited for the big windfall that God would grant us. But, as I said, not everyone is lucky enough to get a windfall, and one was not destined for us. . . .

A month later, our lawyer came and informed us that our company, and many other companies, had decided to stop work in the fields. At that time, many wells had struck oil. So much oil came in that there was nowhere to store it. What good would it do us to reach the real source when there was no way to market it and it would have to be poured down the drain? There was no alternative but to stop work for a short time until a way was found to sell it. Naturally, there was nothing we could do and we had to agree. They stopped further drilling at many wells and laid off hundreds of workers from their jobs.

I remember the fear that Borislav's Jews felt when thousands of unemployed workers set out among the taverns. They ran around like lunatics, because they had no money and they wanted to drink. They beat and murdered. The tavern keepers fled for fear that they would be slaughtered. We too had to flee for our lives with the children in the middle of the night.

We hired a horse and wagon and one dark night we snuck out. We packed the bedding along with a few other things and hit the road.

To get from Borislav to Drogobych, one must cross several streams. During normal times, the streams were quite small, but after a rain they became wild and could wash away houses and bridges. At the time, the streams were small and we traveled quite pleasantly. The children fell asleep. Bundled up in the bedding, they were warm even though it was September and already cold. I held the smallest child in my arms. The servant held the second one, and one slid under the featherbed and slept soundly. We had nearly reached Drogobych and were crossing the last stream when the wagon fell into a pit beneath the water and tossed us all into the cold water. In deadly fear, we barely dragged ourselves out because it was not too deep.

Terrified, the driver started to pull out the bedding and the baggage— and we forgot completely that we were missing a child. The child was only pulled out of the water with the bedding and it seemed as if she had drowned. When we saw that, we began to scream, but we were out in the fields, far from people, and no one heard us. The Gentile, the driver, was a godsend. He was terribly frightened. He took the child on his shoulders, upside down, and he ran with her to look for people. He saw a house lit up, so he knocked on the door and shouted that they should open up to save a Jew child! The Gentile knew that a Jew lived there. They opened up and rushed to revive the child, and they succeeded. They made a warm bath, warmed her up, and by the time we had dragged ourselves over there, half-dead, we found the child alive. The people who lived there were my cousins. We spent the night there and the next day we went to my parents in Drogobych.

And so my luck with Borislav fortunes came to an end. We never returned to Borislav. The oil company soon went bankrupt and that misery was over with.

My father gave us a little money and my husband leased a tavern in Drogobych. But we lost everything in that tavern and closed it before the year was out.

We were deeply in debt, as much from the goods people gave us on credit as from the notes with which my husband had earlier paid his sister and brother their inheritance. Our credit fell and my husband had nothing he could do, so we were almost in despair.

"I will go to America," my husband said. But that scared me. "Go to America? And here we have five small children. What will I do? How will I live with the children when there is no money even for one meal?"

"You will have to go to your parents with the children. There is no other alternative. And in the meantime I will still try, maybe I will earn something without a business. I will go to work."

I agreed to that and we moved in with my parents. We still hoped that sooner or later the fields would open up again and we would be helped by the inheritance.

My husband went off to Borislav and looked for work, but could not earn anything. Due to the closing of the oil wells and the many strikes that took place, it was very bad in Borislav.

My husband had an aunt in America, his mother's sister. My husband had helped out that aunt when her husband, Moyshe Rapeport, went off to America and left her behind with grown children, girls. Since they did not earn anything and suffered deep poverty, he helped them a lot. He remembered this aunt and wrote her a letter, saying that he had failed financially and wanted to come to America. Aunt Rapeport did not even reply, but immediately sent a ship's ticket and twenty guldens for my husband's expenses.

My husband was afraid to tell me that he already had a ticket to travel to America. He still tried various things and still hoped for his vanished fortune. But the fortune from the "gushers," as they were called, did not come and he had to leave for America. He actually intended to go for only a short time—until they returned to work at the oil—because we did not want to believe that everything was already lost. He wanted to go in order to earn enough to pay off his debts, so we would not be charged interest, because we still believed that it would get better again.

When my husband left, I became sick from the hardship. My parents were terribly mortified by our financial failure. And now my father was sued to pay for the notes that my husband had guaranteed for his sister when they had taken money. My father, not wanting to go to court to swear that he had nothing to do with it, paid off the notes that my husband's sister had taken out.

All of these aggravations nearly drove me from the world. The doctor who treated me was a friend of the family and he advised me to occupy myself with something.

"But, Doctor, with what? With whom should I do business?" I asked, not understanding what he meant.

"I am not saying that you should run a business. I am saying that you should busy yourself with something, so you don't think so much about your situation. Read, write, like you used to do when you were a girl! I will put my library at your disposal, as many books as I have, and then you can go to the municipal library. They have quite good books. That will give you something else to do with your life."

The good Dr. Eliashevitsh sent me eighty books with his servant, and I immersed myself in reading. My mother attended to my children, although they had a business and she was a busy person. But it could not be helped. Once she did turn on the doctor angrily: "Doctor, a nice piece of advice you gave to my daughter! Reading books! When she was a girl she had time. But now she has children to take care of."

"Mrs. Shrayer," the doctor answered my mother, "if it weren't for reading you might not have a daughter now. Be happy that she is feeling better and let her read to keep herself occupied."

My poor, good mother kept quiet and let me read as much as I wanted. And my children became hers and she became a "young" mother with young children.

I did not read the books; I devoured them. In a couple of weeks' time I had finished the doctor's books. Then I started going to the municipal library. And so I read, day and night. I did not want to sleep or to eat, only to read. I spent three years reading books until I was finished with the library. Then I found out that the Zionists had a library, so, for the sake of the books, I became a member of the Zionists. And then I became active and enrolled my children in their Hebrew school. This made me happy. My children learned well and sang Hebrew songs at the Zionist events. And I became very friendly with them and took an active part in all Zionist work. And I started to write again.

In 1910, I published a sketch in the *Lemberger Togblat* by the title "Deborah," under the penname "Shoshana."[13] I received a letter from the blessed Moyshe Frost,[14] who was then the editor, saying I should try to write something else and send it to them—for an honorarium, naturally. That also made me happy. And so I wrote for the *Togblat* for two years before I left for America.

Writing placed me in a new world, a new life. I thought that I was already a polished writer. I thought that there was limited room in Galicia for Yiddish literature, but that America would be the right field for me. I started to dream of America. And since my husband was already in America, I started to aspire to go to America. But my husband did not want to stay in America. He would send me money so I could pay off the debts and he could come home. We even paid off the debts of my husband's fellow heirs, who had their greatest revenge in our failure.

In 1911, elections took place for the parliament in Vienna, and the Zionists put forward Dr. Zipper against Dr. Loewenstein. Daszynski of the Socialist Party and Witik of the Ruthenians also ran.[15] People expected a stormy election, because of the vice mayor of the city, Yakob Fayershteyn, who was almost the mayor himself.[16] The Polish mayor let him administer the city, seeing as how Yakob Fayershteyn had great power over everyone and ran everything with an iron fist. Yakob Fayershteyn gave his word to the Polish Republic,[17] who put forward Dr. Loewenstein, that they would win. He assured them that they would win the election.

All the other parties worked with all of their might. The Zionists also threw themselves with all their might into winning the seat in parliament for their party. Dr. Stand[18] came out to us from Vienna and spoke for Dr. Zipper. Dr. Ignacy Schiper, Dr. Pachtman, Dr. Shuster, and Dr. Bankenrot all spoke, agitating the Jews of Drogobych to elect Dr. Zipper, as a Jew and as a Zionist.[19] All of the speakers raged with fire and with pleas to vote only for Dr. Zipper. We, the Zionist supporters, filled the hall and gave the guests a great ovation, and after their speeches and the promises of what Dr. Zipper would do for the Jewish people, we were almost certain that we would win. The other candidates did the same—gave speeches, held meetings—and each one hoped that he would be the winner. But the mayor of the town, Yakob Fayershteyn, decided differently. He decided to force the city to elect his Polish candidate, Dr. Loewenstein. And he really did force it through. What he could not do by the will of the people, he forced through by the will of fire and blood.

I went around with the Zionist Party collecting as many ballots from the voters as possible. I already had something of a reputation in town as a writer, so they had a bit of respect for me. None of my acquaintances refused me; they all gave us their ballots.

Yakob Fayershteyn was a cousin of my father. His mother was my grandfather's sister. He used to do my father favors. If it happened that something came up in his business, where he sometimes had trouble, he would always help him. So Yakob Fayershteyn sent for my father and was angry with him that I, his daughter, was his determined opponent and was working with the Zionists. He had not expected me, a relative, to be against him. My father asked me to give up my work against Yakob Fayershteyn, but I would not hear of it. I remained with the Zionists until the last minute. Unfortunately, our hard work did not bring results. Dr. Loewenstein was elected by the greatest fraud, and by bloodshed in which thirty-seven members of the public were shot to death and tens were wounded.[20] I stood by and saw the terrible catastrophe. I saw a bride, with her wedding dress in her hand in a white bag, fall dead, two days before her wedding. Her bridegroom lost his mind from the pain. That terrible event had such an effect on me that I decided then to flee the city where, out of ambition, a Jew could help a Polish clique win through fraud and blood. (I described the entire incident thoroughly in the newspapers a couple of years ago.) I sent Yakob Fayershteyn a note saying that I was ashamed that he was my relative.

After those events, one could hear the Polish anti-Semites gnashing their teeth that it would not be long before they settled with the *Zydzi*, Polish for "Jews." Let the Old Man close an eye and they would go at the Jews. (By "Old Man," they meant the good Emperor Franz Josef, who was a liberal person and gave the Jews equal rights with all other peoples. They could not stand this.) They hoped that the emperor would die and anticipated what would come later—the world war in which the Poles took back their *ojczynza*, their fatherland.

The Jews heard it all and fearfully awaited the terrible catastrophe, which unfortunately came. Everyone still remembers that war, when the Poles became the rulers over Poland and the Jews suffered.

With all of these experiences and expectations, I decided to flee Galicia. But I knew that my husband would not send for me to come to America. So without waiting I surprised my husband and came on my own, against his wishes.

My husband had been in America for five years and kept writing that he would soon be coming home. But he still did not come. He was earning good money, so he thought it a shame to leave, knowing what kind of fortune awaited him at home.

Now, I knew that my parents would not let me go to America. They were always afraid that they would lose me. I tried to convince my father to let me go to America to bring my husband home. "I will leave you the children, so you will have secure collateral that I will come home." My father even said that he would give me money for expenses to go and bring my husband home. He wanted to turn the business over to us to run, because he did not feel strong enough to work. But when it came time for me to leave, he changed his mind and did not want to let me go. My mother cried that I would die on the ship and would be thrown into the sea. Where she got that idea, I do not know. She must have heard something that stuck in her mind and made her afraid. But I did not allow myself to be held back from going.

I had made up my mind and I went. My father no longer wanted to give me money, and he thought that that would stop me. But I had enough of my own money for expenses. I even traveled second class on a fine ship, the *Augusta Victoria*. But I had already arranged for my cousin to bring my children over, and, in exchange, I brought her to America at my expense.

When I came to say farewell to my parents, they did not want to say goodbye. My mother went into the other room and started to beat her head with both hands. She could not have bewailed me any more loudly if I had lain stretched out on the ground. But there was nothing I could do. I had already sent money to a shipping agency in Lemberg for my ship's ticket, and I had to go. I had decided that I had to go against their will, however much it hurt them. And I left without saying goodbye. At the last minute, my father reconsidered and he and my brother came running to the train when I was already in the compartment. I saw them for the last time only through the window of the train as they stood crying and shouting after me to have a safe and good trip. My children were also at the train station with the cousin, who stayed with them and who later brought them to me in America. And my sister and cousins were there, everyone waving white handkerchiefs to me and wishing me a good trip.

In the compartment, I met two gentlemen who were traveling some-where together. They saw me saying goodbye, so they asked me where I was going. I told them that I was going to America.

"Are those your children?"

"Yes," I answered.

They looked at me in wonderment and asked, "Does a mother leave for America and part with her children, as if it were nothing?" And I saw tears in their eyes. It gripped my heart and I shouted out, "My dear sirs, I have parted with five children! My mother is sitting at home, wailing and cry-ing. She did not want to part with me. My father came running to say goodbye. He did not want to say goodbye either. But I have stayed strong. And you want to break my courage?" The two men did not say another word. But they moved out of the compartment and left me alone.

I got a hold of myself so I would not break down, and traveled on with the same courage. Stubbornly, I decided that I should be calm so that I could travel on.

On board, the *Augusta Victoria* was gorgeous, almost luxurious. Every-thing in the dining hall sparkled with cleanliness and tidiness. At the first lunch I saw butter, cheese, and cold meats on the same plate, and I was immediately seized with fear of the non-kosher food. I sat there without eating. The maitre d' came up to me and asked whether I did not like the food that they had served. If not, they would give me what I wanted.

"No, Mr. Maitre d', I don't want to eat because I see that it isn't kosher. Is it possible to be given just bread and tea?"

"No, madam. We have a table for Jews who don't eat non-kosher food. I will seat you at that table—but it isn't nearly as nice as these tables."

I rejoiced, and he sat me at a long table, like at a Jewish celebration. On both sides of the table sat bearded Jews and women. They received me cordially, and I passed the time amiably with my fellow travelers for the whole trip, during which the sun shone brightly and everyone felt good because of the good weather. And so I made the entire trip in eight days and arrived in America, healthy and fresh.

I sent my husband a postcard that I was coming. But the card arrived three days after I did. They did not make it difficult for me to leave the ship, because I had a letter from my husband.

I had very little baggage, only a small satchel with a couple of things. When I arrived, I did not want to drag around my satchel, so I put it in storage on the ship. I hired a cab—a horse and buggy, which then still existed at the station. I gave the driver my husband's address and he brought me to the house where he was staying with his sister's daughter on Allen Street.

The Surprise in America

On Saturday evening, I went up to my husband's niece on the third floor and appeared as if I had fallen from the sky. Everyone in the house was so surprised to see me that they could not say a word. My husband started to faint from the surprise.

"How? When? Why did you come?" they started asking when they recovered.

"I came by train and by ship, and here I am," I answered with a laugh.

"And where are your bags?" the niece asked, looking at me.

"My bags? In storage. They will bring them to me. I didn't want to drag my bags around," I answered.

"Look at that! A lady from Broadway! So dressed up! And aren't you tired?"

"Why should I be tired? Was I working as I traveled?"

No one could get over me. I wore a light gray little suit with a lovely black hat, with a pocketbook on my arm. That's all.

They could not take their eyes off me, so good did I look.

Only then did they kiss me and start to ask about everyone.

"And the children?" my husband asked. "What did you do with the children?" He thought that I had put the children in storage as well.

I laughed and assured him that the children had remained at home in good hands, that they were beautiful and healthy, and that each child sent him heartfelt regards until they would see him.

My husband considered it scandalous of me to come so unexpectedly without letting him know.

"Why did you come running? Did you think that I had someone else here?"

"Maybe so," I said provocatively. "When a man has been away from his wife for six years, there could be another wife."

"Not Uncle Moyshe," the niece mixed in. "He loves you too much to trade you for another."

"But how can a mother go away and leave behind five children?"

"A mother can do it when she sees no future for her children in poor, dark Galicia," I answered. "Before long you will see what will happen there. War is in the air. The anti-Semitic Poles are sharpening their teeth to settle with the Jews, although the Jews are guilty of nothing. The Jews at home tremble for what is soon to come, but they can do nothing. Anyone who can do so must escape from the fire."

"Oh, those are your philosophical ideas," they all said when they heard me talk. "Even if there is a war, they will take the soldiers. But your children won't be soldiers because they're still little. What does it have to do with those Jews who can no longer be soldiers?"

"Well, you will find out later," I said. "Would that it will be as we hope. But hearing the riled-up anti-Semites speak makes the blood run cold."

"Well, enough already. Since you are here already, good luck," my niece's husband said.

"Better give her something to eat," he said to his wife. "In any case, she must be tired and hungry."

"Really! Look how we got to talking and forgot about that," said Esther, my husband's niece, and she got busy preparing food for me.

Nevertheless, I had a big struggle with my husband until he sent for the children. He wanted me to go back myself, and he still wanted to stay for a little while to make more money in order to open some sort of business back home. But I insisted on bringing my children to America. I cannot say that his niece helped me to fight against him with arguments and evidence of how we would all be happy when the children were in America.

"They will study and go to work to help you out and you will want for nothing," I argued.

I Become a Housewife in America

After much talk and debate, my husband was barely convinced. Two days later, we took a small apartment with a bit of cheap furniture and, with luck, I became an American housewife.

*Landslayt** found out about my sudden arrival and came to get news of their families and fellow townspeople. Some said jokingly that I was the only one who did not trust my husband and so had come uninvited. The main thing was that I could leave my children and travel alone. They also considered it scandalous of me.

It took me long enough to persuade my husband to send for the children. I used to cry through the night from longing and thinking about what my children were doing. But, finally, I broke through my husband's stubbornness and he sent ship's tickets for the children and for my cousin —a girl of twenty-two. She was somewhat educated, and she was not a shallow girl. One could rely on her. And five months later, my children arrived.

When the *Freiheit* was founded, it started to publish my sketches and short stories under the leadership of the Epsteins, and later K. Marmor.[21] Naturally, they did not pay an honorarium. And although I had nothing to do with Communism, my work was good for their newspaper because I wrote about the life of the poor and oppressed in Europe and America. Later, they gradually started to publish my things in other newspapers, like the *Yidishes tageblat,* which still existed then, and in the *Froyen zhurnal* and the *Yidisher Amerikaner.*[22]

When the blessed Louis Miller organized the *Naye varhayt,* I worked for him the whole time, describing institutions until the paper shut down.[23] I will never forget that man and how hard he suffered not being able to continue with his work. On the last day, I went to the office and no one was there but him. It was terribly cold because the steam had been shut off. Only one radiator was still a little warm, and I found him sitting on the radiator, blue and shivering from the cold. That same day, they took him to the hospital, where he died. Unfortunately, more than one great person has had such a bitter end.

When the war ended, I started to receive letters from my family. Every letter included loud complaints about their misfortune and ruination. They rejoiced that God had planted the idea in me to run away to America and save my children from certain death. And I started sending them as much as I could: money, clothing, food.

My father wrote me that I had gone, like Joseph to Egypt, to be their provider, as Joseph was the provider for his father Jacob and his brothers. I lost my only sister in the war, together with her husband. They left behind five children, all of whom I wanted to bring to America. But I only succeeded in bringing one girl. A second was stopped in the middle of the trip and sent back. Now they are victims of Hitler, may his name be erased.

In 1925, I published my first book of stories. In 1930, I published my second book, a novel.[24] I hoped to publish many more books, because I had many novels and stories in print, but unfortunately now is not the time for it. But I still hope that I will live to see a couple more books. In 1935, a play of mine was produced, giving me the means to support my family in Europe, because it was something of a success and brought in a little money for them.

In 1932, I made a trip to Europe. Actually, I went to see my old mother, to whom I had not said goodbye. I still had it on my conscience. I did not enjoy the trip at all, because I found great poverty and desolation there. The houses were shot up and the people went around half-naked. One young woman came to me in a torn man's coat; under the coat, she did not even have a dress. The whole city besieged me when they heard that the American had come. Each person cried, pleaded for help, and begged me to look up their friends and their *landslayt* in America so they could help them. It was a great pity to see everyone so clearly in poverty. Poverty showed on everyone's face. My brother did not even have a tablecloth to lay on the table for the Sabbath. From all his wealth, only a mountain of ash remained, because the Russians had burned his houses. He had lost his pretty young wife and was left with four small children, his old sick father-and mother-in-law, and my old, sick mother. My mother was then eighty-eight years old. She lived to be ninety-two. That shows that one does not die of troubles, when one is destined to live. I used to send her ten dollars a month to live on, but my brother used to take it from her, although I sent him extra.

I visited the *Lemberger tageblat* and the Yiddish newspapers in Warsaw, where they received me nicely.

When I came home, I thanked God properly for the first time that he had led me on the right path to America, the free country where I could make decent people of my children. They are educated professionals and conduct themselves in a Jewish and humane manner. They devote themselves to various charitable works and are ardent supporters of Hadassah.*

My son studied in the Rabbi Isaac Elhanan Yeshiva.[25] He is a pious Jewish young man, a fine cantor by trade.

My husband is what he wanted to be. He is a pious Jew who sits and studies with other Jews. And that is his whole life—to be a Jew. He says that if one wants to be a pious Jew one can be one, no matter where one is in the entire world. No one can keep anyone from being pious.

I continue with my work. I give a little time to the charities to which I belong. And the rest of the time, I work for my family and for my writing, which I publish in various newspapers in the city and out of town, wherever I can. The main thing is that God should grant the true salvation of real peace, to redeem us from our dark exile.

New York
September 3, 1942

NOTES

1. Kislev corresponds to November-December.

2. Franz Josef I of Hapsburg (1830–1916), emperor of the Austro-Hungarian Empire from 1848 to 1916, promoted full legal emancipation of the Jews, which came about in 1867.

3. Many pious Jews are reluctant to swear oaths that they might later unwittingly violate, or that invoke God's name for their own interests.

4. Reb Yitskhok Ayzik Eichenstein (1804–1872) was rebbe of the Zhidachov Hasidic dynasty, which stressed the importance of the kabalistic tradition. *Tsadik* (righteous man) is an alternative term for a Hasidic rebbe.

5. A reference to the local draft board.

6. The ninth day of the Hebrew month of Av, a fast day commemorating the fall of the ancient temples in Jerusalem.

7. Probably Dolgoye, also known as Dolhe Podbuskie.

8. Pious Jewish men wear a garment that fits over their heads and has fringes on the four corners, as specified in the Bible. Usually, this is worn as an undergarment, but Meyer wore it on top.

9. Possibly the Strii.

10. Uri Ha-Kohen Yolles (1833–1910) established his dynasty in Sambor in 1878.

11. Rabbi Meshulem Rokeakh served as rabbi of Borislav at the beginning of the twentieth century.

12. The yeshiva in Khust, in Subcarpathian Ruthenia, was established by Rabbi Moses Schick, rabbi of Khust from 1861 to 1879. Known for its rigorous orthodoxy, it primarily trained rabbis for Hungary.

13. *Shoshana* is the Hebrew word for rose.

14. Moyshe Frostig (1887–1928), Yiddish journalist and Zionist leader, was editor of the *Togblat* (established 1904) from 1909 until the newspaper ceased publication in 1926. In 1922 he was elected to the parliament of independent Poland.

15. Gershon Zipper (1868–1921) was a lawyer and Zionist leader. Nathan Loewenstein (1859–1929), an assimilationist and Polish nationalist, served as a deputy in the Austrian parliament and later in the Polish *sejm* (parliament), as did the Polish Socialist Ignacy Daszynski (1866–1936). Daszynski played a leading role in the establishment of the independent Polish government in 1918.

16. As vice mayor of the town and head of the Jewish community council, Yakob Fayershteyn was known for his efforts to suppress his political opponents.

17. It is unclear what Schoenfeld means by this—perhaps simply the Polish nationalists.

18. Zionist leader Adolf Stand (1870–1919) served as a member of the Austrian parliament.

19. Moyshe Pachtman and Avrom Bankenrot were leaders of the local Zionist organization. Ignacy Schiper (1884–1943), historian and Zionist, served in the Polish *sejm* after independence.

20. Drogobych was indeed the scene of serious disturbances during the 1911 elections. Troops were called in and a number of civilians were killed, though other sources put the death toll at twenty-six.

21. The American Communist Party's Yiddish daily organ, the *Freiheit* (Freedom, founded 1922) was known in its early years for publishing high-quality Yiddish literature. Kalman Marmor (1879–1956), Yiddish writer, journalist, literary critic, and political activist, began as a Labor Zionist before becoming one of the leading Jewish Communist figures in the United States. One of the founders of the *Freiheit,* Shachno Epstein (1883–1945) returned to Russia in 1929. *Freiheit* editor Melech Epstein (1889–1979) later broke sharply with Communism.

22. *Yidishes tageblat,* a New York daily founded in 1885, was one of the first successful Yiddish newspapers in the United States. Representing Orthodox opinion, it merged with the *Morgn zhurnal* in 1928. The *Amerikaner* (founded in 1905) was a very popular Yiddish weekly magazine.

23. Miller (1866–1927) was one of the founders of the Socialist *Forward* in 1897. He left that newspaper in 1905 and established the *Varhayt* (Truth, 1905–19), which had Zionist as well as Socialist leanings, and which he edited until 1916. In 1925 he attempted to start a new newspaper, *Di naye varhayt* (New Truth), but it failed within a year.

24. *Bilder fun lebn* (Scenes from Life) was published in New York in 1925; *Blut farvandshaft* (Blood Relations) was published in New York in 1930.

25. The Rabbi Isaac Elhanan Theological Seminary (RIETS), named for Lithuanian Rabbi Isaac Elhanan Spektor (1817–1896), was founded in New York in 1897. It later became part of Yeshiva University.

Chapter 6

My Future Is in America

Rose Silverman (Eyne fun zeks, One of Six)

b. 1892, Berdichev, Ukraine
To U.S.: 1913, New York

Rose Silverman (fig. 12) relates a complex, gritty, life-or-death struggle to en-sure her future by emigrating to the United States against the wishes of her religious father, whom she feared, resented, and deeply respected. The author details the deadening poverty in which she came of age. Books became both her refuge and her rescue after she taught herself to read and write using a prayer book and a letter-writing manual she found at home. Her palpable desire for knowledge brought her into the sphere of the local intelligentsia, who introduced her to the labor movement to which she became a dedicated, lifelong adherent. In the United States, Silverman partook of the vibrant political culture and social life of the immigrant milieu in New York City. After marriage, she continued to work as a seamstress and was proud to have educated her only son in the spirit of her political and spiritual home, the Workmen's Circle.

One can answer the question in just a few words: because things were bad for me and hardship drove me to leave my old home. It's just that simple.

But I want to return to that time many years ago to recall my child-hood, which, it seems, I never had.

At three and a half years of age I lost my mother. I was the fourth of six children, three sons and three daughters. The youngest was six months old. I was born in Berdichev, Kiev Province. I believe that all six children were born there. To this day, I do not know what circumstances forced us to leave Berdichev and settle in Cheroshne, a small town near Berdichev. There in that small town, we lost our mother.

Fig. 12. Rose Silverman with her son, Philip, in New York, February 1945. Courtesy of Ellen Elias

My father told me of the accident that resulted in her death. It was like this: I had an older sister, and my mother loved her more than me. (This was also an accident. I have a brother eleven months younger than I; we were small children together. Once, when my mother was holding the child in her arms and nursing him, I came to her, asking for a piece of bread. As my father always told me, she was nearsighted as I am and she didn't notice that there was a hole in the bread and that the child had stuck a finger of his left hand in the hole. In this way she cut his finger off. I recall that, as an older child, people used to throw this in my face. This was the reason she didn't love me.) Anyway, once, when my older sister and I were playing outside, my mother looked out and yelled to my sister that we should go play in the shade and not in the sun. To cross to the shady side, we had to go through the stable where my father—apparently it was still in the good times—kept a nice horse and cart. Just then a deaf man was cleaning the stall where the horse was standing. It was a Friday. When we walked through, the deaf man started gesturing with his hand and let out a stern voice. I didn't yet know then that there were deaf people in the world and it really scared me. I fell and fainted with a shriek.

My mother, thinking that it was my older sister—Malke was her favorite—also got a fright. I don't remember what happened next, but on Monday she died.

It didn't take long before my father, who loved me very much, took me by the hand. We went with a gentile driver to a village somewhere nearby. There I accompanied him under his wedding canopy while he married someone else.

I was four years old then. Well, I wasn't alone. As I have said already, we were six children. I did not speculate about their feelings toward our stepmother, so I don't know what they thought and felt. Neither do I think it's that important to tell about it. Stepmothers are an old story. There is already too much said of stepmothers, and mine was no exception. I didn't love her and never spoke with her. Even when I needed to tell her something, I just didn't. When I didn't want to obey her, I told her to do it herself. Life with her was as it is with all stepmothers.

When I was a child, I heard it said that, when a wife dies, she takes everything with her to the grave. Apparently, it was like that with my father. He told me that he had been something of a wealthy man in Berdichev. After my mother's death, everything was lost. I was six years old when I felt hardship and sought work for ten kopeks a week. I don't know exactly what my work was, nor how long I worked there. It seems to me that I had to untangle balls of wool.

My father was one of the first men who had to present themselves for military service at twenty-one years of age. I think that was the reason he had left his birthplace Medzhibozh and settled in Berdichev under a false name. Then, the tsar issued a decree that all those who had resisted the draft in earlier years would be punished, and that they should present themselves again for military service and also register any children they had. My father, being by nature an honest person, was happy to do this because the fear of carrying a false name never gave him any peace. Since his eldest son was of age, he brought him in and presented himself for military service as well. But because of this, he had to return to his birthplace, Medzhibozh.

Of course, he couldn't take the entire family with him, and he abandoned us to our stepmother. As through a thick haze, scenes fly by, pieces of torn, crumbled days, some earlier, others later, of nakedness, going barefoot and hungry—and obviously unhappy. Still more images swim ceaselessly before my eyes. Finally, we are all in Medzhibozh in an earthen gentile house in the peasant settlement, on the bare ground with our bundles at our heads.

We could read the question on my father's face: What now? But we could find no answers anywhere.

My father was a "poor man." He could make the best and most beautiful saddles, for women too. But he didn't have anything to occupy his hands, because Medzhibozh did not need saddles. Although there was a large military camp, they had their own saddles. My oldest brother was nonetheless drawn to the work, but the younger one went to yeshiva.*

I don't recall how long we had to suffer like that, only that I had to drag bundles of straw to heat up the stove. We worked ourselves to death. I understood the situation in the house very well and wanted to earn something, but how? What should I do? Seen through my childish eyes, it seemed that everyone in town was killing himself to make a living and I was no exception.

I couldn't read or write, but I knew that it was very bad if you couldn't. My will is apparently stronger than anything. I found a printed alphabet in a prayer book or a Haggadah[1]—I don't remember. About each individual letter, I asked: What is this? After that, I started to put words together in my head. Then I asked about the punctuation. I kept my head in the prayer book all the time, until I learned to read a bit. But writing, how would I learn to write? Sometimes a coincidence is the best thing. By coincidence, I came upon a Yiddish letter-writing manual in which the Yiddish alphabet was written down, and I quickly comprehended it. I already knew the meaning of all the letters. Reading and writing soon became clear to me.

It didn't take long before I wrote a little letter to my father and handed it to him to read. It began, "My father could . . ." He was amazed and asked me how I had learned to do this. I told him how. Of course, it was chicken scratchings, but for a child in those years and under those circumstances, it was a wonder. My father promised that he would send me to Avrom the

Scribe to learn how to write, and he kept his promise. But he couldn't keep it up for more than a month because he had to pay forty kopeks a month, and we didn't have it.

But this set me on my way. I didn't need any more lessons. As long as I could read printed letters, I didn't take my eyes from the prayer book or the *Taytsh khumesh,** the *Kav ha-Yashar,** and all the *tekhinahs.** I read anything I could get my hands on and copied many things without knowing what I was doing.

As I said, my father was a pious Jew, and he had shown me how to pray daily. During the good times, my older brothers had grabbed some education. They learned a little reading, writing, and praying, how to chant the weekly Torah portion. It was obvious that a Jew had to be able to do these things. My second brother even went to yeshiva and received rabbinic ordination. But as the fourth child in very bitter circumstances, there was no discussion of me going to study. As I said, though, my will was stronger than anything, and, in a very short time, I could write, read, and speak good Hebrew. Another thing appealed to me: my father's chanting of the weekly Torah portion. Nor did it take me long to learn trope, and I could do that too.[2]

Meanwhile time passed. The hard life and the filth around town were not so sweet. I understood that I needed shoes and a dress and none were to be had. To this day, I don't remember a single joyful childlike day, but I found for myself something of a distinct delight in the pages of books. I kept searching for books until I came to a "thirty-two book,"[3] and here I was utterly astonished. I started to look for more. Seek and you shall find. I read whatever came into my hands. What kind of reading material could I get back home some thirty years ago? Shomer's* novels and others, "thirty-two books" and other such things. If something came into my hands, it became reading material to me.

Then my brother, the yeshiva student, became a bit freer in his thinking and started looking at life with different eyes. Of course, he could easily get better books for me. I remember when he brought me the first book, a book by Dineson.* If I'm not mistaken, it was *The Two Sisters.* When I read this, I was so surprised. I quickly understood the difference. I put all the silly stories away and started devouring better literature: Dineson,* Spector, Peretz, Mendele, Sholem Asch,[4] and on and on. All these writers carried me away to other worlds. I saw another life. Then my eyes were opened even more to the filth around the town of Medzhibozh.

Time doesn't stand still. I grew older, not in the course of years but in the course of days that were as long as years to me. Although I was still almost a child, I nonetheless understood that something was not "right," but I didn't know what. I would ask my father why all the people had nothing to eat and went around naked and barefoot. He answered me with a pious expression on his face, "God punishes those who have sinned against God and the punishment is that they have no livelihood or have other troubles. God blesses those who are not sinful with all good things." Not coming into contact with people who were, as they say here, "well off," I thought that all paupers were sinful.

Then I asked him, "What are your sins that you have no livelihood? As far as I can see you are a pretty pious Jew." I paid close attention to my father and noticed that he was not only pious but honest as well.

I started to take an interest in the more well-to-do, as much as I could, being a child. I considered them thoroughly and didn't see anything better about them than my father. So I went to him with a question again: "What's going on? What does it mean, Papa? I've heard of so-and-so, and he is rich and his children go to *gymnasium,** and they have a servant in their house. And here you are so pious, yet you never have anything for the Sabbath." To this, I received a good answer from my father. He simply gave me such a whipping that I kept my mouth shut and didn't ask any more questions. I thought about this on my own a great deal, however, and soon freed myself from everything connected to piety. Yet I didn't dare say a word or do anything about it.

One time, it was the eve of Yom Kippur.* We did everything in the most pious way. According to my father's custom he did not speak until after the final Yom Kippur service. I watched everything. It was indeed melancholy. It is still impossible to forget the trembling of Yom Kippur eve back home. On the evening before Yom Kippur, we ate our meal before the fast and reflected a little. I began to think about the next day, how I wanted to pay close attention to all the pious people, and the still more pious people. My father did not say a word after the blessings following our dinner. I knew it had to be that way from the last meal before Yom Kippur until after the final service.

There was no question that I had to fast, but while being drawn into the holiness of the day myself, I also wanted to look at others at the same time. I could swear that everyone had different faces on this day. The Jews in their white ritual robes gave me the impression that they might have had more access to God than my father because, although my father was a pious Jew, he didn't wear a ritual robe.[5]

Without giving it a thought, I went home. No one was home, and I sat down to record all my impressions. When the time came for the first or second break in the prayers, my father entered the house. When he caught sight of me writing, he just stood there. Unable to speak out loud, he gestured with his hands and screamed, "Huh? Yom Kippur!" I understood what he meant by "huh," and I said that I had forgotten that it is forbidden to write on Yom Kippur. Another "huh" soon followed with which he let me know that in the evening I would get what was coming to me.

Now, after all these years, I can't picture for you how I felt until night came. My father came back from synagogue and found me sitting in fear. He said, "A good week to you," and started smearing the corners of the house with honey. This was supposed to bring a good livelihood to the household in the new year. Then he called me to him and asked, "Why did you write on a day like today, which even a fish in water knows not to do? Don't you fear God at all? Just tell me the truth. If you don't, I'll flay you." I noticed that there were tears in his kind eyes. I started to cry too. I didn't justify myself. I just cried and couldn't stop. I never heard anything else about it. So in my young, but unchildlike, life, I walked around with doubts. It seems that a girl is never a child. I believe this based on my own experience.

Meanwhile, I found friends among the educated group in town. I listened to their talk, and new thoughts came into my head. I kept thinking, and there was a calling in my soul. I asked my friends to give me the reading material that they were talking about. My new friends did not refuse me. They gave me badly printed booklets on thin paper, but to me they were like gold. I was so enthusiastic about this new literature. Of course, I didn't give up my previous reading, but I left out many Russian, French, and German books. Years later my friends called me "the walking library." I read only Yiddish, of course; I didn't know any other language. I tried studying Russian with my knowledgeable friends, but I didn't learn much.

Yet reading and the will to learn did not bring me shoes or dresses. Nakedness, bare feet, and the lack of the necessities of daily life forced me to learn how to sew. When my father got wind of this, he became angry and started yelling, "I need another tailor? I have one already." He meant that my older sister was already earning some ten rubles a year as a seamstress. In other words, he was not so enthusiastic. But I, having already read Socialist books, felt some pride in being a worker. I explained this to my father and showed him that it was not hateful to be a worker, but it was hateful not to have what you need. It seemed to me that I understood the Socialist literature so well because I had already sensed the injustices of life that choked me so. To me, poverty was already an open book. I understood clearly the ways of economic life, thanks also to Karl Marx's *Political Economy.*[6] With tact and childlike fear of my father, I explained the reasons for his poverty. He listened to me and wondered how I had come to this. As usual, he wouldn't and perhaps couldn't give in to me and told me to be quiet, but without anger or reproof. So time passed and I learned to be a seamstress. At first, I didn't make any money. I had to work for free for six months before I would get paid.

This was in 1903. The air was already filled with strike fever, even in our town. I used to get a newspaper through my wealthier friends, and then the educated and well-to-do people founded a library that also had newspapers and journals. The local workers would go there to read, and that's how we knew the meaning of a strike. Soon, a small group of Bundists* and Labor Zionists* formed, of which I later became a member. Although I was a worker with all my heart and soul, I still had something in me that wouldn't let me join the Bund. I was a "party member" against the bourgeoisie, but what did that mean? The poor little town of Medzhibozh didn't give anyone the opportunity to belong to a party in the long run. If one became a party member, he quickly disappeared into a big city.

I can't remember any dates. I only know that during my childhood, and even after I had grown up a little, there were no calendars hanging on the walls. When someone did need a certain date, it was on the Hebrew calendar. Therefore, I am writing things down in order as I recall it. If I were to describe every Sabbath or holiday on which nothing happened to leave me with good memories, and if I were to write about everything that I felt each day, it would take a very long time. Therefore I'll just say that the hardship never let up and accompanied me always. So when I say, living under such circumstances, that "I am what I am," I am satisfied. You can believe me.

At any rate, I learned how to sew. We worked in a kitchen with an earthen floor. The full slop-tub was always standing in there. It was always wet all over, and a rivulet would also sometimes leak out toward the side where we worked. Besides me, two older girls worked there. They were already receiving wages. When something fell down and got soiled, the mistress would scream at us and deduct it from their wages. I hit on a plan and talked it over with the girls, namely that we should go out on strike and that our demand should be that, instead of working in the kitchen, we should work in the parlor. Although they were afraid even to think of such a thing, they listened to me. I spoke with my limited knowledge for so long that I had an effect on them. We went on strike and actually succeeded. I still didn't earn any money at that time, but she didn't want to employ me any more because of the strike.

I was, in other words, no longer a proletarian. But I did not rest. I was already a fourteen-year-old girl and needed a dress. What to do? There was no longer a place for me at home, so I went to Bar, where I had a brother, and found work sewing linens. I tricked the boss and said that I could sew well and received thirty kopeks a week, good wages at that time.

I don't recall how long I was in Bar—a year or less. Meanwhile, I got to know other workers, various "-ists" among them, including a Bundist, a very capable person I particularly liked. He suggested that I go to the city he was from. There, I could stay with his family and study until I accomplished something. I was very enthusiastic about the idea and immediately told my brother. He heard me out and didn't say anything, but he probably sent a telegram or a letter to my father right away, telling him what I wanted to do. My father was apparently afraid of the whole business, and one fine night he came and took me home. I, fearing my father, returned home quietly, absorbed in my thoughts.

Again, what to do? I could not bear the terrible poverty. My kind, wise father could not manage, and I could not rest. I went to a tailor to ask for work. He took me on for thirty rubles a year. I was very happy to be earning something and helping the household. At work, I sang for joy all kinds of little songs, worker songs, religious songs. But when the tailor arrived and heard me singing a sad song, he came over to me, took the work out of my hands and said to me, "If you sing slowly, you work slowly. And if you sew slowly, I don't need you." No more work. I had to go to the union that we had in town to get my wages for the two weeks I had worked there. My reputation as a striker was set.

I was in despair. What to do? I was not a skilled craftsperson and no one wanted to employ me. I got the idea to become a dressmaker myself. Medzhibozh was not a big city, but there were enough tailors, shoemakers, and dressmakers. Nonetheless, it gave me some footing in my meager life. I didn't go around naked and barefoot like before and I still helped out at home. I even made a coat for my father to wear on holidays. Three years passed. During that time, my beloved father got sick. My older sister was already in America. My two older brothers had started working for themselves long before, one in Bar and the other in Khmelnik. My younger sister was also in America. Only I, my younger brother with the cut-off finger, and a little baby from my stepmother were at home.

During these three years, I visited my cousin in a big city. I got to know many students there, all revolutionaries. Through this, I got to know my cousin's son, also a student, in the eighth class in *gymnasium*. He was extremely enthused about me, but I grew flushed when they spoke to me in Russian. When people took to debating contemporary issues, I also took part, but only in Yiddish.

My cousin's son was so madly in love with me "intellectually" that he would tell me that even the girls in the second year in school didn't know as much as I did. This really uplifted me. Although I was not romantic by nature, at seventeen years of age, I too pretty much fell in love. After I had to go back home, a correspondence developed between us. His letters were passionate and admiring, but I was reluctant to express my feelings toward him, knowing that he had more education than I. We corresponded for a long time, and I even received a letter from him in America. He was later killed in World War I.

Now I was back at home. With my feelings somewhat aroused, I started to see all the boys with different eyes. Although I never once spoke of love, my wise father recognized the change in me, and he asked me, "What will the future bring? Nothing will come of your books and meetings. You're already an eighteen-year-old girl. Yes, yes, already an old maid." I felt, however, a little more free with him and suggested that he should let me go to America. Although two sisters were already there, he told me that he wouldn't allow me to go and added that I was his favorite child and he needed to have me with him.

I recall one time when a couple of my friends were at our house, saying things like, "I think they are in America too. I never run into them." We talked up America so much that I once again expressed my desire to go. My father turned his face to me, and, looking over his glasses, he said, "Don't say anything and you're not going."

Feeling somewhat independent, I responded reproachfully, "Before, when I didn't want to accept your poverty as a punishment from God, you called me a scoundrel. Now am I so dear to you because I'm helping you?"

Of course, it was too bold to contradict a father. Without much of a thought, he slapped me right in the face, so hard that it soon swelled up— this was in the presence of my friends—and added, "You will go to America over my dead body."

My stepmother was no longer alive by then, and he needed me to run the household. There was only my younger brother and my stepmother's eight-year-old girl. Although I was earning something, it was very hard to live on what I earned under such circumstances. My father wanted me to have a "purpose." I wracked my brain and didn't hit on anything at all. I didn't see any "purpose" of the kind my father wanted: Of course, he meant that I was supposed to look for a husband. I had truly fine friends of higher standing, both intellectually and economically. I took advantage of the opportunity to taste some of their education, but it was only what would fit on the tip of a knife. The only things in which I found joy were books. We discussed the matter constantly.

It was quite early one morning. My father was walking around wearing his prayer shawl and *tfilin,** praying with great intent. I was then reading Max Nordau's *The Lie of the Wedding* and I said something out loud about it.[7] Once again, it turned into a discussion of "purpose."

But good heavens! I now saw life with different eyes and I could distinguish between people. I started to consider those around me and saw that I wasn't suited to anyone, because those who were intellectually beneath me were hard for me to accept, and those who were above me, well, they were above me. And here I was, thinking of venturing far away into the world. So how could I choose a husband?

So the question arose again, what will be? The passionate letters from my cousin, the student, churned in my head. He wrote to me in beautiful Yiddish and complimented me all the time that I was more intelligent than any of the girl students he knew. But I, understanding that I was far from being a girl of the intelligentsia, suffered from the belief that what he said wasn't true. In my eyes, only people who possessed an education were intelligent. In a word, life did not go on as it did in books. The life portrayed in the few books I had read was not like mine. I had taken an interest only in better literature, which truly changed me. From an ordinary girl, I had become a well-read person who could debate "every issue" in every era. To my great joy, now in middle age, I have come to consider myself intelligent.

So it went, day in and day out, questions flew in the air without answers. I was nineteen years old. I want to note that although I had suffered much during all those years, I still remained good-natured and did not get depressed. I could also tell a good joke. But, go figure, this actually hurt me in making a match. "So?" my father said to me one day, "What's it going to be? Do you think of the future at all?"

Suddenly I found the courage and, without thinking, answered, "My future is in America. Whether you like it or not."

Although I still remembered that earlier slap, I did not feel fear and spoke again.

"Papa, it's no good for a girl like me in this small town." He realized that I was right, and lowered his head. I understood that he would now let me go, and I prepared to leave.

It seems that my father took my leaving to heart, and his prophesy was realized. Just one month before my departure he died. But it didn't happen the way it sounds. First he got sick for two weeks, and his sickness used up some of the money for my voyage. Lying in his sickbed, he told me many things that I have described above and concluded with these words: "See to it, my child, that you are a respectable person in America." The next day he was dead.

What I experienced, what went on in my soul at that time, is very difficult for me to describe today. It's been thirty years and I am now a mother. It is difficult for me to return to all my old thoughts. But I braced myself and left everything behind me. Taking only my "empty" pack on my shoulders and sixty rubles in my pocket, I left for the train station.

I threw a goodbye to everything and everybody, and departed with great hopes on my long journey. The voyage? Well, it was quite an ordinary thing. Everyone's voyage was the same. And that was that. All these things and still others drove me to leave for America.

On August 9, 1913, I stepped onto the free ground of the Golden Land.

What have I gained in America?

My previous fantasies flew off, and I never flew *to* anything. The people around me laughed at all my talk and told me, "Better get a husband and get married!" And all the naysayers didn't keep quiet about it either. They tried their best. I recognized that I couldn't be my own boss in this country either. After being in New York for about two years, I went to Boston, where my two sisters lived. World War I was then going full blast, but America was not affected, as it is now. I did not worry at all; I worked and earned well and felt a bit freer without bosses over me. I joined the Young Circle League.[8] I was somewhat active in Dressmakers' Union Local 44. I say "somewhat" because I was still a greenhorn.* But I made friends there and I was satisfied. Life went on, with meetings, lectures, and other such things that I enjoyed a great deal. They made me forget all my suffering in the Old Country.

When the war quieted down and many of my friends went to New York, I no longer felt the desire to remain in Boston. At any rate, life in Boston is not like in New York. After they all dispersed, it was so empty. As I read somewhere once, you drive nature out the door and it comes back in through the window. I was now around twenty-six years old and I needed to think about a home. I had already realized that I wouldn't go far with my fantasies. When I returned to New York, I got work right away and earned a lot of money. I felt good and self-sufficient. I didn't lack for friends, and I started to attend the theater. I had many companions and completely forgot that one should get married. Maybe the right person hadn't come along . . .

It was fall. I went for a walk along Second Avenue with a few friends of mine. I saw a young man whose appearance I liked, and, in fact, one of my friends knew him. They greeted each other, but he didn't even notice me. Two weeks later, though, when by chance I met him again, I stopped him myself by calling him by name. (That friend of mine told me his name when we first encountered him.) When he heard a strange girl calling his name, it surprised him. How is it that I should know his name? We joked in this way about my boldness and got to know each other, as we met again several times incidentally.

Although I wasn't in love, he was more appealing to me than any of my other acquaintances. In the meantime, I got sick with an inflammation in my lungs and went deaf in both ears. It is easy to imagine what a girl of twenty-six years—alone, living as a boarder, deaf—would feel under such circumstances. But here fate played a trick on me again. Of all my friends and companions, no one came to visit me any more when they heard of my condition.

But the one I had met incidentally did not give up on me. He took me to big specialists and to various hospitals and truly demonstrated great courage to me. After a friendship of two years, we got married. I gave birth to a son. When my child was two years old, I became a dressmaker. Being deaf, I really suffered with my customers, trying to get them to talk to me. So I had no other occupations in life, except mutely sewing. And the child didn't give me much joy, because I could hear neither his cries nor his little bits of wisdom. My husband also lost patience with me . . . and so I suffered. Although I was then a member of Branch 315 of the Workmen's Circle,* I rarely attended meetings, because, for one thing, I was busy with work and, also, I was just so deaf that I didn't hear anything that went on.

But things also got better for me in one sense. I got very sick and the doctors told me to give up my work. Finally, after I underwent two operations, I was freed from having to work. After I recovered from my operation, I had a machine put in that allows me to hear.

Fig. 13. Cover illustration from the annual dinner journal of Workmen's Circle Branch 315, Borough Park, Brooklyn, 1935. Rose Silverman was the branch's protocol secretary. Courtesy of the YIVO Institute for Jewish Research

Here lie my accomplishments: I am the protocol secretary of Branch 315 of the Workmen's Circle (fig. 13). I was also sent as a delegate to the conference that the Scientific Institute had this year.[9] I was active in the reading circle of the Boro Park school where Susel is a teacher. I have a fine son seventeen years old who is also a member of the Young Workmen's Circle and graduated from the Workmen's Circle High School. He reads Yiddish books and is active in his club. My son studies journalism in college and during the day he works as an errand boy. My husband is also a Workmen's Circle member.

Economically speaking, I am an ordinary worker's wife. And that's it.

NOTES

1. Haggadah (Hebrew, "telling") is the book containing the home service for the Passover seder, including blessings and prayers, hymns of thanksgiving, and other material relating to the exodus from Egypt.

2. Each week in the synagogue, a portion of the Torah is chanted according to a traditional trope. As a girl, Silverman would not have been permitted to use her skill.

3. It is unclear what this was—perhaps a series of small, cheap editions.

4. Silverman is slightly mistaken. Dineson's novel was *Di tsvey mames* (The Two Mothers). Mordkhe Spector (1858–1925) was a Yiddish writer, editor, and publisher who played an important role in encouraging the development of modern Yiddish literature. Isaac Leib Peretz (1852–1915) was a Yiddish and Hebrew writer considered one of the founders of modern Yiddish literature. Peretz's works incorporate folkloric themes to further his critique of the hierarchies of traditional Jewish society. Mendele Moykher Sforim (Mendele the Book Seller, pseudonym of Sholem Yankev Abramovitsh, 1835–1917) was sometimes called the grandfather of modern Yiddish literature. Mendele's works are characterized by satirical critique of tradtional Jewish society as well as by affection for the common people. Sholem Asch (1880–1947) was a novelist and playwright known for his sentimental depictions of traditional Jewish life, whose works were widely read both in their original Yiddish and in English translations.

5. On Yom Kippur it is customary for men to wear a white, shroud-like robe called a *kitl*. Silverman may mean to imply that her father could not afford a *kitl*.

6. Silverman may be referring to Karl Marx's *Zur kritik der politischen Ökonomie* (A Contribution to the Critique of Political Economy, 1859) or to his magnum opus, *Das Kapital: Kritik der politischen Ökonomie* (Capital: A Critique of Political Economy, 1867–1894).

7. Max Nordau (1849–1923) was a physician, journalist, social critic, political activist, and one of the founders of the modern Zionist movement. *Der lign fun der khasene* (The Lie of the Wedding) was a Yiddish translation of a chapter from his critique of conventional morality and social institutions, *Die Conventionellen Lügen der Kulturmenschheit* (Conventional Lies of Our Civilization, 1883).

8. The Young Circle League was founded in 1930 as a youth arm of the Workmen's Circle. Silverman may mean to refer to the Labor League, the Massachusetts affiliate of the Workmen's Circle at the time she is describing.

9. A reference to YIVO.

Chapter 7

The Movies Pale in Comparison

Bertha (Brukhe) Fox

b. 1892, Skvira, Ukraine
To U.S.: 1922, New York

Written in two parts, Bertha Fox's dramatic and far-ranging autobiography is a rare account of an Eastern European Jewish woman's life from the turn of the twentieth century through World War I and the Russian Civil War. Fox (fig. 14) endured poverty and starvation as a child and went immediately to work as a youth. Later, she and her brother became photographers and traveled widely to support their family. Fox was the sole supporter of her family in the years leading up to and during the war, often going to great lengths to secure a livelihood. Fox's story has elements of the Socialist autobiography, detailing her conversion to the Bund, her political activism, and the euphoria, chaos, and instability of the Revolution of 1917. Perhaps the most striking aspects of her story are her descriptions of the well-known pogroms in Ukraine in 1905 and 1919–20, along with other incidences of anti-Semitism. Fox's life story, which is translated here by Jocelyn Cohen and Fruma Mohrer, is an important document of survival written by an engaging, perceptive, and shrewd protagonist.

Dear Friend,

My husband is a member of the Workmen's Circle.* Just now, reading over the Workmen's Circle periodical *Der fraynd* [The Friend; fig. 15] after a day of housework, I noticed the announcement about the contest, "Why I left the Old Country, and what I found in America."[1] To answer in a few words: I went through so much that all the movies I have seen pale in comparison. If I were to make my own movie, it would be much more vivid. And what did I find in America? A great deal: material

Fig. 14. Bertha Fox, with her husband, Morris, and her sons, Noel and Reuven, in the Bronx, during the late 1930s. Courtesy of Noel Fox

contentment, free schooling, free lectures in all languages, and, above all, calm. Calm.

It's as if I saved myself from a sinking ship, floating on a piece of driftwood between life and death. After a long time, I was rescued. Oh, how I felt then, lying on a bed in a safe house, no longer frightened by the great big fish in the sea ready to swallow me up in the their big mouths! That's how I feel when I am at home, that *here* they won't break down my door with their big boots and yell, "What are you doing, Yid? What do you have

Fig. 15. The issue of the Workmen's Circle organ *Der fraynd* (The Friend), where Bertha Fox saw the announcement for YIVO's autobiography contest. The caption on the cartoon reads: "The hand that struggles on the labor front and on the war front—The Workmen's Circle begins its campaign for a second half-million dollars in war bonds." Courtesy of the YIVO Institute for Jewish Research

there? Move fast or you'll be a head shorter!" That is why I left the Old Country. Pogroms,* pogroms without end.

And now the details: I came here in 1923. Our family lived in Kremenchug in the province of Poltava. My father, a Russian Jewish teacher in the old style, was a pauper of the first rank. It is amazing that our mother managed to set us on firm footing. All I know is that out of six children, three remained—myself, an older sister, and a brother. As soon as we reached the age of ten, we considered ourselves adults and began to work. A cousin hired me to sort the Wissotsky-brand tea that arrived from Odessa, for which I received four rubles a month in wages. I worked during the day and studied at night. My brother went to work in a photography shop. My older sister got a position as a cashier. And so, we all worked, yet barely made a living. The tsarist system was such that you couldn't keep your head above water. Then the pogroms of 1905 took place. Our home did not escape attack. People fled to wherever fate took them, wherever they could attach themselves to a relative or find some similar opportunity.

After the war of 1914 came the Russian Revolution, when governments were changed like gloves in Ukraine—Petlyura,[2] Denikin, Grigoriev, Wrangel,* and the rest—when Jews drowned in pools of blood.[3] People were swollen with hunger; they ate bread made with sawdust. Like Jews everywhere, we lived through pogroms, pogroms without end. The pogromists always burst into the houses, took whatever there was, and left. Before we could recover, it started all over. My experiences cannot be described. The Jews, powerless, could no longer bear to wait it out alone in their own houses, so they gathered together with neighbors. People from many homes—up to a hundred people or more—gathered in one house, so that their terror would not be so great.

One time, when the hooligans came to break down the doors of our house, I moved quickly to open up, to avert their fury. One of them aimed his rifle at me and stuck it against my chest. Out of terror, I broke into hysterical laughter. Taken aback, he lowered the rifle. When the other one asked him, "So, what are you waiting for?" he answered, "I can't shoot a crazy person."

Another time, they were running around looking for girls. I lay bandaged with gauze so that only my eyes and nose showed, groaning quietly but deeply. To their question, "What is this?" those around me answered, "Typhus." They were afraid of typhus. Out of unexpressed rage, they landed a few blows on my father's thin, stooped shoulders.

A third time, they came in and started harassing my brother, telling him to take off his shoes and jacket and hand them over. Then they put him against the wall and aimed a gun at him. Here my mother proved herself a hero. She pushed the gun away with her hand, placed herself in front of my brother and shouted, "Me first!" I don't know whether the bandit remembered his own mother or whether his drunken head made him dizzy. Luckily, he didn't shoot.

After that, things got quiet. The Red Army arrived and stopped the pogroms, but the papers kept warning that dark clouds still hovered over Russia and that people should remain on the alert, because sooner or later the hurricane would strike.[4] Exhausted, we resolved that even if we had to crawl on all fours, we would leave the country. But how? And to where? All the borders were closed except to those who had papers from relatives abroad. We got some rubles together and sent my brother off to Odessa, to sneak over the border into Romania. Naturally, he was in danger of being shot at the border. After he left, it took a long, long time before we got his first letter saying that he was alive. My father died of grief before his time.

Mother then began to move heaven and earth so that I could leave too. But a girl alone? Where to? How? At this point, a coincidence played into our hands. A family of three—a father, mother, and daughter—had visas for Palestine. Everything was nearly ready, but it turned out that the girl had fallen in love with a commissar and would not go. In short, I became the "daughter" and traveled with them.

Upon arrival in Constantinople, I discovered that Palestine was in crisis and it would be difficult for me to make a living there. Not wasting too much time thinking about it, I went to the Jewish Colonization Association.[5] I told them the secret that I was traveling with false papers and asked for advice on what to do. They told me to stop off in Constantinople, get work, and wait for an opportunity to travel to America. I got work in a photographic studio. Because of my brother, I knew the work well.

I soon received a visa to America through the Jewish Colonization Association. In America, HIAS* picked me up from the ship. A few days later, they took me into a shop. Four years later, I got married. I now live on the outskirts of the city and have two beautiful children. I lead a quiet life and cannot stand any noise. I love quiet and calm, although I am only in my forties.

It seems that the experiences of the past have had an effect on me. From time to time, a deep sigh escapes my heart: Who knows what happened to the others?!

[Signed] Brukhe Fox

I have just finished my letter. How many times was I in danger of being shot, of being torn to pieces? A shudder goes through my flesh recalling my experiences at the hands of those dark, ignorant powers, aroused like dogs by their leaders and a bottle of vodka! But now, so many years later, at a time when civilization has advanced so much (I will not recount all the discoveries of the scientific world in this era), one's thoughts become totally paralyzed when one reads that a doctor—a college-educated doctor —slaughters people in such a cold-blooded way: in gas chambers, cheaply and well, a certain death. Surely no one can escape their grasp. Like beasts in a cage, behind a ghetto wall, they wait each day, each hour, for death. And here comes the doctor, unprovoked, not drunk, without even a gun. With a smile on his lips, he tells them to take a seat and adds, "I will inoculate you against illness." And this is death![6]

I ask myself, why did God create us in order to rule over the beasts? To pride ourselves so much with the honor of being man that a beast can now rule over man? I remember when I learned that Germany as a nation was ranked among the civilized peoples, higher than the Asians, even higher than many other European nations. So how in the world does a nation allow itself to sink so low on account of a single maniac?! A shudder goes through me. I can't work. I would not even be surprised to read that Hitler was eating soup made from Jewish babies and that the people were licking the bones.

In response to Max Weinreich's request for more information, Fox wrote a more detailed account of her experiences.

Dear friend, Dr. Weinreich!

With great respect, I am ready to comply with your request to supplement my previous letter with more details. Perhaps it will even be too much. I hope that you will excuse me for my lack of experience.

I was born in Skvira, in the province of Kiev. I remember that during my childhood years we lived in our own house. According to my mother, we received the money for the house from my uncle in Kamenka Bugskaya who was a very wealthy lumber merchant. He preferred to give my father a little money rather than a job, which would have been much more helpful. The house consisted of two large rooms with long tables and benches on one side, and very little furniture on the other side. As I said in my other letter, my father was a teacher. Children came for lessons during the day and adults at night. We might have been able to make a living, but the tuition was very low, and the students did not always pay anyway. Sometimes the inspector would come and ask to see our permit for running a school, and the children would have to run off and disappear.

The interior side of the wall facing the street was damp and often dirty, so the children would indeed get sick. My brother and I would go from one illness to the next, scarlet fever, diphtheria, not to mention all the other childhood illnesses. I recall that my mother would leave my brother sick in bed with my father to watch over him and run by herself to the rebbe,* Reb* Moyshezon.[7] When she came back, she would say that the rebbe had given her an amulet and promised to pray to God himself. Nevertheless, he told her to call the doctor.

My mother was an intelligent woman, but very pious. She insisted that the children know all the blessings—the morning prayer, grace after meals, the bedtime prayer. She knew the *Taytsh khumesh** by heart. Truly, whatever I know about our history is thanks to Mother. She very much wanted my little brother to become a rabbi. When he was still very young, she wrapped him in a shawl and the teacher's assistant would carry him on his shoulders to *heder,** and he would squeal like a little pig.

I will stop giving details about my early childhood years here, as I don't want to try your patience too much. I could say much more. I recall that there was great poverty and that Mother wanted to help out. She tried to bake bread but it didn't go well, so she learned how to mold galoshes. This provided a livelihood, but only in season. There were times when all the children would cry in unison, "We want to eat!" Then father would leave the house and I would hear Mother saying to herself, "Good for you, you go off to the house of study, to the rebbe. Spare yourself their cries."

I recall how I would close my eyes and fantasize: Oh, how good it would be if, upon opening my eyes, *sweet* tea would flow from the lead samovar, and on the table would be the kind of bagels I had seen the window of the Turkish bakery! On the Sabbath, Mother told us not to cry in front of people, and indeed, she would make every possible effort to see to it that we had something to chew on. Father would even make wine from a few raisins for *kiddush** and *havdalah.** After he came home from synagogue, he made *kiddush* and then all of us sipped from the same little glass. After *havdalah,* he poured out the remnants, wet the tips of his fingers, and stuck them in his pockets to bring a prosperous week. On the Sabbath during the summer, all the women neighbors would sit around Mother on the earthen seats that surrounded all Russian houses while she read to them stories of Hershele Ostropoler.[8] I still remember them. We would roll with laughter.

How joyful it was for me when in the wintertime I would sneak into the tailor shop across the way. There, in a large room, stood a big table, a sewing machine, and a large wooden bed on the yellow sand that people poured over the earthen floors in preparation for the Sabbath. The workers would joke around. They would blow on the coals on which the iron was heated so that smoke and sparks would rise, or grab someone's chair from underneath him. When he went to sit down, he would fall and everyone would laugh. We saw the tailor's grandchild, a little girl with a permanently swollen foot. We would chew up a little bagel with sugar for her and put it into her mouth. All of them are now in America. My sister's friend is here in America, now a doctor's wife. I sometimes run into her.

After consulting with the rebbe Moyshezon, my parents decided to sell the house and move to Kremenchug. Because there were many people from Skvira there and Father even had a nephew, a big businessman, we might be more successful there. No sooner said than done. We sold the house, paid our debts, and left. Upon our arrival in Kremenchug, my father met with his friend, a manager of a tobacco factory, who gave him a job, but not at a machine. My father was pale and thin. Tobacco would settle in the lungs, and many workers got tuberculosis. My father did not make much of a salary, so my brother, sister, and I got jobs at Cousin Shliez's house. I received four rubles a month, my brother three, and my sister eight. At this time, I was fourteen years old.

A year passed in this way, until the 1905 pogrom broke out. A few days earlier, I had heard stories buzzing around my cousin's office: The tsar was giving freedom to the people. People were asking, Do you understand? Freedom! And we Jews—without a trade, without high rank in the merchants' guild—would not only be allowed to live in all the big Russian cities, but even in Tsarskoye Selo, the famous town near St. Petersburg! Hurrah![9]

It didn't bother me that I would sometimes work late and sleep over at my cousin's house. I had a better supper at their table than in my home. And so it was on that day, I slept over there, as usual on the divan in the dining room. I saw the servant preparing Madame Shliez's casual clothing for going out. Her girlfriend arrived and rushed her, "Hurry, hurry, don't you know who'll be there?"

Madame Shliez laughed, "And who *won't* be there? Everyone from the revolutionary underground."

"Hurry, we'll miss the best speaker!"

When they left, the servant closed the front door behind them. Shliez himself, a sick man, went to his room and I to my couch. We extinguished the lamps and it quieted down. I do not remember how long I slept.

I was awakened by the front door bell, the bell of my cousin's room, and the servant's bell. Frightened out of my sleep, I jumped to the floor and heard the hysterical cries of Madame Shliez, "Faster! Faster! Open the door! We are in danger!" The gentile maid ran down the steps from the upper floor and opened the door. Out of breath, the ladies ordered, "Quick, bring all the heavy objects, the press from the office, to barricade the front door." My cousin Shliez came out of his room and asked what had happened.

"What happened? A *massacre*, not freedom!" They explained that thousands of people had gathered in the auditorium. The speakers began to speak. Before long, the Cossacks came in on horses and began to attack, left and right, with their swords, hacking away at heads, arms, and legs. And they, the fancy ladies standing to the side, had managed to escape. And now, there we were, all of us helping the maid barricade the door. We went upstairs, closed the innermost shutters, and put out the lights in the front room. Before long, we heard voices shouting in Russian, "God Save the tsar! Beat the Jews! Hurrah!" Glass began to break all around, and they kept shouting, "Hurrah!" We all left the front rooms and went into the kitchen, which was located in another part of the apartment. It had a door, but this side led to the courtyard, which had an iron gate. Suddenly we heard a shot. Soon bullets flew and the front windows shattered. Shliez told everyone to lie down on the floor. I don't remember how long the shooting lasted, but suddenly it got quiet. Understandably, we did not sleep that night.

The house was located on Aleksandrovski Street; others used to call it Vaksalinaya. The landlord was a Gentile by the name of Padderegin. Downstairs he had a big store, and he himself lived in a side apartment. The gentile maid went downstairs in the morning to find out from him what was going on. He told her that when he heard the glass falling from his store window, he stuck his gun out of his apartment window and shot into the air in order to scare off the Gentiles (he did not know they were collaborating with the military), and the Cossacks responded by shooting up the whole house. Padderegin then realized that he had done the wrong thing. Together with his son, he took all the icons and crosses from his house and, crawling on all fours through the downstairs door to the store, placed them in the window. As it was quite light outside by now, we no longer had to fear shooting, for the crosses were protecting us. We went into the front rooms to see what was going on in the street. Through the slats of the shutters, we saw a devilish activity proceeding across the street at the *tolchok,* the secondhand market, with its rows of stores! Young gentile men and women were pulling sacks and packs from the stores that had been broken into. Others had come from the countryside with horse and wagon and were helping themselves to everything. It tore at our hearts.

We went back into the dining room. The servant brought the samovar and we had tea and something to eat. No one could speak. We sat at the table with our heads bent. The stillness was broken from time to time with sips and gulps. I felt torn by the desperate need to go home, but they didn't let me. I worried about what was happening to my family in the little house with the flimsy little chain on the front door, with no icons or crosses to protect them. Here at Shliez's house, it was dark and gloomy, the shutters drawn. The maid was not free to work, and there was no question of cleaning the rooms. She kept going in and out through the back door, looking for news. She told us terrible stories, that hospitals were packed with the wounded and that there were many dead, among other things. We stayed together in the dining room. There was no discussion of baking or cooking regular meals. The cook brought us whatever was in the icebox, butter and other things. A sadness reigned in the house, as if we were in mourning. Madame Shliez did not care what we ate and did not go into the kitchen as she usually did. A few days passed in this way.

The beds of the gentile servants were off the kitchen. By chance Madame Shliez went into the kitchen for something. We heard a commotion and followed into the kitchen. Oh dear, what have we here? Packages of cut fabric, boxes of dry goods, socks, gloves, and the like. Flushed with color, the maid stood there and defended herself: "Everyone else took things, so why shouldn't I? If the lady of the house doesn't approve, I will leave." They told her to go and she left with all the packages.

I don't recall how long the pogrom lasted, but when it quieted down, my mother came running to see what had happened to us. People had said that the whole Padderegin household had been shot and no one survived. So, thank God, we were all alive. To our questions about what they had experienced, Mother responded that all the neighbors had abandoned their homes unprotected and hidden together in a cellar. And in fact, there had been very serious looting. We did not have much of value, but they did take our most valuable things, the lead samovar and a cushion.

We went out into the street and saw flyers with large letters posted at all the street corners: "In the name of his Imperial Excellency, a decree has been issued that anyone who loots, breaks windows, etc. will be severely punished." They began to board up the stores temporarily. When the people in my cousin's office got together, I heard it said that the police chief had received a nice "present" to quiet things down earlier than in other cities. We walked silently through the streets and spoke quietly. We were not allowed to loiter. Various business people came to Shliez's office and asked each other, "What happened to Kamenyetski and Podolski? I haven't seen them."

"What? You don't know? They were looted so badly that they couldn't get back on their feet. So they scraped together a few rubles and went off to America."

The lives of those left behind slowly picked up. People began to work again just as if nothing had happened. But Mother strictly forbade me from sleeping away from home. I was to come straight home after work, and that's what I did. I now had time once again to read a book and do my homework. (I had lessons twice a week.)

My sister started to come home late. She would have various answers in response to Mother's questions: She had gone to a friend and forgot the time, or she had been invited for tea. When she did come home early, she would sit herself down with both elbows on the table over a book so that the kerosene lamp stood between us and I couldn't get close to her. I asked her, "What are you reading?"

"None of your business. I don't bother you, so don't bother me." Well, I thought, it's probably a novel. She is older than me, I am younger, so she won't tell me.

One night, after midnight, we heard a loud knock at the front door and a harsh voice: "In the name of the law, open the door!" Before we could even move to lift our heads in surprise, there was another knock, the weak little chain on the flimsy door came off, and the door opened. A few gendarmes entered with rifles and shouted, "Where is the lamp?" They found the lamp, lit it, and began to search. Two of them stood watch so we wouldn't run away. The others went into the kitchen and searched everywhere—in the oven, in the chimney, in the pots, everywhere. They told us to get out of bed. We were dressed in our nightclothes. My sister and I looked down, embarrassed.

My mother called out, "At least let us throw something on!"

"Shut up!" was the answer.

When we got out of bed, they began to overturn and grope at the bedding. They looked under the beds, in the small wardrobe, banged on the walls with the stocks of their rifles. Letting loose a few curses of the ugliest kind, they left.

Mother, a sickly woman with chronic rheumatism from that damp house in Skvira, put her hand over her heart and nodded her head as if she were about to faint. We brought her water, rubbed her temples, calmed her, and tucked her in. My sister, pale, her pretty hair loose over her nightgown, smiled strangely and said, "I am smarter than they are. I knew how to hide it!"

"What?!" Mother picked her head up from the pillow. (Father was already asleep on the oven.) "You have those forbidden things?!"

"Yes, mother!" My sister pointed to a white box hanging under the ceiling on a string. "I keep my brochures up there."

"Burn them! Burn them right now!"

With trembling hands, my sister took down the box, took out the two hidden brochures. She went into the kitchen and burned them in the oven. When she was finished, she returned to the bedroom and went over to Mother. With tears in her eyes, she quietly began, "Forgive me, Mother, but understand that things cannot continue like this. They think that when they chop off heads, arms, and legs, they chop off everything. But although they can chop up the bodies of some of the masses, they will never cut away the soul, the collective soul of the greater masses. The Russian people are like a volcano, churning inside, ready to erupt. If they pour cold ashes on the red-hot mouth of the volcano, it doesn't mean that the volcano is extinguished. Yes, Mother, I belong to the Bund* and come what may, I will not stop. But I promise you that I will never bring anything into the house again." And she kept her word.

I swallowed my sister's words like noodles with butter. A few days later, after things had quieted down at home, I went to my sister and asked her to take me along to a meeting. She threw up her hands: "No, and no! Such a little shrimp and she wants in on the action too. Don't even think about it ever again!"

Then I hit upon a plan. I spied on my sister on Yekaterinski Street and saw whom she stopped to speak with. She said something quietly to a man and then went off with another girl. Without much of a thought, I went over to the same person, tugged at his sleeve and said quietly, "I am Rosa's sister, and I want to be a member of the Bund too." I was slim and looked older than my actual age, and my complexion was dark, making me seem older. He sized me up from head to toe and said, "Okay, wait a minute, but don't stand in one place. Keep walking slowly." Before long, I felt a warm hand in mine. Someone said quietly, "Not here. We must walk further." She led me out of the crowd, and only then could I see her face in the moonlight.

I was so surprised, I froze. It was none other than Manya. (I do not wish to state her family name because I do not want to implicate anybody in my story. There are many people here from Kremenchug.) Manya, the daughter of a well-known wealthy man, was an excellent teacher, who had once been recommended to me as a tutor for the *gymnasium** examinations, but I had never been allowed in to see her. The Jewish maids would say, "Of course, child, we'll find out if Manya is home." But their superiors had strictly forbidden anyone to see her. And now here she was.

She noticed me stumbling and asked, "What's the matter, comrade, don't you feel well?"

"Oh no, I just tripped on something!"

Besides excelling in her *gymnasium* studies in Russian, she spoke good Yiddish. She walked around with me for a good few hours, explaining the meaning of the Bund and what would be required of me. I must admit that my young head did not fully grasp the depth of her words, but I was happy that Manya was leading me by the hand and calling me "comrade." That's how I became a member of the Bund (fig. 16), at barely fourteen years of age (but looking eighteen).

I did not understand the book itself, so to speak, but I liked the depiction on the cover. That is, I very much liked how the Bund carried out its work. In the summer, we would mingle with passersby at the *birzhe*,* the "exchange." When we got the signal, we would go to the shore of the Dniepr River. Once there, we would once again mingle and keep watch until everyone had arrived. At the signal, we would pair off and go down to the boats. Again at the signal, we would push off, some to the left, others to the right. Finally, we came together on the same island. We walked deep into a dense forest and sat on the grass in a circle with the speaker, either a man *or* a woman, in the center. We lifted our heads to look at the speaker, who spoke long and passionately, often gesturing with a fist to the sky. A cool wind would blow in from the shore, and those gathered in the circle would nestle together. We sometimes prolonged the reciting of "Di shvue,"* the Bundist oath, at the end.

The winters were not so cheerful. As I remember, we gathered somewhere outside the city, on a lower floor like a cellar in the home of a poor

Fig. 16. Members of the Bund in Berdichev, Ukraine, 1904, from a photograph that appeared in the *Forward* in 1934. Courtesy of the YIVO Institute for Jewish Research

shoemaker. (The cellars in private houses here in America are palaces compared to that one.) The room was packed. We stood crowded together like herring in a barrel. Outside, cadres would line the streets for several blocks to the left and right and keep an eye on things. Then a cadre would come from the courtyard and say, "Disperse! Cossacks!" It was amazing how they were able to carry out the evacuation. You could hear quiet, stern voices: "Calmly, calmly, in pairs. And if they ask you where you're coming from, the answer should be 'from a wedding.'" That's how we did it. We moved so quietly through the streets, along the walls. I never asked if anything had happened at the previous meeting because they wouldn't have told me.

So I became smarter. I asked my cousin for a raise, and he did not want to give me more than one ruble; so I left. Since I looked like an adult, I was able to register with the clerk's union. I immediately got a position as a cashier in a tobacco store. Although he was angry with me, my cousin gave me references. I liked the position. By then, we were working a fixed number of hours a day. Every day the workers received tea and a bagel, and the salary was a whole twelve rubles a month. It continued like this for a while, but the owner had another store that was doing better, so he sold the one where I worked and laid me off.

At the same time—it was summer—I caught a cold. As I was always too thin, the doctor said that in order to protect my lungs I should take a vacation or go to a spa. Since there was no extra money for such luxuries, my parents had a plan. Mother was from Lysyanka, and a sister of hers was still there. I would go there. There were pine trees in the area, so I would get the cure I needed. No sooner said than done. Just as I got to my Aunt Breyne's place, a neighbor suddenly arrived, a mother of three children, who was also unwell. There was no doctor in Lysyanka, so she had no one to ask for advice. If the cure for my illness, similar to her own, was pine extract, then she knew what to do. We hired a Gentile and a horse and wagon and went to Bedeshch, a village near Lysyanka with many pine trees.

I settled into a gentile home and so did my companion, in a house a little further on. We were happy. We had fresh milk, eggs, fresh vegetables, butter, cheese, baked goods, all for a very low price. Things were going well for us. We had heard that in the village there was a nobleman, the landlord of the village, with many servants and other luxuries, but we didn't pay much attention to this. One day we were both sitting under a tree. It was a hot day and a well-dressed man came over to us and asked us in a stern tone of voice, "What are you doing here?"

"We are resting from the heat."

He threw us an angry look and left.

That very night, I was in a deep sleep on a bench near the window when I heard a commotion. The still of the night was shattered by a banging on the door.

"Open up!"

The gentile owner of the house got out of bed. Someone pounded on the door again with a heavy object. "I said open up!"

The head of the house said angrily, "What, there's a fire somewhere again? No firemen here and they still don't let you sleep! Vaska, where's the bucket?"

But at this point there was a harder knock and a yell. "In the name of the law, open up! Otherwise, I'll open it myself!"

When they opened the door it turned out that there was no fire anywhere, but the problem was right there in the house: I was a Jew. The constable had a stick in hand and kept stewing and tapping with his stick, yelling at the Gentile, "Don't you know the law of the tsar? A Jew in your *house*? In a *village*?"[10]

Turning to me the constable said, "Get dressed and come with me!" I got ready, paid the Gentiles what I owed them, said goodbye, and left. The woman followed me to the gate and bid me farewell, adding in Russian, "You are such a beautiful girl."

As we walked a little under the lovely moonlit night, the constable could now take a look at me and get a sense of whom he had been sent him to get in the middle of the night. He said to me in a soft voice, "You don't have to walk so fast. You can walk slowly. You understand, it's not my fault. That's how the tsarist law works. You cannot break the law. I too would prefer to be sleeping and now I have to march with you all night." My heart sank. That meant we were going to Lysyanka on foot. In a little while we got to the village where my girlfriend was staying. She cried. The constable said, "Now, now, don't cry, just come with me." All three of us went out to the highway and marched off. The night, as I said, was wondrous, and the fragrance of the tall, full kernels of wheat and rye and other good things filled our senses. Here in America, under a way of life different from "tsarist law," such a walk would be called a "hike," and we would even be proud of ourselves for doing it.

But the way he handled us! I would have ignored the whole matter, but the young woman kept crying and asking, "What is this? Why me? I have done nothing wrong. I am a good mother, a loyal wife, and efficient housekeeper—and now, such disgrace, being marched like a convict! How will I be able to look people in the eye? Even my own husband?" I tried to calm her, explaining to her that this was no shame, that we were being treated like this not because of any personal wrongdoing but because we were Jews! We were not the first and perhaps not the last. We arrived in Lysyanka in the morning. They locked us up like real criminals, but I requested that we be able to inform our families. It cost a few rubles, but they released us. That same day I traveled to Zvenigorodka and took the train from there to Kremenchug. Thus my vacation ended.

A few weeks after I arrived home, when I was feeling a little better and still unable to find a job, we decided that I should learn the trade of corset making. The best place to learn was Warsaw. Decision made, off I went. I stayed with my brother's boss's daughter, Madame Stein. My brother was already working as an apprentice at the Vitlin photography shop. I worked on Marszalkowska Street and lived on Zakroczymska near the Vistula, the beautiful river that winds through Warsaw. After a time, I learned the work well and went home. After a short rest, I traveled to Kiev to look for a job and stayed with my father's sister, whose daughter was studying to be a doctor. Before long, I got a very good position, in a shop owned by Christians, but for a very good salary. I worked on Vasilkovska Street and slept in Slobodka. I earned money for myself and sent a few rubles home.

Soon there was a commotion in Kiev. This must have been about 1912. They were preparing for distinguished guests: The tsar and his family were coming. The big day arrived, and then the hour. Rows of soldiers with rifles in their hands stretched down the streets. The sidewalks were packed with civilians. The soldiers stood tightly together, shoulder to shoulder so that no one could break through, heaven forbid. Then came the distinguished ones, in carriages upon carriages. The tsar stood, holding himself steady with one hand and responding to the salutes with the other. Standing to the side of the thoroughfare, I could not see their faces, but I did see the big feathers on their hats, waving in the wind as their carriages flew quickly past. The people burst out shouts of "Hurrah!"

That dog Stolypin was with them that day. Then one fine morning you could hear the shouts: "Extra! Extra! Read all about it! Stolypin shot at the theater!"[11] There was a great tumult. When I arrived at work, I saw long faces. I smiled to my fellow workers, but they did not respond. I took a break for a few minutes, and on returning I discovered that the thread had disappeared from my machine and the light-colored corset I had to finish was smeared with black mud. A little while later, in a side room, I had a conversation with the boss. She told me, "You are like a sheep among wolves. They are too many (there were twelve working there), and I don't have anyone I can switch you with."[12] I lost my job and returned home from Kiev.

I later learned from the newspapers that Stolypin had died and that his assassin Bogrov had received the death penalty.[13] When the officer came to get him before his execution, Bogrov looked him straight in the eye and said impudently, "Now you'll have one less mouth to feed."

When I got home I found out that my brother was working in a photography shop in Taganrog. My parents asked me to go there to keep my brother company, as my brother was not physically strong. Upon arriving in Taganrog, it became clear that I could only get a good job making corsets in Mariyampole. My brother sent word and we went to Mariyampole, where he worked in a photography shop and I worked in a corset shop. A few years passed in this manner.

Then World War I broke out. It is impossible to describe all the details of a war breaking out, especially at that time in tsarist Russia. Voices of discontent were everywhere. Why were we fighting and for whom? For *them,* those drunkards, while the rest of us remained ignorant and mute, forever persecuted and pursued by the tsarist law? Though discontent reigned, still they marched with their rifles, drums beating, trumpets blowing, while women wrung their hands and cried in unison. I should add that the Jews in particular had no desire to serve. For whom? For the master? Rather than going to serve, they crippled themselves. Some poked out their eyes, some cut off their ears, others chopped off their fingers.

Before long, the import business was crippled and the corset trade came to a halt. I went home and within a short time learned the photography trade. And indeed photography was a booming business. My brother was called up, but after an in-person medical examination, the doctor gave him a one-year deferment so that he could improve his health. But a year would fly by, after which they might take my brother. Then I would need to be the breadwinner, since my sister was now married. So I came to a practical decision: I would open a photography business. But how? I needed money. My brother and I bought a professional camera and off we went to the mines of Gorlovka, Nikitovka, and others. Making a living was very hard. Many times, waiting for a train at the little stations, we lay down on the wooden benches made for two with our heads on our fists. The mining people lived very poorly. Sometimes they would sing Russian tunes in a monotone: "As a spade, I go down into the abyss, and I know not if I will return."

Thus we traveled until we came to Yenakieyo, a substantial town. There was a large photography shop there by the name of Steskina, swamped with work from the local ironworks. They called those works "Hell," because of the chimneys from which sparks would rain down. No one who stood near the "Hell" chimney was ever sure of his life. In fact, not a week, not even a day, passed without an accident. That is why the tsar did not send workers from there to the front during the war. My brother set to work at Steskina, and I took a look around town to see what was what. Through Steskina we made some acquaintances. We had a few rubles, and money talks. My brother got a job in "Hell" and I took his place in the photography shop.

I cannot say exactly how much time passed in this way, but then news came that the tsar had left the throne. No one believed it. The Jews especially did not make a move, and the dazed Gentiles could hardly conceive of it. Of course they didn't believe the newspapers. The police, although somewhat confused, remained firmly in place. News came every hour. A temporary militia was decreed. A day passed before news arrived with more details. The tsar's entire family was under arrest. Now the workers started to take things seriously. They abolished the tsarist police and temporarily established their own. There was confusion and turmoil. Some danced for joy and others laughed and cried for joy at the same time. We held meetings on every street corner. The Jews no longer had to say prayers for the tsar and his family, mentioning each member by name. Now news arrived that soldiers were getting even with their superiors, a bad general or an officer who slapped soldiers for not saluting and saying "Yes, sir!" fast enough. There was tumult, people ran around in a rush and split the heavens open with their cries: "Let us welcome our freedom! Hurrah!" . . .

Kerensky was appointed as president.[14] People marched in the streets with Kerensky's portrait: "Kerensky, we want Kerensky. Hurrah for Kerensky." They made speeches and rejoiced. Then Kerensky's new currency appeared. Since gold and silver no longer circulated in the country, he issued bills in large denominations, and every pauper who before had counted his life by the *groshn** now dealt in hundreds of rubles. But Kerensky's reign did not last long.

I was drawn to a larger city to experience this event with the masses. People sprang into the air and rejoiced at events. More than anything, they demanded the end of the bloody war that nobody cared about. The army wanted to go home and enjoy the new freedom, but Kerensky planned to fight. Once, as I stood in line for a train ticket, I heard soldiers coming from the front in a rage: "Kerensky should flee abroad. Let's tear him to pieces!"

I went to Kharkov and got a job for one hundred fifty rubles (so-called "Kerenskys") a month. Kharkov was stewing like a caldron. Every political party had its loudmouths, every party wanted power. In the meantime, each felt like the boss. If a certain speaker didn't find favor, then they beat him, sometimes even to death. No arrests were made. People ran rampant with their guns. A truck drove by with a gang of people in it. They shot left and right and hit somebody, but it didn't matter. They just kept going.

I and other cadres from the Social Democratic Party, which had merged with the Bund, ran around distributing leaflets.[15] In relation to this, an episode occurred near a factory at the edge of town. We arrived when the great masses of workers poured out of the factory. I and another student, dressed in student uniforms, began to hand out leaflets. Before the workers could read them, a man with a broken visor and smudged face came forward and shouted in Russian, "Comrades! Do not take the fliers. Don't you see that they are from the bourgeoisie? Do not let them confuse you! Tear up the fliers!"

We understood immediately what this meant. The crowd stood still, like a wolf before it pounces on its victim. I turned to my friend and his face was white as snow. A thought struck me. In photography, I worked in the laboratory using various chemical substances without wearing rubber gloves, as is done in this country. I pulled my gloves off my hand. My fingers and all my nails were black. Lifting up my hands I cried out, "Comrades! Look!" My fingers spoke for themselves. "What kind of bourgeois are we? Perhaps I work even harder than you!"

Then a Gentile came forward and said, "It's true. The intellectual workers keep themselves clean and dress in clean clothes, not like us, always dirty." "True, true" was heard all around. We distributed all of our fliers and left. When we got back to the city, my friend shook my hand to thank me, "I did not think I would get out of that one alive!"

There was unrest in the city:

> A shot here,
> A shot there!
> We know not whom,
> We know not where!

I was working on Yaskovski and sleeping on Zahikovka, almost at the edge of town in a not very cheerful neighborhood. Because the city was packed with people traveling through, it was impossible to get a room in the center of the city. My heart would pound walking home at night, until I opened my door. The anxiety of that kind of life was overwhelming. Indeed, my parents asked me to take pity on them and come home, and I obeyed.

When I arrived home, I found the same kind of thing going on: speakers and more speakers. The Bolsheviks were saying: "Comrades! Open the fronts in the theaters of war! Cry out to the world: We do not want to fight each other! We do not want to shed blood! We want freedom for ourselves and for the whole world! We do not want annexations or tribute states! Let each country live on its own in freedom! Let us declare ourselves brothers, put away our weapons, and take up the hammer and sickle instead!"

Indeed, the Bolsheviks gained the upper hand and remained in power.[16] Now everyone emerged from their cellars, from their dark, forlorn watches. They found their voices on a porch or a corner or a rooftop. Speaker after speaker representing Lenin and Trotsky marched to music through the streets with their deep red flags. People played and spoke and sang. It was lively and joyful. They opened the prisons and freed the political prisoners—arise liberated ones! The streets were packed like Broadway on New Year's Eve when you just have to go with the flow of the crowd. People shouted, "Long live freedom! Long live the Russian people! Long live internationalism! Hurrah!"

At this time, my brother returned home and we opened up a photography shop in Kriukov, a neighborhood across the iron bridge from central Kremenchug, where I experienced the pogroms I described in the first part of my first autobiography.

I must add that I have left out many other episodes for two reasons. First, those who have been here in America for a long time will never be able to grasp that we who have experienced so much could still be full human beings like everyone else. Second, as I write, I relive these moments once again. I get terrible headaches and keep having to swallow aspirins. One example of this: Through the drawn shutters, we saw them leading a poor tailor by the name of Trotsky from Kriukov. He was walking with his hands pressed to his shrunken belly. The Cossack sat on his horse and drove him like a beast. There were many, many episodes like this.

Since I had taken responsibility for the household expenses, my brother went to Romania and I carried on with the photography business by myself. When the situation quieted down, the Bolsheviks came back into power. (In Belarus, they had been around the entire time.) In honor of the Bolsheviks' first five years in power, they arranged for the factory workers of Kriukov to receive new booklets with cards bearing photographs. Since there was only one photography shop in Kriukov, I got the work. I exchanged the Soviet money for gold.

I lived through an episode that might perhaps be of interest to you: the great famine that took place a little while before I prepared to emigrate. People swelled with hunger and died amidst terrible suffering. Even if one could get a piece of bread for a high price, the dough had been mixed with sawdust. I decided to go to some village to get bread for my elderly father and mother. It appeared that it was possible to get bread at Anno-Pokrovka, a village that had earned the nickname "Sinister Bandits" because the villagers had killed the only apothecary there (they didn't have a doctor) along with his family. He helped them in case of illness, and this is how they thanked him, in this sinister way. In this same village, there was a little bread to be had. I hired a Gentile with a horse and wagon and set off.

Upon arrival, I stopped at a gentile home and told them what I could do and what I wanted. The word spread among the youth and things got jolly. They came with their accordions. The gentile women and men, and even older people, played and danced until the streets around the house were packed with people.

I set up a mobile photo laboratory in a shed, glued red paper to the windows and plugged up the cracks so I had a place to change the film. I attached a dark-colored shawl to one side of the house as a backdrop, so I wouldn't have to go under a tree where I was not sure of the reflection. The work flew like hot dogs at Coney Island! Gradually they brought me rye, millet, wheat, groats, and so on. I finished up the orders, gathered my bundles, and arranged for a gentile driver to take me home in the morning. Drivers liked to leave early in order to have the day in the city.

That same night a tall gentile rogue came in and said to me, "What do you think you're doing? So you came to clean out the village? You didn't sow the land or feed the cattle, and yet you take grain?"

"Not everyone has to do the same kind of work. You do your work, and I'll do mine," I answer him.

"Say what you will," he says to me, "You will not take that grain away. I'll be watching you from the mountain leading to the city. You'll end up in the ravine, and the grain will go back."

After he left I went to Ivan in the company of the gentile woman of the house. With tears in my eyes, I begged him to change the departure time and leave town quietly in the middle of the night. I paid him well and he agreed. I don't need to tell you the state I was in as we approached the mountain.

We arrived in Kriukov at daybreak. Everyone opened their windows and marveled at my bundles. Indeed, I saw a hand sticking out of a door that remained ajar. I opened the door. There stood a mother with her baby in her arms. The mother looked like a skeleton, gaunt with sunken eyes. She took the child's little hand and held it out, saying, "I ask nothing for myself, but give a piece of bread to the dear little soul. Don't let it die of hunger!" Her manner brought tears to my eyes, then and even now as I remember her.

Before I left for America, I trained my sister to continue with the photography business. She, her husband, and her child had been living with me for a long time. My father was now dead; my brother was in Romania, or in Odessa, waiting for his final papers and his baggage.

We had to wait for four weeks before beginning our voyage, because of an episode that I did not find necessary to describe in my other letter. In your response, however, you remarked that an event relating to immigration can sometimes be significant.[17] To this day I do not know why the ship had to stop at the Bulgarian port. I was depressed as I traveled and did not pay attention. I had begun to feel weary from the struggle for survival.

The truth is, my heart was not in the voyage. I had begun to fear what I might experience in the big wide world. In Kriukov I was considered a good child who supported her family, but mother had insisted, "Not here. You cannot stay here. The Russian earth is soaked in blood, and one is never certain of what new events may bring." The Bolsheviks themselves admitted this. . . . Because of all this, the route we took did not matter to me, just as long as we traveled.

So, lo and behold, the ship was held up and anchored far from shore. Hours passed and it didn't move from its place. A day and a night passed by. People became impatient. There were various rumors that the ship would be turned back, that they thought we, the passengers, were Communists or propagandists. Women cried and young people walked around preoccupied. Many of them were stowaways and did not want to get caught on the trip back. Several days passed. We had not taken this extra time into consideration when we prepared our food for the trip. Now there was a scarcity of food, as each person had brought his own food aboard ship.

Two men arrived. It was said that one of them was a doctor. No consultation was needed on the second one; a blind person could tell who he was —a tall man with epaulets and a long sword that dragged on the floor. They examined the ship and asked the captain various questions in private. Now they were on the deck where all the immigrants had gathered.

They took away everyone's passport and ordered us to pass by them in a line. The doctor kept a sharp eye on everyone, but that didn't keep old and young alike from crying and begging the officer to let at least one person off the ship to buy food for everyone. The answer was no. Girls tried to smile, looking at the officer with their pretty black Jewish eyes. It didn't help. The answer was still no. The officer spoke fluent Russian; perhaps he was a former tsarist official. I had passed by him and already had my back to him when he called out a command, "Freeze! Why don't you ask for anything? Everyone else is begging and yet you walk by so straight and tall without saying a word?"

"Why should I say anything? Old and young alike are crying and begging you. Little children are crying, yet you have the same cold answer for all of them: No. Why should I make a fool of myself?"

"Look, I'll let you go. Go get ready. After I take the doctor to shore I'll come for you."

There was a great commotion. People pushed money on me from all sides. They even gave me a summer jacket instead of my shawl, so I wouldn't have something hanging over my shoulders. When he came for me, everyone celebrated because they would soon have something to eat. They let me down the emergency ladder from the deck and we were off, three of us in the little boat: the driver, the officer, and me. In my hurry, I had not even combed my hair. I allowed myself to sink into thought about all the orders, trying not to mix them up: meat for one person instead of butter, vegetables for someone else instead of cheese. I noticed how far from shore the ship had set anchor. Not one of us uttered a word.

As we approached the shore, I saw a little white house on edge of a hill. The foundation was covered with boards and jutted out over the water. We approached a gendarme, who made a jerky movement as if he had been poked in the back, saluted, and clicked the heels of his boots. The officer pointed at me and the gendarme ran over to give me his hand, helping me off the little boat. I immediately set out in the direction of the city over the hill, but the officer stopped me. "Where are you going? Do you want to get arrested in the city? You need a permit first. Come to the administrative office. I will give you one."

We entered a small room where a gendarme was seated at a table. He jumped up as if he had been pricked in the seat of his pants. When we entered the next room, the officer took off his summer overcoat and his sword and stated, "Any girl who comes in here goes out a woman!"

I broke out in a cold sweat. I looked quickly around the room. My eyes stopped at the window, through which I could see waves breaking on the shore under the house.

He noticed this and said with an ironic smile, "Are you such a good swimmer?" Not waiting for an answer, he added, "Better not be foolish. Don't jump and don't cry out because it will do you no good. I'm the boss here."

Seeing that I was trapped, I spoke in a low, weak voice, "I won't jump or cry out, but I have no strength left. I am starving. What will you do if I faint here with you?"

"I can send for food!"

"No," I said, "I am religious and I won't touch a thing."

"Okay, I'll give you a permit, but don't think that you can fool me. You will not slip away from me. My men will follow you and you have no other way back to the ship. You will have to go through my office."

When I felt the permit in my hands, my heart beat like a clock. I left. On the first street I came to, I went into a shop and immediately asked, "Jews, do you speak Yiddish?"

"Yes, are you from the Russian ship? What's going on in Russia? Who are the Bolsheviks?"

"I beg you," I interrupted, "don't ask me any questions. As quickly as possible, tell me, where are the leaders of the Jewish community?"

He understood from my behavior that something was amiss, indicated the way, and gave me the name and address. I left with determined steps. It wasn't very far. I went through a door to an upper floor and explained whom I needed to see. Sure enough, a man with the appearance of an intellectual came out and asked me what I wanted. In great haste, I told him that I was from the ship. He interrupted me. "We know about the ship. Since it's been held up, we've been working on the problem from our side." When I told him of my personal situation, he said, "Maybe your experience will help us speed up this process. In any case, don't be frightened anymore. Go and do your shopping. Do not hurry back before the time is up. We will keep an eye on everything."

I was going about my shopping when a very friendly woman came into the shop and addressed me, "Please, come to my store next door." Taking my baskets, she led me into a wine shop. There was a substantial gathering there. People began asking me questions from all sides, which I answered quite willingly. After a while, the door opened and a beggar came in. He had patches upon patches on his sleeves and jacket, but his fine white lining showed beneath them. Someone from among the group gathered there said quickly in a loud voice, "The name of that wine is '*nit gedabert,*'" a mixture of Yiddish and Hebrew meaning, "Don't say anything." I understood right away and answered, "If you don't have a cheaper one then I will have to do business elsewhere," and left.[18]

I sensed that a few hours had passed and set off slowly for the shore. My heart beat with joy when from the hill I saw people carrying crates of goods to and from the ship docked at the shore. A man ran over to me, I know not from where, and helped me carry my bundles down. He pointed me in the direction of the customhouse, where, according to procedure, they looked over the wares. After I boarded the ship, everyone beamed with happiness. They surrounded me and bombarded me with questions from all sides: "Why did it take so long?" "We were waiting and waiting . . ." I did not want to make a spectacle out of myself so I didn't tell anyone anything, with the exception of the old woman, my new "mother."

Now that the work was finished at the port, there was a feeling of joy on the ship. We were finally leaving. But no, a sailor told us we had to return to the place offshore where we had been earlier and wait for our passports. He assured us that it looked as if everything would arrive in one load and we would be on our way. Everyone grew serious because it was quite a distance to Constantinople, and the food I had brought was like a single mouthful to those starving people.

Suddenly we heard shouts from below. "Bertha, Bertha, Mademoiselle Bertha!" We all went over to the handrail of the deck. Below, we saw a little boat with two Jewish men and many boxes of foodstuffs.

"Where is the Bertha who went shopping?"

They pushed me to the front so the men could see me. "You have Bertha to thank for everything!" They waved to me with scarves as a sailor went down and brought up the foodstuffs: plenty of herring, entire sausages with the kosher* stamp, whole cheeses, all kinds of breads, even tea and sugar. It wasn't long before we departed for Constantinople.

We—I and the others going on to America—stayed in Constantinople for a few months. My brother sent me a few liras to cover my expenses. Then I was in America.

As I already wrote to you, I worked in a shop at first, but I realized that I would not make my fortune there. I had to send money to Mother and to my brother, but what I earned was only enough for room and board. On the ship, I had made a few girlfriends who were medical workers. They had immediately gotten positions in hospitals and encouraged me to try a career as a nurse. Here I am reminded of the Russian poem: "If you fall into a patch of wildflowers, you will become fragrant like them." They explained the basics to me, taught me how to take people's temperature, and so on. I got a position at the Montefiore Home and Hospital and worked in the tuberculosis ward. I myself caught cold and underwent a tonsil operation. After I got better I got a job at Israel Zion Hospital. Then I caught the grippe. Upon my recovery I worked at Beth Moses on Myrtle Avenue in Brooklyn.[19] . . . Every doctor is familiar with the long hours worked by the nurses' aides and the undergraduate nurses, sometimes twelve hours a day. You must arrive and leave on time. I always had room and board and didn't buy fancy clothes; instead I sent all the money to Europe. Then my brother emigrated to Palestine. Four years passed.

When the crisis broke out in Palestine in 1928, my brother emigrated to Cairo in Africa, and then to Johannesburg, where he set up a photography business and made a living.[20] I haven't heard anything from him for a few years now. It has been two years since I received the news that my mother could not expect any miracles and had died. Kriukov is now occupied by the Nazis. I did not have the opportunity to bring anyone over. I was not an American citizen, had no home, and the general immigration quota was filled. By the time I got myself settled down and married, it was too late. As the Russian saying goes, "Before the sun rises, the dew will eat out your eyes."

I married a fine man, a housepainter. I have two boys. One of them completed studies at a Sholem Aleichem School last year.[21] We had the great privilege of having the distinguished poet Abraham Reisen[22] distribute the diplomas to the graduates. My younger child, ten years of age, displays a talent for singing, and we are thinking about what to do to encourage him.

So I am the only one in my family saved from death by coming to America.[23] My only fear is that my children will have to live through as much as I did. Let us hope that a wiser day will prevail over the dark night. Humanity will lift up its head in freedom. Then our Jewish duty will be to multiply ourselves and replace the gruesome numbers of victims with new lives.

NOTES

1. *Der fraynd* (The Friend) was the official organ of the Workmen's Circle starting in 1910.

2. Simon Petlyura (1879–1926) was a Ukrainian nationalist and Socialist who assumed leadership of the independent Ukrainian government in February 1919. He denied being an anti-Semite but refused to discipline his army as it perpetrated pogroms.

3. The tsar was deposed in March 1917 and the Bolsheviks took power in November of the same year. From 1918 to 1920, a multi-sided civil war took place, much of it fought in Ukraine and accompanied by pogroms against the Jews. From May to July 1919, Nikifor Grigoryev (1848–1919) led a nationalist rebellion against the Bolsheviks in southern Ukraine, the region including Kremenchug. Anton Ivanovich Denikin (1872–1947), a former tsarist officer, headed the anti-Bolshevik "White Army" in Ukraine. His forces advanced toward Moscow from the spring to the fall of 1919 but then were forced to retreat. In the spring of 1920, Deniken transferred command to Piotr Wrangel. The White Army, which suffered its final defeat in the fall of 1920, was responsible for a large number of pogroms.

4. The Bolshevik Red Army usually defended Jews against attack.

5. Founded by the German and Belgian financier and industrialist Baron Maurice de Hirsch (1831–1896) in 1891, the Jewish Colonization Association (ICA) supported the "productivization" of the Jewish poor. ICA aided Jewish farmers in Eastern Europe, but it was especially interested in encouraging emigration from countries where Jews were persecuted, helping to settle them in the United States, Argentina, Canada, Brazil, Israel, and elsewhere.

6. In the summer of 1942, the first reports reached the West of the Germans' systematic use of gas to murder large numbers of Jews at the Chelmno extermination camp. Since the 1930s, physicians had played an important role in Nazi efforts to eliminate not only Jews and other racial "undesirables," but also individuals with mental and physical disabilities. The outside world was not yet aware of Dr. Josef Mengele, who later came to epitomize this medical collaboration through his participation in the mass murders at Auschwitz.

7. It is not clear which rebbe Fox is referring to. The Skvirer Rebbe at the time was Yitskhok ben Mordkhe Twersky (1812–1895).

8. Hershele Ostropoler was an eighteenth-century Yiddish jester known for his satire of the rich. Stories of his exploits circulated widely throughout Jewish Eastern Europe until the mid-twentieth century.

9. In response to the revolutionary upsurge in 1905, Tsar Nicholas II issued the October Manifesto, promising an elected legislature and more freedom of speech and association. As the revolutionary mood ebbed, however, the government pulled back from its promises and cracked down on opposition groups. The unrest prompted a wave of pogroms, which grew in intensity as the Revolution was suppressed. The Kremenchug pogrom took place in October 1905.

10. The tsarist government's "May Laws" of 1882 severely restricted Jewish settlement in the villages (as opposed to towns and cities) even of the Pale of Settlement, the region of the Russian Empire where Jews were allowed to live.

11. Piotr Stolypin (1862–1911) served as Russian prime minister and minister of the interior from 1906 until his assassination on September 1, 1911. He presided over the suppression of the revolutionary movement after the 1905 Revolution but took no action against anti-Jewish pogroms. The tsar's visit to Kiev and Stolypin's assassination took place in 1911, not 1912 as Fox remembers.

12. The other workers, Gentiles, were angry after Stolypin's assassination and hostile toward her as a Jew and perhaps also as a revolutionary.

13. Dmitri Bogrov (1888–1911) was a leader of the Socialist Revolutionary Party and an informer for the tsarist secret police. His assassination of Stolypin may have been motivated by remorse for his collaboration with the regime.

14. Alexander Kerensky (1881–1970), a moderate Socialist, was premier of Russia from July 1917 until the Bolsheviks seized power in November. His time in power was marked by severe inflation, unemployment, food shortages, and social unrest.

15. A reference to the Mensheviks, Socialists who opposed the Bolshevik seizure of power and called for a constitutional government in Russia and a gradual transition to Socialism.

16. The Bolsheviks (later known as the Communists) were a militant faction of the Russian Socialist movement that called for immediate seizure of power by the working class and peasants and an end to Russian involvement in World War I. Led by Vladimir Ilich Lenin (1870–1924) and Leon Trotsky (1879–1940), they took power in November 1917 and established the Soviet regime.

17. Fox addresses Max Weinreich directly and refers to the letter he sent her after she submitted the first part of her autobiography.

18. The white lining under the "beggar's" tatters betrayed him as a spy in disguise. The local Jews mix Hebrew words in with their Yiddish in order to warn Fox of the danger without the spy understanding.

19. Montefiore Hospital was founded in Manhattan in 1884 as the Montefiore Home for Chronic Invalids. It moved to the Bronx in 1912. Israel Zion Hospital (opened in 1920 or 1921) and Beth Moses Hospital (opened in 1920), both founded to serve observant Jews in Brooklyn, merged in 1947 to form Maimonides Hospital.

20. It is not clear which crisis Fox means. Between 1926 and 1928, the Jewish community in Palestine suffered through an economic depression that led to a high rate of emigration. In August 1929, there were a series of bloody anti-Jewish Arab riots that also led people to leave the country.

21. A secular Yiddish school, which students attended in addition to the public schools, named for the great Yiddish writer and affiliated with the Sholem Aleichem Folk Institute, a Yiddishist organization founded in 1918.

22. Abraham Reisen (1876–1953) was a Yiddish poet and short-story writer whose works express sympathy with the poor and oppressed in lyrical and sometimes gently humorous tones. His poems were often set to music as songs.

23. Fox does not include her brother living in South Africa.

Chapter 8

Why I Left the Old Country and What I Have Accomplished in America

Chaim Kusnetz (Baron von Habenichts)

b. 1904, Duboy, Belarus
To U.S.: 1923, Brooklyn, N.Y.

A true worker-intellectual, Chaim Kusnetz (fig. 17) was unusual for two reasons: First, he remained religiously observant his entire life, even after he fell under the influence of philosophies critical of traditional religion. Second, he was attracted to psychology and to philosophers of the simple life and self-abnegation, rather than to political radicalism. His inclination toward introspection, in turn, leads him to paint a rather dark picture of his inner life—darker, perhaps, than was warranted by his actual circumstances and relationships. He provides an interesting account of his intellectual development, including his reading in traditional Jewish texts, adventure stories, and psychological literature. In addition, he provides informative descriptions of traditional Jewish life in Belarus, of events in South Russia during the Russian Revolution and Civil War, of his first impressions of America, and of immigrant life in Brooklyn in the 1920s. His introspective account of his courtship and marriage stands in contrast to his wife's more straightforward description. Inclined toward introspection, drawn to asceticism while living in a consumerist culture, Kusnetz ends his story on a note of yearning and restlessness.

Duboy is a village in Minsk Gubernia, Pinsk District, seven *versts** from the station at Vidibor, twenty-one *versts* from Stolin (formerly Russia, later Poland). About thirty Jewish families lived there, among about five hundred gentile households.

Duboy had two blacksmiths, both Jews. One of them, Dovid Shloyme,

Fig. 17. Chaim Kusnetz with his wife, Minnie Yezernitsky Kusnetz, his mother, Ruchel Koval Kusnetz, and his daughter Fay,
c. 1943. Courtesy of Fay Minkin

was my father's father. This Dovid Shloyme was an outstanding scholar,
and besides studying on his own—he studied not only at home, but also
in his smithy while the iron was heating—he also studied with the most
eminent householders of Duboy. When he got married, the landowner
gave him a present: lumber for a house, and a cow. And as soon as the
house was ready, my grandfather began to host the *minyan,** and he continued to host it until the Duboy community built a synagogue. My

grandfather had six children: three boys and three girls. One of the boys, Yankev, was my father.

My father only went to *heder** for four or five years because when he was about ten years old, his father (Dovid Shloyme) died, and he was turned over to the other blacksmith to learn the trade. Several years later, he became a full-fledged blacksmith and his own boss in his father's smithy. At the age of eighteen, physically well developed and starting to earn a living, he married a cousin of his, a girl from the big city.

This took place in the middle of the last decade of the previous century.

When my mother arrived in my father's house, the entire Jewish population of Duboy came running to see the novelty. It was not so much that my mother was a big-city girl, something that Duboy had seldom seen before. Nor was it because she was small of stature. Rather, it was because on an ordinary weekday my mother made the house look as if it were Passover* eve.

"Look! You can see the floorboards!"

"Just look! Curtains on the windows, on an ordinary weekday!"

In short, the people of Duboy, especially the Jewish womenfolk, marveled for some time at how a young eighteen-year-old newlywed could be a better, more efficient housewife and housekeeper than the oldest women of Duboy . . . until they too started to imitate my mother, and soon one could see that the floor was made of boards in quite a few Jewish houses, even on ordinary weekdays.

Three years after their wedding, my brother Shloymke was born. Three years later—Leybke. And three years after that—I, the writer of these lines, was born. (This was around the time of the Russo-Japanese War.*)

As soon as I began to walk and was able to use my hands, I started to take an interest in "sculpture." I would knead little people out of clay and mud. I often earned enough for candy from this. "Khayml, here's a kopek. Make me a little 'father'!" I used to hear this tune very often, and thereby come into a kopek. Later I gave up sculpture and began to take an interest in carving. (I remember absolutely nothing about this time in my life. My mother, as well as older Duboy *landslayt,** told me about it.)

At the age of six, I started going to *heder.* There we studied from the end of morning prayers until it was time for evening prayers. On summer days, the teacher would let us go outside to play for fifteen minutes. As pious as Itshe the Teacher was, he was equally ignorant when it came to simple Hebrew. To this day I cannot read Hebrew as one should, that is, grammatically. I studied for several years with this traditional teacher, learning to pray and to write, as well as studying Khumesh* with the commentaries of Rashi,* along with the early Prophets. Then I started to study with a modern teacher, first with one, then with another who took the first one's place. With the modern teachers, we studied Russian and arithmetic, along with Khumesh with Rashi and *Tanakh.**

Es khato'ay ani mazkir, "I must make mention . . . of my offenses."[1] Because of me, the second teacher, Khlavne, did not teach in Duboy for more than one term. Here is the story. Of all the boys in Duboy, I was the only one who liked to immerse myself in the written word. I was bit of a ne'er-do-well when it came to all "worldly" things. For example, when it came to playing *myatshik* (baseball, in the local lingo), or swimming, or to getting around the forest that surrounded Duboy, or climbing trees, or the like, I was among the less accomplished.[2] Yes, I would do all of these things, or take part in them, but what I did with true pleasure was to immerse myself in the stray pages of Jewish holy books that were stored under the reading desk in the synagogue, or read the holy books in the synagogue—like *Kav ha-yashar,* *Khovot ha-levavot, Reshit khokhmah, Ein Ya'akov,** each with an old-fashioned Yiddish translation—or the books at home—like my mother's *Tsene-urene* and *Nofet tsufim,* and my father's Khumoshim loaded with commentaries.[3]

Khlavne, the teacher, was more of a modern teacher than a traditional one, so he used to try to get through the Khumesh with Rashi one-two-three. But I used to pester him. At every step, I would ask him questions, which I would get from the *Tsene-urene* and from the many commentaries in my father's Khumoshim. And he could not answer them. When this reached the fathers of Duboy, they sent a "committee" to test him in Khumesh. He taught us Khumesh as the committee listened. With all eyes on the teacher and on me, my "ambition" began to soar. I had to show them, the Jews of Duboy, that I, a mere boy, was a better scholar than the teacher—and I pelted him with questions. Seeing that he did not know how to answer them, the householders on the committee asked me if I knew the answers. When I answered all of the questions, the teacher saw that he would not be hired for another term. And that is what actually happened.

The following term, I went with several other boys of my age to study with Shmuel Khaym, the ritual slaughterer. He hardly knew any Russian at all. He could barely creep through a Russian sentence, and even then he would understand one word in ten. But he had a mind like a steel trap. He went through both Iurevich's and Evtushevskii's mathematical textbooks with us and there was not a single problem that he was not able to solve.[4] He mainly studied Tanakh and Gemara* with us, and in this area he was truly gifted. He would digest and explain even the hardest question so that a child could understand it.

Yes, my father had also studied with this Shmuel Khaym, but this was before I started *heder*. Duboy was not acquainted with any parties or "isms." Everyone, from the oldest man to the youngest *heder*-boy, was strictly Orthodox in his piety and went to synagogue three times a day. And the greatest respect (or, more precisely, esteem) was reserved for the talmudic* scholars. And since my father was one of the most prominent householders, not to be able to study was not becoming of him. So he hired this Shmuel Khaym (who, besides being the ritual slaughterer, was also circumciser, synagogue Torah reader, and something of a rabbi) to study Mishna* with him every evening. My father was a hard worker. He used to get up at two or three in the morning every workday and work until late in the evening. But every evening, he would take a break for an hour to study Mishna, no matter how busy he was.

My father was pious, as were all of Duboy's Jews. He wore a beard and, while he was praying, a kind of long coat with a belt. On Fridays he would work for only half a day. During the second half of the day, he would go to the bathhouse, review the Torah portion for the week, recite the Song of Songs, and in general prepare for the Sabbath. Of course, he never worked during the intermediate days of holidays.[5] And my parents were great adherents of the commandment to be hospitable to guests. When the Berezner rebbe* or a preacher or an emissary, or simply a poor man, came to town he would stay with us.[6]

In short, life in Duboy was an authentically Jewish one, a deeply rooted one. Besides the house and the smithy, we had a stall with two cows, a garden, a bit of an orchard, our own well, and several chickens. So there was no lack of food, and my father was able to save up a few rubles, especially since my mother was one of the best seamstresses and also earned something.

But once it happened that someone set fire to the smithy. It was not insured, so it cost my father quite a pretty penny, almost everything that he had saved up, to rebuild it.

Some time later, in 1910, my father found out that ten young men from Duboy, married and unmarried, were preparing to go to America. He had almost no money, he was working hard day and night, and the family kept on getting bigger. Khane had been born three years after me, and a year after her, Moyshke, and my mother was already several months pregnant again. So he figured that he would go to America as well, accumulate a bit of a fortune, and return to Duboy to live a little easier.

No sooner said than done. At the end of winter, 1910, he took what was left of his money, borrowed some more, and left for America, where he settled in New York (more precisely, in Brownsville).

Left alone with five little children—the oldest, Shloymke, had just reached bar mitzvah* age—my mother cried and cried. Her crying made me and the other children very sad. But at the same time I had a kind of feeling of satisfaction that my father had gone away. My mother could no longer threaten me: "Wait, wait. When your father comes, I will tell him everything, and he will give it to you."

My mother cried in Duboy, Russia, and my father in Brownsville, America. He simply cursed his life. Arriving in America, he went right to work in an iron shop. As a greenhorn,* he was given all the hardest work: pounding with the heavy hammer, hauling heavy pieces of iron, and the like—labor worthy of a chain gang. What's more, he had to be a lodger in someone else's house, eating in restaurants and sending money home. And he earned all of six dollars a week.

For a half a year, he slaved away, until, with God's help, something happened that stood him back on his feet. This is what happened. The shop where he worked had to make a gate with a complicated "artistic" ornamentation, and no one in the shop could do it. Hearing the boss and the foreman conferring about what to do about the gate (they had decided to get a specialist from somewhere else), my father told them that he could make it if they let him. In any case, he would try. Hearing such talk from the "green" laborer, the foreman started to ridicule my father: "No one in the shop can do it, not one of the old, experienced tradesmen. And this greenhorn is going to undertake to do it! The nerve of that greenhorn!" But the boss told him to let my father make the gate. "Let him try. Maybe he really does know something."

Allowed to have a go at it, my father got down to work and both the boss and the workers in the shop could not get over their amazement at the job my father did. It was worthy of being displayed in an exhibition! Seeing that my father had golden hands as well as a head on his shoulders, the boss began to take him along on jobs and showed him how to take measurements and lay out the work. Very soon, he laid off his old foreman and made my father foreman in his place. Of course, he raised his wages at the same time.

When my father began to make better money and lose his "greenness," he had his picture taken and sent it to us. My mother was delighted as she opened the big package from America and called out, "Children, look what we have received from America!" She took out the card . . . and began to faint. Recovering a little, she started to cry and wail. In short, my father had left for America a distinguished Jew with a beard, and on the card was a picture of a clean-shaven young man who did not look anything like a Jew.

Later that same day, a neighbor came to see us and asked my mother to show her my father's picture. My mother did not want to, because she was embarrassed. When the neighbor strongly insisted, my mother grabbed the picture and tossed it on the ground, saying, "I don't want to look at such a picture. I don't even want to have it in the house. If you want it, take it, but never give it back to me!"

To my mother's chastising question, "How in the world can a Jew go and shave off his beard?" she received an answer from my father saying that she should not be so upset about this. America is not Duboy. In America, even rabbis go without beards. Some time later a Duboy Jew returned from America. His news of my father was that not only did he shave, but he also worked on the Sabbath. This was something that no one in Duboy believed. A Jew working on the Sabbath? Utterly impossible! For months and months, my mother was ashamed to show her face to the Jews of Duboy, especially to the women. But one gets used to everything, and my mother too got used to the idea that her husband was clean-shaven.

My father got used to it a lot more easily—not only to shaving, but also to working on the Sabbath and eating forbidden leaven on Passover. He boarded with Jews—and worked with workers—who were completely devoid of Judaism, and they went at him until he finally behaved as they did. The first couple of times, he found working on the Sabbath very difficult. His heart pounded and ached, and he literally cried. It was the same with eating leavened food on Passover. But with time, he got so used to it that it became a natural thing for him. He used to love to say, "The cart you are riding on, that's whose song you sing," or "When you come to a place, follow its customs," which he found somewhere in a midrash.[7]

Once he had been in America for a couple of years and saved up a little money, my father started to think about returning to Duboy. But when his boss found out about this, he started to dissuade him from going. "What is the point of making your whole life miserable in a village in darkest

Russia? And what sort of prospects can your children have there?" In short, he offered to give him a raise and lend him as much money as he needed to bring his family to America.

My father allowed himself to be convinced and inquired of my mother if she would like to come join him in America. My mother's answer was no. She could not do it. It would be a shame to take Shloymke out of the yeshiva* and she was afraid that in America the children would become Gentiles. It would be better if he came home.

How did Shloymke, my eldest brother, come to be in a yeshiva? The story was this: After my father had gone to America, the emissary of the yeshiva in Zvihil visited us in Duboy, and my mother consulted with him about what to do with Shloymke. He was already bar mitzvah age and she had to develop some sort of plan for him. So the emissary advised my mother to let him take Shloymke to Zvihil, where he would enroll him in the yeshiva and arrange "eating days"* for him. Shloymke had a good head; he wanted to study. With time, he might turn out to be a rabbi! My mother immediately seized on this, and before long Shloymke, together with a friend of his, was sitting and studying in the Zvihil yeshiva.[8]

Instead of coming home, my father wrote to Shloymke that since America was a dear land, and since a family from Duboy was coming to America that year, he should leave the yeshiva, go home, pack up, and travel together with that family. So in 1913, Shloymke joined our father in America. Soon we received a letter from them with requests, arguments, and demands that our mother sell everything and come to America with the children. This time it was my mother who allowed herself to be convinced, and at the end of 1913, she sold the house, the stalls, and the smithy —absolutely everything—for three hundred rubles. For the time being, we moved in with a neighbor who lived not far from our house.

But before we knew it, World War I broke out, and nothing came of the idea of going to America. We even stopped receiving money from America. What should we do? Since my father had relatives (a sister, a brother, and an uncle, with their families) in the nearby town of Stolin, my mother hired a couple of carts, packed them full of all our "junk," and in 1915 we arrived in Stolin. There were my mother and five children, Leybke and I, and the three children who were born after me: Khane, Moyshke, and Leye.

I did not really miss Duboy much. True, Duboy had been a lively world for me. All the boys of Duboy were my friends. We would all go swimming together. We would walk in the woods, gathering nuts, mushrooms, and berries. We would catch fish in homemade nets, steal pears and plums from other people's orchards, wage war against Duboy's non-Jewish boys, play ball, go skating, roll snowballs, collect and trade "thousands" (the papers from candies), go for walks on the dam to the "signal," climb trees, and many other such activities. But Stolin had other things, absorbing things that interested me. First, it was a new place with which to get acquainted. Everything was new and different: sidewalks made of boards, masonry buildings, a marketplace, fairs, and three synagogues on one square! There was a study house, a communal synagogue, and the rebbe's synagogue. And all the synagogues were conducted in the Sephardic style, like in Duboy.[9]

There was another synagogue in Stolin, one belonging to the *misnagdim*,[10] the opponents of Hasidism. Though we lived opposite this synagogue, I went to the Sephardic ones to pray. The point was that I would go from one synagogue to the next, catching bits of the service—*kedushes, barkhus, omeyn yehey shmey rabos,* and simple amens.[11] In Duboy, I would not have been able to "collect" all the "things" in a whole month that I collected in one morning here in Stolin, especially since many *minyanim,* one after the other, prayed in the study house.

I quickly became acquainted with Stolin, and acquired a couple of friends. (They considered me to be very knowledgeable. I could read Russian just as easily as Yiddish, while they had only recently learned the Russian alphabet from the signs on the stores.) I went to study in the yeshiva at the study house. When they threw me out of that yeshiva after two days of study, I started studying Gemara on my own in the *misnagdic* synagogue across from where we lived.

I was thrown out of the yeshiva for the following reason: When I arrived to study at the yeshiva, they were already at the Gemara chapter *Ezehu neshekh,* "What is biting usury."[12] After the head of the yeshiva had taught us the lesson, he told us—all little pipsqueaks nine to fourteen years of age—to review it out loud. So they all went right to it, and I . . . I looked at them and burst out laughing. When the head of the yeshiva asked me why I was laughing and why I was not reviewing the passage together with everyone else, I answered that I did not have to review because I already knew what he had just taught us almost by heart. And that is why I was laughing at them for even needing to review it. "Nevertheless," he said, "you must review it. You may remember it now, but if you don't memorize it you'll forget quickly." So I held in the laughter, and pretended to repeat the passage.

The next day, it was the same story. Again, I burst out laughing when I saw the group rocking back and forth as it reviewed the newly learned lesson. And when the head of the yeshiva told me that I had better stop laughing and review instead, I laughed even harder. So he took me by the hand and led me out of the yeshiva, saying as he did so, "This is a place for studying and not for laughing."

So I spent my mornings in the synagogues. I used to "lunch" at the rebbe's synagogue, where they would pray at about noon. I loved to watch the rebbe, Reb Yisroeltshe Perlow, and his sons, all dressed in long black silk kaftans as they stood at the eastern wall and prayed.[13] And I loved to see how the Hasidim would always stand up when the rebbe walked by. During the day, I would walk through the streets of Stolin, collect cigarette butts and watch the Jewish market women plead and argue as they haggled with the peasants. The late afternoons and evenings, I spent in the *misnagdic* synagogue.

None of us children earned anything. Less and less remained of the three hundred rubles that my mother had brought from our household in Duboy. My father's relatives were no small paupers who themselves needed help. And who knew how long the war would last? So my mother decided to go to Melitopol (formerly Tavricheskiy Gubernia, Crimea; recently in Yekaterinoslav Gubernia, Ukraine). There she had her entire family—her mother, sisters, and brothers—and there she would be able to find prospects for the children. It was a big city with big possibilities!

Of course, we needed an internal passport. And, in general, how would we go? Well, since some sort of relative of ours was a big shot on the refugee committee, he registered us as refugees, and soon the committee sent us away from Stolin, though my mother paid for the tickets herself.

We traveled for about three days. At every station, there were large signs with warnings: "Beware of thieves!" But I was not as concerned about thieves as about finding some corner where I could put on *tfilin** and pray without being disturbed. I remember that the following incident happened to me in Poltava. When the train arrived at the station, it was already midday. It was swarming and teeming with people, and I was completely unable to find a place to put on my *tfilin* and pray in peace. The train was supposed to stop for a couple of hours, so we decided to see the city. "In the meantime," my mother said to me, "eat, and you'll find a place to pray in the city." But I did not want to eat before praying, so I set out for the city hungry. I walked a while, until I started to faint. It was near a restaurant, and a man ran out of the restaurant, helped me recover, and gave me a glass of milk. He wanted to give me a whole meal, but I turned it down. (Who knew whether it was kosher*?) Only after I had prayed did I eat lunch.

We arrived in Melitopol in the summer of 1916 and went right to the synagogue courtyard, along with all the other refugees. At that time, Melitopol was full of Jewish refugees from Kurland, Mitava, Kaunas, and from those general areas. Many had already become residents of Melitopol, and others continued to arrive. All went to the synagogue courtyard, where they remained until a committee provided them with places to live and, for many of them, with jobs.

So we stood there in the courtyard with our bags and baggage. Suddenly, an elderly, dignified woman came up to us and embraced my mother. They both started sobbing.

"Come home with me, children, and you'll have something to eat," the elderly woman said to us.

"Children," our mother said to us, "this is your grandmother!"

My grandmother lived right opposite the synagogue courtyard, and, since she was expecting us to arrive in Melitopol at about this time and a cart had driven up with refugees, she had come over to see who had arrived.

We found a place to live immediately. It consisted of one room, and we, my mother and the five children, moved in. Later, when we had gotten to know the city a little, we rented a place not far from my grandmother. A woman had a three-room apartment in a small house made out of clay, and she rented us two rooms.

Leybke and I were already big lads—I, the younger, had already become bar mitzvah—so we had to think of practicalities. Since Leybke had already learned tailoring in Stolin, he went off to work for a tailor. And I . . . Really, what should they do with me? My mother consulted with her brothers, who had a *ribnoia,* or, as it would be called here, an "appetizing business," and they said that since I was a capable lad they would take me into the business.[14] But I would also have to be there on the Sabbath—not "also," but "especially," since Saturday was the main source of income. Desecrate the Sabbath? That put an immediate end to that idea, as was the case with all sorts of businesses in Melitopol. Just as Duboy and Stolin were authentically Jewish and strictly Orthodox, Melitopol was "gentile" and heavily Russified. All Jewish businesses and factories were open on the Sabbath, and it was seldom that a member of the younger generation could speak Yiddish.

So, if it was not going to be business, I had to learn a trade. My mother went to the committee that dealt with refugees, and very soon thereafter I went to work at a metal, laticework, and plumbing *mastiersakaia,* or workshop. That is, I became a locksmith and plumber.

My boss, Mikhail Grigorovich Leker, or, as they called him, simply "Khoma," was a Jew, but so gentilized that he barely knew anything about Judaism. When I asked him to let me go home earlier than usual on the eve of Purim,* and to his question of "why" answered that I wanted to hear the Megillah read, he fixed both of his eyes on me and asked with surprise, "What *mohila*?" which means "grave" in Ukrainian.[15] But when it came to putting up a tree for Christmas, he never missed it. Despite his gentileness, he never forced me to work on the Sabbath or on a holiday. I did not even work for him on the intermediate days of holidays. The first month, I worked for free. The next month, he started paying me four rubles, and from time to time he gave me a raise of a couple of rubles.

When I came to the trade, the workday was from six in the morning until six in the evening, six days a week. We had half an hour for lunch and half an hour for supper. In the beginning, my work consisted mainly of sitting and pumping the bellows, but as soon as I had become a bit of a tradesman, the boss took in another "*maltshik,*" apprentice, and I became a helper to the tradesman.

At the beginning of spring 1917, a major upheaval took place in Melitopol. People were literally dancing in the streets. There were constant demonstrations and there was singing, mainly "Otrechomsia ot starogo mira."[16] People starting calling each other *grazhdanin,* citizen, instead of *gospodin,* mister. In short, the entire city had a holiday atmosphere. Out with "Nicky"![17]

Social issues, politics—these things were still alien to me then. I knew only the "shop" and the synagogue. Every day, after coming home, I would wash and run right to the synagogue, the study house that was not far from our house—not so much for the public prayer as for the fact that the study house and the synagogue courtyard served me as a "club" where I met with friends and passed the time until after evening prayers. So the Revolution was a matter of indifference. But there was one thing that it did accomplish for me. Now that Nicky was no more, I gave myself permission to come to work at seven o'clock instead of six. Seeing what I was doing, the other couple of workers started to arrive at the same time as I.

Soon Melitopol was full of German soldiers, and things got lively. Those Germans were a fine and lively bunch. The public did business with them, and they paid for everything generously—sometimes in kind, with such products as brown sugar, cigarettes, and the like. My mother started to go among the barracks with a basket of apples and earned very good money. The two smaller children also started to peddle and earned something, so we were not living badly at all.

Soon after the Germans left Melitopol, the affair of the "Whites," "Reds," and "Makhnovists" got underway.[18] The years 1918, 1919, 1920 were three years of constant tension, constant exchanges of power. Now the Whites (the followers of Wrangel*) ruled over us, and now the Reds. Now the Reds, and now the followers of Makhno. No pogroms on the Jews or on the general population took place in our city. But what did happen? When the Whites would arrive, they would search out Communists or Communist sympathizers wherever they might be (there were more than enough informers), arrest them, and shoot them without trial.

Once, when they captured Melitopol after a bitter battle, they gathered together all of our city's Chinese, with their wives and children, took them all to the outskirts of town, forced the Chinese to dig a trench, lined them all up at the edge of the trench, and started to shoot them with a machine gun. Those dead and half-dead who did not fall into the trench they pushed in and immediately covered up. What they had against the Chinese is not known. Probably, there were a couple of Chinese among the Red Guards whom they had captured.

Neither did the followers of Makhno make any pogroms in our town. On the contrary, they strove to show the public that they were on the side of the people and working for the people's welfare. Thus, for example, they once caught a scoundrel who had attacked a house, beaten the inhabitants, and robbed them. I remember one evening when a cart rolled up to the marketplace with a man standing on it. Around him sat Makhnovists with guns in their hands. A large crowd immediately gathered, and one of the Makhnovists opened the "people's tribunal," as he called it. He recounted what the man had done and said that the people should try him. He himself demanded the death sentence for the man, but if the public decided that he deserved a lighter punishment, the public's will would be carried out. I do not know how it ended. I only know that most of the speakers from the crowd asked that the man's life be spared, and after everyone had had their say, the wagon went off.

So the followers of Makhno did not carry out any pogroms on us, but they did rob the stores. As soon as they entered the city, they would impose a heavy tribute on the population. But since no one gave freely of their money, they would break into the larger stores, fill up large freight wagons with goods, and disappear.

The Reds? They certainly did not make any pogroms. On the contrary, as soon as they arrived in town, the city was filled with joy and with a holiday spirit of celebration. The first thing they used to do was to exhume or to collect all those who had been shot by the Whites, and with pomp, music, and song ("Vy zhertvoiu pali v bor'be rokovoi") rebury them in a common grave.[19] When May Day came, things got lively. The entire Melitopol population would take part in a parade that lasted almost the whole day. And all the young folk used to receive packages of sweets. What's more, there were constant meetings and demonstrations. More than anyone else, the workers felt proud and exalted.

I remember that when I went home from work with filthy hands, all smudged up, I felt like a doctor in a small town—proud and self-confident. And when people asked me what my occupation was, I would answer with pride and self-satisfaction: "a metal worker." I simply pitied my uncles: shopkeepers, poor things.

There was one thing about the Reds that I did not like: their demonstrations against religion. Our forebears had let themselves be killed and died all sorts of terrible deaths for the sake of their religion. And here came Jews who had just left slavery for freedom and wanted to tear religion out by the roots. Yes, Jews—because the majority of the activists and leaders of the anti-religious front, the main ones, were our brothers, the children of Israel. And for the same reason, it upset me when they also made fun of the gentile religion—not "also," but *especially.* Instead of making heretics *bezbozhnikes,* atheists, as they called them) of the Gentiles with their mockery, they made those same Gentiles into anti-Semites and potential pogromists.

The following incident comes to mind. One Sunday morning, when the Gentiles were supposed to be leaving church, the Communists staged an anti-religious demonstration across from the church. One man was dressed up as a rabbi, wearing a prayer shawl and *tfilin.* A second was dressed up as an authentic Russian priest. The crowd carried parodies of icons as they marched opposite the church, giving speeches ridiculing religion. After the speeches, they made a fire and threw in the prayer shawl and the *tfilin,* as well as, let the distinction be noted, the priest's garb and the icons. When the Gentiles came out of church and saw that they were making fun of their saints, they . . . well, they could not actually do anything. But I saw that they were getting worked up among themselves. Several gentile women made threatening gestures in the direction of the demonstration, and I heard isolated words in Russian, such as "mangy Jews."

I recall another incident. At that time Melitopol had three synagogues: a study house that was open all day, from dawn until after evening prayers, where people were not only continually praying, but also continually studying; a communal synagogue, which was open only in the morning and the evening; and a choral synagogue, which was open only on the Sabbath and the holidays, and where the bourgeoisie of Melitopol used to hold "services." All three synagogues were located on one courtyard.

Va-yehi hoyoym, one day, the Communists wanted to requisition the choral synagogue and turn it into a club. I read the announcement that in such and such a place, and at such and such a time, there would be a grand anti-religious meeting at which the question of requisitioning the choral synagogue would be discussed and the public would be able to speak out. Even the defenders of religion would be allowed to take the floor and present their side. So I went.

The first speaker happened to speak logically and seriously: There was a shortage of houses. The choral synagogue was closed anyway, except on Sabbaths and holidays, and if the bourgeoisie wanted to pray, it could do so in the other two synagogues. And a club was needed, etc. etc.—logical arguments. But the rest of the speakers simply made fun of religion in general, and Judaism in particular. One Jewish woman spoke up about how she had once been pious, had blessed the Sabbath candles, kept kosher. But now she could see. Now she was liberated from all of these silly and nonsensical superstitions. Now Communism was her religion.

After the son of the Kaunas Preacher (Rabinovitsh) finished his speech —delivered in a broken Russian and with the melody of a traditional sermon, calling for the choral synagogue not to be turned into a club—after his speech, a couple of speakers attacked him with such contempt and derision that I found it nauseating, and I left.

But the same Communists who were doing everything they could against religion made it possible for me to avoid going astray and desecrating the Sabbath. This was the story. One Tuesday—was it in 1919 or the summer of 1920?—I came home from work and discovered that a tough from the White Guard had come to our house that day and informed us that the next day I was to report to such and such a place, in Semionovka, a village about seven *versts* from Melitopol.

This was a big surprise for me. Up to that time, power in our city was continually shifting. Now it was with the Reds, now with the Whites, and so on. No one bothered with such young lads. And now, suddenly, something new! I asked around, and found out the following from a friend and neighbor: The White Guard had also been to his house, and he too had to report to Semionovka the next day. What for? Every young man over the age of sixteen was being taken to dig trenches. Everyone had to dig, and that was it.

In short, I did not sleep that night. I got up at dawn and together with my neighbor marched off. We finally arrived at the appointed place. There they registered us, gave each of us a pick and shovel, and ordered us to go to a field about ten *versts* from the village. It was not really a field, but a stretch of flat land consisting of dried clay. There was not a tree, not a trace of grass—a wasteland. Only a can of water stood, warming in the sun.

Having drunk—there could be no talk of resting—we had to get to work immediately. We started to dig, but the earth would not be dug! It had to be broken up first with the pick. And so we worked until evening, only digging half a trench. We rested a little and set off for home. At dawn, we set out on foot again, this time, directly to the field. Again, we worked with the pick until with God's help, we finished one trench, long and wide —but only in the evening.

The next day, Friday, I stood there hacking at the earth with a bitter and heavy heart. The sun burned mercilessly. The earth was hard as stone and tomorrow was the Sabbath! Would I have to desecrate the Sabbath? That would have been worse for me than exile! I asked my neighbor what he thought about it. He said that he was afraid that the next day, the Sabbath, we would have to work. So I hacked at the earth and thought: Should I pretend to be sick? Or should I ask the supervisor to let me go for the Sabbath? Hush. What will happen the *next* Sabbath? At the rate I was working I would be working on the seven trenches for the next month. And who had the strength to walk seventeen *versts* every twenty-four hours, without enough to eat or enough sleep?

While I was sunk in such dark thoughts, I suddenly heard a whistle, and immediately after the whistle a voice: "Hand in your tools, now!" I turned my head and saw that the supervisor was taking everyone's pick and shovel. "Faster, faster! The Reds are coming." He started to rush the crowd and, after a while, he disappeared. Hearing that the Reds were coming made us all very happy and, with joy in our hearts, we began to march home. When we arrived in the city, the Reds were already in power.

I did not like the fact that they, the Reds, requisitioned my uncles' appetizing store either. But, on the other hand, I *did* like it when some time later, these uncles of mine were sent away somewhere in Crimea, where they were settled on the land together with other relatives and, in general, with all other formerly bourgeois and currently "déclassé" elements. (Years later, when we were already in America, all of our relatives asked us for help. But the uncles who lived in the Jewish colonies in Crimea were the only ones who never needed help.)[20]

At the end of 1920, Wrangel met his final defeat, and the constant exchange of power came to an end. But instead of becoming better, times got harder.

In the years 1918, 1919, 1920, we did not live badly. I worked—and no longer for wages, but on a fifty-fifty basis. That is, if I did a job and got a thousand rubles for it, I would give half of it to the boss and take half of it for myself. My mother and the other children sold bread, bagels, apples, or saccharine, and we earned very good money. True, many things were unavailable. Instead of kerosene, we used oil for lighting (a cotton wick in a vessel with oil). Instead of sugar we used saccharine or hard candies. Instead of shoes, we wore *kolodkas* (flat wooden soles with a pair of leather straps). For bedding, we used sack material.

Personally, I did not suffer from the civil war at all. It was a time of suspense, which made us savor life even more. Besides the general tension, I was also kept in suspense by the books that I read. Read? I would literally devour the books of Jules Verne, Mayne Reid, Fenimore Cooper, and, in general, the books from the Russian series "Adventure on Land and Sea."[21] Later, I also devoured textbooks on physics, chemistry, botany, and the like. Whether I understood them or not, I kept devouring them.

My passion for books of the Jules Verne type was so great that I once became a common thief because of it. I was then extremely pious. Once, I realized in the middle of the street that I had forgotten to put on my *arbakanfes,* my ritual fringed garment—and one is not permitted to go more than four ells without *tsitsis.*[22] I fell into such a muddle that I literally had no idea what to do. Miraculously, I had an ingenious idea. One may go four ells without *tsitsis,* so I made four strides and stood still for a while. Then I made another four strides, and again stood still, all the way home. It was really quite a distance, but I did not go more than four ells at a time.

And I was also strictly ethical. When I once found some money that a gentile woman had lost, I ran after her for quite a ways, until I caught up with her and gave her the money. And when she wanted to reward me with some of the money, I refused it.

But once, it happened that I was called to a house to open a lock and make a key for it. The lock was on a bookcase. A young woman showed me the lock that I was supposed to open, while she herself went into the kitchen. Having opened it, I took a look at the books and—what do I see? Jules Verne's book, *Voyage to the Center of the Earth!*[23] In short, I had to read it. Should I ask the woman to lend it to me? What if she doesn't want to? I thought and thought, and I figured: I'll take the book with me without the woman's knowledge. I'll read it overnight, and tomorrow, when I return to install the lock, I'll put the book back in its place. And that is what I did. I read all evening until I fell asleep reading. The next day, I reinstalled the lock, but not the book, because I had not yet finished it and I wanted to know how it ended, as if my life depended on it. And so the book stayed with me until the famine, when I sold it, together with all of my religious and secular books, for half a pound of bread.

Besides reading books, I had my work cut out for me reading all the decrees posted on the walls. New decrees were constantly being posted. For the most part, they dealt with sabotage, speculation, and weapons, and the punishment, in all decrees without exception, was *v'plot do rastrelu,* up to pain of death.

For a little while, I also busied myself with teaching *Ein Ya'akov* to a group between afternoon and evening prayers. I taught together with Zvi Krol, who later became a fine lyric poet in the Land of Israel and a historian of Jewish Socialism.[24] He interpreted the *Ein Ya'akov* for the group, and I discussed everything according to the various commentaries.

I had work the whole time, both under the Whites and under the Reds, if not for civilians, then for the Whites and the Reds and their institutions —for example, fixing plumbing, opening locks and safes, making keys, fixing rifles and revolvers, and the like. And I was paid for everything. With the Reds, besides being paid, I received rations for a time (a half a loaf of bread, sugar, tea, and a few other things).

But when in 1920 the Reds secured their position in our town and began to establish order (perhaps it was half a year earlier), my brother

Leybke and I came down with typhus. We lay in bed for two weeks until the fever broke, and for two weeks after it broke. Then my mother and the other children came down with spotted typhus. So we, Leybke and I, left our beds and, barely able to move our feet, began to hover around the other patients. After spotted typhus, we went through stomach typhus, and three times "recurring typhus."

Later, I started in with the business of "universal training," and for three evenings a week, two or three hours an evening, I had to take part in military exercises (along with all youths between sixteen and military age).

In 1921, there was a terrible drought in the Volga region and famine broke out. Very soon, the famine moved in with us in Melitopol as well. For a while, it did not bother us, because we had prepared some sacks of flour, barley, and so on. And we also had a bit of an income. But soon Melitopol filled up with soldiers (Red ones, of course), and a half a *minyan* of them were quartered in our house. (House? It was an apartment of two rooms in a clay hut.) Well, after their two-month stay with us, nothing remained of the sacks of food, and in the winter of 1921–22 we also tasted hunger.

There was enough bread on the market. There was even enough white bread, let alone bread made of cornmeal. But it was so expensive that I would not have been able to buy more than about one pound for a full week's wages. Everything that we children earned we would hand over to our mother, and she would buy food for the day and divide it up equally. The portions got smaller and smaller as time went on, as did the means to buy them. So my mother's two brothers, who had the appetizing store (they were back in business), had pity on us and gave my mother a little money every day to buy something to eat. And every day our food for six people consisted of half a pound of bread made of chaff, a half a quart of milk mixed with half a quart of water, soup made of a sort of straw (apparently the husks of threshed or pounded grains of barley), and boiled water with saccharine. There was a time that we stuffed ourselves with oilcake, the "bricks" that are left after the oil is pressed out of sunflower seeds. But very soon, the cost of oilcake began to climb steeply. And the oilcake itself was harder than stone.

So we lived the entire winter on the above-mentioned foods. From time to time, we would get hold of something sweet. When I fixed some pipes, or did some other kind of work in a wealthy house—the rich did not know the famine at all—I would sometimes ask for something to eat instead of money. Sometimes, I would get a loaf of real white bread, or a couple of potatoes, or a glass of barley, and I would bring it home and share it with everyone. But this happened rarely.

There was nothing to use for heating. We had barely enough horse and cow dung to fuel the fire to cook a little soup and bring the teapot to a boil. So we children used to lie in bed far into the middle of the day. But when spring came that was the end of *sheves akhim gam yakhad,* of "brothers dwelling together."[25] First thing in the morning, each of us would go off to the market and wander around there, each on his own, poking around and looking for something to eat. There was plenty of horsemeat, as well as "bricks" of congealed blood that the gentile women used to bring to the market to sell. But there was no question of bringing that home. Despite the famine, everything at home was kosher.[26] Leybke did used to have a bit of congealed blood from time to time, but in such a way that no one knew. I never even tasted any blood. I did try to eat horsemeat, but it was so tough and tasteless that after a few minutes of chewing I had to spit it out.

Cats and dogs could not be found anywhere. But all the trash heaps at the market were full of dead and half-dead people. The half-dead used to whisper continually, "Food! Bread!" And the dead lay covered, surrounded by flies. Most of them were all swollen. Hundreds of people would pass by without paying them any attention. During the day, long wagons would arrive at the marketplace and sanitary workers would throw into them all the dead bodies that were lying around on the trash heaps. And the next day, the same procedure would repeat itself.

When an acquaintance died, of hunger of course, we all envied him: lucky person! In general, the hunger dulled both the mind and the ability to feel, and filled a person with a dull apathy. Young children would leave the house for a whole day, dragging themselves through the market and making the rounds of the wealthy houses begging for food, and it did not begin to bother their parents.

I had accumulated a couple dozen religious and secular books, which were my pride and joy—books to which I was attached with body and soul. But during the famine years I once figured, "What do I need them for when I can't eat them?" So I brought them all to the market and sold them to the peasants to use as rolling papers. And for all the money that I made, I bought half a pound of bread for myself. (I ate half of it immediately, and the other half I brought home.)

Finally, in the summer of 1922, Melitopol began to receive assistance from the American ARA.[27] Every day, the ARA distributed a meal to every hungry family. People also began to receive parcels, food packages, from America.

Now that it was possible to contact America, we began to barrage my father with letters asking him to send us money or parcels and, if possible, to bring us over to him in America. Soon, we began to get letters from my father, and in several of the letters we found American money—here a five-dollar bill, there two dollars or one dollar—and we began to recover. True, the inflation was tremendous. A simple envelope cost fifty thousand rubles. At the beginning of the summer sending a letter to America cost half a million rubles, and at the beginning of the fall, a whole million. Rye bread cost about three million rubles, a pair of shoes, 120 million. One could barely get by for two days on a dollar. But now, with father's help, it was a little easier. For a couple of weeks, we could eat a little more and better. My father wrote that he was enclosing several dollars with every letter, but since very soon (actually at the beginning of summer 1922) we began to receive his letters opened, we wrote him that he should not enclose any more money in his letters.

At the beginning of fall 1922, we received a parcel. A little later, we got three more, and then seven all at once. Every parcel consisted of white flour, sugar, tea, cocoa, condensed milk, vegetable shortening, and a kind of thin groats. So we kept the first four parcels for ourselves (dividing up perhaps half of them). The other seven we sold, lending the money we made to a relative to expand his business. In return, the relative paid us a certain sum every day, enabling us not only to live comfortably, but to save something up as well. And when at the beginning of spring 1923 we received another twelve parcels at once, we became truly wealthy.

During the famine, I had only one thought and one dream: to eat bread until I was full, to sit in a secluded room over a five-pound loaf of bread and eat until my belly protruded. When we started to receive parcels this dream of mine came true. Over the course of several months, I ate a whole pound of fresh white bread at every breakfast. I would eat up the pound of bread plain, by itself, as a kind of appetizer to breakfast.

As they recovered, people started to leave for America, so we worked on our father, once again asking him to bring us over to him. Not knowing how to go about this, my father turned to Jacob Mark's agency, which, for a substantial sum, promised him to bring all of us all the way from Melitopol directly to Brownsville, New York.[28]

Suddenly, we received a letter from Riga saying that we should take out passports and come to Riga to such and such an agency, where all the necessary papers would be made up for us and we would be sent off to America. We replied to the agency that we could not get passports for the oldest two children, Leybke and me, because being close to draft age it would, of course, be impossible for us to leave Russia legally. The agency informed my father of our difficulty and said that if he would agree to pay four hundred dollars (in addition to the 212 dollars for our second-class ship tickets), the agency would bring us to America. My father immediately agreed to pay the four hundred dollars, and soon we received another letter from the Riga agency, which was managed by Yitskhok Mark, Jacob Mark's son. It said that we, Leybke and I, should go to a town on the border with Latvia, and from there we would be brought to Riga. Nothing could be done for us if we did not go to that town.

But we could not go to that town, because to do so we would have needed a pass, which we could not get. So it was decided that we would go to a larger city, a little further from the border, and there we would see what to do. Without a second thought, we stuffed our pockets full of necessities. (In order to avoid suspicion that we were speculators or who knows what, we did not want to carry any luggage.) A speculator who was a neighbor of ours was getting ready to travel to Polotsk, a city not far from the Lithuanian border, and since he was a cunning fellow, we gave him a few rubles and he saw to it that we traveled in peace.

We arrived in Polotsk on July 1, 1923. The speculator brought us to a certain house and we stayed there for a couple of days. A few days later, the innkeeper informed us that some carts were there from a small village right on the Lithuanian border. Two Gentiles had come to town in the morning to shop for something, and in the evening they would be going back. So, if we wanted, they could take us, my brother and me, to the village with them. It would only cost us a couple of silver rubles. Once we were near the border we could easily sneak over, because guys were smuggling both goods and people across almost every night.

We eagerly accepted his suggestion, and by evening we were already riding on the carts. I was on one cart, and my brother on the other. We traveled on an unpaved road through a forest. You could see nothing besides the sky and the earth. When it became good and dark, the carts turned off of the road and went deeper into the forest, where they stopped. The Gentiles unhitched the horses, made a fire, and sat down to eat. I burrowed into the hay on the wagon and covered myself with a tarpaulin. It did not even occur to me that we should be afraid. After all, we were carrying several silver rubles and a whole fifty dollars in cash, and here we were at night with two Gentiles! But it did not occur to me at all to think about that. I burrowed into the hay and fell right asleep.

I awoke at dawn, washed my hands in the morning ritual, and since I had brought my *tfilin* instead of the notebooks with my writings, I was able to pray in them. It became light, the Gentiles hitched up the horses, and off we went. Only in the late afternoon did we see peasant cottages from a distance. By the time we entered one of the cottages, it was dark. We washed our hands and drank down glasses of milk. Then they led us to a barn to take a nap in the hay until midnight, when they would wake us up to cross the border.

About twelve at night we heard a voice: "Come!" We began to walk: Leybke and I, another couple of youths, a couple of young Gentiles with bundles of flax, and a young man, the guide. We strode through a thick forest. Suddenly, the guide stopped near a cabin. He told us to wait while he approached the cabin by himself. A Red Army soldier came to meet him and asked how many people we were. They conversed and went into the cabin together. After a while, the guide came out and we continued on our way. The forest became sparser. We went downhill, forded a stream about three feet deep, climbed up the other bank. "We are now on the Lithuanian side," said the guide.

We started forward. Suddenly, we heard a whistling. The guide gestured to us with his hand to lie down on the ground. From afar, we saw riders on horseback: it was they who had been whistling. When it quieted down and the riders were no longer to be seen, we stood up and set off on our walk. We left the forest and were now in open fields. We walked like this for a whole night, without stop until dawn, when we fell into a peasant hut and immediately went to sleep.

In the morning, a man came in and said that he was our agent. He wanted fifty dollars as a down payment for taking us directly to Riga. The rest of the money he would get at the Riga office. We gave him the fifty, climbed onto a cart, and came to a station, where we boarded a train. And on Friday, July 6, 1923, we arrived in Riga.

First off, the agent brought us to a hotel, which was strictly kosher and charged eighty cents a day. And from there we immediately left for Mark's agency, where the agent received another sixty dollars from Mark for smuggling us over the border. After the Sabbath, we reported to quarantine, a kind of barracks for emigrants on Kosakenstrasse, where we stayed for almost a month. We paid eighty cents a day. The first time that we sat down to eat dinner they served us sausages and something that appeared to be butter on the same plate. There was an immediate uproar and a couple of older Jews went off somewhere to find out about *kashrut.** A while later, they came back with a Jew who looked like a rabbi. He said that he was the *kashrut* supervisor of the quarantine and he assured us that everything was completely kosher. The fatty substance that looked like butter was not butter, but margarine, a vegetable fat, neither meat nor dairy.

We spent the whole month in Riga as tourists. We walked around the city almost every day, spending time by the Dvina River, munching on chocolate. (Leybke mostly went to the movies.) We did not buy clothing there. A cloth suit there cost between fifteen and twenty dollars, a pair of shoes not less than four dollars. And they told us that everything was cheaper in Hamburg.

Oh yes, my brother Leybke already began to lose his "greenness" in Riga. Our barrack consisted of over twenty cots, and our fellow inmates were all young men. So for the first couple of days, Leybke and I got up an hour or two earlier than usual, when everyone else was still asleep, washed our hands, put on our *tfilin,* and prayed. But one time, a fellow got up while we were in the middle of prayers. Seeing us in our *tfilin,* he woke up several friends and they made fun of us. We could barely finish our prayers. The next day, Leybke said that he was not going to pray anymore! And he kept, and has kept, his word ever since!

I, too, stopped praying, but only in quarantine. I started going to synagogue every morning, a distance of about fifteen or twenty minutes.

On August 2, we received our visas, and we began to prepare to leave Riga. We went to the agency and settled our account. The agency had 150 dollars that our father had sent us. So we paid off the loans that it had given us—forty dollars for the quarantine and ten dollars for transit cards. (From the four hundred dollars that the agency had received from our father, it laid out 160 dollars for the Latvian passes and sixty dollars for the smuggler.)

On Saturday evening, August 4, we left Riga, and on August 6, we arrived in Hamburg. As soon as we arrived, they disinfected our things with steam. A doctor vaccinated us against smallpox, and off we went to quarantine, which was in Hamburg-Veddel (the emigration halls—barrack number fifteen).

In the Hamburg quarantine, we paid thirty-five cents a day, a wild bargain compared to Riga. In general, compared to Riga, everything was cheap in Hamburg. A cloth suit then (August 1923) cost around ten dollars, shoes two dollars and fifty cents. But the inflation was terrible. For example, I would go to the Hamburg black market exchange and change a dollar for, let's say, fifteen billion marks. When I arrived back at the quarantine, the dollar was worth twice as much. We greenhorns* (emigrants) did not want to sell anything for marks.

But in the fall and winter of 1923–24, the inflation became literally insufferable. We were no longer in Hamburg at the time. But our mother and the rest of the children were there then. They had left Russia legally. It cost a fortune. For all the documents in Russia, my mother paid twenty-seven and a half billion rubles. The trip from Melitopol to Moscow cost her ten billion rubles, and from Moscow to Riga, twenty-five billion. Quarantine now cost sixty cents a day. Breakfast consisted of bread, raspberry juice, butter, and tea with sugar; lunch of bread, meat and potatoes, cucumbers, soup, and compote; dinner of bread, herring or sardines or sausage and potatoes, tea with sugar. The general prices in Hamburg at that time were: a woman's dress, eleven dollars; bread, fifteen cents a kilo; butter, fifty cents a pound; meat, thirty cents a pound; cocoa butter, twenty cents a pound; and sugar, twelve and a half cents a pound.

And for "dessert," the Germans had no other name for the emigrants than "Russian swine!"

On August 25, we boarded the ship *Finland* of the American Line—a small ship with just one smokestack. We were supposed to travel on deck, where dozens of cots stood one on top of the other, but we found an empty cabin with four cots and moved into it. On the ship, Leybke lost even more of his greenness. When it came time for dinner, the pious Jews asked that they be given a separate table with kosher food. So first of all, they sat us at a separate table. But since there was no kosher cooked food, they served us baked potatoes with herring. Seeing such a meager dinner, and noticing the full plates of meat and soup on the other tables, Leybke went right over to the "gentile" table, where he dined quite nicely. A couple of hours later, he became yellow. Really, without exaggeration. He became yellow, and started to vomit violently.

On September 6, the ship arrived in New York harbor, and then sat there for all of six days. They did not allow any of the passengers to disembark. Even before we left the ship, we got a taste of America's goodness. Almost every day that we were on the anchored ship, our father and older brother came to visit us, and each time they brought us all sorts of good things. In a small boat, they would come right up to our ship and tie the gift packages to a rope that we would lower. What did they not bring us? Roasted chicken, fresh fruit, and sweets were all a lot more tasty than the bread, potatoes, and herring I had been eating for the almost two weeks of the sea journey.

Finally, on Wednesday, September 12, the second day of Rosh Hashanah,* they let us off the ship. They led us, together with quite a few other passengers, to a certain building, and before they let each person through a kind of small doorway they stopped him, asked him something, and opened a book for him. There was a man there with several books in front of him, and this was the man who did it. When they came to me, the man asked me if I could read. In response to my answer that I could, he asked me in which language. As soon as he heard that I could read and write Yiddish, Hebrew, Russian, a little German, and a pinch of English to boot, he gestured for me to go.

I left one area and entered another. There I found a real celebration. Many of my fellow travelers were greeting, hugging, and kissing their relatives who had come to take them home. I looked for my father and brother, but there was no sign of either. It was already late afternoon and the hall where we were was emptying out. So I went up to a man who was bustling around and asked him what to do. He pinned a white piece of paper with the word "HIAS"* to my jacket, and said that I should not worry, they would take care of me. He did the same thing to my brother and a couple of other fellows.

A while later, a young man of about thirty-five came up to us and told us to follow him. In short, we crossed some water, traveled a little on a train that went underground, and then got into a sort of yellow automobile. We traveled a little ways, and the guide let one fellow out, but only after the man gave the guide a couple of dollars. A while later, a second man got out, but the second man also gave the guide a couple of dollars— to pay for the automobile, that is.

We did not have our father's address, only the address of the store where our older brother, Shloymke, worked: 1098 Manhattan Avenue, Brooklyn. We gave this address to the guide. He said that he had never heard of such a street in Brooklyn, but he would enquire about it. So the automobile sped on and I became interested in looking at the strange clocks it had in it. I found one face where the numbers changed occasionally to be especially novel. Now it was forty, and suddenly, fifty, and a while later, sixty. The further we went, the bigger the numbers got, until suddenly there was a one with two zeroes, a one with a ten, and then a twenty. And now there was a two with some figures to the side, then a three and a four. I thought, "There is probably some sort of gadget in the automobile that records how many *versts* it has gone. If so, America is not only a rich country but a smart one as well."

We went on and on, stopping several times for the guide to get out to speak with people. Finally, the automobile came to a stop and the guide told us to get out. I glanced at the changing numbers. They were no longer changing. A six and two zeroes stood frozen. I thought to myself, "It probably means that we have traveled six *versts* or miles." Since he had ridden with us for so long, I gave the guide a two-dollar tip. He took the two dollars and gestured for me to give him another six dollars.

"Eight dollars?" I called out in amazement.

"*Ja wohl!*" he said. He had to pay the taxi eight dollars.

It occurred to me that the "six" in the automobile must mean "six dollars." And so I said to the guide, "But the automobile only ticked off six dollars!"

"That is true," he conceded, but he wanted two dollars for wasting so much of his time with us.

I started to argue with him in German, of which he understood one word in ten. He did not understand Yiddish at all. Then a girl approached us and asked in Russian if we were by any chance Sam's brothers. Hearing Russian was really a pleasure for me. I could now untwist my tongue. I told her about the guide and the automobile. She started to speak to him in English and on her advice we gave him the required six dollars.

She told us that Sam [that is, Shloymke] worked downstairs in the store and that he had told her that he would be having guests in the coming days: a couple of green brothers. So she understood right away that we were they. Since the store was closed and it was already late, we should stay the night at her house.

The next morning, we went down to the store, and a while later Sam arrived. Yes, it was he! We embraced, kissed, and started to talk. When we had finished our conversation, he telephoned our father, and by evening we were already in a seven-room apartment having a feast.

After Sukkot* we started to think about what to do to make a living. Since I had a sharp mind when it came to reading and writing, I desired to become a lawyer. But my father worked for someone else and we still had to bring over my mother and the rest of the children. So it was decided that I would work during the day and go to school at night. But what should I do? People advised me to discard my trade and get experience in a delicatessen store. Once I had experience and a couple of dollars saved up, I could open a business myself. In short, one morning I looked through the "Help Wanted" section of the *Morgn zhurnal,* and then went off to a delicatessen that wanted a "green boy."[29] Shloymke went with me.

Yes, I could start work, but I would have to work from seven in the morning until around ten or eleven at night, and even later on Saturdays. In exchange, I would receive ten dollars a week. When I heard that I would have to work on the Sabbath, I left immediately. The next day, and subsequent days, I continued to look for a job in various businesses. But I heard the same tune everywhere: Saturday was the main moneymaker, the really busy day.

"Well," I thought, "I'm not going to be a businessman. I'll have to go work in a shop." So Shloymke brought me to a metal novelty factory, where they wanted to pay me twelve dollars for fifty hours of work. While Shloymke spoke with the foreman, I contemplated the workers at the machines. There was a whole variety of machines, and next to every machine sat a young man making rhythmic motions with his hands and feet, every once in a while straightening his back. Seeing how they were breaking their backs and hearing what the wages were, I turned the job down and later told my father to take me into his shop, Mirken's iron shop, where he was the foreman. At first he was reluctant, but when I persisted he finally brought me into the shop on October 15, 1923. It was a real pleasure for me. It was almost next door to our house, there were eight hours of work a day, something to which I was accustomed, there was no work on the Sabbath, and the pay was twenty dollars a week!

My mother and the other three children did not arrive in America until a week before Passover, 1924. So for half a year, I was the cook and a bit of a "homemaker" in general. Every day, the butcher would bring us a cleaned kosher chicken and, since I ate lunch at home for half an hour, I would start the chicken cooking with all the fixings over a low flame. By evening, I would find it completely ready. And not only did we have chicken. Almost every day, my father brought home all sorts of good things: baked goods, vegetables, fruit, and the like.

We had a seven-room apartment (seventy-five dollars a month in rent) for just four men; we had food and drink, all sorts of good things. But until my mother arrived I felt like I was in exile the whole time, more precisely, like a Marrano.[30]

It started from the very first day that I was together with my father. The *korzinka*, a kind of trunk made of woven reeds, with all of our things, including my *tfilin*, remained on the ship. The first morning, I asked my father where he kept his prayer shawl and *tfilin*, and he responded that he did not have any *tfilin*. He had once had a pair, but they were lost. In the evening, when it was time for dinner, my father sat down at the table without covering his head. Shloymke did the same. Seeing what they did, Leybke also uncovered his head, or more precisely, took off his hat. Seeing that I ate with my head covered, my father started to lecture me: That was well and good in Duboy, but not in America. In America, everyone ate without covering his head and I should not put on such pious airs. In short, it was a new country and a new life, and I had to start acting like a proper person! I thought it over: I have already said a blessing. Honoring one's father is also an important thing. So instead of opposing him, let me oblige him. This was on Friday evening, and, of course, *kiddush** and the Sabbath songs were out of the question.

The next time that we ate dinner together I pretended that I had completely forgotten about the American etiquette and did not remove my hat. But this time, my father did not say anything to me. He just stretched out his hand and took the hat off of my head. I do not know what came over me, but I did not protest. (Can it be that I was afraid of picking a fight with my father?) From this time on, when it came time for dinner, I would first go into my room, say the blessing, and come out and sit down at the table with my head uncovered. After eating, I would go back into my room and say the blessing after the meal. Of course, in both cases, I would close the door.

On Friday evenings, I used to wait for my father to get into the bathtub. When he was in the very middle of soaping himself, I would quietly say *kiddush* for myself and take something to eat.

On the first day of Sukkot, my father told Leybke and me to get dressed and come with him to visit a *landsfroy** in New York.

"But today is Sukkot!" I said.

"Look at him, the rabbi!" my father started screaming excitedly. "He came to carry on his rabbinate in America! Get dressed and let's go!"

Seeing how upset he was, how his hands and feet were trembling, I thought for a second: It is a matter of life and death. Perhaps I should do as he says. But my immediate response was: Travel on a holiday?[31]

"I'm not going," I told my father firmly.

"Leybke, come!" And they left.

This was my first experience in America: being in exile with my own father. More precisely, it was my first unpleasant experience, because besides that I had several pleasant experiences in my first days here. The first time that I went down to buy a newspaper for my father (it was a Sunday morning), I went into a candy store and asked for a *Morgn zhurnal*. "The *Morgn zhurnal* is outside on the stand," said the storekeeper. "Go take one." I paid him the three cents, went out, took a *Morgn zhurnal,* and thought, "Imagine, he keeps his wares outside with no one even guarding them!"

I stood there thinking and looking at the newspaper stand. A man came up, took a newspaper, put something down on the stand, and left. A while later, another man did the same thing. Out of curiosity, I took a look at the stand and saw several nickels and quite a few pennies. I thought, not for nothing do they call America the "blessed land." A person keeps his wares outside, without a guard, and not only do people not simply take them, but everyone pays for them, knowing that no one is watching. What's more, no one even tries to steal a couple of cents.

Late one evening, I went out to look at Pitkin Avenue. Most of the stores were already closed. But the greatest surprise to me was that not a single store had shutters. The show windows were full of merchandise. One could easily break the glass and take everything out! At night, one could certainly cart entire stores away without so much as a rooster crowing about it. There was no other conclusion one could come to than that America is not only a blessed land, but also a land of pure saints, of strictly honest people.

Another pleasant and surprising experience: One evening, at the end of October, I went out for a walk on Pitkin Avenue. I saw a man standing on a platform, with a crowd of men and women around him. The man was speaking with such force and enthusiasm that I went up to the platform. I heard the speaker say things that nearly made me tremble with fear. He thundered against the president of the United States and against the entire government. He ended his speech with the words, "Long live the Communist Party of America!"

Instinctively, I looked around to see if there was a policeman nearby, and I thought, how can he not be afraid to speak like that against the president and the government? If he had said half as much in Russia against

Lenin and Trotsky, or against the Communist Party, they would have stood him against a wall at the very beginning of his speech and shot him like a mad dog! Now that is what I call a free country! You can even speak against the government!

And last but not least: From the time that I began to read, I had always envied writers, especially because they got to see their names in print. What I would have given to see my name in print in black and white! My hope was to see my name in print above an article, a story, or a poem. In reality, I would never get to see that. But when I got older and started to earn something, I would subscribe to a magazine, and every week I would see my name on the front cover itself—and my address as well.

Once, I was leafing through the Sunday *Morgn zhurnal* in my early days here in America. My eyes lit up when I saw a puzzle in Hebrew with a lengthy list of names of those who had solved the previous week's puzzle. Well, here was my chance to see my name in print! All I had to do was solve the puzzle and send the *Morgn zhurnal* the solution. I did it right away. For a whole week I was full of impatience and suspense. Finally, finally, the long awaited Sunday arrived. I went down at dawn, bought a *Morgn zhurnal,* and, still standing at the newsstand, started to look for my name among the dozens of others.

And what did I see? My personal and family names, black on white! Hah? Maybe I was imagining it; I took another look. Yes, it really was my name. I went back upstairs and took another look at my name. I could not get enough of looking at it. It would seem for a moment I had already gotten a good look at my name in the *Morgn zhurnal* and could put it aside. But a while later I would pick up the *Morgn zhurnal* again and look at my name once more.

Later, dissatisfaction started to gnaw at me. I was seeing my name in print, but who else saw it besides me? And anyway, what was the trick in solving a puzzle? Now if I myself composed a puzzle and the *Morgn zhurnal* printed it, then, yes, then who would compare to me? My name would then be printed prominently, by itself, not *im kol ha-neorim,* a name among dozens of other names.[32] And all the puzzle-solvers would work over MY puzzle and see my name!

When this desire of mine was also fulfilled, dissatisfaction started to gnaw at me again. Oh, if only I could see my name printed in a magazine as a real writer! I wrote a fable in verse and sent it to the *Groyser kundes.*[33] (I had already started to write stories in verse in Melitopol in 1919, but they were very clumsy.) A couple of weeks later my story was published!

And, what's more, the names of all of the contributors to the magazine were given on the very top of the front cover, and my name was among them. If I have ever in my life known what it is to feel happiness and joy, that was it!

Later, I started to publish humorous pieces, poems, short features, jokes, and witticisms in various newspapers and magazines. But this was already "matter of fact." There was no joy, no thrill. I would read them over, cut them out, and put them away somewhere.

A week before Passover, 1924, my mother arrived with the other three children. She brought my redemption with her. My father started to eat with his head covered (more precisely in a hat or a yarmulke*), and to say *kiddush* on Friday evening. And when I said the blessing after the meal, I did not have to hide behind closed doors. Rather, we said the entire blessing out in the open.

I was happy. I only worked forty-four hours a week—nine hours a day, seven-thirty to five, with half an hour for lunch, the whole week from Monday to Thursday, and eight hours on Friday. From time to time, I also worked half a day on Sunday, but for that I was paid separately, and time-and-a-half besides. From the first day on, I worked as a real ironworker, not as an apprentice or laborer, though at our place of work that was not difficult. Since my father was a kind of foreman in the shop, he made sure that they did not bully me. (There was a real foreman in the shop at the time, a German, but he only took care of the structural work. He did not get involved with the ornamental work, leaving it all to my father.)

True, I did not have any money. During my first year, all of the twenty dollars or more that I made I gave to my father. But I did not need any money. I had more than enough of everything. My father bought everything for me, as he did for the whole family. He was generous, buying only the nicest and best things.

In the evenings—three times a week—I went to night school. In the couple of months that I attended school I learned how to read English quite well, and also to understand. I did not have the patience to continue with school for more than a couple of months. You try repeating, like a first-grader: "I stand up. I sit down. I turn the knob," and so on. Instead, I started to study and read English on my own, like a non-matriculated student studying for exams in Russia.

In my free time, I would stretch out on the sofa and read (mostly poetry) or write. I had nothing to do with my brothers and sisters. Each one of them had his or her friends. So I spent my time peacefully and cheerfully with my newspapers, magazines, and books. Girls, love-*shmuv*. I was as far from that as Hitler is from justice. "People have no sense," I thought. "Look at what they waste their time on!"

If I was at all unhappy that I received only twenty dollars a week when all the other workers received thirty-three dollars, that unhappiness only lasted less than two years. Then, I too started to receive thirty-three dollars. After having worked for several months, I asked the boss for a raise in my wages. But he laughed, "You're still a greenhorn, you know! Work a while longer, and then we'll see." I finished a year of work and asked the boss again for a raise. "Everyone else is getting thirty-three dollars, so let me get at least twenty-five." But try as I might, the boss would not give me more.

I spoke with my father, and we went to see an acquaintance who said that if I was willing to work for twenty-five dollars, I could come and work for him the very next day. So the next day, my father told my boss that I did not want to work anymore for twenty dollars a week. If he gave me a raise of five dollars, fine; if not, I would leave. So the boss said, "He doesn't want to? So let him go." So I left and started to work for my father's acquaintance. A couple of weeks later, my previous boss told my father that he wanted to give me twenty-five dollars a week and that I should come back to work. I came back and worked another several months until a strike broke out. After three weeks of striking in the middle of the summer, the bosses gave in and renewed the agreement on the old conditions. And when we returned to work, I started to receive the same wages as everyone else.

So, where were we? Oh yes, personally, I was happy. My mother, though, suffered deeply, and the cause was nothing other than that my father was no longer the pious philanthropist that he had been in Duboy. During the week, he neither donned his prayer shawl and *tfilin* nor prayed. He did not even do the morning hand-washing. He just got up, washed his hands with soap, ate without ritually washing his hands, without a blessing and without the blessing after the meal, glanced at the newspaper, and went off to work.

The Sabbath. My mother would go to synagogue in the morning, and my father would go off somewhere for the whole day—in the winter to the theater, to a burlesque, or to a movie, and in the summer to swim at Coney Island. She kept begging my father to become a Jew, but her entreaties did no good. On the contrary, they only alienated him from her even more. Sometimes he used to answer her, "If you are such a pious woman, you should know that you have to obey your husband. So why not obey me and go with me on Saturday to the theater, or to Coney Island to swim?" After such a response, my mother would go into the other room and have a good cry.

Once, my father really lost his temper, and made my mother want to die. Once? Dozens of times! But this time cut the most. In her piety and loneliness, my mother used to go every Sabbath afternoon to listen to a rabbi, and my father did not like this. They used to have frequent arguments, all because my mother wanted to set him straight. During an argument he would rage at my mother, "You've been conspiring with the rabbis, God's thieves!" And he heaped scorn upon the rabbis.

Va-yehi hoyoym, one day my mother happened into a synagogue where the Doliner rebbe led prayers. She liked his praying so much that from then on every Sabbath and holiday she used to go to where the Doliner rebbe led the prayer. He was a God-fearing Jew, and a rebbe besides. Once, my mother went to him to talk about my father's impiety and asked his advice and blessing. The rebbe gave her a religious tract and told her to give it to my father to read. He hoped that after my father read it, his Jewish heart would reawaken and he would become the pious Jew he had once been.

Well, when my mother gave him a religious book that she had come across, he began to read it. As soon as he realized that it was a moralizing book that scolded and chastised those Jews who had transgressed against Jewish law, who did not put on *tfilin,* who desecrated the Sabbath, and so on, he blew up and really gave my mother a piece of his mind (besides flinging the book away): "That's it! It seems you're informing on me to your Doliner rebbe!" (He knew that my mother was praying with the Doliner rebbe because she had told him a couple of times what a wonderful prayer leader the rebbe was.) "Let him @#&%! I am not afraid of God. Am I going to be afraid of her &*%$# rebbe? They'll find out soon enough!"

But all of this was only a sort of introduction for what followed. The High Holidays* were approaching. (These were my mother's second in America. During the first High Holidays, my father had bought my mother a seat for ten dollars in the same synagogue where he went to pray. It was a large synagogue where no one knew him and where a famous cantor led services. So on those High Holidays they had gone to synagogue together.) As the High Holidays approached, my father wanted to buy my mother a seat in a synagogue where a great cantor was to lead services. But my mother suggested that it would be better for him to buy two seats, for himself and for her, in the synagogue where the Doliner rebbe was going to pray. First of all, he would save a few dollars, and second, no more delightful a prayer-leader than the Doliner rebbe could be found.

"Again with your rebbe?" Father fell upon her with such anger and wrath that not only his voice but his hands and feet trembled. "She's taken a lover and she can't tear herself away from him! Alright, you go to your lover. I'll buy a seat for myself where *I* want to go." He made such a scene in front of her that my mother cried for weeks on end.

Nor did my mother derive any pleasure from my father when it came to charity. Buy my mother clothes, or shoes, or a hat? That he would do, and only the nicest and the best. But give her a dollar, or fifty cents, for a synagogue, for a *yortsayt** or the like, that he would *not* do. "Let those parasites go to work!" he would argue. So she would save for this in whatever way she could without my father's knowledge.

But when it came to sending money to her family, there was trouble. We were pelted with letters from all sides: "Help! Send a couple of dollars!" So he regularly sent ten or fifteen dollars, and sometimes more, every month to one sister who lived with her young children in deep poverty in Poland. From time to time, he also sent a few dollars to another sister, and to a brother, too—both in Poland, as well. But when it came to sending help to my mother's family in Russia, especially to my mother's mother, my father refused to do it. He was sending enough. Let the children send some, as well!

My mother did not want to take too much from her children, nor would she have been able to. So she washed everyone's laundry and did all the other housework, and sent her family the few dollars she would have spent on laundry or on a black maid. She regularly sent money to her mother every month, of which the children contributed more than half. Later, when the Torgsin stores opened in Russia, my mother also had to send dollars to those members of her family who did not need help so badly.[34]

One year passed after another. My older brother, Shloymke, got married. Later, the second one, Leybke, did as well. The youngest daughter, Leye, finished business school and began working. But the situation at home did not change. My father remained the same impious man, and my mother's Sabbath days and holidays were spoiled. And what's more, my father developed a habit of complaining to his *landslayt** and bad-mouthing his children. "In proper families where there are so many children the father does not have to work at all!" Such and such a *landsman,** is in much better health than he, my father continued, and you know he doesn't work, and he is having a great time of it. His children support him in grand style. And he, my father, must still toil, now even more than before! If the children were only decent people. . . . And his daughters are bad characters, common whores. The older one tramps around with boys every Saturday, Sunday, and holiday, and does not come home until the middle of the night, one or two o'clock. And how she can't bring herself to part with them! As if it weren't enough that she comes home so late, she stands in the hall who knows how long and keeps on whispering with the boy! And the younger one? She is no better than the older one, maybe even worse! Have you ever heard of such a thing? When she was not yet sixteen years old, he once caught her standing in the hall holding hands with a *boytshik*!

To stand in someone else's shoes, to understand another's feelings— these were things that my father could not do. I have already told of the time that he took the hat off of my head. Now I will recall a couple of similar incidents.

Khane once lost her millinery job and was unable to find another job so quickly. So my father asked around among his acquaintances. One, who had a concession stand in a theater selling candy and drinks, promised her a job as a salesgirl. Arriving home, he happily gave Khane the news. It was clean work, easy work, and the wages were not bad. Having heard him out, Khane exclaimed that at a job like that she would have to work every Sabbath and holiday. And, well, that was all she needed! Father became a hunk of agitation incarnate and started to scream at her, "Children of rabbinical families work on the Sabbath here, and she, the little saint, doesn't want to work on the Sabbath! She wants to be more pious than anyone in the world! She came to America to be a rabbi's wife!" And he went on in that vein. Of course, Khane did not accept that job, and my father was beside himself with distress for a while, until she got another job.

There was a similar incident with Leye. She worked in a place that did multigraphing, mimeographing, typing, and mailing. She was skilled at all of these jobs and the boss liked her, so she managed to get him to allow her not to work on the Sabbath. Things once got slow at her place, and she was laid off for a while. She looked for another job, but she would have had to work on the Sabbath everywhere, which she did not want to do. One Friday evening, in the middle of eating, she told the household about this. Well, she really caught an earful from my father:

"What a big nothing! She has barely sprouted from the ground, and she's already putting on pious airs! She came to America to be a rabbi's wife!" And so on.

Leye: "But I can't work on the Sabbath!"

Father: "I can't work on you either!"

I wrote earlier that I was happy personally, but this was only true until the end of 1925. At that time, I experienced a psychic earthquake that threw me completely off balance and caused my peace of mind to disappear forever and ever. *Cherchez la femme?* Correct!

When I left Melitopol, I was already a young man of about nineteen years, but I could not understand at all why my friend Motl became so enraptured every time he spotted a girl. A neighbor of ours, a young girl, used to drop by sometimes. As soon as Motl saw her, if he was visiting, he would run right over and embrace her, especially in the vicinity of her breasts.

"For heaven's sake, Motl," I used to argue with him. "What do you get out of embracing her? And what do you get out of groping her breasts? Do you want to touch human flesh? You can touch your own hand."

"What in the world do you know?" he used to reply. "Anyway, it's so delicious, so delicious!"

"What a savage," I used to think to myself. If he had said that one of Jules Verne's novels was delicious, I would have believed him. But that someone could have a taste for embracing a girl . . . eh!

Later, while traveling on the ship, I could not understand why a gentile girl was trying to sit as close to me as possible. The gentile girl was still quite young and spoke only Ukrainian. Hearing me speak Russian, she came up to me and asked me something. The next day, I was sitting around on the deck, when my gentile girl appeared, sat down next to me, and started to talk. So I moved away from her and she moved closer to me. It seemed to me that there was a lot of room, but she, the little devil, had to sit where I was sitting!

When my mother and the children arrived in America, our house immediately became a regular youth club. Male friends used to come to visit the boys and girlfriends came to visit the girls. Every weekend the house was lively. But I did not take part in the parties. I would go into another room and immerse myself in a newspaper, a magazine, or a book. Sometimes, Khane, who was two or three years younger than I, would beg me, "Chaim, come in, spend some time with us!" But I would wave her off and go on reading.

One Saturday or Sunday, during the day it was, at the beginning of summer 1925, Khane insisted adamantly that I come in and spend some time with her company. This time I did what she asked. I sat down near a girlfriend of hers, a red-haired girl of about seventeen. When she spoke to me, I responded, and, by and by, a lively conversation developed. Becoming a little more familiar, she put one of her arms around me, and with the other hand she took my arm and wrapped it around her waist. Seeing that I felt a bit uncomfortable and embarrassed, she pressed herself closer to me and said with a smile, "Don't be afraid. I won't eat you."

The next Sunday, the girls insisted that I had to go with them to Prospect Park. And the boys helped them out. Well, alright. The whole bunch of us youths and girls went off to Prospect Park. The whole time, the red-haired girl clung to me and put my arm around her waist. And so began a chapter in which we went to Prospect Park almost every Sunday. With time, I learned to hold her by the hand and even to embrace her. To kiss her—this I did not dare. If I wasn't thinking of marrying her, how could I kiss her?

Marrying her was out of the question, not so much because I lacked the slightest urge or desire to get married, as because the girl was not for me. First, she was a regular "Gentile," and second, she kept on criticizing me. "Oh, if you would only stop messing around and would dress like a respectable person—with a crease in your trousers, a shine on your shoes, and a nice tie—then I would love you."

Once, when I missed her a lot, I asked myself, "Listen, Chaim, if this X were a boy instead of a girl, would you want to have him as an intimate friend?" And I had to answer myself, "No. If she were a young man, I would have no interest in him."

She wanted me to come to her house and "pick her up" like all the other "sweethearts" did. But I could not do it. If I was not going to marry her, I could not take up her time or make her fall in love with me even more. So we used to "go out" only in company. And she always came to see her friend Khane at our house. When there was no company, I would take her to the movies. Seeing that she would not be able to make anything of me, and that instead of getting closer to her I was actually becoming more distant, she started visiting us less often. And when she did come, it was only to see Khane. She ignored me completely. And, with time, she stopped coming altogether.

With her disappearance, my peace of mind also disappeared. Such a yearning, such a painful longing settled into my heart that I felt like killing myself. Whatever I did, my mind was elsewhere. After I had finished reading a magazine or a book, it was as if I was awakening from a stupor. "What? Did I just read something?" The weekdays were still tolerable, but when Saturday and Sunday arrived, hell opened up for me. Unable to do anything, I would sit in the house and look out the window. And when a girl who resembled or dressed like the redheaded girl went by, my heart would constrict and such an uneasiness would come over me that I was literally unable to find rest.

This condition continued in my soul for half a year, after which I gradually began to recover. At the same time, I began to keep a diary. At the end of the winter of 1926–27, I became sick with the grippe and came down with a heavy cough. The doctor ordered me to go to Lakewood for a couple of weeks.[35] I was the only young man in the hotel, and the daughter of the hotelkeeper was the only young girl. So we quickly became friends and often went for walks together. On rainy evenings, we would sit in the lobby, just she and I, and she would sing such heartfelt, delicious Russian songs that my heart would melt with bliss. When I came home after spending two weeks in the hotel, I felt completely cured of my longing for the redhead. Now I longed for the girl from the hotel. . . . But I never did regain my peace of mind.

In July 1927, I met Sam Z., and a light went on within me. This was a person unlike any other. Pearls of wisdom poured from his mouth—such deep and profound psychological thoughts and observations. He looked me over, saw my handwriting, heard how I spoke, and analyzed me in such a way that I saw myself in my psychic nakedness. I am an introvert; my functions are thought and feeling. And he gave me a whole lecture about this, mixing in Freud and Adler and Jung and everyone else.[36] That man was a real psychologist.

Later, in November of the same year, when Professor Fischel Schneersohn came to New York, I did not miss a single one of his lectures, and with each lecture that I heard I somehow became more adult, more perceptive—but also more unhappy.[37] *Da es atsmekho*, know yourself! But there was so much to learn and to know, and I was a real ignoramus.

In the summer of 1928, I met a seventeen-year-old girl. She had pitch-black hair and burning eyes and her whole being breathed love and passion. The morality of the herd was foreign to her and she was completely free of inhibitions. She was like a hybrid of Isadora Duncan and George Sand, and she wrote—and still writes to this day—wonderful lyrical poems.[38] The very first time we met, she covered my whole face with kisses and acquainted my sense of touch with her anatomy. . . . We lived far away from one another—a three-hour trip—so I was at her place a couple of times, and she was at mine a lot more than that. We went no further than kissing and petting.

It was a time of prosperity and success. In every newspaper and magazine there were screaming advertisements: "Success! Learn this, do that, and you'll have success!" And I sat year in, year out at the punch machine and punched holes. In October 1928, I felt that, if I had to continue to sit and punch holes, I would have a nervous breakdown. I talked it over with my father and with the boss, and someone else took my place.

What should I do now? Should I remain an ironworker my whole life and slave away in the shop forever? People advised me to become a draftsman. I inquired at Cooper Union, but it was not for me.[39] One had to have a high school education. In the meantime, my union organized a class on blueprint reading—how to read and understand a plan. Now that was what I needed! So I joined immediately.

For several weeks, twice a week (every Monday and Wednesday), I went to the blueprint lectures in New York. On my way to the lecture, I would read a book on philosophy and, on my way from the lecture, I read a book of poetry. So I did not get all that much out of the lectures. As a rule, I should have occupied myself with mathematics and books about blueprints and mechanical drawing. But what could I do when I literally could not breathe without a book of poetry?

Nevertheless, after the course, I could see where once I had been blind —I mean when it came to work in the shop. I started to understand what I was doing, and by looking at a blueprint I now could lay out a piece of work by myself.

On March 25, 1929, we moved out of Brownsville to Coney Island. My father very much loved to swim, which he did eight months out of the year, and he wanted to live near the ocean. It was slow in the shop, so he now had enough time to go swimming. And when, with God's help, we went out on strike at the beginning of May and struck until the middle of July, he certainly had the time.

It is worth describing this strike at a little greater length. The administration of the union was then in the hands of the left wing, and although a deep crisis already reigned in our trade (perhaps more than half the members of our union were without work), the union nevertheless decided not to give in to the bosses by working according to the old agreement—thirty-six dollars for a forty-four hour week—but to go out on strike. Toward that end, it called a special meeting for Tuesday, April 23, 1929. Let me quote here from my diary of the time:

> I left for the meeting of my union at a quarter after seven in the evening. The hall was full. About 800 people were there, two-thirds of our membership. At about nine o'clock the meeting began. After the financial secretary, A.R., a lively little, familiar sort of Jew, illuminated the situation in the trade, a discussion began.
>
> The first speaker from the crowd, a full-bodied, bald Jew, an ardent union man who mainly went idle, spoke bitterly against the bosses and for a strike and was warmly applauded. After him spoke an older, old-worldly Jew with a steady job. He spoke politely, calmly, and logically against the union officers and against a strike—and the crowd hooted him down. A third spoke heatedly and passionately for a strike and the crowd applauded him with enthusiasm. After him spoke K, a big shot in the union, an empty poser and a cheap demagogue. He spoke angrily and bitterly against the Jew who had spoken against a strike, calling him a "representative of the bosses," and giving him a good, all-around scolding. After him the shop delegate K-N spoke for a strike. "This is," he said, "the only solution to the current situation. If we vote against a strike, it will mean that we admit our weakness, and it will mean the death of the union."
>
> One more person spoke, calmly and to the point, against a strike. "First," he said, "we have to organize ourselves. In the meantime, however, we must remain with the old contract, because if we go out on strike, not only will we not win, but we will also most likely lose the old conditions. We should not fool ourselves. We are a minority in the trade. Most shops are open shops and more than half of the workers are non-union men. And besides that, there is now a lot of unemployment. What we need now is to have another conference with the bosses and if we don't win our new demands perhaps we can maintain the old conditions." I applauded him passionately, but the crowd booed him and hooted him down.

The next speaker spoke for a strike. "We need," he said, "to accept the bosses' challenge. We need to fight! It is better to fight and lose than to give in without a struggle!"

After the "discussion" the crowd voted on a strike by secret ballot. There will apparently indeed be a strike. Most of the workers are unemployed and embittered, with nothing to lose. They will certainly vote for a strike. I voted "no." The bosses may really be my "most bitter enemies," with whom I must "fight to the death," but I know that they are right, after all. There is no work. Most of the shops sit idle and the planned strike does not even begin to worry the bosses. On the contrary, they are quite happy. But they nevertheless do not want to take advantage of this opportunity to lower wages or add a few hours. All they want is for us to wait another year and work under the old conditions for the time being. And they are absolutely right. This is not the time to demand a four-dollar raise.

In the end, we struck from the beginning of May until the middle of July and lost the strike—not only the strike, but the union as well. When the bosses informed us in the middle of July that we should return to work under the old conditions, my father went to the strike headquarters, but the hall was locked and there was no sign of the officers. No more union!

We worked from the middle of July until September, when our shop closed completely for several weeks. I started to look for another job, but in vain. I would have been happy to work for twenty dollars a week, but that did not do any good either. For fifteen dollars a week, I *would* have been able to get a job doing upholstery. But I would have had to work on the Sabbath. In the middle of October, my father and I went to work in an iron shop and worked there for several weeks.

In the middle of March 1930, we went back to work in our old shop under the old conditions. But the bosses soon thought it over and—since wages were being cut everywhere and since they had to follow the lead of the other bosses even though they did not have the heart to do as the others—they decided that we should work forty-eight hours instead of forty-four. We worked forty-eight hours a week for a while for the same thirty-six dollars. But the bosses saw that they could not afford it and they cut wages. They kept on cutting until my father's wages went from fifty-two dollars to twenty-five dollars, and mine from thirty-six dollars to seventeen dollars.

There were times of "slack*" and times of "busy,"* until around 1932, when work came to a complete stop. At first we searched everywhere for a job, but not being able to find one, we, both my father and I, stopped looking and started to live off the other members of the family.

My mother never despaired of returning my father to the right path. Whenever my father was in a good mood and wanted my mother's attention and love, she would set a condition for him: Wash before you eat, pray, and so on. She kept it up for so long that he began to oblige her. He began to put on his prayer shawl and *tfilin* every morning and to wash before eating.

He became a bit of a Jew, so my mother grew closer to him and he grew a little closer to my mother. He even began to go to synagogue on the Sabbath. True, he did not go with my mother to the neighboring synagogue, but alone to the Jewish Center of Coney Island, where men and women prayed together, gentile girls sang, and an organ played.[40] But as long as he went to synagogue, my mother was happy.

This is how he started going to pray at the Jewish Center: My mother insisted one Sabbath that he go with her to synagogue. Wanting to get out of it, he replied that praying in the *misnagdic* style (that is, *nusakh Ashkenaz*) did not appeal to him. So my mother said that she knew of a synagogue where they prayed in the Hasidic style (*nusakh Sfard*). Well, now he had to go with her. Passing the "temple" of the Jewish Center on the way home, he heard the organ music and female voices, so he told my mother to wait and he himself went in to see what was going on there. He came out full of enthusiasm.

By the following Sabbath, he was praying at the temple. When he came home after services, he could not say enough to my mother in praise of the temple or its decorum. "Listen to this," he told my mother. "One Sabbath, I entered a nearby synagogue, and they immediately called me to the Torah in exchange for a *shnoder,* a pledge of a donation. Feh! I hate those moochers. You see? At the temple they also called me to the Torah and gave me the honor of saying the blessing, but there was no trace of a *shnoder.* That is what I call real gentlemen! From now on, I'm going to the temple!"

When he was not working, he was continually going swimming, eating, and relaxing, and my father acquired a belly like a real bourgeois. He had always been a "sport." He would shave three times a week, wear a ten-dollar hat, a three-dollar shirt, and a fifty-sixty-dollar suit. His trousers always had a sharp crease and his shoes always had a fresh shine. Now that he had acquired a truly distinguished belly besides, he looked like a magnate, especially since a heavy, double, golden chain that shone in one's eyes stretched from one vest pocket to the other, and a pin with a hefty diamond was stuck in his tie as if he were a real millionaire. And, in fact, he quickly became prominent at the temple, and they began to give him honors. They gave him an important seat, a fat *aliyah** without a *shnoder,* and the like. And since he was a fine teller of stories and anecdotes (he knew almost by heart all of *Oytser fun ale midrashim* and *Ale agades fun talmud*) —and real spicy stories as well—the common folk, the ordinary worshippers, Jews his age, fell in love with him.[41] Before long, he was elected as a trustee.

Well, in the middle of the week—when he prayed three times a day with the ordinary Jews in the small synagogue under the temple—he felt completely at home. But on the Sabbath and on holidays, when he stood on the platform of the temple with all of the elite, he apparently did not feel so comfortable. For, as soon as he became a trustee, he and a few other old-fashioned Jews went to work and soon turned the temple into an Orthodox synagogue.

My mother was redeemed. My father went to synagogue three times a day, day in and day out. He now stayed at home on the Sabbath and did not even go to the beach. And when my mother occasionally needed a dollar for a *yortsayt,* or a *shnoder,* my father gave it to her with all due respect and from the goodness of his trustee's heart. He literally did my mother's health significant good by saying such things as, "Rokhele, I have you to thank for all of it. You were the one who led me back on the right path. Really. What was I before? Now, look at the honor that I have."

I was also happy. Since I did not have to get up every morning and waste the day in the shop, I took to reading at an amazing pace. Whenever I found an anthology of Yiddish, English, French, German, or Russian poetry, I would devour it. And I literally could not tear myself away from books on psychology. I steeped myself in Freud, Jung, Adler, Schneersohn, and Watson.[42] And I continued to write as well: poems and meditations.

On summer Sundays, I felt like a fish in water. I would spend the whole day on the seashore together with a bunch of young people—young men and girls, almost entirely a college crowd. Not only did I enjoy myself emotionally spending time with the girls—who were familiar and intimate with me—but intellectually as well. In a word, when talk turned to psychological or philosophical issues, I was the main speaker. And when a couple of girls of my acquaintance took sociology, normal and abnormal psychology, and philosophy in college, I would hold entire lectures for them, and for the rest of the gang as well, on those cool Sunday evenings. With them, I was the top of the heap.

And another thing. The more I steeped myself in post-Freudian psychology, the younger I started to feel—younger and freer. All of the moss and mold of my childhood education and traditional civilization disappeared from my mind as a scab falls off a healed wound. It dried up and fell off! And when I read Freud's *The Future of an Illusion*, I felt that this was the book that I should have written! That man simply robbed me . . . ![43]

Spiritually, I became free and independent. I lost all respect for all revered authorities. But in my behavior, in my day-to-day life, I remained the same as before. For example, I might be giving a lecture for a group on "religion as a compulsive neurosis," or "religion and the primary principle," or "religion, infantilism, and magical thinking," and when I saw that it was time for afternoon prayers, I would ask the group to wait while I went into the next room to say my prayers. To this day, I pray three times a day and strictly avoid non-kosher food and the desecration of the Sabbath. I do not even carry a handkerchief on the Sabbath.[44]

My mother was happy. But her joy did not last long. On Sunday, November 12, 1933, at about ten in the morning, my father felt like going for a swim. Mother started to beg him, "True, the sun is shining. But it is so cold! Enough swimming." But he did not listen to her. What he did promise her was that he would not be in the water long. He would just take a short swim and then get dressed right away.

It was nearly eleven and my father was not back yet. Mother became uneasy. Moyshke, my younger brother, and I also became afraid. It was already eleven o'clock, and mother asked Moyshke to go to the beach to see what was taking father so long. A while later, our telephone rang. Mother was lying in bed and her heart was pounding so hard that it nearly sprang out of her. I went to the telephone, picked up the receiver with a trembling hand, and with a dry mouth asked who it was. It was Moyshke. He was speaking from the morgue. Father was there. I hung up the phone and tried to save my mother.

A while later, Moyshke returned, bringing father's coat, which he had been wearing on the way to the beach. Well? What had happened? When? How? This is the story he told: He got to the beach where father usually swam, but did not find him. A circle of people was standing there, so he asked if anyone had seen an older man swimming. They replied that a man had been swimming there not long before. More precisely, he had tried to swim. As soon as he entered the water and started to swim, he returned immediately to the shore. But now he was not swimming, but wobbling. And when he reached the shore, he fell right down with a cry. He tried to raise himself up but fell down again. An ambulance came, a doctor gave him an injection, and . . . they took him to the morgue.

We sat through *shiva,** the seven-day mourning period, and after living for another few months in Coney Island we had to escape from there. The sea, the street, the house, everything reminded us of our tragedy. We moved back to East New York. After father's death, we distributed all of his things to poor relatives and acquaintances. Before distributing them, I went through all of his pockets, and they were full of receipts for three or five dollars from the Jewish Center of Coney Island.

My two older brothers were married. My two sisters, the same. So that put an end to all the company. No girls came to visit us anymore, and without the girls, what would the boys have done with us? So, not a trace remained of them either. It became gloomy.

The poetess with the pitch-black hair got married and no longer came to visit me. One of the girls whom I would often see in Coney Island, and with whom I went together as a sweetheart, became a bride. And soon Moyshke fell in love with a neighbor girl and I no longer even had anyone to go for a walk with. When he got married a short time later and I remained alone with my mother, we moved out of East New York and into Brownsville. Like a grandpa and a grandma: my mother and I.

All my sisters, brothers, and male and female friends were married. Being by nature a homebody, it would have been easier for me to get a Ph.D. than to acquire new friends, so a time of great hunger began for me—not for bread, of course, but for female companionship.

If I did happen to become acquainted with a girl and went out with her several times, she or her parents would start to speak of getting down to "business," either directly or indirectly through hints. And since I did not want to get married, just as a self-satisfied philistine does not want to die, I would soon be left alone again with my hunger.

I was working again. For a year and a half, I worked for the old wages. But when my union reorganized in July 1935 (this time with a "right-wing" administration affiliated with the AFL), I received a raise of twenty-five percent, along with all the other workers in the shop. At the end of the year, we got another raise and I was now earning sixty cents an hour. I still took pleasure in books and magazines on psychology, philosophy, sociology, and poetry. But the hunger, the sexual frustration, never left me, especially on Sundays.

Va-yehi hoyoym, and one evening in May 1936, an acquaintance of mine comes up to me and tells me the following story: A couple of days earlier, he had by coincidence met a girl in a park. He saw a girl looking into a notebook with handwritten Yiddish poems, so he went up to her and started a conversation. It turned out that she was the author of the poems. So he told her that he had a friend who also wrote poems and asked her if she would be interested in meeting him. Since it turned out that his business partner's wife was a friend of the girl's sister—and she was also in the park—the girl agreed. In short, they agreed that the girl would come to his house the next Sunday. And so, he came especially to invite me to his house the following Sunday. And, for God's sake, I must not refuse.

So I promised right away that I would come, and I kept my word. . . . The girl was no great beauty, but she was not ugly either. She was slim and a tiny bit shorter than I. She was a familiar sort of girl from a good family, who spoke a juicy White Russian Yiddish. She had studied in a Sholem Aleichem School in the Old Country, and wrote lyrical poems that were not bad at all.[45] We chatted for a while and I took her out to a Yiddish play. By the time we left the theater, we were already good, old friends.

For a couple of weeks we exchanged letters (fig. 18), and my girl fell in love with me. So a problem arose for me—the problem of to be or not to be married. We saw each other another couple of times and I saw that the girl did not believe in simply "going out." If one was going out, it had to be for a purpose. I started to struggle with the idea. If she had been a beauty, or a scholar, or a deep artist, perhaps I would not have had to think for long. But as it was, I could not decide.

Not to marry? What would happen in the future when my mother would die and I would have to become a boarder? Then if I wanted to marry, I would have to take an old woman!

One Sunday I went with her to Sam Z., the psychologist who had once psychoanalyzed me, and he helped me make peace with the idea. For years and years, he had lived all alone in a room in Greenwich Village. And he complained to me, "It is hard to live like this!" The entire room and everything in it nodded their assent, "True, true." And I thought, "If he, who has been used to living alone all his days and sustaining himself with wine and cigarettes, feels that it is hard to live like this, how will I feel when I must

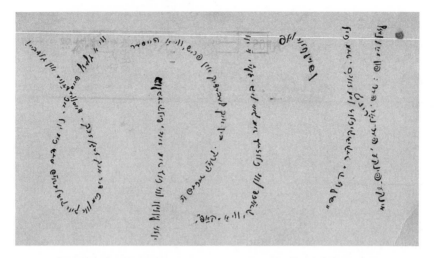

Fig. 18. A note from Chaim Kusnetz to his fiancée, Minnie Yezernitsky, discussing in rhyming verse his recent recovery from a cold. The note is laid out so that it spells her nickname, "Minke." Courtesy of Fay Minkin

live alone? I, who am accustomed to a cozy home and to a proper life in general?

He spoke of my girl with real enthusiasm: She was a healthy, normal person. She could be depended on and one could build something with her. She was made to measure for me. Later, I calculated her virtues and faults, and it came out that her virtues had the upper hand when it came to married life. And most of her faults could actually be seen as virtues. I decided that I would have to leave it up to her. If she wanted to marry me, I would agree. . . .

When we started to go out "steady" on Saturday evenings and Sundays, I found out from her that her heart was burdened. I consoled her: If it turned out she was not a virgin—if she had been raped or seduced—it absolutely did not to matter to me in the least. Does it matter to me that her upper mouth is not a virgin? That it opens up several times every day and something—a spoon, a fork, food—is put into it? It is biology, nothing more! Nor would it bother me much if she happened to be a widow or a divorcee. I am not a *kohen,* a member of the priestly caste.[46]

She told me the story, and it turned out to be none of those things. She was here illegally! So I consoled her again. Since I was a citizen (on my father's papers), she had nothing to fear.[47]

At Passover time, 1937, I received a card from her. She was at Ellis Island, because someone had informed on her. In the middle of work, a government agent had come to her shop and taken her away. If that was the case, there was no time to lose. As soon as she was released on bail, we went to City Hall and got married. A week later, on the first day of the month of Iyar, we were married again according to the laws of Moses and Israel. No one from my family was present, and from her family only her sister and the sister's husband, with whom she lived.

I was also present at her hearing at Ellis Island, and we managed to get a ruling that she could leave the United States voluntarily, at her own expense. It is a story of "pull," of documents, and of HIAS. (Her brother-in-law met with his congressman and the latter did not spare the letters and telegrams whenever and to whomever it was necessary—and all for free, without a fee.) In the end, she traveled to Canada, and immediately reentered legally as the wife of an American citizen.

Now that everything was on the up and up, we moved into a five-room apartment—my missus, my mother, and I—and I furnished it with the most modern furniture. For me personally, this was an absolutely unnecessary thing. My old rocking chair and my homemade desk were all that I needed. (Needed? What I don't need!) But if she wanted everything as it was in fine homes, and if she wanted to boast or make a display for her family and friends, let her have the pleasure. I felt like an adult who buys a toy for a child: Let the child play with it and enjoy it. And for this same reason, I also bought her an engagement watch set with diamonds for fifty-something dollars, as well as two diamond rings.

Even before we had started to go steady, I told her that I did not believe in going along with the herd in the practice of the bride and groom giving each other presents. Before I marry a girl, she is a stranger to me, after all. So why should I give her a present? This is nothing more than a payoff, bribery, graft, to make her love me more. I want her to love me for myself, for my personality, and not for my presents! And when I do marry her, after all, I hand over to her all of my earnings. Then she can buy whatever her heart desires.

But when she wanted an engagement present, poor thing (although she did not speak openly about it or mention it), I bought her the watch that cost fifty-something dollars instead of the twenty-seven-dollar one that she picked out. Let the child have something to play with and enjoy, as I have already said.

Just as I did not want to get married, so—and maybe even more so—I did not want to become a father. I therefore only had relations with my wife (naturally, "as God commanded") in the times when according to the medical books she would not conceive. But this only worked for a little over a year and a half. Suddenly, she became pregnant, and on September 21, 1939, she gave birth to a girl.

Conclusion: Unfulfilled Intentions

When as a boy I steeped myself in moralistic religious books, I would think: I am truly pious, but not pious enough. With this kind of piety, I will not merit a vision of Elijah the Prophet. And I must have quite a few sins. When I grow up and stand under the wedding canopy, all of my sins will be forgiven. Then I will begin a new life for myself, strictly avoiding even the smallest sins and only accumulating good deeds. Well, I got married and . . . my intentions went unfulfilled.

When I later started to steep myself in philosophy, I felt a tremendous affinity to Diogenes, to Buddha, to Schopenhauer, and to Tolstoy.[48] When I possess something, it means that the thing possesses me. I will try to be a Diogenes and not possess anything, not even want to possess anything! If I have to possess anything at all, let it be myself. Then, I got married and . . . my intentions went unfulfilled.

Seventeen years ago, when I was wriggling around in the net of love and my heart was like a wriggling, cut-up snake, I used to think: If the girl became one of my own people, and I married her, who could compare to me? It would be an end to my sadness, my sorrow, and my loneliness. I got married and . . . my intentions went unfulfilled.

Externally, my life is the petty life of a settled, happy petit bourgeois. I have a fine little wife who is a wonderful housekeeper and is devoted to me and to our home with body and soul. I have a three-year-old girl who is the soul of my neighborhood. Everyone envies me for the treasure that I possess. She is healthy, pretty, and full of charm. She speaks a fluent, natural Yiddish, is good buddies with everyone, and knows about fifty songs by heart—both words and melodies. I have a steady job and make quite good money. (Without strikes, we kept on getting raises until most of the workers make forty-six dollars now and I get forty-eight dollars.) I have a nice few dollars in the bank and in bonds, and, as I mentioned, a fine spacious home with all the conveniences. I am respected in my shop; I am assistant foreman and the bosses would not trade me for the world. I am also prominent in my *landsmanshaft* society. (Besides the union, I belong to the Duboyer Society, nothing else.)[49] But . . .

I always have the feeling that none of this has anything to do with me. It is just the shell of my life. Under this shell is a kind of eerie hollowness, a kind of emptiness, a no man's land. Life, I always feel, does not flow through me, but passes me by from afar. It passes me by and does not even touch me.

I am someone who does not belong, who is unconnected—an uprooted tree that lies on the ground and rots. The sun shines on it, reptiles and insects crawl on and in it, and it lies peacefully on the ground and rots.

And the thorn of loneliness in the desert of my life burns eternal.

NOTES

1. Genesis 41:9. Translation from *Jewish Publication Society Hebrew-English Tanakh,* 2d ed. (Philadelphia: Jewish Publication Society, 1999), 86.

2. *Myatshik* (Russian: small ball) may refer to a variety of particular games.

3. *Khovot ha-levavot* (Duties of the Hearts, c. 1080), by Bahya b. Joseph ibn Paquda, is a very influential work that focuses on the Jew's inner spiritual and moral life. Originally written in Arabic, it was translated into Hebrew in 1161 and, subsequently, into other languages, including Yiddish. *Reshit Khokhmah* (Beginning of Wisdom, 1579), by Elijah ben Moses de Vidas, deals with morals from a kabalistic perspective in a popular and engaging style. *Tsene-urene* (Hebrew, "go and see") is a Yiddish paraphrase of the Bible together with interpretative and illustrative material, divided according to the weekly Torah portions. Composed by Jacob ben Isaac Ashkenazi in the late sixteenth century, it achieved abiding popularity among women unable to read the Hebrew original. *Nofet Tsufim* (Honeycomb, before 1480), by Judah ben Jehiel (Messer Leon), is a book on Hebrew rhetoric. Influenced by the Renaissance, it analyzes the Torah from an aesthetic perspective.

4. Vasilii Andrianovich Evtushevski (1836–1888) composed several mathematical textbooks.

5. The first and last two days of Passover are considered full holidays on which work is forbidden. Work is permitted during the intermediate four days. Similarly, the first two days of Sukkot are full holidays, as are Shmini Atseret and Simhat Torah, which follow immediately after the end of Sukkot. In between are five intermediate days, on which work is allowed.

6. The Berezner rebbe at the time that Kusnetz describes was Avrom Shmuel Petshenik (d. 1914/15 or 1917), also known as Reb Shmelke.

7. See Genesis Rabbah 48:14. Translation from Marcus Jastrow, *A Dictionary of the Targumim, the Talmud, Babli and Yerushalmi, and the Midrashic Literature*, vol. 2 (New York: Title Publishing Co., 1943), 905. The term "midrash" refers both to a method of extrapolation on the text of the Torah and to several collections of such extrapolations.

8. The yeshiva in Zvihil (also called Novogrod Volinskiy), known formally as Yeshiva Or Torah (Light of the Torah), was founded by Rabbi Yoyel Sharin (1870/71–1926/27) in 1896/97 and moved to Zvihil in 1901/02.

9. Prayer in Stolin was not actually conducted in the style of the Sephardic Jews (the Jews of Spain and their descendents). Rather it was in the style of Rabbi Isaac Luria (Ha-Ari, 1534–1572) as adopted by the Hasidim. Since it resembled the Sephardic rite in some ways, it was commonly referred to as the Sephardic style.

10. The *misnagdim* (Hebrew, "opponents") were the opponents of Hasidism within Eastern European traditional Judaism. They emphasized talmudic study and criticized the focus on charismatic leadership within Hasidism. After a period of sharp conflict at the beginning of the nineteenth century, both groups made common cause against the Haskalah and other challenges to tradition.

11. A reference to sections of the synagogue service. The *Kedushah* is a section of the Amidah prayer during which the congregation sanctifies God's name. *Barkhu* is the call to prayer. *Ameyn, yehey shmey raba* (May his great name be blessed) is from the *Kaddish* prayer.

12. Tractate Bava Metsia, folio 60b.

13. Israel Perlov (c. 1869–1922) was the rebbe of the Karlin-Stolin dynasty at the time. An innovator, he encouraged secular studies and supported the education of girls.

14. An "appetizing store," in New York lingo, was a store that sold prepared fish, diary foods, salads, and baked goods.

15. The Megillah, literally "scroll," is the Book of Esther, which is read in the synagogue on Purim.

16. "We renounce the old world": the opening line of the "Workers' Marseillaise," a popular revolutionary song.

17. A contemptuous reference to Tsar Nicholas II.

18. During the Russian Civil War (1918–1920), much of which was fought in Ukraine, there was a multisided struggle for power among the Reds (Bolsheviks), the Whites (tsarist counterrevolutionaries), Ukrainian nationalists, and others. The Makhnovists were followers of Nestor Makhno (1889–1934), Ukrainian Anarchist and leader of the Revolutionary Insurrectionary Army of Ukraine from 1918 to 1921. The White Army, especially, was responsible for many pogroms. The Red Army generally defended the Jews against such attacks. Makhnovist units also carried out a number of brutal pogroms, though Makhno himself condemned antiSemitism and had a few Jewish supporters.

19. "You fell victims in the final struggle": the opening line of a revolutionary "Funeral March."

20. In the 1920s, the Soviet government placed many Jews in collective farming settlements in the Crimea and elsewhere in an effort to find a solution to the problems of petty traders and others whose economic situation had been undermined by the Revolution.

21. French novelist Jules Verne (1828–1905) has been credited with virtually inventing the modern genre of science fiction. His works were very popular in Yiddish and Russian translation. British author Mayne Reid (1818–1883) was known for his adventure novels set in the American West. American writer James Fenimore Cooper (1789–1851), who depicted life on the frontier, was especially famous for his novel *The Last of the Mohicans* (1826). The works of Verne, Reid, and Cooper were available in Yiddish and Russian translations.

22. Pious Jewish men wear a garment called an *arba-kanfes* that fits over the head and has fringes, *tsitsis,* on the four corners, as specified in the Bible. This is usually worn as an undergarment. An ell is equivalent to forty-five inches.

23. *Voyage au Centre de la Terre,* originally published in 1864.

24. Tsvi Krol (1907–1948) settled in Palestine in 1925.

25. Psalm 133:1.

26. Horsemeat is not kosher. Blood, even of kosher animals, is not kosher.

27. The government-funded American Relief Administration (1919–1923), headed by Herbert Hoover, was the main agency for American aid to Europe after World War I. It operated in Russia from 1921 to 1923.

28. Jacob Mark was a steamship agent on the Lower East Side.

29. The *Morgn zhurnal* (Jewish Morning Journal) was a Yiddish daily published in New York beginning in 1901. Conservative politically and Orthodox in its religious orientation, it was the only Yiddish morning newspaper for many years and therefore well known for its help-wanted classified section. It merged with the *Tog* (Day) in 1953 and ceased publication in 1971.

30. Marranos were Spanish Jews who converted to Christianity to avoid persecution by the Inquisition but continued to practice Judaism in secret.

31. Travel on holidays and on the Sabbath is forbidden by Jewish law.

32. *Im kol ha-neorim* ("With all the youths"): phrase by which pre–bar mitzvah boys are called to the Torah on Simhat Torah.

33. The satirical periodical *Der groyser kundes* (The Big Prankster, often called The Big Stick), appeared in New York from 1909 to 1927.

34. Torgsin (abbreviation of *torgovlia s inostrantami,* trade with foreigners) refers to stores that offered goods otherwise unobtainable in the Soviet Union, but only for hard (i.e., foreign) currency.

35. A resort town near the New Jersey shore.

36. Sigmund Freud (1856–1939) was the founder of psychoanalysis and the

most important proponent of the modern psychological theory that the exploration of the unconscious mind can help heal emotional illness. Alfred Adler (1870–1937) was one of Freud's early followers but broke with his mentor over Freud's insistence on the centrality of sex as a cause of neurosis. Carl Jung (1875–1961), another early associate who broke with Freud, is best known for his theory of the collective unconscious.

37. Fischel Schneersohn (1887–1958), an experimental psychologist and expert in child psychology, wrote psychological works in English, Russian, German, Hebrew, and Yiddish, and also wrote novels and stories in Yiddish.

38. Isadora Duncan (1877/78–1927) was a pioneer of modern dance who stressed freedom of movement and expression. Known for her powerful personal presence, she was attacked by some segments of the American establishment in the 1920s for "indecency" as well as for her sympathies with the Soviet Union. George Sand (pseudonym of Amandine Aurore Lucie Dupin, Baronne Dudevant, 1804–1876) was a French novelist who advocated equal rights for women. She achieved notoriety for her numerous affairs and for dressing in men's clothes.

39. Cooper Union was founded in 1859 as an institution of higher education in New York specializing in engineering, art, and architecture. It does not charge tuition.

40. Founded in 1914 as Temple Adath Israel, the Jewish Center of Coney Island was located on West Fifth Street until 1931, when it dedicated its building on Ocean Parkway.

41. *Der oytser fun ale midrashim* (The Treasury of All Midrashim; published in New York in 1926) and *Ale agades fun Talmud* (All Legends of the Talmud; published in several editions in New York, 1922 and 1926) are compilations by the Yiddish writer Israel Joseph Zevin (also known by the pseudonym Tashrak, 1872–1926).

42. John B. Watson (1878–1958), an experimental psychologist and originator of behaviorism, viewed human behavior as a response to outside conditioning. By the 1920s he had left his earlier academic career and become an advertising executive and popular authority on psychology.

43. In *The Future of an Illusion* (1927) Freud critiques religion, which he compares to a childhood neurosis, as an irrational attempt to come to grips with human powerlessness.

44. Carrying is considered a category of work and therefore forbidden on the Sabbath.

45. A secular Jewish school, with Yiddish as the language of instruction, named for the great Yiddish writer.

46. A *kohen*, a man who is a member of the hereditary priestly caste in Judaism, is forbidden to marry a divorced woman.

47. As the wife of a citizen she would have been able to regularize her status. As a minor, Chaim Kusnetz became a citizen automatically when his father did.

48. Diogenes (c. 412–323 B.C.E.) was a Greek philosopher who extolled the virtues of the simple life and gave up all material possessions. Buddha (The Enlightened One, born Siddhartha Gautama, c. 563–483 B.C.E.) was a prince in what is now Nepal who renounced his power and wealth to seek enlightenment through meditation and simple living. Arthur Schopenhauer (1788–1860) was a German philosopher who taught the ethics of sympathy with the pain of others and believed that only the rejection of desire and of the will could overcome the main causes of conflict in society. Count Leo Tolstoy (1828–1910) was a Russian novelist who preached nonviolence, the virtues of simplicity, the rejection of the state and the church, and Christian love. He too eventually gave up his material wealth.

49. *Landsmanshaft* refers to a society made up of immigrants from the same town in the Old Country. The Duboyer Society was the association of immigrants from Duboy.

Chapter 9

I Haven't Lost Anything by
Coming to America

Minnie Kusnetz (Mrs. Baron fon Habenikhts)

b. 1912, Ruzhany, Belarus
To Canada: 1929
To U.S.: 1930s, Brooklyn, N.Y.

Minnie Kusnetz's spirited, optimistic story conveys the vicissitudes in the life of the youngest writer in this anthology, including her experiences as a child during the Polish–Soviet war. Unable to enter the United States directly because of the restrictive immigration laws then in place, Kusnetz (fig. 19) went to Canada and subsequently immigrated to the United States illegally. A proficient seamstress and active union member, Kusnetz gives a lively portrayal of work in the garment industry and clashes between workers and bosses in both Montreal and New York. She describes her courtship with Chaim Kusnetz, whose autobiography also appears in this collection. Notable for their rejection of the ethos of domestic consumption, and for their adherence to the Jewish dietary laws, the couple offers a rare glimpse at gender relations in marriage from the perspectives of both husband and wife.

I was born in 1912 in the town of Ruzhany (fig. 20), Grodno Province (formerly Russia, now Poland), to pious and genteel parents, though they were not wealthy. My father was a carpenter and barely made a living for the family. We were three girls and two boys. I, one of the three girls, was the fourth child. My mother helped my father earn a livelihood, trading grain, honey, and various other things.

When my oldest sister turned eighteen she went to America with my mother's mother, who was a widow. Her children in America had sent my

Fig. 19. Minnie Kusnetz. Courtesy of Fay Minkin

grandmother money to cover her expenses, and my sister had her own money that she had saved working as a threader-girl at a weaving mill.

When I turned seven years old, I was handed over to a teacher from whom I learned Hebrew very quickly and fluently. At eight years, my parents sent me to study at a Sholem Aleichem Folks Shule, where I learned well.[1] All of my teachers—there were six of them, a different teacher for every subject—all loved me very much. For this reason, the other pupils in my class called me "the privileged one." (This nickname hurt my feelings.) For me, school was more light-hearted than home, where I merely spent the night and got up in the morning. I particularly had dramatic abilities, such as singing, reciting, and the like. The teachers would put on shows for every holiday, and I almost always had the lead, so the whole town loved me. My parents always sat in a place of honor for the performances, and the teachers would not sell my parents tickets. They would say, "Never mind, you can come without tickets. Your daughter brings in enough money for the school with her theatrics!" On the first night the school gave a performance for the pupils, and on the second night for the towns-people who had bought tickets.

Fig. 20. The ruins of a castle in Ruzhany, Minnie Kusnetz's hometown, during World War I. Courtesy of the YIVO Institute for Jewish Research

Once, during the intermediate days of Passover,* the teachers put on an operetta, "Adam, Eve, and the Snake." I played the role of the snake and made such a hit that the audience actually bombarded me with flowers, packages of chocolate, and all kinds of candy. I was so busy singing and dancing and bowing for the audience that I simply had no opportunity to gather together all the goodies. Only when the curtain closed did I do so, with help of a few other children, before going home with my parents, full of joy. Apparently, I had had too much excitement and enthusiasm that evening and it damaged my health. I awoke the next morning with a high fever, stammering, unable to speak one word correctly. My parents got a good fright and called for the doctor. He immediately ordered them to put ice to my head until the fever went down. Neighbors charmed away the evil eye. They said to my mother, "They really ate her up, looking at her so. It's no trifle, performing like that! No harm should come to her, such a bright child!"[2]

I was laid up like that for an entire week. My mother did not leave my bedside, all the while putting ice on my head. When my teachers came to visit, my parents told them that I was no longer allowed to act in plays, but when I became well I was drawn back into acting, as a fish to water. It seems to me that that time was the happiest in my life.

When the war broke out between Soviet Russia and Poland, there were bitter battles in Ruzhany.[3] I was still a child and did not understand much that took place. There was great hunger, and we could not buy a thing because whoever had grain, potatoes, gas, or salt hid them. We had a few hundred rubles, but there was precious little we could do with them. My father worked very little, and the small amount we had stored up was quickly depleted. Hence, my parents took me out of school. They just couldn't pay for me. When I didn't come to school for a few days, the teachers started to ask what had happened to me. When a girlfriend told them that I could not pay, they sent for me and I went on learning there for free.

I went to school, my older brother went to learn to be a shoe stitcher, and my youngest brother went to *heder.** My sister accompanied Mother to gather berries and mushrooms in the forest about ten or twelve *versts** from home. They would sell some and we ourselves would eat the rest. We would also cook a kind of grass called orach. At any rate, very soon we all lay ill with dysentery, first father, my sister, and my two brothers and, a week later, I as well. It was a miracle that my mother did not get sick and could move around among us until finally she asked a neighbor to take pity and notify the hospital. Her strength was giving out. It became too difficult for her to tend to so many sick people. And indeed, first thing the next morning my sister and older brother were taken to the hospital because they were more sick than the rest of us.

From time to time, a neighbor would push open the door and give Mother cereal. The doctor had attached a note to the door saying that no one should enter our house because of an infectious disease. And so we suffered. The neighbor truly kept us alive. Because of the bran in the cereal, we started to improve. With God's help, we all came out of it with our lives. We suffered like this for a year.

I remember as if it were today: My mother and sister left for the forest. Father had worked somewhere and received a few potatoes as payment, so he brought them home and said to me, "Here, take two potatoes and peel them!" He went out and cut grass near the fence, brought it back to the house, sorted through it, washed it, cut the potatoes into small pieces, chopped the grass, put everything in a big copper pan with boiling water, and put it up to cook on the hearth. We would all eat when my mother and sister returned from the forest. Father said to me, "Take care that, God forbid, it doesn't boil over. And put woodchips on the fire so it doesn't go out." Then he went to synagogue with my older brother for evening prayers. I was hungry, so I set a chair near the hearth, took a wooden spoon, and started to sip slowly. I let my brother sip too.

By the time my father came from synagogue and my mother and sister returned from the forest, there was only a little bit left in the pan. My sister shouted, "You little glutton! Such a big pan of soup? Where on earth did you put it?" I burst into tears and said, sobbing, "I was hungry." My parents cried bitterly looking at such a scene. My father soon calmed down and said, "We now have the mushrooms and a few potatoes left. There's still grass too. How long could it take? In a half an hour there will be something to eat."

With God's help, the war ended. Then my sister from America started to send us packages of food and clothing as well. Our world brightened and we truly came back to life. The neighbors, who had no one in America, would come look at the good things that we received. They were jealous of us for our good fortune. My mother distributed foodstuffs and clothing among the neighbors. Yes, my sister sent money too, dollars. With that "green paper" we could buy many good things. Only then, did my parents once again begin to pay for me to go to school.

A little while later, my next sister went to America with the help of our oldest sister. After that, my older brother departed for Cuba, because one could no longer travel to a brother or sister in America. Parents could go to children, and so it became a chain.[4] My youngest brother also went off to Cuba with the help of the older brother, and I remained with my parents. My father started to work and earn quite well. An excellent craftsman, he built up his clientele, and we also had the support of the children abroad. I especially did not lack for anything.

By the time I finished school, all the youth had dispersed, some to Palestine, some to Argentina, some to Cuba. I, too, felt the desire to leave my small town and travel into the wide world I always dreamed about. I was eighteen then, and full of life.

Since we had a relative connected with immigration in Winnipeg, Canada, I found his address and wrote him a letter. He was then a man of around forty-five years old, with a wife and three children. Anyway, he replied that the only way that he could bring me over was if I applied for permission to emigrate as a servant. If I agreed, he would send traveling papers and a ship's ticket at a cost of two hundred dollars. I sent off a letter to my sisters at once, proposing this plan and they sent me one hundred fifty dollars. My parents added the last fifty dollars, and I sent the money to our relative in Winnipeg. My parents did not want me to leave them, but I wanted them to go to America. By this time, my sisters had married and were well off, so they could bring our parents over to them, but I was in their way. Though I decided to go away mainly for this reason, my parents are still in Europe to this day. My father does not want to part from the house he owns.

The papers and ship's ticket arrived three months later. During those three months, I peeled potatoes, grated carrots, made *tsimes,** and washed dishes. I even did this kind of work for the neighbors so that my hands would not look too refined. I was going as a servant, after all! I was then eighteen and a half years old, and the authorities wouldn't let me go as a servant because I was under the age of twenty-one. Under Polish law, you belonged to your parents until the age of twenty-one and were forbidden to do what you wanted to do independently. I got an agent who made up a birth certificate for me saying that I was twenty-one, a passport, and all other important papers. My parents paid him fifty dollars to do this.

Now everything was ready, but my heart felt sad. Somehow, I had suddenly lost all my courage. I would have a good cry, taking care that my parents did not notice, but my wise mother noticed anyway that I was going around distraught. She said to me, "You know, my child, forget about the money you've already spent and don't go. What are you lacking for here? May nothing bad come of it if I say so, but all that's good is here at home. Why do you need to venture into the wide world and be lonely, and bear the burden of making a living besides? Listen to me, stay here with your parents!"

I assured my parents not to worry. I would not get lost, I would manage. I couldn't hide behind my mother's apron forever!

I was to depart right after Rosh Hashanah,* but as I would have been on the ship on Yom Kippur,* my parents would not let me go. I had no desire to go then either. I enquired at the HIAS* office in Warsaw (fig. 21) how long I could wait. They replied that the last intermediate day of Sukkot* was the final deadline, October 4, 1929.

My mother accompanied me to Brest. I received the Polish visa there, said a heartfelt goodbye to my mother, and, weeping, departed for Warsaw. On the way I got to know other immigrants going to Canada, but to other cities like Toronto and Montreal. Upon arriving, we checked into a hotel, and from there a girl led me to HIAS. At HIAS I coincidentally got to know a girl from Volkovysk. After speaking for a good while, I discovered that she was going to the same relative as I was. She should have

Fig. 21. At the HIAS office in Warsaw, 1920s. Photo by Alter Kacyzne. Courtesy of the YIVO Institute for Jewish Research

been in Winnipeg some months before, but it happened that her trip was postponed. She was also going as a servant, and boarding with a woman where he had rented me a room also, because there was no room for us with my relative. We were both very heartened and were soon staying at the same hotel. Neither of us took a step without the other one.

Three days later, we were on the ship *Polonia,* quickly getting used to life among the immigrants. I traveled third class and enjoyed the voyage very much, even though I did not feel so well for the first few days. But after that I felt right at home. The only thing I didn't like was the food. First, there was not one piece of familiar rye bread, just sliced white hal-lah* or whole wheat, like regular chaff, without a "Jewish flavor." There were separate tables for Jews and Christians, and a kosher* supervisor with a red beard for our tables. He said that he came from Lodz, and he was always agitated and distracted.

Once, when I found him in a better mood, I had a word with him: "Mr. Supervisor, I want to ask a favor of you. Would you please ask the cook to make different dishes for us?"

He burst out, "See here, you don't like it? Perhaps you'd like to be the cook?"

"Indeed, why not?" I responded.

"Really? What would you cook, then?"

"I would peel potatoes, cut them into small pieces, put them in boiling water with some chopped onions, a little black pepper and salt. The passengers would lick their fingers. That would be a delicious soup—with black bread and butter or a piece of herring."

My mouth was watering as I spoke. He heard me out and at lunch the next day we actually had potato soup. The passengers liked it, but there still wasn't any bread like we had back home. I'm ashamed to tell you (keep it a secret) that I had taken with me a few pounds of black bread ("pumpernickel," as they say here) with a substantial piece of sausage from home. So after every meal, I would go down to my cabin and eat a little piece of sausage with bread. In this way, we traveled by ship for eleven days.

The final supper was not an ordinary one, but something very festive: a quarter chicken, noodle soup, plum compote, and large glasses of beer. So I asked the supervisor, "What is this?"

"Eat, daughter, this is the last meal!" he replied.

"What, we're getting off?"

"Of course! Of course!"

We arrived at the port of Halifax. Many immigrants were going on to the United States, so they remained on the ship, but the ones going to Canada all got off. I felt so sad and empty inside saying goodbye. I had the feeling that I would never get off the ship, that the ship would never stop, but instead keep going forever. I said goodbye to my fellow travelers, almost all of them young girls and boys. We all cried bitterly, not wanting to part.

When we got off the ship, they examined everyone's documents, and at dusk we were all put on a train going to various Canadian cities: Montreal, Toronto, and Winnipeg. It took more than three days before I disembarked at Winnipeg Station at nine o'clock on November, 15 1929. As we descended, my fellow traveler, Sheyne, and I heard a man shouting, "Sheyne! Minke!" (my name is Minke). Waiting for us was the man who had sent us the papers. He took us in an auto to the family where he had rented us a room.

On arrival, we encountered a woman from Warsaw, some thirty years of age, with three small children. Her husband was a hard worker. She led us up to the second floor, where there were two rooms, one occupied by a boarder, a man in his seventies, and the other for Sheyne and me.

"Girls," our landlady said, "Take a bath first, and then have a bit to eat and take a laxative." Well, if she says so. We did as we were told and went to sleep.

I slept the night away, like after a wedding. It was already ten o'clock in the morning when Sheyne awakened me. We went to the kitchen. The landlady made us a breakfast consisting of a bit of cocoa—more water than milk—and a little piece of black bread with butter, spread very thinly. Never mind, better than nothing. Supper was also very meager. Sheyne would usually buy something for both of us for dinner.

"How much are you charging us for the room and two meals?

"Four dollars a month."

"Very good!"

My parents had given me twenty-five dollars. I had spent five dollars for fruit aboard ship. An apple had cost five cents, and so had an orange. Since I was not happy with the food aboard ship, I had bought fruit quite often. So I had twenty dollars left. Sheyne had addresses of several of her *landslayt*,* so we went to visit a different *landsman** every other day. We were very well received, but we could not find jobs. There were very few factories, we discovered. The houses were so far from each other and the cold was terrible. Girls in Winnipeg wore wool socks over their silks (that means two pair). I had to do the same, and yet I was still cold.

Although Sheyne's *landslayt* and my relative very often made parties (they would bake latkes* and drink tea with cake, play cards, play the Victrola, dance, and sing), I was often sad at heart and felt very foreign. I had a desire to return home, but Sheyne mixed in with the *landslayt*. They received greetings from their families and friends from her, and they were therefore more interested in her than in me. Four weeks were idled away in this way, especially for me, until one day I spoke up to Sheyne: "You know, I have a married cousin in Montreal. I'm going to ask him if it's possible to go to Montreal. Maybe I can get some work there." She was enthusiastic about the idea, as she had many *landslayt* in Montreal. "If you're going, Minke, I'll go too."

And so it was. My cousin wrote me to come right away, that Montreal is a big city with many factories. I immediately sent off a letter to America to my sisters asking them to send me fifty dollars, because I needed that much for traveling expenses to Montreal. In fact, they sent seventy dollars right away. Sheyne's sister also sent her ninety dollars. I spent a few dollars paying off my room and board, bought a ticket for fifty dollars, as did my friend, and we were on our way. I had been in Winnipeg for two months.

We arrived at Montreal station safely after traveling for two days. My cousin was waiting for me and took me to his home. His wife received me warmly. They had two small children, boys. My cousin worked in a millinery, but they lived very poorly. Yes, I also met my cousin's sister there, a girl of sixteen years. She had come to them from Europe six months earlier. She worked as a hat finisher, earning ten dollars a week. A week after my arrival, my cousin took me out to the dress factory, two blocks from my house, where his brother-in-law worked as a cutter. My cousin had a discussion with him, after which the brother-in-law had a talk with the boss in English. I did not understand a word. The boss considered me, then asked, "You'll do anything to earn a few dollars?" He led me to a large area. My eyes could barely take in the 140 machines at which girls sat sewing dresses.

He assigned me the job of turning the cotton dresses right-side-in after they had been sewed and said he would pay me twenty cents an hour. But after a day's work, I told the forelady that my hands ached a great deal and that I would no longer do the work. She called in the boss and he came to me and said, "I'm happy with your work. I'll pay you twenty-five cents an hour, alright?"

"No," I said, "I don't like the work."

"What kind of work do you want?"

"Like that," I said, pointing to an operator sitting by her machine and sewing cotton dresses. The boss smiled, took me to one of the girls, and said, "Show her, teach her to sew dresses."

I thanked him very much and sat down at the machine standing next to the girl's. Three days later, I could already sew a straight bodice. After that I sewed belts and helped the girl with everything. I did whatever she told me to do.

When I had finished a week's worth of work, at seven o'clock Friday evening, I asked the boss's father, who was the manager, "When is payday?"

"Tomorrow, after work."

"On the Sabbath?!"

"Yes, yes. You must work tomorrow until noon." I burst into tears.

"What are you crying about? I am a man over sixty and I work on the Sabbath. Don't you need to eat on the Sabbath? If you don't like it, you can go home and find yourself another job."

Now what would I do? I had no money and no idea how and where to look for another job. I thought to myself, he's ordering me to do it; it's his sin! The next day, on the Sabbath, I went in to work. But instead of singing while I worked, as I did every other day, tears streamed from my eyes.

The next week, I bought the girl who had shown me how to work a smock as a thank-you gift. She thanked me very much for helping her with her work. Now I worked on my own and the girl showed me how to sew some things whenever necessary. We earned by the piece. Though I still earned very little, I tried to give a few dollars to my cousin.

We worked on the cotton dresses on the fifth floor, but on the fourth floor the boss had installed thirty machines to work on regular silk dresses. Through my cousin's brother-in-law I worked my way up and started to work on the fourth floor. The forelady of the silk dresses was very good to me and showed me every step stitch and taught me how to make piping. One time, an order for a lot of Georgette dresses came in.[5] When she gave me a dress to make, I broke into a cold sweat. I got so scared that my hands trembled. When the forelady noticed this, she said to me with a smile, "Don't be afraid. Here's the sample. Just look at it and sew. You don't need to rush." The color of the dress was "solid light blue." I set to work and worked with difficulty, until I finished. The dress was soaked in machine oil and I in sweat. The forelady took it to put on the manikin, biting her lip. She liked the dress's fit—but the oil! "What did you do to that dress?" she whispered to me, actually putting her head in her hands. The designer noticed and burst out screaming in English. I knew that he was giving it to me good because of the dress. The forelady tried to calm him down. She washed the dress out in benzene, and the spots came out.[6] I was no longer afraid. From then on, I was proud of myself and put out truly good work. The boss would take my piping and make a fuss over it, showing the other workers how nice it looked.

Many French and Jewish girls worked at that shop. More than a half of the Jews were greenhorns,* not long in the country. The boss used to say that a greenhorn girl worked much better and quicker than a Canadian girl. The greenhorns were healthier and had fresh energy. He knew what he was talking about. I knew it from my own experience. I practically lived for morning, when I would run to the shop. A single dream lingered always before my eyes: dresses, machines, the forelady. I worked with such zeal and appetite. I spoke only of the shop with my cousin, the sixteen-year-old girl. I now earned twelve dollars a week. I worked by the piece from eight in the morning until seven in the evening, with an hour for lunch. There was no union there.

I went to public night school, three times a week. I flourished in school, where I got to know new girls and boys. We were a class of about thirty-five pupils. The teacher was a woman of fifty or sixty. I understood very little of what she said to us, and it was the same for the others. So what did we do? We wrote notes to each other (girls to boys and boys to girls), so the teacher wouldn't notice, of course. In this way, we spent the evenings. Gradually, though, I started to understand and sat closer to the teacher in order to listen to her more attentively. I learned a bit of reading and writing, but very little speaking. My cousin and I formed a nice group of friends, male and female. Every Sabbath evening we had a gathering, and Sundays we went out to swim and picnic. I had a very good time. So a year passed.

I now made fifteen dollars a week and repaid my cousin for the time when I had earned very little and could not pay the six dollars for room and board. I paid off every penny, although they did not feel so comfortable with it. My cousins were like my own parents to me. I loved them very much.

At the end of winter—it was a Friday, after work—I came home, lay right down in bed, and cried bitterly. The entire time I had been abroad, I had missed home very much. But when I felt out of sorts or just sick, my yearning would flare up, and only then did I feel the loneliness. When my cousins asked me what had happened, I said I did not feel well and my ears hurt. My cousin took my temperature, 102 degrees, and called the doctor. I had the grippe. I lay in bed for two days, and Sunday in the middle of the night I was really crawling the walls. My ears were infected. In the morning, the doctor came to examine me. He said that he had to operate and would do it right then and there, at my cousin's house. He sterilized the necessary instruments, gave me ether and performed the operation with the help of my cousin (the girl who lived in the room with me). He opened the abscess in my ear. During my recovery, my other cousin, the wife of the house, wet my brow, washed me, and tended to me. She took very good care of me and did not want me to be taken to the hospital, even though since my arrival she had had a third child and it was very difficult for her to tend to me. But with God's help, within two weeks I had recovered. I was very thankful to my cousins.

I went back to the shop, worked a full week from Monday to a half-day on Saturday, and suddenly my hand started to irritate me. I gave it a scratch and large blisters formed, as if my hand had been scalded. The more I scratched, the more blisters I got. I ran home and called the doctor. He didn't know what it was but gave me the address of a skin specialist. My cousin and I went straight to the skin specialist, who told me the minute he saw it not to worry at all. It would go away quickly. He gave me a big white tablet to dissolve in water and drink, and told me to smear myself with Calamine Lotion. By now I had the same blisters all over my body and they itched terribly.

The condition subsided in two days and I went back to work, but after four days I came home with a headache and pus running from my ear again. The doctor came and examined me. He told me to spray it with warm water twice a day. My cousin did this, but the fever went from 101 degrees to 103 in one day, and the pus had turned green. The left side of my head, the side with the bad ear, started to hurt more. The doctor then called a major ear specialist. That call cost me ten dollars, and his visit was no less than twenty-five dollars. But my cousin asked him to lower the price since I earned very little and was, moreover, very alone. When she told him that I had no one here, that she was a complete stranger to me, it helped. He asked me for no more than ten dollars. After he examined me he immediately said that I had to go to the municipal hospital, where he himself would operate. I had a mastoid that could no longer be neglected. He told me to be at the hospital at two o'clock and gave me the address. I had a good cry over my "good" fortune, as it was the Thursday before Purim.* That Purim, the club to which I belonged, the Ruzhany-Volkovysk Provincial Society, was giving a concert in which I was to appear with a recitation. We also had a choir in which I sang. A teacher of mine from Europe, who had rehearsed with me at my old folks-shule events, now lived in Montreal with his family. He was also performing with the club choir, in which I was an alto.

With the last of my strength, I sat down and wrote a letter to my parents, saying that all my needs were taken care of, that I was well, that I was working and earning very well, that I was appearing in a show that Purim singing and reciting, and that they should not worry about me. My cousins asked me to send a telegram to one of my sisters in the States right away, asking one of them to come to Montreal and be at the operation, simply because they, the cousins, were afraid to take everything on themselves. I agreed, and my cousin sent a telegram. Instead of someone coming, the next day I received all of ninety dollars with a telegram that they could not come because both sisters had infant children, but not to worry, they would not abandon me. But I did not need money. I had a few hundred dollars saved up and even sent my parents ten dollars from time to time.

I was now in the hospital, where they took an x-ray of me. Friday at one o'clock I was given ether. I felt as though I was falling into a deliciously sweet sleep, but as though my head was leaving me to go somewhere far, far away.

I woke up only when I felt someone slapping my cheek. It was the nurse. My cousin sat by my bed. I threw up a lot. My head hurt tremendously, as if in a haze. (I would feel very weak and sick yet for many months.) I asked for water, but they didn't give it to me. My cousin read me the telegram from my sisters saying that they couldn't come. They were very sorry; they were sending me ninety dollars. I cried hard and said to my cousin, "My own sisters wouldn't come to see their sister in situation like this. God knows if I'll ever be able to see them again!" I knew full well that the operation was a dangerous one, but I also said God would help me. If I did escape death, I wouldn't write even a single word to my sisters. My cousin comforted me and calmed me down.

On the third day, Sunday, at around five o'clock in the evening, my condition took a turn for the worse. The doctor was there, and two nurses gave me a few injections. Neither of them left my bedside the entire night, taking my temperature all the while. I did not sleep that night. I just kept moaning as I lay there delirious. My cousins told me all of this later. I vaguely remember feeling a terrible pain in my head. Only in the morning did I come back to my senses a bit and understand, as the nurses confirmed, that I was out of danger. That night had been the crisis. On the fifth day, the doctor replaced the bandage, and two weeks later I left the hospital, paying thirty dollars for the hospital and ten dollars to the doctor for the operation. Thank God, I arrived home safely. A week later, I returned to work.

I continued to go to the first doctor for treatments three times a week, after work, for five weeks, until he told me that my ear had healed. This doctor belonged to our club; he was a so-called society doctor.[7] I gave him my heartfelt thanks and handed him ten dollars. This made him happy because he was not owed anything as I paid dues to the society for the doctor's care. I even sent off a letter to my sisters forgiving them. Really, how could they have left small children to come to me? During the time I was laid up in the hospital, they had telephoned several times to find out how I felt.

My highest wages were from fifteen to seventeen dollars a week, but this was enough for me. I dressed quite well and now had a boyfriend. Still, I was drawn to be with my sisters. One of my brothers-in-law, my younger sister's husband, came to visit me on Rosh Hashanah. I was so delighted to see him that I decided to sneak across the border to America. But I would need money. I myself had no more than seventy-five dollars in all, but my brother-in-law assured me, "Just get a man who will smuggle you over and write me how much he wants. I'll send it to you. Leave the money with your cousins, and when you arrive safely in the States, telephone them and tell them to pay the man the price you agreed upon."

My brother-in-law left after a two-day stay. A week later I hired such a man. He wanted two hundred dollars, not a penny less. I notified my sisters, who sent the sum. I left the money with my cousins and made an arrangement with the man as my brother-in-law had instructed me to do, and he agreed to the conditions. Two days before Sukkot, I packed up all my things, withdrew my own few dollars out of the bank, and asked my cousins to send me my things and the money order for the seventy-odd dollars as soon as I arrived in the States. I was traveling by car and could not take anything with me.

The man led me to the border, and there, next to a forest, stood a car with New York license plates and two Christian men. I transferred to their car, said goodbye to the Jewish man and assured him that, as soon as I arrived at my sister's, I would call my cousins and they would pay him. Not to worry. We waited a good while in the forest and then we got on our way, traveling through fields. I had left the house at eight in the morning, and by the evening we were already in Albany. On the way, two officers approached us and asked for papers and the driver's license. The man sitting with me in the back seat told me not to look in the direction from which the officers had come. The driver showed them all the necessary papers and we departed. Around six in the morning, we were in New York City on First Avenue. My older sister lived in Brooklyn, and the men took me to her place. When we arrived at my sister's address, I thanked him, put two dollars in his hand, and got out of the car. He did not make a move after I got out but said, "Ring the bell to your sister's apartment. As soon as you're convinced that your sister lives here, let me know and then I'll leave." I did as he said and indeed found my sister. I burst out crying hysterically, seeing my eldest sister whom I did not remember at all except from pictures she had sent when I was still in Europe. I drank down a glass of milk and fell asleep.

A few months later, I went to Manhattan with my brother-in-law, a cutter in a dress shop, and found a job in a dress shop. Since the job was on Twenty-fifth Street and Sixth Avenue, not far from my younger sister, I moved in with her.

I worked at that place for about one year, and suddenly people from the union stopped us workers from working. It was an open shop and they wanted to organize it. The result was that the boss moved away and I got another job on the same street sewing silk dresses. I made more than six dollars on the first day, as we earned by the piece there. The boss was very happy with my work and so was I, since this was a union shop. Two weeks later, I became a union member, and worked for four years at the same place. During that time, earnings for A-line dresses went down from ten dollars to $2.89 to $1.89 to $1.25, in such a way that I ended up making eighteen cents a dress. But I would still earn my twenty-two to twenty-three dollars a week. I paid my sister six dollars for room and board. In fact, I saved a few dollars. Most of the time, I sent my parents several dollars, dressed quite well, and had a good time.

At the place where I worked, I became one of the best "hands," a good union member—paying my dues on time, serving on the shop's wage committee, a position for which the other workers had selected me (we were four on the committee, two Jews and two Italian girls), always fighting for higher wages. This irked the boss. More than half of the workers there were Italian girls in a shop consisting of about forty machines. He used to tell me that I spoiled his business, because if I hadn't been on the wage committee, the others would have worked for wages that he set. To this I would reply: "Let them work as they please, I don't tell them anything!" He would also rebuke me: "Greenhorn, did you come here with a rake to rake up the money?" It grieved him that I made good wages. I was a good "hand" and quick, and yet I still fought for higher wages. He couldn't—or wouldn't—understand this. When he handed me my pay envelope, he'd say, "A swollen envelope!" to which I replied, "And it cost my health plenty!"

I went out with my girlfriends, swimming in the summer and to dances in the winter. But I almost never made appointments on Sundays, not with girls or boys, because if I went to a dance Saturday night, I was exhausted on Sunday, first from dancing and second from arriving home late at two or three o'clock in the morning. On the other hand, if I went swimming, I felt exhausted all week. So Sundays, I cleaned my sister's house, and then took a notebook with a lead pencil and went to a little park nearby. There I wrote poetry, read the poems I had written earlier (I did this with excitement), or just read a book—all in Yiddish.

It happened one day that I was sitting in this way in the park and a girl-friend of my sister came over to me with her husband and asked after my sister. They introduced me to a couple who was walking with them. Their husbands were partners in the fur business. We all sat together on the bench and the partner asked what kind of notebook I had there.

"Oh, it's nothing. Little poems I write."

"May I see?"

"Why not?"

Looking a few of them over, he asked me a question, "Do you want to meet a boy who also writes poems?"

"A poet?" I say, "Is he normal?"

He smiled and replied, "Well, sure he's normal!"

"If so, I would indeed like to meet him." Here his wife got involved and asked me to come visit them the following Sunday. They would see to it that the boy came, too.

That's how it happened. I did not tell my sister and brother-in-law any-thing about it. I only said that Sunday at one o'clock on the twenty-fourth of May I had a date. I arrived at the time we had set, but the boy was not yet there. Meanwhile, I had a conversation with them about what sort of boy he was. They told me that he lived with his mother, that he was a very pious and quiet boy. In his free time, he was always busy writing and read-ing books, journals, various literature. Before a half hour had passed, he was there! He was dressed shabbily but was noble in appearance. We were introduced and spoke together. He was very pleased to hear me speaking such a familiar Yiddish, because he himself had only met American girls who seldom spoke a Yiddish word. Hearing my Yiddish, he said, "You are one of my people!" Like me, he was from White Russia.

He took me out to the Yiddish theater and back to my house, and we talked like good, old friends. As he escorted me to the door, he asked me, "What is the number here?"

"What number?"

"The number for your house," he replied.

"Oh, here's the number!"

"Good night!" he said "I'm delighted to know you!"

"Good night!" I answered, and he left. I stood there a while, shrugged my shoulders, and went into the house. It was around nine o'clock in the evening, and I found my sister and brother-in-law sitting in the living room. "So, what's the news? Did you have a good time?" I told them the whole story and remarked, "But I don't understand. A boy escorts me to the house and doesn't even ask me for another date. That's the first time that's happened to me, particularly when I noticed and felt that he liked me."

"Do you like him?" they both asked.

"What kind of question is that?" I answered shortly.

But three days later I received a very lovely note from the boy, expressing much love for me. I was so inspired that that same evening I wrote him a reply, and we corresponded in this way for five weeks because I went on vacation for several weeks, so we did not have an opportunity to see each other.

Anyway, we wrote to each other only in verse (see fig. 18), until he came over to my house at my request. He was very shy and barely said one word —not to my brother-in-law either (perhaps because they were from such separate worlds). So my sister was not enthusiastic about him.

After he left she said to me, "He is an egoist! What's the matter, it doesn't suit him to talk to us?" I assured her that he was not an egoist, but quite simply a quiet, shy person. After all, this had been his first time in my house with complete strangers. I myself would feel as he did.

"I'm sure that after he comes a few more times, you'll see for yourself that he'll feel more at home. I assure you that you will then have a different opinion of him."

And so he came to my house quite often and I truly fell in love with him—perhaps not so much with him as with his speaking and writing. My sister had a daughter, six years old, and she loved him a great deal. She would kiss and hug him, because he paid attention to her and told her all sorts of stories. It appeared that he was also not indifferent to me, but he did not propose. Rather, he simply said one time, "You know, I live with my mother and you'll have to live with her. Would you like that? And you'll have to keep a one-hundred-percent kosher kitchen."

I smiled and said, "Why not?"

Then he once said to me while we sat in the theater, "I feel a heavy burden that I'll have to go to City Hall and get a marriage license."

"What's the matter, is that such hard work? That's a heavy burden to you? I have a greater burden than you!" I told him the whole story about how I entered the country illegally. He bit his lip.

"What?" I said fearfully, "Aren't you a citizen?"

"Come out of the theater," he ordered. Once outside, he said, "My father's citizenship papers declare me a citizen."

"So good," I said.

"Yes," he said, "but why haven't you told me this the whole time?"

"It didn't come up."

We went to my house and spoke until four in the morning. He did not promise me riches. He said he would buy me neither jewelry nor any new furniture. I would have to move in with old furniture and live together with his mother, because she wouldn't move in with the other children because their homes were not kosher. He said his mother did not, God forbid, need to go to her children because she had a few thousand dollars that her husband had left her through a life insurance policy. I consented to everything.

A few weeks before Rosh Hashanah, he introduced me to his mother, along with his entire family. His mother invited me to stay with them over the holiday. My family did not like the looks of this.

"A boy," they said, "goes out with a girl for almost six months and, from what we understand, is going steady with her, and he hasn't even given her a ring!" But I kept insisting that jewelry meant nothing to me, as long as he himself was a good man from a respectable family who made a living. He was a welder and had worked in the same place since coming to America.

I was at my boyfriend's house for the two days of Rosh Hashanah. His mother baked and cooked as if for a bride. The Sabbath followed the holiday, and his mother and he insisted that, of course, I must stay over to Sunday, at least until lunch. I allowed them to persuade me, and the next morning at around eleven o'clock my boyfriend's brother arrived with his wife.

"Come," they said, "Let's walk a bit." We walked and talked. When we walked by a jewelry store we stopped. My boyfriend asked me, "What kind of watch would you choose for yourself?"

"What's the use of choosing, if I won't buy it?"

"Maybe I'll buy it for you."

Anyway, I chose a beautiful watch with four little diamonds. He, however, bought me a watch with twenty-four little diamonds that I had looked at but never dreamed I could have. There was no limit to my happiness. I kissed my boyfriend out of sheer joy, and my future brother- and sister-in-law also, because I understood that the thing had been decided.

When we returned to my boyfriend's house, I kissed his mother and cried for joy. His mother was very happy and actually told me that she encouraged him to buy me the watch—if not a ring, then a watch.

After dinner, he escorted me home. When my sister and brother-in-law saw the watch, they wished me well. A few weeks later, my sisters held a surprise engagement party for us and the family. I got to the shop for work, and, when all the workers noticed me wearing such a beautiful watch, they wished me well. They already knew that I was engaged.

And so every Friday after work I went to my fiancé's place, and he would take me home Sunday evening. I was the happiest girl in the world that my mother-in-law liked me and received me very warmly. My groom didn't know what to do with me or where to take me out.

It went like this until three weeks before Passover, when my boss came to me and asked me for my name and address because some matter was starting up about "social security cards."[8] When I got wind of this, I asked my brother-in-law for advice and he told me to ask my boss not to submit my name. When I made this request, the boss protested, "Oh . . . you're here illegally! I'm very sorry but I must submit your name. If you don't want me to, then go work somewhere else." I told him that he had not guessed right: I was here legally. I didn't want him to submit my name for a different reason. But nothing helped. He simply reported me and came to me nearly every day saying, "You know, Minnie, I would advise you to go work at a different place, because whatever happens, don't blame me, I'm warning you!" I replied that I wasn't afraid of anyone and that he should worry less about me.

I decided to keep working at the same place, because if he had turned me in, they would find me wherever I worked. So it was. On Thursday, April 1, at around two o'clock in the afternoon, the boss came to me and said that a man wanted to see me in the office. Yes, the boss introduced him to me as a detective. I felt the color leave my face and all my hopes for happiness dissolve. I controlled myself and answered all of his questions. At around three o'clock, he took me to Ellis Island. On the way, I went to a drug store and telephoned my brother-in-law at his grocery store and told him that I had been turned in and that a detective was now taking me to Ellis Island. Tears stuck in my throat. My brother-in-law assured me that he would come with a lawyer first thing in the morning to bail me out. I quickly wrote my fiancé a postcard that I would not be able to come this Friday, but I did not write the reason.

Upon arrival at Ellis Island, they asked me questions, took fingerprints and photographs—just as they would of a real criminal. I had no food at all and didn't sleep all night. I could not stop crying. At one o'clock the next day, my brother-in-law came with a lawyer and put up five hundred dollars. I was released. When I got home, my sister burst into tears at the sight of me and I cried bitterly, too. My lawyer advised me to go to my fiancé and tell him what had occurred. He, the lawyer, said that my only recourse was to get married in court as soon as possible.

I changed my clothes and went to see my fiancé, who was already home from work. When I entered the house, he got up from his chair, came over to me, and asked in astonishment, "What happened?" I burst into tears. He let me cry for a while and then calm down a bit, and then I told him what had happened. He heard me out and said, "Alright, we can even go on Monday to City Hall and get married." I was glad because it would cost much effort, health, and money before I crawled out of this mess. But he agreed to everything. I assured him that my brother-in-law would help me get myself out of trouble. He knew a lot of politicians. So we agreed to go to City Hall on Monday, take out a marriage license, and get married right there.

So it was. I was in seventh heaven because the lawyer assured me that now I need not fear anything and could go back to work in the shop. In fact, I went right back to work on Tuesday. The boss was surprised to see me, and, smiling, asked, "What, you took a vacation?"

"I got married and that's why I took a few days off. Am I not entitled to that?"

"Alright, alright. Get to work!" he said angrily. He didn't even wish me well, but I am well, thank God, without his good wishes. The shop workers told me that, as soon as the detective had led me away to Ellis Island, the boss said to some of them, "Good riddance! There's no one in the shop dictating to me now that Minnie's been sent back to Europe." I sat and worked as if nothing had happened. Everyone in the shop congratulated me, seeing that I now wore a wedding ring.

I got married on April 5, 1937, in court. On April 11, the first of Iyar on the Hebrew calendar, we went to a rabbi and got married under Jewish law without a ceremony. On April 8, I went to a hearing on Ellis Island with my new husband, my brother-in-law, and my lawyer. At the hearing, I had to convince them that I had in fact married my husband. I had to present my husband's letters to me and my letters to him, and a translator read the letters. The lawyer had prepared me beforehand and told me what to say. I told the following story: I had met a boy in Montreal at a dance. We went out for a good while. When he asked me if I had family in the States, I told him that I had sisters.

"Why don't you go to them?"

"How can I? You need the proper papers, you know!"

"I can get them for you. I'm going there by car next week. If you want, I'll take you to your sisters." I was more than eager to go and did not understand that he was taking me illegally. When I got engaged to my current husband, he explained that his father's papers declared him a citizen. I only discovered that I was here illegally when I was taken to Ellis Island. The official asked me if I knew the name of the boy who had brought me across the border from Canada to the States. I told them that I had not seen him since that time. He said his name was Harry, and he was a tall blond boy. That's all I knew about him.

I said all this as the lawyer had instructed me. I was to leave the States until my husband received his own citizenship papers and I got a visa. The lawyer made a motion that they allow me to leave the country on my own. But since my brother-in-law knew high-placed politicians well, he convinced the U.S. Commissioner of Immigration based at Ellis Island to let me stay in the States. I was even allowed to work at the shop while I waited to be called to get my visa in Montreal. Meanwhile, my brother-in-law also worked it out for my husband to get his own citizenship papers. It was not easy since my husband did not have a birth certificate. With God's help, in a mere three months, my husband had his citizenship papers.

A short time later, I was called to get my visa. Of course, I had to have all the necessary papers: my birth certificate, marriage license, pictures, and so on, dozens of papers that my brother-in-law and my husband helped me get. With the entire pack of papers, I set off for Montreal. Officials stopped me at Rouses Point to look everything over.[9] They swore me in to give testimony and asked various questions. As soon as I showed them the letter that the commissioner had given me to take with me, they stopped asking questions and I departed for Montreal. My cousin went with me to the American Consulate, and, after a day of many questions, I finally got the visa. Eight days later, I was with my husband.

My husband sent me to the country to rest and recover from all my experiences. I stayed there for three weeks and came home to four small rooms with old, used furniture. But this did not bother me at all. I was overjoyed that I had crawled out of such a horrible mess. A year after my wedding my husband bought me a beautiful diamond ring, and half a year later we moved into five lovely rooms in which he had set up new furniture according to my taste.

Thank God, we have everything we need. My husband makes a fine living. I have a beautiful, bright daughter of three years. I am so busy now with the house and child that I not only don't have time to write poems, I don't even have time to look at the newspaper. My husband is very good to me. I still live with my mother-in-law. She is a good mother to me, and I love her. My child also loves her very much. It's easy to love her.

As you see, I haven't lost anything by coming to America.

NOTES

1. A modern, secular Jewish school, with Yiddish as the language of instruction. Such a school was founded in Ruzhany in 1920.

2. According to Jewish folklore, excessive praise may do someone harm by bringing the "evil eye" on him or her.

3. The war between the Soviet Union and Poland lasted from June to October 1920. The Peace of Riga in March 1921 fixed the border between the two states, with Ruzhany in Poland.

4. The Immigration Act of 1924 placed severe restrictions on the number of immigrants who could enter the United States, with especially low quotas on Eastern and Southern European countries whose people were considered particularly undesirable. The law granted preferences to children and spouses of residents or citizens of the United States, but not to siblings.

5. A Georgette dress is made from a double layer of chiffon.

6. A solvent for oil, benzene was commonly used in the dry-cleaning process in the nineteenth century.

7. Like many hometown societies, the Ruzhany-Volkovysk Provincial Society contracted yearly with a doctor to serve its members for reduced fees.

8. The Social Security Act of 1935 provided for such government programs as unemployment insurance, old-age pensions, and aid to dependent children. In November 1936, the Post Office distributed applications for Social Security cards through employers. The first cards were issued that same month.

9. Rouses Point, New York, was the site of two border inspection stations constructed toward the end of Prohibition.

Glossary

aliyah: The honor of being called up to the platform to say the blessing for the Torah reading during services. It was common in American synagogues to auction off this honor in order to raise money for the congregation.

bar mitzvah (Aramaic, Hebrew; "son of commandment"): At age thirteen, Jewish boys become "bar mitzvah," that is, subject to carrying out the commandments. The term has also come to refer to the ceremony and celebration that attend a boy's thirteenth birthday.

Bava Batra (Aramaic, "The Last Gate"): Talmudic tractate dealing with issues of real estate, partnerships, contracts, and inheritance. It is the third tractate in the talmudic order Nezikin (Damages).

birzhe (Yiddish, "exchange"): In late tsarist Russia, a street on which revolutionaries would promenade while surreptitiously distributing illegal literature, discussing underground operations, or exchanging political information.

borsht (Yiddish): Beet soup, served hot or cold, with meat or dairy.

Bund (Yiddish): Jewish Socialist party founded in the Russian empire in 1897. The Bund opposed Zionism and promoted the development of the Yiddish language. Its full name was the Algemeyner yidisher arbeter bund in Lite, Poyln un Rusland (General Jewish Workers Alliance in Lithuania, Poland and Russia).

busy: In slang among immigrant workers, a noun meaning "busy season."

Castle Garden: Also known as Castle Clinton, a former fortress and theater on the southernmost tip of Manhattan, and New York's official immigrant reception center from 1855 to 1890. Even after Ellis Island opened in 1892, many immigrants continued to refer the immigration station as Castle Garden.

Dineson, Jacob (1852/56/59–1919): Novelist and educator who pioneered the modern Yiddish novel. His sentimental and didactic works were widely popular.

eating days (Yiddish: *Esn teg,* literally "to eat days"): The practice by which yeshiva students away from home would eat meals with a different local household each day of the week.

Ein Ya'akov: A popular compilation, by Ya'akov ben Shlomo ibn Haviv (c. 1450–1516), of stories from the Talmud, together with some commentaries by ibn Haviv and others.

Ellis Island: An island in Upper New York Bay on which the busiest immigration station in the United States was located from 1892 to 1954.

Forverts: See ***Forward***

Forward (Yiddish: *Forverts*): Yiddish daily newspaper published in New York. Founded in 1897, the *Forward* espoused Socialist politics and soon became the most widely read and influential Yiddish daily in America.

Gemara (Aramaic, "teaching" or "tradition"): The Talmud. The rabbinic discussion and analysis of the Mishna compiled c. 200–500 C.E.

green: See **greenhorn**

greenhorn: A recent immigrant, often pejorative. The adjective "green" was also applied to new arrivals.

groshn (Yiddish; Polish: *grosz*; Russian: *grosh*): Half a kopek; a coin of very small value; a penny.

gulden: A gold or silver coin of some value, also called a *guilder* or *florin.* The basic Austrian monetary unit until 1892.

gymnasium (Russian: *gimnaziya*): A secondary school stressing classical studies in preparation for admission to university.

Hadassah: The Women's Zionist Organization of America. Founded in 1912 as the Daughters of Zion, the organization adopted the name Hadassah in 1916. It was known especially for its sponsorship of medical facilities in Palestine and later Israel.

Hakhnoses Orkhim: The Hebrew name for the Hebrew Sheltering House Association, founded in New York in 1889. The group took its name from the term for the traditional precept of inviting guests into one's home. In 1909, it joined with the Hebrew Immigrant Aid Society (founded 1902) to form the Hebrew Sheltering and Immigrant Aid Society (HIAS).

hallah (Hebrew): The rich white egg bread, usually in the form of a twisted loaf, eaten by Jews at the Sabbath meal and on holidays.

Hanukkah (Hebrew, "dedication"): Holiday celebrating the re-dedication of the Temple in Jerusalem after the victory of the Maccabees over Antiochus of Syria in the second century B.C.E. The holiday lasts for eight days, during which a special eight-branched lamp is lit, beginning with one light and adding an additional light each day.

Hasid, Hasidic: See **Hasidism**

Hasidism (from the Hebrew *Hasid,* "pious one"): A Jewish religious movement characterized by ecstatic prayer. Founded in the eighteenth century by Israel ben Eliezer, known as the Bal Shem Tov (Master of the Good Name, c. 1700–1760), the movement soon divided into sects centered on individual charismatic leaders known as *rebbes* or *tsadikim.* Each sect was known by the name of the town where its *rebbe* kept his court, and these positions of leadership evolved into hereditary dynasties.

havdalah (Hebrew, "differentiation"): The ceremony on Saturday evening marking the end of the Sabbath and the beginning of the week.

heder (Hebrew, "room"): The traditional Jewish elementary school in Eastern Europe, usually a very small private school attended by boys. Girls sometimes attended separate *heders.*

HIAS (Hebrew Sheltering and Immigrant Aid Society): The main communal organization providing aid and guidance to newly arrived immigrants, with its own representatives at Ellis Island. HIAS was founded in New York in 1909 from the merger of two older organizations, the Hebrew Sheltering House Association (sometimes called by the Hebrew name, Hakhnoses Orkhim, founded 1889) and the Hebrew Immigrant Aid Society (also called HIAS, founded 1902).

High Holidays: Rosh Hashanah (Jewish New Year) and Yom Kippur (Day of Atonement). Also called the Days of Awe (*yamim nora'im*).

Kaddish (Hebrew, "sanctification"): A doxology in praise of God. The *Kaddish* is recited by the congregation several times in slightly different forms during the service. One form, known as the *Mourner's Kaddish,* is recited daily by the children (traditionally, by sons) of a deceased parent during the first eleven months after the parent's death, and then each year on the anniversary.

kashrut (from Hebrew *kasher,* "fit, proper"): The laws regulating what Jews may or may not eat. In general, certain animals may be eaten while others may not. But even permissible animals must be slaughtered in a prescribed fashion and the meat drained of blood. The combination of meat and dairy is also prohibited.

Kav ha-yashar (Hebrew, "Measure of Righteousness"): An ethical tract written in 1705 by Zevi Hirsch Koidonover (d. 1712). Widely translated into Yiddish, it reached a mass audience in Eastern Europe with its lively descriptions of the torments awaiting the wicked and the rewards awaiting the righteous.

Khumesh (Hebrew): The first five books of the Bible, also called the Pentateuch.

kiddush (Hebrew, "sanctification"): The blessing recited over wine at the start of the Sabbath or holiday meal.

kosher: See *kashrut*

kreuzer: In Austria, a coin of small value, equal to one-sixtieth of a gulden before 1859 and one-hundredth thereafter.

landsfroy: See *landsman*

landslayt: See *landsman*

landsman (Yiddish): Compatriot; among immigrants, a person from one's hometown, region, or country. A woman may also be called a *landsfroy*. The plural is *landslayt*.

latke (Yiddish): Pancake, often made of potatoes and fried.

maskil (Hebrew, "enlightened one"): A supporter of the Haskalah, the "Jewish Enlightenment" that began in Germany in the late eighteenth century and spread eastward into Russia in the nineteenth century.

minyan (Hebrew): The quorum of ten adult Jewish males needed in order to recite certain parts of the public synagogue service.

Mishna (Hebrew, "learning" or "repetition"): A compilation of the oral law as discussed and debated by rabbis, dating from about 200 C.E. Composed in Hebrew, it forms the basis of the Talmud. Within the work as a whole, the term *mishna* also refers to each individual discussion of a particular question.

Passover (Hebrew: Pesakh): A spring holiday commemorating the exodus from Egypt. Passover lasts eight days (seven in Israel), during which time no leaven may be eaten or even possessed. The first two evenings are marked by a special service, called a *seder,* read at the table and accompanied by a festive meal. The first two days and last two days are full holidays during which no work is performed. During the intermediate days, work may be performed and regular business transacted.

pogrom (Russian): Anti-Jewish riot.

Purim: Holiday celebrating the deliverance of the Jews from Haman, minister to the Persian King Ahasuerus, who plotted to exterminate them. The Scroll of Esther, where the story is related, is read in the synagogue. During the reading children use noisemakers to blot out Haman's name whenever it is mentioned. Other customs include sending gifts of food to friends and neighbors and drinking to intoxication.

Rashi (acronym of Rabbi Shlomo ben Yitskhak, 1040–1105): Medieval French commentator on the Bible and the Talmud. Rashi's commentaries, which include both explications of the plain meaning of the text and homiletic interpretations, became standard in traditional Jewish learning.

Reb (Hebrew, Yiddish): An honorific used before a man's first name.

rebbe (Hebrew, Yiddish; "teacher"): The charismatic leader of a Hasidic sect. Rebbes were often referred to by the names of the towns in which they held court. The word was also used to refer to a traditional Jewish elementary school teacher.

Rosh Hashanah: The Jewish new year. Rosh Hashanah is considered a day of judgment and is therefore solemn as well as joyous. The central custom associated with the holiday is the blowing of the *shofar,* a ram's horn, during the service.

Russian blessing (Yiddish slang): Curses and abuse.

Russo-Japanese War: War fought 1904–5 over competing claims to Manchuria and Korea. Japan's defeat of Russia stunned the world and contributed to the outbreak of the 1905 Russian Revolution.

shiva (Hebrew, "seven"): The seven-day mourning period after the death of a close relative. Mourners abstain from regular business and remain mainly in the house, sitting on low stools and receiving visitors who come to comfort them.

Sholem Aleichem (pseudonym of Sholem Rabinovitsh, 1859–1916): Yiddish and Hebrew writer, considered one of the founders of modern Yiddish literature. Sholem Aleichem's works, which were tremendously popular, are characterized by folksy humor and affection for the common people as well as by critique of the traditional social order.

Shomer (pseudonym of Nahum Meyer Shaikevich, 1849–1905): Yiddish novelist and dramatist whose romantic adventure stories were extremely popular in Europe and the Americas.

"shvue, Di" (Yiddish, "The Oath"): The anthem of the Bund, composed by S. Ansky (Shloyme Zanvil Rapoport, 1863–1920).

siddur (Hebrew, "arrangement"): The prayer book used for daily and Sabbath services.

Simhat Torah (Hebrew, "Rejoicing of the Law"): Joyous holiday at the end of the High Holiday season that marks the end of the previous year's cycle of weekly Torah readings and the beginning of the new year's cycle.

slack: In slang among immigrant workers, a noun meaning the slow production season.

sukkah: See **Sukkot**

Sukkot (Hebrew, literally "booths"): Seven-day holiday commemorating the period the Israelites spent wandering in the desert after the exodus from Egypt. The principle custom is the erection of temporary outdoor booths (*sukkot*; singular: *sukkah*) in which meals are eaten. The first two days are full holidays during which no work is performed. The following days are intermediate days, when work may be performed and regular business transacted. Sukkot is followed immediately by Shmini Atseret and Simhat Torah, which are full holidays.

Talmud (Hebrew, "teaching" or "study"): The Gemara. More loosely, the Gemara together with the Mishna. Following the order of the Mishna, the Talmud is organized into six "orders," which are further divided into tractates.

talmud torah (Hebrew, "study of Torah"): In Eastern Europe, a school for poor children sponsored and supervised by the community. In America, a supplementary or day school with a religious orientation.

Tanakh (Hebrew acronym for Torah, Neviim, Ktuvim[c], Pentateuch, Prophets, Hagiographa): The Hebrew Bible.

Taytsh khumesh: A Yiddish translation or paraphrase of the first five books of the Bible intended for those who could not read the original, and therefore read mainly by women.

tekhinah (Hebrew, "supplication" or "prayer"): A prayer or collection of prayers composed in Yiddish and intended for women.

tfilin (Hebrew): Phylacteries. Small leather boxes containing certain verses from the Bible. Traditionally, a Jewish man strapped one of these boxes to his arm and another to his head during morning services, except on the Sabbath and on holidays.

Torah (Hebrew, "the teaching" or "the law"): Most narrowly, the Pentateuch, or first five books of the Bible. More broadly, Torah refers to the entire Bible together with the "oral law"—the Mishna and Talmud. Finally, most broadly, the term encompasses all traditional Jewish learning.

Tosefos (Hebrew, "additions"): Commentary on the Talmud by authorities who followed Rashi in the twelfth to fourteenth centuries. They are usually printed alongside the text upon which they comment.

treyf (Hebrew, "torn by wild beasts"): Not kosher; ritually unfit to eat or use.

treyfene: See *treyf*

tsholnt (Yiddish): A stew prepared with meat, potatoes, legumes, and other ingredients for eating on the Sabbath. Because of the prohibition against cooking on the Sabbath, the *tsholnt* is prepared the day before and baked slowly overnight.

tsimes (Yiddish): A stew of carrots, or other vegetables or fruits. In slang, a fuss.

verst (Russian): Russian unit of distance equivalent to .6629 of a mile.

Workmen's Circle: Jewish labor fraternal order. Originally founded in 1892 as a mutual aid society, it became a multibranch fraternal order in 1900. It included members with a variety of political opinions but was dominated by Socialists.

Wrangel, Piotr Nikolayevich (1878–1928): Russian general who joined the counterrevolutionary "White" army in 1917 and took over command in the spring of 1920. His defeat that November signaled the end of the Russian Civil War. Under his leadership, White forces were responsible for numerous pogroms.

yarmulke (Yiddish): Skullcap worn by Jewish men in conformity with the custom of keeping one's head covered out of respect for God.

yeshiva (Hebrew): An academy of higher talmudic learning.

Yom Kippur (Hebrew): The Day of Atonement. A solemn fast day, considered the holiest day of the Jewish year, on which the synagogue service includes a recitation of sins and pleas to God for forgiveness.

yortsayt (Yiddish): The anniversary of a death, observed according to the Jewish calendar. Survivors recite *Kaddish* and light candles in memory of their deceased parents.

Zionism: The nationalist movement that arose in the late nineteenth century with the aim of establishing a Jewish homeland in Palestine.

Index

About the Editors

Jocelyn Cohen earned her doctorate degree in history from the University of Minnesota. She has taught American and Jewish history at the University of Minnesota, Fordham University, and Brooklyn College. Among her appointments, Dr. Cohen is a Research Associate of YIVO's Max Weinreich Center for Advanced Jewish Studies.

Daniel Soyer is Associate Professor of History at Fordham University. His book *Jewish Immigrant Associations and American Identity in New York, 1880–1939* (1997) was co-winner of the Saul Viener Prize of the American Jewish Historical Society. He is the editor of *A Coat of Many Colors: Immigration, Globalization, and Reform in the New York City Garment Industry* (2005).